THE CATHOLIC UNIVERSITY OF AMERICA
CANON LAW STUDIES
No. 115

THE PASTOR'S OBLIGATION IN PRE-NUPTIAL INVESTIGATION

AN HISTORICAL SYNOPSIS AND COMMENTARY

A DISSERTATION

Submitted to the Faculty of Canon Law of the Catholic University of America in Partial Fulfillment of the Requirements for the Degree of

DOCTOR OF CANON LAW

BY

JAMES JOSEPH DONOVAN, J.C.L.
Priest of the Diocese of Great Falls

THE CATHOLIC UNIVERSITY OF AMERICA
WASHINGTON, D. C.
1938

Nihil Obstat:

VALENTINUS T. SCHAAF, O.F.M., J.C.D.,
Censor Deputatus.

Washingtonii, D. C., die 11 Maii, 1938.

Imprimatur:

EDUINUS VINCENTIUS O'HARA,
Episcopus Greatormensis.

Greatormensi, die 12 Maii, 1938.

Printed by
THE PAULIST PRESS
New York, N. Y.

TO

THE HOLY FAMILY

IN

GRATITUDE

TABLE OF CONTENTS

CHAPTER IV

PART TWO

COMMENTARY

CHAPTER V

CHAPTER IV

FOREWORD

Happiness in the marriages of her subjects has always been desired and sought after by the Catholic Church. The reason is obvious. Happy unions tend to promote the interests of religion, the good of society, the security of the home, the well-being of the family and the betterment of the individual. To aid in effecting happy unions, the Church has surrounded the sacred institution of marriage with many legal safeguards. And one of the most prominent of these safeguards is the disciplinary measure obliging pastors, who have the right to assist at marriages, to make diligent and careful pre-nuptial investigation concerning the freedom to marry of prospective brides and grooms.

No fair-minded person can fail to recognize the legal, spiritual, moral and social values of pre-nuptial investigation by the pastor. Pastors from their professional experience appreciate those values keenly and even right-minded nupturients cannot be oblivious of the signal service the Church has rendered them by enacting such a precautionary measure as pre-nuptial investigation to insure the valid and lawful celebration of marriage.

Many circumstances in modern life have made it imperative on pastors to be very diligent and careful in the pre-nuptial investigation of prospective brides and grooms. Neo-pagan marriage standards have penetrated many of the legal systems of the world; there is considerable propaganda for a greater laxity in marriage morality; divorce and re-marriage after divorce are tolerated in many countries by law and social custom; temporary, trial and companionate marriages are being advocated; in many circles the sanctity, unity and indissolubility of marriage are derided and as a result there are many who contract marriage from unworthy motives. Although propaganda against Christian marriage has mainly affected the non-Catholic population, not a few Catholics have been infected with the contagion. Moreover, because of the concentration of large masses of the people in the cities, the mobility of the population and the fact that the past history and background of nupturients are often unknown to the local pastor, concealment of impediments to marriage is comparatively easy. Carefully and diligently conducted pre-nuptial investigation will go a long way in preventing illicit and invalid unions; it will prevent hasty marriages; it will promote more intelligent selection of married partners and it will help to ensure a sufficient instruction for nupturients in their prospective marital and familial obligations.

This dissertation attempts to outline the pastor's obligation in pre-nuptial inquiry. It is divided into two parts. The first part discusses briefly the notion of pre-nuptial investigation and presents a summary history of its development from early Christianity to the present time. The second part is devoted to commentary and considers chiefly the investigating pastor, his competency to investigate and the manner of conducting the investigation. Separate chapters are devoted to the investigation of Catholic marriages and mixed marriages, as they differ somewhat from each other in matrimonial discipline. In the final chapter pre-nuptial investigation in certain extraordinary circumstances will be treated. This study does not presume to give an exhaustive treatment of all the problems that may confront the pastor when conducting the investigation. Much is left to the intelligence and prudence of the individual pastor because all the possible cases that may arise are too manifold to be treated in any one volume.

The writer wishes to express his sincere gratitude to the Most Reverend Edwin V. O'Hara, D.D., LL.D., Bishop of Great Falls, for the opportunity of advanced study and for his kindly encourgement. An equal expression of thanks is due to the Faculty of the School of Canon Law for their helpful direction and generous assistance at all times. Likewise an earnest word of appreciation is extended to those pastors and priests who furnished many useful suggestions garnered from their experience, to the librarians of the Catholic University for their willing assistance and to many friends who so generously lent their time and aid in the preparation of the manuscript.

Part I

HISTORICAL SYNOPSIS

CHAPTER I

PRELIMINARY DISCUSSION

ARTICLE 1. NOTION OF PRE-NUPTIAL INVESTIGATION

THE Code of Canon Law does not give a formal definition of canonical pre-nuptial investigation. It simply states that the pastor, who has the right to assist at marriage, is obliged to institute pre-nuptial inquiry and then it proceeds to summarize in a general way the subject matter of that inquiry.[1]

To formulate in one sentence a comprehensive and scientifically precise definition of pre-nuptial investigation is not an easy task because of the wide field that such investigation is intended to cover. Consequently the intention here is not that of giving a concise definition of it but rather one of setting forth and explaining its notion.

Etymologically the word "pre-nuptial" signifies "before marriage" or "antecedent to marriage." Pre-nuptial investigation, therefore, means investigation that precedes marriage. The duty of making this ante-nuptial investigation is imposed by ecclesiastical law on the pastor. The basic purpose of pre-nuptial investigation by the pastor is twofold: (a) to establish the *status liber* of the parties who manifest to the pastor their intention of marrying; (b) to find out whether the parties are sufficiently instructed in Christian doctrine. A brief explanation of the meaning of *status liber* is in order here. *Status liber* is a technical expression denoting canonical freedom to marry. It is known also as *libertas status, free status* or *free state* and may be defined as immunity from any impediment affecting the lawful and valid celebration of marriage.[2] To offset any confusion concerning the precise meaning of the phrase *status liber* a brief explanation of the meaning of matrimonial impediments in the comprehensive sense and of matrimonial impediments in the strict and proper sense

[1] Canon 1020, §§ 1, 2.

[2] *Cf.* Felix M. Cappello, *De Sacramentis,* III: *De Matrimonio* (3. ed., Romae: Marietti, 1933), n. 145.

is in order here. Matrimonial impediments in the comprehensive sense are those circumstances which according to the prescriptions of divine law or human ecclesiastical law prevent marriage from being contracted validly and licitly. It makes no difference whether those obstacles arise from an internal source such as defect of matrimonial consent, etc., or whether they proceed from an external cause such as consanguinity or affinity. Matrimonial impediments in the comprehensive sense are therefore very numerous. Matrimonial impediments in the strict and proper sense are less numerous and may be defined as those external circumstances which from the prescriptions of divine law or human ecclesiastical law either render a *person* incapable of marriage or bar *him* from the lawful contracting of marriage. It is in the strict and proper sense that the Code considers matrimonial impediments in canons 1035-1080. Marriage impediments in this sense directly and immediately affect only the persons intending marriage. To put it more aptly they are impediments *ex parte personae,* whereas impediments in the comprehensive sense include not only impediments *ex parte personae,* but also impediments *ex parte consensus* and *ex parte formae;* as a matter of fact they include all obstacles which preclude either the validity or the lawfulness of a contemplated marriage.[8] As far as the *status liber* is concerned it is well to remember that canonical freedom to marry implies (a) immunity from matrimonial impediments in the strict and proper sense, (b) immunity from matrimonial impediments in the comprehensive sense.

The treatment of the notion of pre-nuptial investigation would be incomplete without some discussion of the questions: who are interrogated and are there any means employed to support the replies of those interrogated? In reference to the first of these queries the pre-nuptial inquiry is primarily a joint and separate personal interrogation of the prospective bride and groom by the pastor. Ordinarily the interrogation is made orally. To interrogate the man and not the woman, or *vice versa,* is not in accordance with the true notion of pre-nuptial investigation; both should be questioned. The Code is

[8] *Cf.* Cappello, *De Sacramentis,* III, n. 195; Petrus Card. Gasparri, *Tractatus Canonicus de Matrimonio* (ed. nova ad mentem Codicis I. C., Typis Polyglottis Vaticanis, 1932), nn. 204, 205.

decidedly clear on that point, "*Tum sponsum tum sponsam etiam seorsum et caute interroget.*"[4] *A fortiori* interrogation of the parents or guardians of the parties, or of their friends or relatives or others, to the exclusion of the questioning of the parties themselves, is not pre-nuptial investigation as the law intends it. The reason why the inquiry is chiefly concentrated on the contracting parties is evident; they are generally better informed than others are regarding the presence or absence of matrimonial impediments in their case and they can also testify more directly to their knowledge of Christian doctrine. Besides, the parties themselves are often the only ones who can furnish information on certain points, *e. g.*, in regard to matrimonial consent. However, interrogation is not always to be confined solely to the parties themselves. Not infrequently for the purpose of establishing the free status of the parties it will be necessary to address questions to parents, relatives, friends or others who can give reliable information on the freedom of the parties to marry. This will be especially true when doubts arise in the mind of the pastor concerning the existence of marriage impediments.[5]

To support the replies of both the parties themselves and of the witnesses to the interrogations of the pastor the production of authentic documents is of great utility. At times it can even become obligatory. Legal and reliable documents are a convenient and satisfactory means of supplying the desired information, *e. g.*, in proving the reception of Baptism and Confirmation, the death of a former spouse, the declaration of nullity of a previous marriage, dispensations from impediments, etc.[6]

Another aid of real value to the pastor in making pre-nuptial investigation is the publication of the banns of matrimony. The banns are a distinct canonical institution and they complement the personal interrogation of the parties and witnesses made by the pastor. They play an important rôle in the detection of matrimonial impediments known to others. The banns of marriage are public announcements of a future marriage made in church according

[4] Canon 1020, § 2.

[5] Canon 1031, § 1, 1°.

[6] Armandus Gougnard, *Tractatus de Matrimonio* (7. ed., Mechliniae: H. Dessain, 1931), p. 61.

to the prescriptions of Canon Law.[7] Unlike personal inquiry by the pastor, they are not an interrogation of persons, but they bear a close relationship to the investigation by the pastor, not only because they were instituted for the detection of impediments to marriage, but also because of the fact that the pastor, before he admits parties to marriage, must make sure that the banns of marriage have been published and must have testimony of the fact that they were published and of what was the outcome of their publication. The obtaining of this testimony forms part of the pre-nuptial inquiry.

In bringing to a conclusion this article on the notion of pre-nuptial investigation, it is in order to state that pre-nuptial inquiry is not intended to be a mere cursory and superficial investigation of the *status liber* of the nupturients consisting of a few general questions addressed to the parties; rather, both the prospective bride and groom should be subjected to a comprehensive, thorough and somewhat systematic interrogation. A discussion in detail of the various points and phases of that interrogation will be given in the commentary which is to follow.

Article 2. Division and Scope of Pre-nuptial Investigation

In this article the purpose is to set forth the usual divisions of ecclesiastical pre-nuptial investigation mentioned by authors and to state what items are to be covered by the investigation.

Ecclesiastical pre-nuptial investigation may be sub-divided as follows:

1. *Judicial* and *Non-judicial*. *Judicial* is that which requires the formalities of a judicial process, which formalities are found in the Fourth Book of the Code. *Non-judicial* is that which is exercised in a purely administrative fashion without judicial formality or procedure.

2. *General* and *Special*. *General* investigation signifies interrogation of the parties as to whether all the requirements for the valid and lawful celebration of marriage are fulfilled in their case. *Special*

[7] *Cf.* canons 1022-1026; James Brendan Roberts, *The Banns of Marriage* (The Catholic University of America, Canon Law Studies, n. 64, Washington: The Catholic University of America, 1931), pp. 9, 10.

investigation is of two kinds: (a) examination of the parties concerning the sufficiency of their instruction in Christian doctrine and the obligations of the married state; (b) special examination of witnesses to prove the *free status* of the parties.[8] Here there is reference to the special examination of witnesses, which was prescribed by Clement X in his instruction *Cum alias* issued in the year 1670 by the Sacred Congregation of the Holy Office.

3. Pre-nuptial investigation of the *external* and *internal* forum. The *external forum* concerns the external government and administration of the affairs of the Church and has direct reference to the public good of the faithful as members of the visible society of the Church. The *internal forum* has immediate and direct reference to the private good of the individual and aims at the private sanctification of the individual man. Because it concerns the relations of man's individual conscience with God, it is also known as the forum of conscience.[9] The internal forum is sacramental and extra-sacramental. Pre-nuptial investigation of the external forum may be regarded as pre-nuptial investigation of the contracting parties in so far as the inquiry affects the public good of the Church and society. Pre-nuptial investigation of the internal forum is investigation of the parties in so far as the inquiry affects the private good and sanctification of man. Pre-nuptial investigation of the internal sacramental forum is that investigation which is made in the Sacrament of Penance or on its occasion. Pre-nuptial investigation of the internal extra-sacramental forum is that investigation in the internal forum which is made outside of the Sacrament of Penance. In the external forum the external observance of the marriage laws of the Church suffices; in the internal forum not only is external compliance with the laws of the Church required, but also internal compliance with them.

The present dissertation, strictly speaking, embraces within its scope only ecclesiastical pre-nuptial investigation, *i. e.*, investigation

[8] Franciscus Wernz, *Ius Decretalium*, IV: *Ius Matrimoniale* (Romae, 1908-1913), n. 129.

[9] *Cf.* Raymond A. Kearney, *The Principles of Delegation* (The Catholic University of America, Canon Law Studies, n. 55, Washington: The Catholic University of America, 1929), p. 104; Pacificus Capobianco, "De Notione Fori Interni in Iure Canonico," *Apollinaris*, IX (1936), pp. 343-365.

conducted under the authority of the Church by ecclesiastical officials and according to the rules of Canon Law. Civil officials are not authorized to conduct the investigation and pronounce the parties canonically free to marry. This does not mean, however, that the Church never takes cognizance of the juridical effects of the civil laws of marriage. She does recognize the State's right to enact marriage laws in its own proper sphere and will co-operate with the State by giving consideration to those laws in canonical pre-nuptial investigation, provided the marriage laws of the State are in accord with faith and morality. In many countries the State has taken it upon itself to enact marriage laws for its Catholic citizens, which interfere with the rights of the Church. While the Church resents this interference with her rights, it will be necessary for the pastor, in order to prevent conflict with the State, to comply externally with many of these regulations in making his pre-nuptial investigation. Furthermore, many civil governments insist on a civil pre-nuptial investigation for their citizens. Though the results of such civil pre-nuptial investigation may be an asset to the pastor in determining the free status of the parties, it cannot be considered a sufficient substitute for ecclesiastical investigation,[10] because the Church, as a juridically perfect society,[11] claims for herself the right to inquire into her subjects' canonical freedom to marry. Moreover, many civil codes and statutes reject several canonical impediments to marriage; in numerous instances admit divorce and permit divorcees to re-marry: all of which is contrary to Catholic teaching.[12]

Excluded from the scope of pre-nuptial investigation by the pastor is any form of investigation that requires the intervention of an ecclesiastical tribunal. Pre-nuptial investigation by the pastor is not judicial; it is strictly non-judicial and purely administrative. Consequently, if in the course of the pastor's interrogation and examina-

[10] Gasparri, *Tractatus Canonicus de Matrimonio,* n. 126; Benedictus Ojetti, *Synopsis Rerum Moralium et Iuris Pontificii* (Romae, 1899), pp. 541, 542.

[11] Alaphridus Ottaviani, *Institutiones Iuris Publici Ecclesiastici,* I, *Ius Publicum Internum* (ed. altera emendata et aucta, Romae: Typis Polyglottis Vaticanis, 1935), 185-209.

[12] Joseph Rossi, *De Matrimonii Celebratione iuxta Codicem Iuris Canonici* (Romae: Pustet, 1904), n. 5.

tion of the parties difficulties arise that require judicial procedure for a solution, the pastor cannot there and then make a decision, but is obliged to refer the matter to the ecclesiastical tribunal, which will make judicial investigation of the case and decide accordingly. As will be noted later in this study, there are a great many circumstances in pre-nuptial investigation when the pastor, even in purely administrative points, must refer the matter to the ordinary. This limits his freedom in certain instances to decide the question of the *status liber* of the parties.

It is important to note here that this study does not properly include within its scope pre-nuptial investigation in the internal sacramental forum made by the pastor as confessor. Circumstances, however, will necessitate sometimes allusions to the internal sacramental forum.

From the point of view of the matter treated, the general scope of the pastor's investigation can be summed up in the three following questions: (a) Is there any impediment to the valid and lawful celebration of the marriage? (b) Are the parties willingly and freely consenting to the marriage? (c) Are they sufficiently instructed in Christian doctrine? To develop these points further would be superfluous here, for their development properly belongs to the commentary and will be presented in later chapters.

This brief sketch of the notion, the division and general scope of pre-nuptial investigation by the pastor, will suffice for the present. The next three chapters will be devoted to presenting a historical conspectus of its development from faint beginnings in early Christianity to its more complete development in the Code of Canon Law.

CHAPTER II

PRE-NUPTIAL INVESTIGATION PRIOR TO THE FOURTH LATERAN COUNCIL

IN pre-Christian legislation, whether civil or religious, one seeks in vain for traces of juridical pre-nuptial investigation. Even the highly developed Roman legal system, which contained so much jurisprudence and legislation on marriage [1] and which considerably influenced Christian matrimonial legislation, is silent on the subject. It is true that the seventy-fourth Novel of Justinian forbade those of illustrious rank to marry without a dotal contract and required those who occupied positions of less importance, but pursued honorable occupations, and desired to marry without entering into the ante-nuptial contract, to go to a house of worship and declare their intention to the defender of the Most Holy Church. The defender was to draw up a statement testifying to the marriage. The statement was to be signed by the parties married, by the defender himself and three or four clerics who acted as witnesses. The document was to be placed in the Church archives.[2] The dotal contract in the case of the illustrious and the appearance before the defender of the Most Holy Church in the case of those above mentioned do not seem to have involved any juridical pre-nuptial investigation. Apparently the intention was to have proof of the marriage, which proof was sufficiently established either by the solemnity of a dotal contract or the recording of the marriage in the archives of the Church. Registration would serve to prevent fraudulent contracts.

Why was Roman Law silent on the subject of pre-nuptial investigation? It certainly was not that Roman Law tolerated complacently invalid and illegal marital unions. Undoubtedly it did desire to leave marriage a social institution unhampered by legal restrictions; yet, despite that fact, it did enact marriage legislation when it deemed

[1] D. 22-25; I. 1 (10); C. 5 (1-26); Novellae, 2, 12, 22, 74, 78 (3), 91, 97, 98, 100, 117, 119 (1), 137, 140, 143.

[2] Nov. 74 (4) 2; *Cf.* etiam Nov. 117 (4).

it really necessary. Apparently the reason for the absence of juridical pre-nuptial inquiry lay in the fact that Roman Law was content to protect the validity and lawfulness of marriages by means of drastic and severe penalties imposed on the parties after they had entered invalid or unlawful unions.[3] Moreover, the Romans as a rule were respecters of law, who did not desire to have their good name and reputation sullied by subjection to legal penalties, and consequently the sanctions of the law would sufficiently deter them from entering forbidden unions, thereby making pre-nuptial investigation more or less unnecessary. In addition, the common practice of betrothal,[4] the dowry arrangements,[5] the solemnity of the ceremonial accompanying the *confarreatio* and the marriage *cum manu* as well as the custom of the *deductio in domum, i. e.*, public bringing of the bride to the husband's house, publicized the marriage and thus contributed to prevent prohibited marriages. Furthermore, the necessity of obtaining the consent of the *paterfamilias* aided in securing valid and lawful marriages; [6] for a *paterfamilias* really interested in the welfare of those subject to him and desirous to uphold his own honor in the community would hardly consent to a marriage which would violate the laws of Rome. From these observations it is easy to conclude that juridical pre-nuptial investigation was juridically unnecessary in Roman Law.

Article 1. Marriage with the Consent of the Bishop

In the quest for the primary traces of ecclesiastical pre-nuptial investigation early Church organization cannot be overlooked. The original Christian churches were urban,[7] because the Apostles, their

[3] I. (10), 12; D. 3 (2) 1; D. 23 (2) 51, 66, 68; C. 5 (5) 2, 3, 4, 6; C. 5 (98) 2; C. 5 (9) 1, 2.

[4] D. 23 (1) 1-18; C. 5 (1) 1-5; Percy Ellwood Corbett, *The Roman Law of Marriage* (Oxford: Clarendon Press, 1930), pp. 1-23.

[5] D. 23 (3); C. 5 (12); J. Declareuil, *Rome the Lawgiver*, translation by E. A. Parker (New York: Alfred A. Knopf, 1926), pp. 109-113.

[6] I. 1 (10); D. 23 (2) 18; C. 5 (4) 5; R. W. Leage, *Roman Private Law* (London: MacMillan, 1932), p. 99.

[7] *Cf.* William Moran, *The Government of the Church in the First Century* (New York, 1913), p. 60; Clement Bastnagel, *The Appointment of Parochial Adjutants and Assistants* (The Catholic University of America, Canon Law Studies, n. 58, Washington: The Catholic University of America, 1930), p. 4.

early successors in the episcopate as well as the priests and missionaries of early Christian times largely concentrated their activities in the cites and towns. These urban churches were presided over by bishops who exercised the care of souls somewhat after the manner of present day pastors. These episcopal pastors were assisted in their work by priests and deacons who, however, required the authorization of their respective bishops before they could perform spiritual ministrations or ecclesiastical functions.[8] Thus it appears that the relationship between the bishops of early Christian times and their priests resembled in a sense the present day canonical relationship existing between pastors and their assistants.

Evidently one of the duties of the bishops of the infant Church was to give their approval and consent to the marriages of those under their pastoral care, as a passage in the letter of St. Ignatius to Polycarp indicates: "It becometh men and women too when they marry to unite themselves with the consent of the bishop that the marriage may be after the Lord and not after concupiscence." [9] The text considers it altogether seemly for those intending marriage to consult the bishop and receive his approbation for the marriage. The positive purpose of such consultation was to ensure the contraction of marriage in accordance with the laws of God. It seems legitimate to conclude that the bishop would not place his stamp of approval on a marriage without having made some kind of pre-nuptial inquiry, at least in a cursory manner. Otherwise how could he conscientiously determine whether the marriage was "after the Lord

[8] "Presbyteri et diaconi absque sententia episcopi nihil pergant; ipse enim est, cui comissus est populus Domini a quo de animabus eorum ratio poscetur." —Francis Xavier Funk, *Didascalia et Constitutiones Apostolorum* (Paderbornae, 1905), I, 577; Charles Koudelka, *Pastors, Their Rights and Duties According to the New Code of Canon Law* (The Catholic University of America, Canon Law Studies, n. 11, Washington: The Catholic University of America, 1921), p. 8.

[9] Πρέπει δὲ τοῖς γαμοῦσι καὶ ταῖς γαμουμέναις μετὰ γνώμης τοῦ ἐπισκόπου τὴν ἕνωσιν ποιεῖσθαι, ἵνα ὁ γάμος ᾖ κατὰ Θεὸν μὴ κατ' ἐπιθυμίαν. —St. Ignatius, *Letter to Polycarp*, c. 5—*MPG*, V, 723. Translation from J. B. Lightfoot, *The Apostolic Fathers* (London and New York, 1889), II, 573; *Cf.* M. J. Rouët de Journel, *Enchiridion Patristicum* (3. ed., Friburgi Brisgoviae: Herder, 1920), n. 67.

and not after concupiscence?" From the above passage in the letter of St. Ignatius there can be deduced no juridical obligation on the part of the parties intending marriage to consult the bishop; for the quotation is couched in the language of a counsel rather than a command and probably was written in approval of a custom prevailing at the period, namely, the custom of seeking the bishop's advice prior to marriage.[10]

Article 2. Non-Episcopal Pastors

About the end of the third century or the beginning of the fourth parishes committed to the care of priests who were not bishops began to come into being.[11] They first appeared in the rural districts and manifested themselves in the East before they spread to the West. Their development was not rapid; it was slow and gradual. As a matter of fact, excepting the cities of Rome and Alexandria, they did not appear in urban areas till the eleventh century.[12]

With the growth of parishes which were presided over by non-episcopal pastors many of the duties and functions that were previously performed by episcopal pastors or by priests delegated by the bishop began to be exercised by priests acting in their own name. Though prior to the time of Charlemagne there is not any explicit or express mention of juridical pre-nuptial investigation as being exercised by non-episcopal pastors or priests, it is probable that betrothed parties consulted their pastors concerning the desirability of their marriages, just as they were accustomed to consult the bishop in the time of SS. Ignatius and Polycarp. This theory is supported by the widespread custom of the religious marriage ceremony which will be treated in the next article.

[10] Roberts, *The Banns of Marriage*, p. 3.

[11] Thomassinus, *Vetus et Nova Ecclesiae Disciplina*, p. I, lib. II, c. 21; Wernz, *Ius Decretalium*, II, n. 689; Septimus Vecchiotti, *Institutiones Canonici* (3. ed., Paris, 1880), pp. 22, 23; Koudelka, *Pastors, Their Rights and Duties*, p. 3; Bastnagel. *The Appointment of Parochial Adjutants and Assistants*, pp. 8, 22.

[12] John Joseph Coady, *The Appointment of Pastors* (The Catholic University of America, Canon Law Studies, n. 52, Washington: The Catholic University of America, 1929), p. 12; Koudelka, *Pastors, Their Rights and Duties*, p. 9.

Article 3. The Religious Celebration of Marriage

Christ raised marriage to the dignity of a sacrament. It was only natural, therefore, that the early Christians should express in an external manner the dignity and sanctity of the sacrament by the solemnity of a religious ceremony. Thus the presence of the priest at the marriage ceremony, the nuptial Mass and the nuptial benediction of the parties became popular. In this article an endeavor will be made to present the evidence for the religious celebration of marriage during the early centuries of Christianity. The reason for including this article in the present chapter is the close relationship that the religious celebration of marriage had with the early beginnings of ecclesiastical pre-nuptial investigation. Were it not for the fact that the presence of the priest at marriage became established by custom and by law the development of ecclesiastical pre-nuptial investigation would not have been very effective or rapid. The religious celebration of marriage facilitated the introduction of juridical pre-nuptial investigation. That there was no definitely juridical pre-nuptial investigation by the pastor before the time of Charlemagne is not surprising, because the early Church only gradually acquired jurisdiction over marriage independently of the secular power; and it took some time before matrimonial legislation by the Church developed. However, it was the duty of the early clergy, just as of the clergy today, to protect the marriage laws of God and of the Church and it is inconceivable to think that any of the conscientious clergy of the early Church would assist indiscriminately at the marriages of the faithful without first making some effort to discover if the parties were entering a valid and lawful marriage. It has been already pointed out that the custom prevailed of parties getting the consent of the bishop prior to entering marriage; when pastors who were not bishops came into being it is very probable that the parties asked their consent likewise, for there is a wealth of testimony to prove that priests were wont to assist at the marriages of the faithful and that nuptials were celebrated with the nuptial Mass and the nuptial blessing.

Tertullian (d. 222) emphasized the happiness of that marriage which "the Church *conciliates* and the *sacrifice confirms,* the *bene-*

diction seals, the *angels announce* and the *Father holds ratified*."[13] He also observed that marriage without the approval of the Church ran the risk of being adjudged as adultery and fornication, an evidence that the Christians of the African Church, for which he was a witness, generally favored only those marriages which were contracted with religious ceremonial.[14]

Clement of Alexandria (d. 215) indirectly called attention to the sacerdotal blessing, when he opposed the practice of a bride wearing false hair, by stating that "when a bride adorns herself in this way, it is not on her head that the *benediction* descends, but on the head of the dead woman whose hair she wears."[15]

Pope Siricius (384-399) also referred to the *blessing* which the priest imposes on "the woman who is about to be married."[16] St. Ambrose (d. 397) considered it obligatory that marriage be sanctified with the sacerdotal veil and benediction,[17] which apparently was the custom at Milan. Pope Innocent I (402-417) not only mentioned the blessing which was bestowed on the bridal party by the priest, but also affirmed it to be the accepted teaching that the blessing was the "observance of a law instituted long since by God."[18] Pope Hormisdas (d. 523) explicitly mentioned the blessing of the priest at public marriages,[19] and St. Isidore of Seville (560-636), an outstanding canonist and witness for the Church in Spain, referred also to the nuptial blessing.[20]

The thirteenth canon in the ancient collection of decrees known as the *Statuta Ecclesiae Antiqua* is decidedly explicit on the priest's part in the marriage celebration: "When the bridegroom and the bride are to receive the priest's blessing, let them be conducted by their parents or by the bridesmaids; and when they have received the

[13] Tertullian, *Ad Uxorem*, lib. II, c. 9—*MPL*, I, 1302.

[14] Tertullian, *De Pudicitia*, c. 4—*Corpus Scriptorum Ecclesiasticorum Latinorum* XX, 225.

[15] Clement of Alexandria, *Pedagogus*, lib. III, c. 11—*MPG*, VIII, 638.

[16] Siricius, *Letter to Himerius*, c. 4—*MPL*, XIII, 1136.

[17] *Letter to Vigilius*, c. 7—*MPL*, XV, 984.

[18] *Second Epistle to Victricius*, c. 6—*MPL*, XX, 475.

[19] C. 2, C. XXX, q. 5.

[20] *De Ecclesiasticis Officiis*, lib. II, c. 20—*MPL*, LXXXIII, 810.

benediction, let them out of respect for the blessing remain the same night in virginity." [21]

The sacramentaries, which are ancient liturgical collections, clearly confirm the foregoing testimony. The Leonine Sacramentary, found in the library of the Cathedral Chapter at Verona as preserved in a manuscript of the seventh century but containing liturgical formulae of an earlier date, gives excerpts from the nuptial Mass of the early centuries of the Christian era.[22] The nuptial blessing, as well as portions of the nuptial Mass, is found in the Gelasian Sacramentary,[23] attributed to Pope St. Gelasius (492-496), and also in the Gregorian Sacramentary,[24] which dates from the time of Pope Gregory the Great (590-604).

It may be concluded that such extensive evidence, coming from Popes, Fathers of the Church, ecclesiastical writers and early Church liturgy and at the same time representative of various countries, constitutes undeniable proof that the practice of public religious rites in the celebration of Christian marriage was widespread during the early centuries of Christianity.

Article 4. Suggested Reasons for the Absence of Definite Pre-nuptial Investigation in Early Christianity

The practice of consulting the bishop or priest prior to marriage probably involved some pre-nuptial inquiry, as was pointed out above. At most, however, the inquiry would have been very indefinite, as the extent and diligence of the investigations depended on the conscience of the consulted priest or bishop and not on a definite law. Conse-

[21] Carl Joseph Von Hefele, *Conciliengeschicte* (2. ed., Freiburg im Breisgau, 1875-1890), II, 71; *Cf.* Cicognani, *Canon Law* (2. ed., Philadelphia: The Dolphin Press, 1935), p. 222; A. Van Hove, *Commentarium Lovaniense in Codicem Iuris Canonici,* I, *Prologomena* (Mechliniae-Romae: H. Dessian, 1928), pp. 115, 116; H. Denziger-C. Bannwart, *Enchiridion Symbolorum Definitionum et Declarationum de Rebus Fidei et Morum* (17. ed., Friburgi Brisgoviae: Herder, 1928), n. 150, footnote.

[22] Ludovicus Antonius Muratori, *Liturgia Romana Vetus* (Venetiis, 1748), I, 446, 447.

[23] Muratori, *Liturgia Romana Vetus,* I, 721-723.

[24] Muratori, *Liturgia Romana Vetus,* II, 244, 245.

quently it could not have followed any uniform rules. Apparently the sources of Canon Law contain no vestiges of definite and specific pre-nuptial inquiry before the Carlovingian period of history. Several reasons taken conjointly are responsible for this. One of the chief reasons is that matrimonial legislation was yet in its infancy, and the laws on marriage impediments were not well developed. Unquestionably, the early persecutions, the struggles against heathenism, the early heresies and doctrinal controversies considerably retarded the evolution of marriage legislation. When the persecutions ceased after the first three centuries, other factors contributed to the same end. Chief among these factors were the interference of emperors and rulers in strictly ecclesiastical affairs, the political upheavals and the invasions and ravages of the barbarian and Arab hordes. Despite these disadvantages, however, a certain number of matrimonial laws came into being either by custom or legislative enactment. Severe penalties and penances were imposed for breaches of matrimonial discipline,[25] and they to some extent prevented prohibited marriages, thereby constituting another reason for the absence of definite pre-nuptial investigation. Moreover, Christianity was born into a world where betrothal and ante-nuptial parental consent were customary, *e. g.*, among Jews, Romans, Greeks, and Germanic peoples. The Church, realizing the utility of these practices, received betrothal[26] and the practice of obtaining ante-nuptial parental consent into her

[25] *Cf.* Council of Elvira (305), cc. 8, 9, 10, 14, 54, 61, 66—Mansi, II, 7-15; Council of Arles (314), c. 11—Mansi, II, 472; Council of Ancyra (314), cc. 10, 24—Mansi, II, 531-534; Council of Neo-Caesarea (314-324), cc. 1, 2, 3, 7, 8—Mansi, II, 540, 541; Council of Valence (374), c. 2—Mansi, II, 493; Council of Toledo (400), cc. 4, 19—Mansi, II, 999, 1001; Council of Chalcedon (451), cc. 14, 27—Mansi, VII, 377, 380; Council of Arles (circa 452), cc. 21, 46, 52—Mansi, VII, 881, 884; Council of Tours (461), cc. 2, 6—Mansi, VII, 945, 946; Council of Agde (506), c. 25—Mansi, VIII, 329; Council of Arles (511), c. 13—Mansi, VIII, 353, 354; Council of Epaon (517), c. 32—Mansi, VIII, 563; Council of Auvergne (circa 541), cc. 6, 12—Mansi, VIII, 861; Council of Arles (538), c. 7—Mansi, IX, 14; Council of Paris (557), c. 6—Mansi, IX, 746; Council of Rheims (625), cc. 8, 23—Mansi, X, 595-597; Council of Rome (721), cc. 1-9, 11—Mansi, XII, 263, 264.

[26] Council of Elvira (305), c. 54—Mansi, II, 14; Council of Ancyra (314), c. 11—Mansi, II, 518; St. Basil, *Letter to Amphilochius,* c. 22—*MPG,* XXXII, 722; Council of Trullo (692), c. 98—Mansi, XI, 986.

legislation.[27] Betrothal afforded the affianced parties the opportunity for sober reflection in regard to their choice and so publicized their forthcoming marriage that hidden impediments to their union were likely to be brought to light. On the other hand, parents as a general rule would hardly consent to prohibited marriages of their children. All these considerations together with the stability of the communities of the period, the simplicity of social life, the lack of facilities for frequent and extensive travel, the strength of public opinion and the fact that the spouses were from the same locality, contributed to prevent illegal and unwise marriages, and consequently a detailed and definite pre-nuptial inquiry by the pastor did not develop in early Christianity.

Article 5. Local Legislation on Definite Pre-nuptial Investigation

A decided step forward in the development of the pastor's obligation in pre-nuptial investigation was made between the end of the eight century and the Fourth Lateran Council (1215). This period witnessed no universal legislation on the subject. A few local councils, however, took the initiative and enacted laws prescribing a definite pre-nuptial inquiry to be made by the priest. These laws were primarily directed towards finding out whether the parties intending marriage were related by the ties of blood within the forbidden degrees of kindred. The reason for this was the prevalence of forbidden incestuous and consanguineous marriages. Marriages of *affines* were also by no means rare. An evil of even greater proportions was that of secret and clandestine marriages, that is, marriages celebrated without due publicity, without solemnity, without the nuptial Mass, without the nuptial blessing and without the assistance of the priest and witnesses. Because of their occult nature secret unions helped to increase incestuous, consanguineous and bigamous marriages. A consideration of these abuses is in order here.

[27] Tertullian, *Ad Uxorem,* II, 9—*MPL,* I, 1302; Council of Arles (541), c. 22—Mansi, IX, 117; Pope Nicholas I, *Responsa ad Bulgaros* (866), c. 3—Mansi, XV, 402; c. 3, C. XXX, q. 5; St. Basil, *Letter to Amphilochius,* cc. 40, 42—*MPG,* XXXII, 727-730.

That the prohibited marriages of relatives must have become a very grave menace to society may be judged from the numerous councils in various countries that legislated against them.[28] Likewise the decree of Gratian in its second part devotes considerable space to them and treats at length of the laws governing the accusation of such marriages,[29] thereby indicating that the validity of these marriages was frequently questioned. The spread of the abuse was encouraged by the difficulty of travel, the lack of social intercourse between marriageable people of different localities and the fact that married couples usually belonged to the same locality where many of the inhabitants were related by consanguinity or affinity. Moreover, opportunity in the selection of a suitable mate was further restricted by the numerous prohibited degrees to which the impediment of consanguinity extended. Though the extent of the impediment was not universally uniform, it did reach as high as the seventh degree of consanguinity until the Fourth Council of the Lateran reduced it to the fourth degree inclusive.[30]

The seriousness of the evil of clandestine marriages was attested by several councils, especially by those celebrated in England and in France. These councils reprobated such unions, either *directly* by expressly condemning them, or *indirectly* by insisting that marriages

[28] Council of Agde (506), c. 61—Mansi, VIII, 355; Council of Auvergne (535), c. 12—Mansi, VIII, 861; Council of Orleans (538), c. 10—Mansi, IX, 14; Council of Tours (567), c. 21—Mansi, IX, 800; Council of Paris (614), c. 14—Mansi, X, 542; Council of Toledo (527), c. 15—Mansi, VIII, 768; Council of Rheims (624), c. 8—Mansi, X, 595; Council of Rome (721), c. 8—Mansi, XII, 263; Council of Verberie (753), c. 1—Harduin, III, 1990; Council of Compiegne (757), cc. 1-3—Harduin, III, 2004; Council of Mainz (813), c. 30—Harduin, V, 14; Council of Bourges (1031), c. 17—Mansi, XIX, 505; Council of Rheims (1049), c. 11—Mansi, XIX, 472; Council of Rome (1063), c. 9—Mansi, XIX, 1026; Council of Rouen (1072), c. 14— Mansi, XX, 38; I Lateran Council (1123), c. 5—Mansi, XXI, 283; II Lateran Council (1139), c. 17—Mansi, XXI, 503. *Cf.* also St. Ambrose, *Letter Ad Paternam—MPL,* XVI, 1183-1186; St. Augustine, *De Civitate Dei,* c. 15—*MPL,* 485.

[29] Cc. 1-11, C. XXXV, q. 6.

[30] C. 50—Mansi, XXII, 1035, Francis X. Wahl, *Impedimnts of Consanguinity and Affinity* (The Catholic University of America, Canon Law Studies, n. 90, Washington: The Catholic University of America, 1934), pp. 18, 19.

be celebrated *in facie ecclesiae,* in the presence of priest and witnesses and with the nuptial Mass and blessing.[31] Ecclesiastical writers also testified to the serious illegality of secret marriages. According to John of Orleans numerous marriages were celebrated without any ecclesiastical solemnity, a practice which he vehemently condemned.[32] The pseudo-Isidorian decretals affirmed that marriage was not legitimate unless celebrated with the priestly blessing and the nuptial Mass.[33] Burchard of Worms in his *Interrogatory on the Sacrament of Penance* instructed confessors to ask the penitent whether he was married in church and whether the nuptial blessing was imparted.[34] Peter Lombard enumerated some complications to which clandestine marriage gave rise.[35] Hugh of St. Vicar looked on them with disfavor[36] and Bandini considered them illegal.[37] In the decree of Gratian clandestine marriages were strictly prohibited and public marriage with the blessing of the priest and the Sacrifice of the Mass was prescribed.[38]

From these testimonies the evil of secret marriages is easily deduced. No doubt they opened an avenue for unscrupulous people to declare, even under oath, that they were not married when in reality they were; to affirm that they were married when the opposite

[31] Council of Laodicea (343-381)—Mansi, II, 577; Council of Friuli (791), c. 8—Mansi, XVII bis, 373, 374; Council of Rouen (1072), c. 14—Mansi, XX, 38; Council of London (1102), c. 32—Mansi, XX, 1152; Council of London (1174), c. 18— Mansi, XXII, 151; Council of London (1200), c. 11—Mansi, XXII, 719. For a discussion of the different meanings of the expression *"in facie ecclesiae"* see Joyce, *Christian Marriage,* pp. 109, 110.

[32] *De Institutione Laicali,* lib. II, c. 2—*MPL,* CVI, 170.

[33] *Decretales Pseudo-Isidorianae et Capitula Angilramni,* ed. Paulus Hinschius (Lipsiae, 1863), p. 87.

[34] *Liber Decretorum,* XX, c. 5—*MPL,* CXL, 958.

[35] Petrus Lombardus, *Libri IV Sententiarum studia et cura PP. Collegii S. Bonaventurae in lucem editi* (Ad Claras Aquas: Typographia Collegii S. Bonaventurae, 1916), lib. IV, D. XXVIII; cc. 1, 2.

[36] *De Sacramentis,* lib. II, c. 4—*MPL,* CLXXVI, 483.

[37] *De Ecclesiasticis Sacramentis,* lib. IV, D. XLV—*MPL,* CXCII, 483.

[38] Cc. 1-5, C. XXX, q. 5. The civil practice of exchanging marriage vows before the *Fürsprecher,* as was common among the Germans, and before the *orator,* as was prescribed by Lombardic law, was probably introduced to offset the difficulties offered by clandestine marriages. *Cf.* Joyce, *Christian Marriage,* p. 49.

was true and to conceal matrimonial impediments quite easily. As such marriages were difficult to prove, they paved the way for the desertion of lawful spouses and entry in new but adulterous unions. In the Eastern Church but not in the Western, there was a tendency to consider the nuptial blessing as something essential to a valid marriage. This doctrine was taught the Bulgarians by certain Greek priests. Pope Nicholas, however, refuted this false doctrine in his famous reply to the Bulgarians. Recalling the marriage ceremony as it existed in Rome, he denied that the religious marriage ceremony with the blessing of the priest and the imposition of the heavenly veil was necessary for a valid marriage.[39]

It was becoming evident that the old methods of securing lawful and valid marriages were inadequate to curb the evil of consanguineous and clandestine marriages. Consequently the Council of Friuli (791) not only directed attention to the pre-nuptial investigation of the impediment of consanguinity, but also prohibited secret and clandestine unions. It prescribed that a certain interval of time should elapse after the espousals for the purpose of finding out from the neighbors and the older people of the locality, who were acquainted with the genealogy of the espoused parties, whether there existed between the nupturients any blood-relationship that would prohibit marriage.[40] Although there is not any evidence from the Council of Friuli that the inquiry was made by a priest, the fact that it was made marks a certain evolution in pre-nuptial investigation. The Synod of Ratisbon (799) repeated substantially the legislation of the Council of Friuli,[41] but the authenticity of this legislation of the Synod of Ratisbon is doubted.[42] Charlemagne attacked the problem of consanguineous marriages in a Capitulary (802),

[39] *Decreta Papae Nicholai I*—Mansi, XV, 402; c. 2, XXVIII, q. 2; Leo VI, the Philosopher, in the 74th Novel prescribed that the pre-nuptial blessing was necessary for the validity of marriage. Benedict XIV declared that this law, being a civil law, did not bind in conscience—*cf. De Synodo Dioecesana,* lib. VIII, c. 12, n. 6.

[40] C. 8—Mansi, XIII, 848.

[41] C. 12—*MGH, Leges,* III (edit. Georgius Henricus Pertz, Leipzig: Hiersemann, 1925), 456.

[42] Hefele, *Conciliengeschichte,* III, 375.

wherein it was decreed that nobody should dare to marry until the bishops and priests together with the older people of the vicinity had made a diligent inquiry concerning the blood-relationship of the parties. If the inquiry was favorable, the parties could be united in marriage with the customary blessing.[43] The inquiry was to be a *diligent* one, indicating that it was not to be superficial and careless, but rather detailed and careful. Moreover, the bishop and the priest or pastor played an active part in the investigation, which was of a somewhat public nature. Benedict the Levite expressly mentioned in his collection of Capitularies that pre-nuptial investigation should take place in church and was to be conducted by the priest in whose parish the marriage was to be celebrated. The people assisted at the inquiry. It encompassed not only the impediment of consanguinity in all its forbidden degrees, but also the factors of previous valid marriage or espousal and the possible admission of adultery.[44] The Canons of Isaac, Bishop of Langres, in treating of the pre-nuptial investigation repeated *verbatim* what was contained in the collection of Benedict the Levite.[45] The Council of Rouen (1072) forbade occult marriages and decreed that the priest inquire diligently regarding the relationship of those about to be married. If he discovered that the parties were related within the seventh degree of consanguinity, he was forbidden to marry them. The penalty of deposition was the punishment prescribed for a priest who violated this law.[46] Odo, Bishop of Paris (1196-1208), ruled that before assisting at a marriage the priest, under penalty of excommunication, must ask the people about the legality of the marriage of those espoused. In case a doubt should arise about the legality of the marriage, Odo directed that the priest consult the bishop, a pre-

[43] "Ut omnes omnino episcopus [!] et presbyteros suos omni honore venerentur in servitio et voluntate Dei; ut incestis nuptiis et se ipsos caeteros maculare audeant coniunctiones facere non praesumat [!], antequam episcopi presbyteri cum senioribus populi consanguinitatem coniungentiun diligentur exquirant; et tunc cum benedictionem [!] iungantur.—Capitulary of Charlemagne (802), c. 35—*MGH, Leges,* I (edit. Georgius Henricus Pertz, Leipzig, Hiersemann, 1925), 95.

[44] *Collectio Capitularium,* lib. III, 179—*MPL,* XCVII, 820.

[45] C. 6—*MPL,* CXXIV, 1094.

[46] C. 14—Mansi, XX, 38.

scription similar to that of canon 1031, § 1, 3° of the Code.[47] Authors generally agree that the credit for introducing the banns of marriage should go to Odo of Paris,[48] which likewise demonstrates his zeal for promoting thorough pre-nuptial investigation.

It may be concluded that before the Fourth Council of the Lateran a definite pre-nuptial investigation to be made by the pastor had been established by particular law in some localities, especially in France. The exact extent of the practice cannot be precisely determined. The inquiry was public rather than private and was directed primarily, but not exclusively, to the impediment of consanguinity. Although it lacked the authority of universal ecclesiastical legislation, it undoubtedly paved the way for the general legislation which was to follow.

[47] *Constitutiones Synodales Udonis Parisiensis*, c. 7—Mansi, XXII, 679.

[48] *Cf.* Roberts, *The Banns of Marriage*, pp. 10, 11.

CHAPTER III

FROM THE FOURTH LATERAN COUNCIL (1215) TO THE DECREE "CUM ALIAS"

(AUGUST 21, 1670)

THE period from the Fourth Lateran Council to the decree *Cum alias,* which was issued in the reign of Pope Clement X, was a most important era in the development of Canon Law. During this time the two outstanding general councils, the Fourth Council of the Lateran and the Council of Trent, were celebrated, and the widely used Decretals of Pope Gregory IX, the *Liber Sextus* of Pope Boniface VIII, the *Clementinae,* the *Extravagantes* of John XXII and the *Extravangantes Communes* were compiled. It was the golden era of Canon Law. Matrimonial law underwent considerable evolution and pre-nuptial investigation was notably developed.

Before discussing the development of pre-nuptial investigation during this celebrated period, it may be well to mention briefly an important decision which was handed down by Pope Alexander III prior to the Fourth General Council of the Lateran and which ended a controversy intensely contested between the schools of Paris and Bologna concerning the efficient cause of matrimony. The decision is somewhat pertinent to the topic of pre-nuptial investigation, because it finally decided the exact time that the marriage contract is effected, thus rendering clear-cut the point of time that distinguishes pre-nuptial investigation from any investigation subsequent to the marriage itself. The School of Bologna maintained that consummation was necessary for a true, valid and sacramental marriage. This theory was known as the *copula* theory. The School of Paris, on the other hand, contended that a real, valid and sacramental marriage was effected by matrimonial consent alone, without any consummation of the marriage. Celebrated among those who supported the latter opinion were Pope Innocent II [1] and two other very outstanding personalities of the period,

[1] *Quinque Antiquae Compilationes,* ed. Aemilius Friedberg (Leipsic, 1882) Compilatio I, c. 10, IV, *De Sponsalibus et Matrimonio,* I.

namely, Hugh of St. Victor [2] and Peter Lombard.[3] Celebrated among those who supported the opinion of the Bologna School were the Magister Gratian [4] and Roland Bandinelli before he became Pope Alexander III.[5] Their advocacy of the *copula* theory of the Bologna School is not surprising because they taught there. However, when Roland Bandinelli became Pope he decided in favor of the opinion of the Paris School.[6] Another matter that caused confusion was the signification of the word *desponsatio*. Sometimes it was used by authors to signify *betrothal*, and at other times to mean *marriage*. Peter Lombard cleared up the situation by using the words *consensus per verba de futuro* to signify betrothal, and the words *consensus per verba de praesenti* to mean marriage.[7] The words *sponsalia per verba de futuro* and *sponsalia per verba de praesenti* were used in a similar signification.

Article 1. The Fourth Lateran Council

The Fourth Lateran Council, presided over by Pope Innocent III, was solemnly convened on November 11, 1215. Among the matters discussed at the council was that of the reform of the universal Church.[8] Naturally the current problems of clandestine and consanguineous marriages came up for discussion and called for remedial measures. As a result of the deliberations of the fathers of the council, the impediments of consanguinity and affinity were restricted to the fourth degree of relationship inclusive; a strict observance of the prohibited degrees of kindred was prescribed; clandestine marriages were entirely prohibited and the clergy were

[2] *De Sacramentis*, lib. II, p. IX, c. 50—*MPL*, CLXXVI, 485.

[3] *Libri IV Sententiarum studia et cura PP. Collegii S. Bonaventurae in lucem editi* (Ad Claras Aquas: Typographia Collegii S. Bonaventurae, 1916), lib. IV, D. XXVII, cc. 3, 4.

[4] Cc. 16, 17, C. XXVIII, q. 2.

[5] Friedrich Thaner, *Die Summa Magistri Rolandi nochmals Papstes Alexander III* (Innsbruck, 1874), p. 32.

[6] C. 3, X, *de sponsa duorum*, IV, 4; Joyce, *Christian Marriage*, p. 35; Esmein, *Le Mariage*, I, 140.

[7] *Libri IV Sententiarum*, lib. IV, D. XXVIII, cc. 1-4.

[8] Hefele-Leclerque, *Histoire des Conciles*, Tom. V, part 2, p. 1316.

forbidden to be present at them.[9] Up to this time clandestine marriages embraced: (a) marriages contracted without the presence of witnesses and which consequently could not be juridically proved; (b) marriages entered into without the prescribed solemnities. After the Fourth Lateran Council another type of clandestine marriage was distinguished, namely, that celebrated without the publication of the banns.[10] The fathers who were present at the deliberations of the council saw a positive antidote to the widespread abuse of consanguineous and clandestine marriages in two heretofore local practices, namely that of pre-nuptial investigation by the clergy and that of the publication of the banns of marriage. Consequently they incorporated both practices into the general legislation of the Church by canon 50 of the council.

> Cum inhibitio copulae coniugalis sit in tribus ultimis gradibus revocata; eam in aliis volumus districte observari. Unde praedecessorum nostrorum inhaerendo vestigiis, clandestina coniugia penitus inhibemus: prohibentes etiam, ne quis sacerdos talibus interesse praesumat. Quare specialem quorumdam locorum consuetudinem ad alia generaliter prorogando: Statuimus, ut cum matrimonia fuerint contrahenda, in ecclesiis per presbyteros publice proponantur, competenti termino praefinito: ut infra illum qui voluerit et valuerit, legitimum impedimentum opponat: *et ipsi presbyteri nihilominus investigent, utrum aliquod impedimentum obsistat.* Cum autem apparuerit probabilis coniectura contra copulam contrahendam, contractus interdicatur expresse, donec quid fieri debeat super eo, manifestis constiterit documentis.[11]

Thus the Fourth Lateran Council became the first general council to legislate definitely on the pastor's obligation regarding prenuptial investigation. This legislation was later inserted into the decretals of Gregory IX.[12] The words of the council *"et ipsi presbyteri nihilominus investigent, utrum aliquod impedimentum obsistat"* are the important words as far as pre-nuptial investigation

[9] IV Council of the Lateran (1215), c. 51—Mansi, XX, 1038, 1039.

[10] Esmein, *Le Mariage,* I, 205.

[11] IV Council of the Lateran (1215), c. 50—Mansi, XX, 1038.

[12] C. 3, X, *de clandestina desponsatione,* IV, 3.

by the pastor is concerned. They indicate that the investigation was to be performed by the *presbyteri*. *Presbyteri* evidently referred to pastors.[13] This view seems to be confirmed by the Council of Trent, which re-stated some of the Lateran legislation, but substituted the word "*parochus*" for the word "*presbyter*." Moreover, prior to the Fourth Lateran Council the practice was established of ascribing individual priests, who were called *presbyteri*, to individual parochial churches for the care of souls. Their duties were really pastoral.[14] Doubtless *presbyteri* embraced both regular and secular clergy, because in establishing sanctions for the violation of canon 50 the council made mention not only of the parochial clergy but also of the regular clergy.[15] The duty of the pastor to make the indicated pre-nuptial investigation was essentially, but not exclusively, intended to be an examination of the contracting parties themselves and was presumably intended to cover all species of matrimonial impediments, as is indicated by the unrestricted character of the Lateran law. Because of the prevalence of marriages between relatives, it would appear that the impediments of consanguinity and affinity were to be given particular attention. The council also prescribed what should be done in case a priest or pastor discovered a doubtful impediment. He was expressly to forbid the marriage until manifest evidence concerning the impediment was forthcoming and then decide on what course he should follow.

To make the law more effective, a marriage contracted without the publication of the banns did not enjoy the favor of law of a "putative marriage." Therefore, if the banns were not published, the children of a forbidden consanguineous marriage were not to be considered legitimate, even though the parents were ignorant of the presence of a forbidden degree of relationship. The children were likewise to be considered illegitimate if, though the marriage took place in church, the parties knew at the time that there existed between them a prohibited degree of relationship. Moreover, parish

[13] Gasparri, *Tractatus Canonicus de Matrimonio* (Paris, 1891), n. 141.

[14] Bastnagel, *The Appointment of Parochial Adjutants and Assistants*, p. 28.

[15] IV Council of the Lateran (1215), c. 51—Mansi, XX, 1038.

priests who did not prohibit such forbidden unions, and members of the regular clergy who assisted at such marriages were to be suspended from office for three years and, if the quality of their fault demanded it, they were to be punished even more severely. These sanctions go to show how seriously the fathers of the council looked on the law they formulated. Furthermore, anyone who maliciously presented an impediment for the purpose of frustrating a legitimate marriage was not to escape ecclesiastical punishment.[16]

Article 2. After the Fourth Lateran Council

The Fourth Lateran Council gave a notable impetus to the celebration of local councils by decreeing that provincial councils be celebrated annually for the reformation of morals.[17] Subsequent to the Fourth Lateran Council numerous local councils and synods were held throughout the Christian world, many of which manifested much initiative in the formulation of legislation. Several of them, especially those in Italy, France, Germany and Great Britain propagated the Lateran decree concerning the priest's duty in pre-nuptial investigation. Some expressed the Lateran enactment *verbatim;* others re-stated it substantially, while in many instances suitable additions and directive norms were added for the guidance of the pastor.[18] The Synod of Treves (1227) declared that if anybody knew of the presence of the impediments of consanguinity, affinity, compaternity and such like hindrances affecting a given marriage, they were to reveal them. But if the priest discovered

[16] IV Council of the Lateran (1215), c. 51—Mansi, XXII, 1038, 1039.

[17] IV Council of the Lateran (1215), c. 6—Mansi, XXII, 991.

[18] Constitutions of the Synod of Dublin (date uncertain)—Mansi, XXII, 1127; Council of Oxford (1222)—Mansi, XXII, 1177; Council of Scotland (1225), c. 50—Mansi, XXII, 1242; Provincial Council of Treves (1227), c. 5—Mansi, XXIII, 29; the *Praecepta Antiqua* of the Diocese of Rouen (1235), c. 68—Mansi, XXIII, 384; Council of Treves (1277), c. 5—Mansi, XXIV, 196; Synod of Cologne (1298), c. 10—Mansi, XXIV, 356; Synod of Nîmes (1284), c. 4—Mansi, XXIV, 904; Synod of Würzburg (1298), c. 18—Mansi, XXIV, 1194; Council of the Armenians (1342)—Mansi, XXV, 1264; Council of Prague (1355), c. 50—Mansi, XXVI, 401; Council of York (1367), c. 9—Mansi, XXVI, 471; Council of Salzburg (1420), c. 12—Mansi, XXVIII, 1013.

no impediment either from the parties themselves or from the people of the parish, he was to proceed with the marriage.[19]

Special difficulties were bound to beset pastors in making pre-nuptial inquiry when a parishioner intended to marry somebody from another parish, or when both parties came from other parishes and presented themselves for marriage before a pastor who did not know them. The problem became increasingly difficult when the party or parties had no fixed abode. It was an easy matter for such people to conceal marriage impediments, if they desired. During the period under consideration many marriageable men and women were likely to seek partners in marriage outside their own communities, for intercommunication between different communities, towns and even countries was well established. Moreover, the thirst for adventure, the increased commercial activity, the crusades to the Holy Land and the flocking of students to various universities occasioned marriage unions of men and women whose native towns were far distant from each other. In such circumstances it is easy to appreciate the difficulties under which pastors labored in those days in making pre-nuptial investigation, especially when it is borne in mind that many of the modern and efficient means of rapid communication were not yet invented.

The Fourth Lateran Council made no express mention of the manner of investigating such non-parishioners. Hence local councils, spurred on by necessity, took the initiative to enact legislation to cope with the situation. They began to forbid pastors and other priests to assist at the marriages of *peregrini* and other unknown persons, unless they produced testimonial letters proving their freedom to marry and testifying to the fact that the banns of marriage were published in their own respective parishes. The same requirements were demanded of those who acquired a new domicile shortly before the marriage. Usually the testimonial letters were issued by the proper bishop of the parties.[20]

[19] C. 5—Mansi, XXIII, 29.

[20] Constitutions of Richard of Sarum (1217), c. 56—Mansi, XXII, 1125; Provincial Council of Treves (1227), c. 5—Mansi XXIII, 29; Council of Cologne (1536), c. 45—Mansi, XXXII, 1268; Council of Mainz (1549), c. 58—Mansi, XXXII, 1413.

Article 3. Clandestine Marriages

The general effectiveness of the pre-nuptial investigation in preventing illicit and invalid unions was seriously hampered by the clandestine marriage evil, which it sought to cure. The reason was that clandestine marriages defied pre-nuptial inquiry. Pre-nuptial examination of those intending to contract secret marriages was impossible. Local councils continued to combat the evil. Councils, particularly in Spain, Italy, France, Germany and England, with unusual consistency condemned, reprobated and heavily punished these forbidden unions. Reverence and respect for the sacred character of marriage were inculcated. Marriages were to be celebrated in decent places and not in taverns or such like places and, moreover, they were not to be made the matter of jest.[21] Marriages before lay officials were prohibited.[22] The practice of exchanging matrimonial consent at *the doors* of the church in the presence of the priest was prescribed by some councils [23] and the faithful were encouraged to celebrate their weddings with the nuptial Mass and blessing. Such legislation emphasizing the necessity of the religious celebration of marriage must have had some influence in restraining clandestine marriages. There was one great drawback, however, in the fact that clandestine marriages were recognized as valid marriages until the Council of Trent in its celebrated decree *Tametsi* remedied the situation.

Article 4. The Council of Trent

A signal service was rendered to the efficacy of pre-nuptial investigation by the Tridentine precept, contained in the decree

[21] Constitutions of Richard of Sarum (1217), c. 56—Mansi, XXII, 1123; Provincial Council of Treves (1227), c. 5—Mansi, XXIII, 29; Council of Treves (1277), c. 5—Mansi, XXIV, 196; Synod of Oxford (1287), c. 7—Mansi, XXIV, 793; Council of Magdeburg (1370), c. 32—Mansi, XXVI, 583; Council of Salzburg (1420), c. 13—Mansi, XXVIII, 1014.

[22] Provincial Council of Treves (1227), c. 5—Mansi, XXIII, 29; Council of Magdeburg (1370), c. 32—Mansi, XXVI, 583.

[23] Old Precepts of the Diocese of Rouen (1235), c. 66—Mansi, XXIII, 393; Synodal Statutes of the Church of Le Mans (1247)—Mansi, XXIII, 748; Synod of Bayeux, c. 69—Mansi, XXV, 74; Council of Langeais (1278), c. 3—Mansi, XXIV, 213; Synod of Oxford (1287), c. 7—Mansi, XXIV, 1194; Council of Lyons (1449), c. 14—Mansi, XXXII, 97.

Tametsi, which declared null and void those marriages which were not celebrated before the pastor or a priest delegated by the pastor or ordinary and two or three witnesses.[24] All contracting parties therefore who wished to marry validly were required to appear before the pastor or a priest delegated by the pastor or ordinary and two or three witnesses. The Tridentine decree in this instance uses the words *praesente parocho,* which would seem to signify *any pastor.* A reading of the context, however, seems to indicate that it is the *parochus proprius* that was meant. Canonists interpreted the words *praesente parocho* as referring to the proper pastor of either of the parties,[25] *i. e.,* the pastor of the place where either of the parties had a domicile.[26] This teaching was confirmed by the Holy See.[27] After much disputation on the part of jurists in regard to quasi-domicile, it was decided by the Holy Office in 1867 that a *parochus proprius* was also obtained by means of a quasi-domicile.[28]

The Council of Trent was responsible also for an important de-

[24] Conc. Trident., sess. XXIV, *de ref. matrim.,* c. 1.

[25] Carberry, *The Juridical Form of Marriage,* p. 27.

[26] Thomas Sanchez, *De Sancto Matrimonii Sacramento Disputationum* (Lyons, 1699), lib. III, disp. 23; John M. Costello, *Domicile and Quasi-Domicile* (The Catholic University of America, Canon Law Studies, n. 60, Washington: The Catholic University of America, 1930), p. 44.

[27] Urbanus VIII, const., *Exponi nobis,* 14 Aug., 1627—*Bullarium Romanum,* XIII, 537; Benedictus XIV, const., *Paucis abhinc,* 19 March, 1758—*Fontes,* n. 447.

[28] S. C. S. Off., litt. encycl., 7 Jun., 1867—*Coll.,* n. 1407. For a more thorough knowledge of the development of the institution of quasi-domicile the following references will prove helpful: *Cf.* Sanchez, *De Sancto Matrimonii Sacramento Disputationum,* lib. III, disp. 23; P. Fourneret, *Le Domicile Matrimonial* (Paris, 1906), p. 115; F. Suarez, *Opera Omnia,* lib. II, c. 14; Paulus Laymann, *Theologia Moralis* (Paris, 1627), lib. I, tit. IV, c. 12; Enricus Pirhing, *Ius Canonicum Novo Methodo Explicatum* (Dilingae, 1728), lib. II, tit. II, n. 18; Anacletus Reiffenstuel, *Ius Canonicum Universum* (Venice, 1735), lib. II, tit. II, nn. 2 ff.; Franciscus Schmalzgrueber, *Ius Ecclesiasticum Universum* (Romae, 1843-1845), lib. IV, tit. III, nn. 149, 150; Cronin, *The New Matrimonial Legislation,* pp. 162-179; Neil Farren, *Domicile and Quasi-Domicile* (Dublin: Gill & Son, 1920), pp. 43-65; Costello, *Domicile and Quasi-Domicile,* pp. 73-94.

velopment in general Church legislation concerning the pre-nuptial investigation of *vagi* and those of no fixed residence.

> Multi sunt, qui vagantur, et incertas habent sedes, et, ut improbi sunt ingenii, prima uxore relicta, aliam, et plerumque plures, illa vivente, diversis in locis ducunt. Cui morbo cupiens sancta Synodus occurrere, omnes, ad quos spectat, paterne monet, ne hoc genus hominum vagantium ad matrimonium facile recipiant: magistratus etiam saeculares hortatur, ut eos severe coerceant: parochis autem praecipit, ne illorum matrimoniis intersint, nisi prius diligentem inquisitionem fecerint, et, re ad Ordinarium delata, ab eo licentiam id faciendi obtinuerint.[29]

The purpose of the fathers of the Council of Trent in issuing this disciplinary measure was to safeguard the faithful against the danger of illicit and invalid unions when they intended to contract marriage with *vagi* and transients. Obviously, as the decree indicates, many of these *vagi* and transients had taken occasion of their condition to conceal from the pastor the fact of their former marriages and afterwards entered into bigamous and polygamous unions. Consequently the council not only urged the secular authority to punish the violators of the marriage laws, but also decreed that *vagi* be not easily admitted to marriage. Furthermore, it was made obligatory on pastors not to assist at such unions until they had first made a diligent inquiry into the free status of the contracting parties and, after having sent the result of the investigation to the ordinary, had obtained his permission to proceed with the marriage.[30] Local councils undertook to make this law more widely known by ordering that it be most diligently observed or by re-stating it at least substantially in their decrees.[31] A pro-

[29] Sess. XXIV, *de ref. matrim.*, c. 7.

[30] Conc. Trident., sess. XXIV, *de ref. matrim.*, c. 9.

[31] Council of Milan (1569), c. 26—Mansi, XXXIV A, 113; Council of Rouen (1581), c. 13—Mansi, XXXIV A, 626; Council of Bourges (1584), c. 112—Mansi, XXXIV A, 919; Council of Aachen (1585)—Mansi, XXXIV bis, 957; Council of Florence (1573), c. 5—Mansi, XXXV A, 767; Council of Naples (1576), c. 40—Mansi, XXXV bis, 844; Council of Genoa (1574), c. 13—Mansi, XXXVI bis, 577; Council of Cambrai (1631), c. 13—Mansi, XXXVI ter, 180.

vision of the decree *Tametsi* which required that the pastor have a special book for the registration of marriages, in which he was to enter the names of the married parties and the witnesses to the marriage as well as the day and place of the marriage, was a further aid towards satisfactory pre-nuptial investigation. It furnished legal proof of the marriage and, should a party attempt another marriage, the pastor had written evidence of the presence of the impediment of *ligamen.* The Council of Trent also urged that before their marriage, or at least within three days before the consummation of their marriage, the parties were to make a diligent confession of their sins and piously receive Holy Communion.[32]

There was one serious drawback to the universal efficacy of the Tridentine precepts. That was the fact that the decree *Tametsi* was not universally promulgated. The result was that it had no binding force in many parishes, dioceses and even countries.

Subsequent to the Council of Trent local councils continued to play an active part in legislating on pre-nuptial investigation. According to the Council of Milan (1576) the interrogation of the man and woman was to precede the banns of marriage. They were to be separately questioned as to whether they consented to the union. Moreover, for the sake of propriety it was prescribed that the woman be questioned in a decent place in the sight of friends. She was to be sufficiently distant from them that her answers could not be overheard and that her restraining sense of modesty would not deter her from freely expressing her mind to the pastor.[33] A later Council of Milan (1582) was even more specific. It explicitly mentioned as matter for investigation the impediments of *ligamen* and the vow of chastity, as well as the impediments of consanguinity, affinity and spiritual relationship.[34] The Council of Sienna (1599) stressed the interrogation of the parties as to their freedom of consent and the precautions to be taken in the interrogation of the woman.[35] When a priest discovered a doubtful impediment

[32] Conc. Trident., sess. XXIV, *de ref. matrim.*, c. 1.

[33] C. 9—Mansi, XXXIV A, 315, 316.

[34] C. 27—Mansi, XXXIV A, 527.

[35] C. 16—Mansi, XXXVI bis, 539-542.

he was to refer the matter to the bishop,[36] the vicar-general[37] or the *officialis*[38] for a final decision.

Several particular councils insisted that pastors, both secular and regular, were to receive written testimony concerning the free status of nupturients from other parishes before admitting them to marriage and also concerning the fact that they were not excommunicated.[39] Those who came from other dioceses to be married were to present to the pastor properly authenticated testimonial letters from their proper bishop or bishops,[40] or from the vicar-general or *officialis*.[41] The legislation of the various particular councils on the matter was not uniform, but a concentrated effort to make pre-nuptial investigation more efficient was noticeable. Later some of these regulations on pre-nuptial investigation found their way into the general legislation of the Church.

In summary it may be said that the Fourth Lateran Council, seeing the utility of pre-nuptial investigation by the pastor and the efficacy of the publication of the banns of marriage, introduced both institutions into the general legislation of the Church. Subsequent particular councils made the precepts of the Fourth Lateran Council more universally known, especially those councils celebrated in Italy, France, Germany and Great Britain. Though the Lateran enactment contributed to some extent in preventing the evils of consanguineous and clandestine marriages, it was not entirely satisfactory, mainly because clandestine marriages were still legally

36 Ancient Synodal Statutes of the Church of Nevers (date uncertain), c. 34—Mansi, XXXII, 294.

37 Council of Sienna (1599), c. 16—Mansi, XXXVI bis, 539-542.

38 Council of Besançon (1571), c. 8—Mansi, XXXVI bis, 60.

39 Council of Milan (1569), c. 26—Mansi, XXXIV A, 113; Council of Mechlin (1579), c. 3—Mansi, XXXIV A, 583; Council of Rouen (1581), c. 13—Mansi, XXXIV A, 626; Council of Aachen (1585)—Mansi, XXXIV bis, 957, 958; Council of Ravenna (1568), c. 5—Mansi, XXXV A, 624; Council of Urbino (1569), c. 5—Mansi, XXXV A, 627; Council of Benevento (1571), c. 13—Mansi XXXVI bis, 60.

40 Council of Mechlin (1570), c. 5—Mansi, XXXIV A, 583; Council of Aachen (1585)—Mansi, XXXIV bis, 957, 958; Council of Bordeaux (1583), c. 6—Mansi, XXXIV B, 1564; Council of Benevento (1571), c. 23—Mansi, XXXVI bis, 17.

41 Council of Besançon (1571), c. 14—Mansi, XXXIV bis, 60.

valid. This drawback was removed by the Council of Trent, which decreed that marriages not celebrated before the pastor, or before a priest delegated by the pastor or ordinary, were to be considered null and void. The most direct contribution of the Council of Trent to pre-nuptial investigation was the precept requiring the pastor not to assist at the marriages of *vagi* until he had made a diligent inquiry into their *status liber* and, having sent the results of the inquiry to the ordinary, had obtained the ordinary's permission to assist at the marriage.

CHAPTER IV

FROM THE DECREE "CUM ALIAS" TO THE PRESENT TIME

Article 1. Juridical Examination of Witnesses

It became evident after the Council of Trent that the Tridentine matrimonial enactments were not completely satisfactory in preventing invalid and unlawful marriages, especially bigamous and polygamous unions. Consequently a new method of pre-nuptial investigation came into being in the determined effort to promote valid and lawful unions and particularly to protect the unity of marriage. This method took the form of a summary juridical process by which two witnesses for each party to the marriage were required to make depositions before a designated ecclesiastical official for the purpose of establishing whether or not both parties were free to marry. Though this special examination of witnesses was not necessary for the validity of marriage, it would have been unlawful for a pastor to admit the parties to marriage unless witnesses had juridically testified to their free status.[1] Even though their free status was otherwise evident, the juridical proof of it could not be omitted.[2]

The main document emanating from the Holy See and treating of this special examination of witnesses was the decree *Cum alias*. It was issued by the Sacred Congregation of the Holy Office on August 21, 1670 with the approval of Pope Clement X. Later a number of instructions and responses, elucidating certain points of the decree *Cum alias* and clearing up certain doubts that were raised, was issued by the same Congregation.[3] In the introductory paragraph of the decree *Cum alias* mention is made of two previous in-

[1] Bouix, *Tractatus de Iudiciis Ecclesiasticis* (Paris, 1855), II, 463.

[2] Bouix, *Tractatus de Iudiciis Ecclesiasticis*, II, 464.

[3] S. C. S. Off., instr., 13 Jan., 1869—*Fontes*, n. 1008; instr., 22 Aug., 1890—*Coll.*, n. 1740; resp., 2 Apr., 1873—*Fontes*, n. 1025; resp., 9 Dec., 1874—*Fontes*, n. 1036.

structions of the Holy Office issued in the years 1658 and 1665 respectively,[4] which called for an interrogation of witnesses to prove the free status of those intending to marry. In many places, according to the decree *Cum alias,* those instructions were either totally neglected or observed only imperfectly. Few authors make mention of them, and they are not to be found in the usual collections of decrees and instructions of the Holy See.

To detail every point in the juridical process outlined in the decree *Cum alias* would be impossible in the present short historical synopsis. The important points, however, will be touched upon and occasional references will be made to those later instructions and responses of the Holy See, which clarified certain features of the decree. The decree may be divided into three general divisions: 1. The ecclesiastical officials who took the depositions of the witnesses. 2. The witnesses themselves and their qualifications. 3. The actual interrogation of the witnesses.

A. *The Ecclesiastical Officials Who Took the Depositions of the Witnesses*

In the city of Rome the witnesses were to be questioned before a notary and another official specially delegated by the cardinal vicar: outside of Rome they were to be interrogated before the bishop and his vicar-general or some special delegate of the bishop.[5] Vicars foranc and their chancellors could be chosen as suitable delegates by the bishop, but the depositions made before them had to be transmitted to the ordinary together with the testimony of the parties' baptism and confirmation.[6] The instruction to the Oriental bishops stated that in the episcopal city the juridical examinations of witnesses was to be made by the vicar-general, while in other parts of the diocese it was to be made by the pastor.[7] Those delegated to make the pre-nuptial inquiry could be delegated for one particular case or for all cases. From the foregoing it is evident that there was

[4] *Cf.* S. C. S. Off., decr. *Cum alias,* 21 Aug., 1670—*Fontes,* n. 742.

[5] S. C. S. Off., decr., *Cum alias,* 21 Aug., 1670—*Fontes,* n. 742.

[6] S. C. S. Off., resp., 24 Feb., 1847 ad 7—*Fontes,* n. 900.

[7] S. C. S. Off., instr., 22 Aug., 1890—*Fontes,* n. 1228.

not complete uniformity as regards the officials who conducted the interrogation of the witnesses.

B. *The Witnesses and Their Qualifications*

At least two witnesses were required to testify to the *status liber* of each party to the marriage. The same two witnesses could testify for both the man and the woman, provided they were capable of furnishing the necessary information.[8] Men or women, Catholics or non-Catholics, could act as witnesses, provided they were trustworthy. It was desirable, however, that non-Catholics be admitted only when suitable Catholic witnesses were not obtainable. As a general rule, the oath to tell the truth was not to be administered to non-Catholics.[9] Blood relatives, as being usually better informed about the parties than others, were to be preferred as witnesses.[10] Even near blood relatives, such as fathers, mothers, brothers and sisters were to be admitted as well as those more distantly related to the parties.[11] Soldiers and *vagi* were not to be permitted to act as witnesses except for a just cause. The presumption apparently was that they were not well qualified, because of the character and nature of their life and the fact they were more or less continually moving from one place to another. The notary was obliged to declare in writing that the witnesses were well known to him. If they were unknown to him, he was not to admit them to give testimony, unless another reliable witness, known to the notary, testified to the name, address, surname and reliability of the said witnesses.

C. *Interrogation of Witnesses*

The witnesses were to be examined individually under oath. The preliminary questions put to a witness were general in character and concerned the Christian name, surname, country, age, occupation and residence of the witness and whether he was a citizen of the place or whether he came from elsewhere. If he had come from

[8] Gasparri, *Tractatus Canonicus de Matrimonio* (2. ed., Paris, 1892), n. 129.

[9] S. C. S. Off., decr., *Cum alias*, 21 Aug., 1670—*Fontes*, n. 742.

[10] S. C. S. Off., resp., ad Vic. Apost., Constantinop., 2 Apr., 1873—*Fontes*, n. 1025.

[11] S. C. S. Off., resp., 24 Feb., 1847—*Fontes*, n. 900.

elsewhere, he was questioned as to how long he had lived in the place where he was making the depositions. These general interrogations were valuable for the purpose of ascertaining the reliability of the witness.

After having been questioned about the circumstances that led up to his appearing as a witness, the witness was interrogated about his particular knowledge of the party for whom he was testifying; how long he knew him; whether he knew what his state in life was; whence he knew him and whether or not he was a citizen of the place. Should the contracting party prove to be an extraneous person, he was not permitted to contract marriage until testimonial letters concerning his freedom to marry were obtained from the proper ordinary. If the party to be married was an inhabitant of the place, the witness was to be interrogated concerning the parish or parishes in which the party lived prior to the time of the depositions. The witness was next questioned as to whether the party was impeded from entering marriage on account of any impediments, such as *ligamen,* sacred orders or religious profession.

If the witness during the course of the interrogation replied that the party was not married, he was questioned as to how he knew that such was the case and as to whether it would have been possible for the party to enter marriage unknown to the witness.

The remaining interrogations of the decree *Cum alias* concerned the case where the witness asserted that the party was previously married, but that his partner in marriage had died. The witness was to be questioned concerning the circumstances of the death of the deceased spouse. If possible, authentic and legal documentary proof of death was to be submitted before permission for the new nuptials was to be granted, but in the absence of such documentary evidence other reliable proofs would be admitted.[12]

The depositions of the witnesses were to be written down and certified by the signatures of the witnesses, of the notary and of the ordinary or the delegate appointed by the ordinary to take the depositions.[13] If the testimony of the witnesses satisfactorily proved

[12] S. C. S. Off., decr., *Cum alias,* 21 Aug., 1670—*Fontes,* n. 742.

[13] Gasparri, *Tractatus Canonicus de Matrimonio* (2. ed., Paris, 1893), n. 130.

the *status liber* of the parties, the ordinary was to grant the pastor permission to publish the banns of marriage.

The juridical examination of witnesses in the case of the marriages of *vagi* and *exteri* presented problems not found in ordinary cases. In regard to *vagi,* the decree *Cum alias* repeated the legislation of the Council of Trent,[14] while in regard to those who were not *vagi,* but who belonged to another diocese, authentic testimony of their free status was to be obtained from their own ordinary or *vicar-general* before they were admitted to marriage,[15] a practice that was already prevalent in many ecclesiastical provinces. Should a party after puberty have resided in several dioceses outside his own proper diocese, testimony from the ordinaries of these various dioceses concerning his freedom to marry was required. It sometimes happened that it was impossible for *vagi* and *exteri* to provide witnesses to prove their *status liber.* To meet with this contingency, it was sufficient that their assertions concerning their freedom to marry be supported by a suppletory oath. The faculty of tendering the suppletory oath was to be received from the Congregation of the Holy Office.[16]

What was to be done should a party desire to marry *in articulo mortis?* He was exempted from the obligation of providing witnesses to prove his free status. Should he recover, the process of the juridical examination of witnesses had to be put into effect before he was permitted to live maritally with his married partner.[17] Many local councils explicitly insisted on the observance of the above juridical examination of witnesses as outlined by the decree *Cum alias.*[18] But the decree was scarcely observed in places outside the

[14] Conc. Trident., sess. XXIV, *de ref. matrim.,* c. 7.

[15] S. C. S. Off., decr., *Cum alias,* 21 Aug., 1670—*Fontes,* n. 742 .

[16] Gasparri, *Tractatus Canonicus de Matrimonio* (3. ed., 1904), *Allegatum,* III, iv: II, p. 489.

[17] Gasparri, *Tractatus Canonicus de Matrimonio* (3. ed., 1904), *Allegatum,* III, iv: II, p. 489.

[18] Council of Naples (1699), c. 2—Mansi, XXXVI ter, 757; Council of the Ruthenians (1720), tit. III, § 8—Mansi, XXXV bis, 1504; Synod of Westminster (1852), c. 22—Mansi, XLIV, 742; Council of Ravenna (1855), c. 8—Mansi, XLVII, 220; Council of Smyrna (1869), c. 1—*Coll. Lac.,* VI, 579-581; Council of New Granada (1868), c. 11—*Coll. Lac.,* VI, 521; Coun-

papal states, for in those places it was either never accepted or, if it was accepted, it soon fell into desuetude. This was probably due to the many difficulties of securing proper witnesses and to the strictness of the character of the decree. Before the Code of Canon Law was promulgated many doubts arose as to whether or not the juridical examination of witnesses was abrogated by custom in those places where it was not observed.[19] These doubts seem to be solved by the Code, for the Code is ominously silent concerning the juridical examination of witnesses, except for cases where doubts arise concerning the existence of a matrimonial impediment.[20] With this one exception, therefore, the juridical examination of witnesses to prove the *status liber* of parties intending to marry may be considered abrogated.

Article 2. The Marriage of Conscience

Though it was the earnest desire of the Church that marriages be celebrated publicily, and not secretly and clandestinely, there were at times grave reasons why certain marriages should not be publicized. Hence there arose a certain form of secret marriage which was previously and is today known as *marriage of conscience.* The celebrated canonist Pope Benedict XIV issued an encyclical letter *Satis vobis* dealing solely with this type of marriage. The letter was addressed to patriarchs, primates, archbishops and bishops.[21] A marriage of conscience is one which is celebrated without the publication of the banns before a pastor or before a priest who has the permission of the pastor along with two witnesses, who are obliged to keep secret the celebration of the marriage.[22] Though such marriages are perfectly legitimate, they are not altogether desirable, particularly

cil of Urbino (1859), c. 66—*Coll. Lac.*, VI, 25; Council of Ravenna (1855), c. 4—*Coll. Lac.*, VI, 168.

19 Gasparri, *Tractatus Canonicus de Matrimonio* (2. ed., Paris, 1892), n. 139; Julius De Becker, *De Sponsalibus et Matrimonio* (2. ed., Louvain, 1903), pp. 289, 290; Bouix, *Tractatus de Iudiciis Ecclesiasticis,* II, p. 465.

20 Canon 1031, § 1, 1°.

21 Benedictus XIV, litt. encycl., *Satis vobis,* 17 Nov., 1741—*Fontes,* n. 319.

22 Franciscus Mazzeus, *De Matrimonio Conscientiae* (Romae, 1766), p. 3.

because of certain social evils which are likely to result, such as injury to the reputation of the parties and perhaps doubts in society regarding the legitimacy of the children born in such wedlock. Moreover, unscrupulous people might take advantage of marriages contracted in this form to make them a stepping stone to bigamous and polygamous unions. Consequently, the encyclical letter *Satis vobis* stressed the point that the parties entering a marriage of conscience should be diligently examined before marriage. In particular, earnest inquiry was to be made concerning the character, rank and condition of the parties; whether they were *sui* or *alieni iuris;* whether they bore ill-will to a father, who justly refused to consent to their marriage; also whether they were in minor orders and whether there was any question involved of their obtaining ecclesiastical pensions of benefices. The reason for the last inquiry was to check the abominable retention of ecclesiastical benefices and pensions by those in minor orders who entered the married state. It was especially required that the parties to a marriage of conscience present unquestionable and authentic documents to prove their free status in order thereby to avert any danger of polygamy. The responses given to the above questions would certainly provide the ordinary with ample knowledge to form his judgment as to the advisability of admitting them to marriage. No doubt judicious care was to be exercised and all scandal was to be avoided. Moreover, instructions were to be imparted to the man and the woman regarding their obligations towards the baptism and education of the children born of their union.[23]

Article 3. Investigating the Alleged Death of a Former Spouse

Solicitude in protecting the unity and indissolubility of marriage has always been characteristic of the Church. This solicitude has been very manifest in her painstaking efforts to obtain moral certitude of the death of a previous spouse before permitting the surviving partner to enter new nuptials, as is manifest from the decretals of

[23] Benedictus XIV, encycl. letter, *Satis vobis,* 17 Nov., 1741—*Fontes,* n. 319.

Gregory IX [24] and from various replies and instructions of the Holy See on the subject.[25] There are two outstanding instructions which emanated from the Sacred Congregation of the Holy Office in the nineteenth century and which pertain to the investigation of the alleged death of a former spouse. One is entitled *Ingentes bellorum clades*,[26] and the other is the instruction *Matrimonii vinculo*.[27] Both instructions contain certain similarities, but the instruction *Matrimonii vinculo* is the more complete. This latter instruction, though not abrogating previous instructions on the investigation of the alleged death of a former spouse, did eclipse them in the detailed character of the directions it introduced for proving the death of the missing former partner in marriage.

The instruction *Ingentes belloroum clades* [28] repeated the provisions of the decree *Cum alias* in those matters which concern the necessity of obtaining documentary evidence of the death of a former spouse and the qualifications of the witnesses who testified to the free status of the parties. Moreover, the instruction *Ingentes bellorum clades* did enlarge somewhat on the decree *Cum alias* by admitting that moral certainty of the death of a former spouse was also obtainable by a sufficient cumulation of individual proofs, even though these proofs taken separately did not produce moral certainty. Furthermore, it provided that consideration be given to conjectures, presumptions, public opinion and to those authentically approved facts which pointed to the death of the spouse. Even those witnesses who *tempore non suspecto* heard of the death of a former

[24] C. 19, X, *de sponsalibus et matrimonio*, IV, 1; c. 2, X, *de secundis nuptiis*, IV, 21.

[25] S. C. S. Off., decr., *Cum alias*, 21 Aug., 1670—*Fontes*, n. 742; S. C. S. Off., resp., ad Vic. Apost., Transvaal, 23 Jun., 1671—*Fontes*, n. 745; S. C. de Prop. Fide, instr., ad Pro-Vic. Apost. Tenk. Occid., 1792—*Fontes*, n. 4632; S. C. S. Off., resp., Nank., 22 Mar., 1865—*Fontes*, n. 982; S. C. S Off., resp., ad Vic. Apost., Corea, 12 Sept., 1855—*Fontes*, n. 934; S. C. S. Off., resp., ad Vic. Apost., Pondicherry, 28 Jun., 1865—*Fontes*, n. 984; S. C. S. Off., resp., Tchely Meridio-Occid., 21 Nov., 1866—*Fontes*, n. 997.

[26] S. C. S. Off., instr., *Ingentes bellorum clades*, 22 June, 1822—Feije, *De Impedimentis et Dispensationibus Matrimonialibus* (3. ed.), pp. 816-818.

[27] S. C. S. Off., instr., *Matrimonii vinculo*, 13 Maii, 1868—*Coll.*, n. 1321.

[28] Feije, *De Impedimentis et Dispensationibus Matrimonialibus*, pp. 816-818.

spouse from trustworthy witnesses were to be given attention, when these latter were immediate and direct witnesses and when they could not themselves testify, either because they had died, or because they were absent or on account of some other cause.[29]

War, shipwreck, earthquakes and such catastrophes have been responsible frequently for husbands not returning to their wives. Sometimes wives disappear and fail to return to their husbands, but it is a more frequent occurrence for husbands not to return to their wives, no trace of them being evident. Many husbands having left their homes on business or other missions of one kind or other have failed to return either intentionally or unintentionally. Apparently about the middle of the nineteenth century the number of petitions sent to the Holy See by wives asking permission to enter new nuptials because their husbands failed to return was considerable. The presumption was that their husbands were deceased. In order that ordinaries might be able to take care of such cases in their territories and not be unduly inconvenienced by having too frequent recourse to the Holy See, the instruction *Matrimonii vinculo* was issued in the year 1868.

The instruction did not regard mere absence over a long period of time as proof of a spouse's death. Hence it outlined certain norms to facilitate the forming of judgments concerning the moral certainty of death. The instruction distinguished between full and legal proof of death and incomplete proof. Full proof was considered established in two ways: (a) by authentic documentary evidence, (b) by the sworn and concordant testimony of two reliable witnesses. All other proofs fell short of full proof.

According to the instruction of 1868 documentary testimony of the spouse's death was first of all to be sought after and taken either from the registers of the parish, from the files of the hospital or from the records of the army, as the particular nature of the case might indicate. This direction was substantially similar to the prescription of the decree *Cum alias*.[30] When no testimony of the death of a former spouse was to be found in the church registers, authentic

[29] S. C. S. Off., instr., *Ingentes bellorum clades*, 22 June, 1822—Feije, *De Impedimentis et Dispensationibus Matrimonialibus* (3. ed.), pp. 817, 818.

[30] S. C. S. Off., decr., *Cum alias*, 21 Aug., 1670, § 11—*Fontes*, n. 742.

testimony from the death records of the civil government of the place where the spouse was supposed to have died was sufficient.[31]

ARTICLE 4. LATER DEVELOPMENT OF THE PASTOR'S OBLIGATION IN PRE-NUPTIAL INVESTIGATION

The special examination of witnesses, as prescribed by the decree *Cum alias* for the purpose of juridically proving the free status of nupturients, did not abolish the obligation placed on the pastor by the Fourth Lateran Council and the Council of Trent to interrogate the parties themselves concerning their freedom to marry.[32] Rather, this private pre-nuptial investigation of the contracting parties still remained obligatory on the pastor, and was notably developed during the period now under consideration.

In a meeting of the Sacred Congregation of the Inquisition held in the presence of Pope Innocent XII on June 11, 1697, it was decreed that the banns of marriage were not to be announced in church by the pastor until he had found out that the parties were sufficiently instructed in the rudiments of their religion.[33] A similar declaration is found in the encyclical epistle *Etsi minime* of Benedict XIV, in which it is stated that the pastor should interrogate the contracting parties and, if he discovered that they were ignorant of those things which were necessary for salvation, he should refrain from assisting at the marriage. Furthermore, it was the duty of the bishop to warn pastors subject to him of this obligation and even to punish them if they were negligent.[34]

In a later encyclical epistle entitled *Nimiam licentiam,* Benedict XIV was more explicit and extensive. This epistle was directed to the archbishops and bishops of Poland for the purpose of reforming

[31] S. C. S. Off., *Matrimonii vinculo,* 13 Maii, 1868, § 2—*Coll.,* n. 1321: *Cf.* L. Kaas, *Kriegsverschollenheit und Wiederverheiratung nach staatlichem und Kirchlichem Recht* (Paderborn: Ferdinand Schöningh, 1919), pp. 7-222; *cf.* etiam W. Ursprung, *Verschollenheit und Todeserklärung* (Aarau: H. R. Saurlander & Co., 1918).

[32] De Becker, *De Sponsalibus et Matrimonio,* p. 376.

[33] *Cf. Bullarium Clementis XI* (Romae, 1723), n. 11, p. 376; De Smet, *De Sponsalibus et Matrimonio* (ed. 1909), p. 47.

[34] 7 Feb., 1742, 11—*Fontes,* n. 324.

abuses which existed in that country. It declared that before the publication of the banns of marriage it was the duty of the proper pastor to make a separate and careful examination of the man and woman as to whether they were freely and willingly consenting to contract marriage. The reason for the separate examination is evident. The parties would more freely and frankly express their minds when interrogated separately, and would more readily reveal such impediments as might be present. According to the encyclical epistle *Nimiam licentiam* the pastor was also to inquire as to whether either of the parties had been betrothed previously to a person other than the one whom he or she now intended to marry. Furthermore, he was to ask them if they had obtained parental consent for the marriage. If any other impediment became known or if other important matters which called for inquiry were brought to light, the parties were to be accurately examined regarding this new information. And if the investigation revealed the existence of a matrimonial impediment or a defect in the consent of the parties, then the publication of the banns was to be suspended, and the matter of further procedure was to be referred to the bishop.[35] A comparison of the encyclical epistle *Nimiam licentiam,* § 10 with canon 1020, § 2 of the Code demonstrates how closely they resemble each other in regard to the investigation of the parties' freedom from matrimonial impediments and their freedom of matrimonial consent. As a matter of fact, the resemblance is so close that it can with truth be said that the Code actually adopted some of the language of the encyclical epistle *Nimiam licentiam.*

Benedict XIV's constitution *Firmandis* is also worthy of note, because it directed that the bishop in his personal visitation of the pastor was to question him as to whether, before admitting parties to marriage *in facie ecclesiae,* he was wont to make and was making the necessary inquiries of them about the existence of matrimonial impediments, their freedom of consent and their instruction in Christian doctrine, particularly in the principal mysteries of religion.[36] It is interesting to note that the pre-nuptial inquiry referred to here covered the same three major points as does canon

[35] 18 Maii, 1743, § 10—*Fontes,* n. 337.

[36] 6 Nov., 1744, § 9—*Fontes,* n. 349.

1020, § 2 of the Code, namely, (a) the examination of the parties concerning their freedom from matrimonial impediments; (b) the investigation of their freedom for matrimonial consent; (c) the investigation of their knowledge of Christian doctrine.

In his work *De Synodo Dioecesana,* Benedict XIV devotes considerable space to the treatment of the investigation of the parties concerning their knowledge of the rudiments of faith, giving a historical conspectus of the teaching on that point and emphasizing the pastor's obligation in regard to it. Knowledge of the Lord's Prayer, The Apostles' Creed, the precepts of God and His Church was particularly stressed. Those who were uneducated or dull of intellect were not forbidden to marry, but should be taught, according to their capacity, the principal mysteries of faith, such as the Unity and Trinity of God, the punishment of the wicked and the rewarding of the good, the Incarnation of Christ for the redemption of mankind, the essentials of the sacraments of baptism and penance and the precept of charity.[37]

In his encyclical letter *Cum religiosi* to the patriarchs, archbishops and bishops of Italy, Benedict XIV again called to mind the pastor's obligation of instructing his subjects before admitting them to marriage, if they were ignorant of truths which are necessary for salvation by necessity of means.[38]

After the time of Benedict XIV there was not any great development in the fundamental regulations on the pastor's obligation in pre-nuptial investigation, but the necessity and importance of that investigation were frequently stressed, especially in instructions and replies from the Holy See and in various particular councils. Prenuptial investigation was definitely insisted on; [39] doubtfully public sinners, if they refused to confess their sins before marriage, were not to be admitted to marriage except for very grave reasons. Oc-

[37] Lib. III, c. 14, nn. 1-6.

[38] 26 Jun., 1754, § 4—*Fontes,* n. 429.

[39] S. C. S. Off., resp., ad quartum dubium (Vic. Apost., Oceaniae Central), 18 Dec., 1872—*Fontes,* n. 1024; resp. (Siouxormen.), 18 Maii, 1892—*Fontes,* n. 1155; Council of Soissons (1849), c. 2—Mansi, XLII, 595; Council of Bordeaux (1850), c. 8—Mansi, XLIV, 88; Council of Toulouse (1850), c. 75—Mansi, XLIV, 392; Council of Quebec (1854), c. 13—Mansi, XLVII, 40; Council of Port of Spain (1854), c. 2—Mansi, XLVII, 65.

cult sinners were not to be excluded from marriage, but were to be given a salutary admonition in regard to their obligation.[40] A reply of the Sacred Penitentiary left it to the prudent judgment of the ordinary to determine the necessity or utility of examining the contracting parties themselves as well as the witnesses for the purpose of verifying matrimonial impediments and the causes of matrimonial dispensations.[41] Particular councils likewise displayed an earnestness in putting the Benedictine pronouncements on pre-nuptial investigation into practice. Contracting parties were to be examined particularly in regard to their knowledge of their religion. Pastors were to refrain from admitting to marriage those ignorant of the rudiments of faith,[42] but were rather to instruct them diligently in the elementary truths of faith prior to admitting them to marriage. Practically all the outstanding authors of the period who wrote on marriage gave consideration to the subject of pre-nuptial investigation, and made frequent references to the Benedictine epistles. The examination of witnesses prescribed by the decree *Cum alias,* though not observed in many places, was not totally neglected.[43] Particular attention was devoted by local councils to the examination of the free status of *vagi, peregrini* and *ignoti.*[44] Care

[40] S. C. de Prop. Fide, resp. (Quebec), 17 Apr., 1820—*Coll.* n. 2261.

[41] S. Poenit., resp., 5 Sept., 1898—*Fontes,* 4716.

[42] Council of Palermo (1850), c. 2—Mansi, XLIV, 47; Council of Thurles (1850), c. 8—Mansi, XLVII, 1139; Council of Urbino (1859), c. 69—*Coll. Lac.,* VI., 26; Council of Ravenna (1855), cap. VIII, n. 3—*Coll. Lac.,* VI, 167; Synodal Convention of the Bishops of Pisa (1850), cap. I, n. 3—*Coll. Lac.,* VI, 237; Council of Quito (1863), decr. III, n. 14—*Coll. Lac.,* VI, 402; Council of New Granada (1863), tit. IV, cap. 11—*Coll. Lac.,* VI, 521.

[43] Council of the Ruthenians (1720), tit. III, § 8—Mansi, XXXV bis, 1504; Council of Westminster (1852), c. 22—Mansi, XLIV, 742; Council of Urbino (1859), tit. II—Mansi, XLVII, 872; Council of Ravenna (1855) cap. VIII, n. 4—*Coll. Lac.,* VI, 168; Synod of New Granada (1868), tit. IV, cap. 11—*Coll. Lac.,* VI, 521; Council of Smyrna (1869), cap. V, n. 6—*Coll. Lac.,* VI, 572.

[44] Council of the Ruthenians (1720), tit. III, § 8—Mansi, XXXV bis, 1504; Council of Rouen (1830), c. 20—Mansi, XLIV, 47; Council of Sens (1850), c. 8—Mansi, XLIV, 235; Council of Toulouse (1850), c. 75—Mansi, XLIV, 392; Council of Westminster (1852), c. 22—Mansi, XLIV, 742; Council of Quebec (1854), c. 13—Mansi, XLVII, 40; Council of Tuam (1817),

was taken to provide for the proper investigation of the reported death of a former spouse, and pastors were forbidden to assist at the marriages of those who had no domicile in the parish, unless permission had been obtained from the proper bishop or pastor of the contracting parties.[45]

After the so-called Reformation in the sixteenth century there was a tendency on the part of the State to usurp certain rights over marriage which properly belonged to the Church. However, civil or secular marriage, *i. e.*, marriage as regulated entirely by the State, was immediately due to the false philosophies that became so rampant in the eighteenth century. The tendency towards secularism in marriage became very pronounced towards the end of the eighteenth century at about the time of the French Revolution and civil marriage became obligatory. In France it was given permanence by the Napoleonic Code, which legal system influenced the spread of the practice into other countries. In due course civil marriage was adopted by almost all countries, though not to the same extent and degree. In some countries it became absolutely compulsory; in others it was optional. Such a state of affairs presented a new problem to the pastor in pre-nuptial investigation. On many occasions lax Catholics did not scruple to marry civilly and without any religious ceremony whatsoever; divorces also, especially among non-Catholics, became more and more frequent. This necessitated a more careful pre-nuptial inquiry into the impediment of *ligamen* by investigating pastors. Where the State set up her own marriage laws and regulations, she usually had sanctions more or less serious to protect the observance of these laws. Hence many local councils prescribed that pastors were to take care that the contracting parties observe the civil regulations and formalities of marriage for the purpose of obtaining the civil effects of marriage.[46]

c. 10—*Coll. Lac.*, III, 764; Council of Thurles (1850), c. 16—*Coll. Lac.*, III, 783; Council of Port of Spain (1854), art. VI, n. 2—*Coll. Lac.*, III, 1099; Council of Ravenna (1855), cap. VIII, n. 4—*Coll. Lac.*, VI, 167.

[45] Council of Quebec (1854), c. 5—*Coll. Lac.*, III, 648; Council of St. Louis (1858), c. 9—*Coll. Lac.*, III, 319; Council of Port of Spain (1867), art. V, n. 1—*Coll. Lac.*, III, 1113; Council of Halifax (1857), decr. XVII, n. 6—*Coll. Lac.*, IV, 749.

[46] Council of Soissons (1849), c. 2—Mansi, XLIII, 595; Council of Rouen (1850), c. 20—Mansi, XLIV, 47; Council of Bordeaux (1850), c. 8—Mansi,

A few decrees on pre-nuptial investigation were issued by councils held in the United States of America, and are worthy of mention. According to the First Diocesan Synod of Baltimore (1791), *vagi* and *peregrini* were not to be admitted to marriage before the publication of the banns and especially not unless sufficient testimony that they were free to marry had been obtained from the pastors of the places from which they had departed:

> Vagi et peregrini ad matrimonium non sunt admittendi, nisi post tres publicationes factas iuxta praescriptum Concilii Tridentini, et presertim nisi testimonium omnino sufficiens habuerint a Pastoribus loci unde discesserunt, ipsos conjugali vinculo liberos esse.[47]

This synod furthermore required that the contracting parties possess a knowledge of Christian doctrine, at least of the principal mysteries of faith:

> Nullus ad matrimonium admittatur qui doctrinam Christianam aut principalia Fidei mysteria ignoret.

The same synod expressly required the pastor, who was to assist at mixed marriages, to make the necessary previous investigation concerning other possible matrimonial impediments:

> . . . adhibita tamen prius debita inquisitione, ne forte alia impedimenta matrimonio obstent, v. g., defectus Baptismi, consanguinitas, aut quid aliud.[48]

In the First Provincial Council of Baltimore (1829) it was decreed that pastors be solicitous in disposing the faithful for the proper reception of the Sacrament of Marriage:

XLIV, 88; Council of Clermont (1850), c. 8—Mansi, XLIV, 483; Council of Port of Spain (1854), art. VI, n. 5—Mansi, XLVII, 65; Council of Quebec (1854), decr. XIII, n. 2—*Coll. Lac.*, III, 647; Council of Rheims (1849), tit. XI, cap. 2—*Coll. Lac.*, IV, 126; Convention of the Bishops of Austria (1856), tit. I, § 69—*Coll. Lac.*, IV, 1295; Council of Coloza (1863), tit. III, cap. 12—*Coll. Lac.*, IV, 658; Council of Utrecht (1865), tit. IV, cap. 12—*Coll. Lac.*, IV, 840.

[47] Diocesan Synod of Baltimore (1791), sess. IV, c. 18—*Coll. Lac.*, III, 4.

[48] Diocesan Synod of Baltimore (1791), sess. IV, c. 18—*Coll. Lac.*, III, 4, 5.

> Pastores animarum monemus ut, sui officii memores, omnem adhibeant sollicitudinem ad rite disponendos fideles qui sacramentum Matrimonii suscipere velint; nec se peccato immunes existiment, si temere quoslibet manifeste indignos iungant.[49]

After the American Civil War (1861-1865) doubts arose in the minds of many wives as to whether their absent husbands had been killed in the fighting. To facilitate the investigation of these presumed deaths, an instruction was inserted in the decrees of the Second Plenary Council of Baltimore (1866) with the admonition that before these wives could pass to new nuptials, certainty of the death of their husbands should be established. Moreover, the council decreed that the faithful should be admonished in their preparation for the devout reception of the Sacrament of Matrimony to make a diligent confession of their sins, and to profit by a pious reception of the Holy Eucharist.[50] The Third Plenary Council of Baltimore (1884) was silent on the subject of pre-nuptial investigation by the pastor, except for the fact that it stressed the utility of an accurate examination by those having the care of souls into the canonical causes required for the granting of a dispensation from the impediment of mixed religion:

> Quum totum hoc caput ecclesiasticae disciplinae gravissimi sit momenti, curent omnes quibus animarum cura concredita est, ut mala ex matrimoniis mixtis enascentia efficacissimis quibusque mediis praecaveantur, aut si tolli omnino non possunt, saltem maxima ex parte minuantur. Ad hunc autem finem maxime conducit: . . . 3° examen accuratum de canonicis et gravibus causis quae requiruntur pro dispensatione super hoc mixtae communionis impedimento concedenda.[51]

On August 2, 1901, a letter was issued by Cardinal Ledochowski, Prefect of the Sacred Congregation of the Propagation of the Faith, to Cardinal Gibbons relating certain abuses that prevailed in certain

49 C. 26—*Coll. Lac.*, III, 31.

50 *Concilii Plenarii Baltimorensis II, Acta et Decreta,* tit. V, cap. IX, nn. 328, 329.

51 *Concilii Plenarii Baltimorensis III, Acta et Decreta,* tit. IV, cap. II, n. 33.

dioceses in the United States in connection with pre-nuptial investigation, especially in reference to mixed marriages. The letter stated that these abuses were reported to the Sacred Congregation for the Propagation of the Faith, and it requested Cardinal Gibbons to bring them up for discussion at the next meeting of the archbishops. The abuses consisted in the use of the telegraph system of communication for obtaining matrimonial dispensations and in totally neglecting, at least in urgent cases, to mention any canonical causes in the petition for the dispensation; in the suppressing of circumstances and annotations which the Holy See had declared to be entirely necessary; in the fact of considering the dispensation as obtained in urgent cases as soon as the petition was mailed; in the wrong application of the principle in virtue of which a doubtful baptism is considered as valid *in ordine ad validitatem matrimonii:* and finally in the fact that the investigating priest, when interrogating non-Catholics about their baptism, simply accepted as true their statement that they were baptized, without requiring any document or proof of their baptism, and in consequence assisted at the marriage for which only a dispensation from the impediment of mixed religion was granted, when a dispensation from the disparity of cult might actually have been needed. The letter, furthermore, stated that as a result of this latter abuse many of the contracted marriages were really invalid, in view of the existing impediment of disparity of cult; for many non-Catholics were not baptized, despite their ready affirmation to the contrary.[52]

The decree *Ne temere* did not modify the manner of proving the *status liber* of the parties desiring to contract marriage, but it did facilitate and expedite such proof by permitting the pastor in all ordinary cases to be the final judge as to the freedom of the parties to be married. Abstracting from extraordinary cases, it was not any longer necessary, as it was heretofore, to refer the matter to the ordinary for final decision, except in the case where the contracting parties were *vagi*.[53] This concession to the pastor was highly prac-

[52] *ASS*, XXXIV (1901), 640.

[53] S. C. C., decr., *Ne temere*, 2 Aug., 1907, V, §§ 1, 4—*Fontes*, n. 4340; *cf.* John T. Creagh, *A Commentary on the Decree, "Ne temere"* (Baltimore: Furst Co., 1908), pp. 41-44.

tical. Previously the referring of the proofs of the *status liber* to the ordinary had proved cumbersome and, at times, exceedingly difficult. Moreover, it had not been universally observed.[54]

There was another influence of the decree *Ne temere* on the examination of the contracting parties by the pastor which was important, though indirectly so, in character. It consisted in the fact that the juridical form of marriage was made obligatory for the validity of marriage in the universal Church, *i. e.*, marriages were to be contracted in the presence of the local ordinary, or of the local pastor, or of a priest delegated by either, along with at least two witnesses.[55] Such a regulation healed the long-standing weakness of the decree *Tametsi*, which, because of the fact that it was promulgated only in some parishes, dioceses and countries, did not obligate the universal Church. With the decree *Ne temere* obligating everywhere, all couples who intended to marry validly were brought within the reach of the pastor's investigation. Previous to the decree *Ne temere*, the proper pastor of the parties had the exclusive right to assist validly at marriages of his subjects, and difficulties frequently arose as to what pastor was the proper pastor. The decree *Ne temere* simplified the matter of valid assistance at marriage by prescribing that the bishop in his diocese and the pastor in his parish could validly assist at the marriages of all who approached them, irrespective of the places from which the contracting parties came.[56] Since the pastor who assisted at the marriage had also the obligation of making the pre-nuptial inquiry, the said ruling had a least an indirect effect on the duty of pre-nuptial inquiry. The Tridentine precept which required the registration of marriages was renewed by the decree *Ne temere*, and a distinctly new and valuable precept was added which obliged the pastor who assisted at the marriage to take care that the marriage was entered in the baptismal register, wherein the parties' baptisms were recorded.[57] Such a safeguard was ususually valuable in the investigation of the impediment of *ligamen*; for

[54] Charles J. Cronin, *The New Matrimonial Legislation* (New York: Benziger, 1908), p. 190.

[55] S. C. C., decr., *Ne temere*, 2 Aug., 1907, III—*Fontes*, n. 4340.

[56] *Cf.* Carberry, *The Juridical Form of Marriage*, p. 40.

[57] S. C. C., decr., *Ne temere*, 2 Aug., 1907, IX—*Fontes*, n. 4340.

in seeking testimony in regard to the baptisms of the contracting parties, a pastor would also conveniently detect whether or not the parties were previously married, provided that the records were really well kept and accurate.

Apparently many pastors were negligent of their duties in regard to pre-nuptial investigation following the appearance of the decree *Ne temere.* Moreover, some pastors who assisted at marriages failed to transmit notification of these marriages to the pastor of the place where the parties were baptized. That such was the lamentable situation is indicated by an instruction issued by the Sacred Congregation of the Sacraments on March 6, 1911. As a consequence of the aforesaid negligence of some pastors many people already bound by ties of marriage dared to enter new but invalid nuptials. Hence the instruction prescribed that ordinaries see to it that the pastors subject to them attend to n. V, § 2, of the decree *Ne temere,* which declared that it was not lawful for pastors to assist at marriages unless the free status of the contracting parties had been established. In addition, the testimony of the parties' baptism was to be requested, if they were baptized in a parish other than the parish of their marriage. The regulations of the decree *Ne temere,* n. IX, § 2 were to be properly observed, *i. e.,* the marriages were to be recorded in the baptismal register. If the parties were baptized in a place other than the parish of their marriage, notification of their marriage was to be sent to the parish of their baptism. The following points were to be mentioned in this notification: the Christian names and date of their marriage together with the Christian names and surnames of the witnesses to the union. The document was to be signed by the pastor and sealed with the parochial seal. If it happened that the pastor of the place of the parties' baptisms discovered on notification of their marriage that one or other or both of the parties had been married previously, he was obliged to notify as soon as possible the pastor who had assisted at their marriage. To add to the effectiveness of the instruction ordinaries were therein empowered to punish, if necessary, the transgressors of the foregoing prescriptions.[58]

The Code of Canon Law, which was promulgated by the constitution *Providentissima Mater Ecclesia* on Pentecost day, May 27,

[58] S. C. de Sacramentis, instr., 6 Mart., 1911—*AAS,* III (1911), 102, 103.

1917, and declared to be in force from May 19, 1918, adopted the prevailing law on pre-nuptial investigation, stressing the three major points: (a) immunity of the contracting parties from matrimonial impediments; (b) freedom for matrimonial consent; (c) interrogation of the parties on their instruction in Christian doctrine. However, the Code did change the extent and character of some matrimonial impediments, which change naturally necessitates a change in the interrogations of the pastor. The succeeding chapters will seek to develop the interpretation of the law of the Code on the subject, thereby rendering superfluous any treatment of the matter here.

On July 4, 1921, another instruction was issued by the Sacred Congregation of the Sacraments to ordinaries. It demanded more careful pre-nuptial investigation of the free status of parties contracting marriage and laid special emphasis on the pre-nuptial inquiry of workingmen who emigrated from Europe. The instruction was occasioned by the complaints of many local ordinaries that pastors, especially those in distant countries to which workingmen emigrate from Europe, had not observed the rules of Canon Law concerning the investigation of the canonical freedom to marry, and failed to send notification of the marriages contracted to the parishes in Europe where those emigrants had been baptized. The instruction re-stated the regulations of the instruction issued by the Congregation of Sacraments on March 6, 1911, perhaps for the purpose of showing that the said instruction still obtained and was not revoked by the Code. Reference was made to the Code Law on the subject of pre-nuptial investigation and workingmen recently immigrated from European countries were not as a general rule to be admitted to marriage without consulting the local ordinary. Finally, ordinaries were reminded of their obligation zealously to see that the precepts of the instruction were faithfully observed and to punish, if necessary, the violators of these precepts.[59]

Summary of the History

As far back as the beginning of the second century in the time of St. Ignatius of Antioch there is evidence that marriages were entered into with the consent and advice of the bishop, who at that time

[59] S. C. de Sacramentis, instr., 4 Jul., 1921—*AAS,* XIII (1921), 348, 349.

performed many of the parochial duties which are performed today by pastors. There is reason to believe that before giving consent to the celebration of marriage that the bishops of early Christian times made some kind of pre-nuptial investigation at least in a superficial way. The seeking of the bishop's consent to marriage arose from custom rather than from legislative enactment. When priests, who were not bishops, began to exercise the pastoral office about the fourth century, it is probably correct to state that they, like the bishops, were consulted by those contemplating marriage. In the time of Charlemagne the first traces of juridical pre-nuptial investigation appeared in the prescriptions of local law. The primary purpose of this local legislation on pre-nuptial investigation was to find out whether the impediment of consanguinity barred the marriages of nupturients. Priests and people assisted at this pre-nuptial inquiry. The inquiry was of a public nature. The Fourth Council of the Lateran was the first general council to impose an obligation of pastors to institute pre-nuptial investigation. The Council of Trent emphasized the Lateran precept and urged that *vagi* and transients be given particular attention in the matter of pre-nuptial inquiry. After the Tridentine Council a special kind of pre-nuptial investigation was introduced in which witnesses were juridically examined to establish the free status of the contracting parties. In the course of time this species of pre-nuptial investigation became obsolete. However, the examination of the contracting parties themselves was further developed, due particularly to the influence of a number of instructions and responses from the Holy See. In the more recent development of the institution in question the instructions of Benedict XIV played a very prominent part. His regulations on the matter were adopted by the Code of Canon Law with the exception of a few minor variations.

Part II

COMMENTARY ON THE LEGISLATION OF THE CODE

CHAPTER V

THE INVESTIGATING PASTOR

To promote reverence for the sacred character of marriage, and to protect the well-being of the individual, of the family and of society the Church lays down the law that before a marriage is celebrated it should be evident that there is no obstacle to its validity and lawfulness.[1] To ensure that validity and lawfulness canon 1020, § 1 states that "the pastor who has the right to assist at a marriage ought to investigate diligently at a suitable time beforehand whether there is any obstacle to the marriage." Before entering into a discussion of pre-nuptial investigation itself, it is but logical first of all to ascertain who are included under the term "pastor," and then more precisely to determine what pastors are competent to make the investigation and finally to outline the gravity of their obligation.

ARTICLE 1. THOSE INCLUDED UNDER THE TERM "PASTOR"

The term "pastor" may be accepted either *in a strict sense* or *in a broad sense.* A pastor in the *strict sense* is an individual priest or moral person on whom a parish is conferred *"in titulum"* with the care of souls to be exercised under the authority of the local ordinary.[2] According to Woywod the phrase *"in titulum"* may be translated "with rightful possession" and it designates the pastoral office itself together with the various rights and duties attached to the office.[3]

Ordinarily a parish is given to an individual physical person, but, as canon 451, § 1 explicitly states, it can also be given to a moral person, *e. g.*, to a monastery or religious congregation. The moral person in this case is the pastor of the parish in the strict sense, but it is necessary that an individual priest, who acts in the capacity of

[1] Canon 1019, § 1.

[2] Canon 451, § 1.

[3] Stanislaus Woywod, *A Practical Commentary on the Code of Canon Law* (3. ed., New York: Wagner, 1929), n. 325.

a parochial vicar, be entrusted with the actual care of souls.[4] That which the moral person (*parochus habitualis*) holds *in titulum,* the individual priest (*vicarius actualis*) exercises *in administrationem.* When a parish is given or united with a moral person, it is the parochial vicar—and not the members of the collegiate moral person, nor the operative agent for a non-collegiate moral person—that enjoys the right of assisting at marriages in the parish, and of instituting the required pre-nuptial investigation.[5] It is merely a matter of mention to recall that the order of priesthood is a necessary requirement for the active exercise of the pastoral office. Consequently, a lay person, or a person in minor orders or even a person ordained to sub-deaconship or deaconship is incapable of appointment as a pastor.[6]

Personal Pastors. The definition of "pastor" in canon 451, § 1 indicates that the Code intends that the exercise of the pastoral office be connected with a strictly defined territory. However, for reasons of expediency and sometimes of necessity the care of souls in certain circumstances requires that the bond of relationship between pastor and people arise from a personal element rather than a territorial one, or that it arise from both elements together, personal as well as territorial. Consequently, personal pastors have come into existence. Two kinds of personal pastors are distinguished: (a) *personal pastors in the broad sense* and (b) *personal pastors in the strict sense. Pastors are personal in the broad sense* when they have jurisdiction over certain persons, families or groups of persons in a particular territory in such a way that their power over their subjects is both personal and territorial, *e.g.,* when pastors exercise the care of souls over members of a certain race or nationality or language in a certain diocese, town or community. The pastors of most of the national parishes in the United States of America are personal pastors in the broad sense, because their jurisdiction is usually limited to a certain town or district and is exercised only over immigrants who came from

[4] Ludovicus Fanfani, *De Iure Parochorum ad Normam Codicis Iuris Canonici* (Turin: Marietti, 1924), pp. 73, 74.

[5] Canon 452, §§ 1, 2; canon 471, §§ 1, 4; Carberry, *The Juridical Form of Marriage,* p. 50.

[6] *Cf.* canon 453, § 1.

non-English speaking countries or over the descendants of these immigrants. Chaplains and rectors of pious places, orphanages, convents of sisters, boarding schools, homes for the aged, the blind and the crippled and such like institutions are considered equivalent to personal pastors in the broad sense, if they enjoy full parochial power over their subjects.[7] *Pastors are personal in the strict sense* when they have jurisdiction over certain persons or groups of persons and accompany them wherever they go, *e. g.*, when chaplains are given full parochial authority over a certain noble family, or over a regiment of soldiers. Their jurisdiction is purely personal and is not circumscribed by territorial limits. If they are not given full parochial power over their subjects, they have not the status of pastors, and would not *per se* have the right to assist at the marriages of their subjects. The question of the respective rights of personal pastors both in the broad sense and in the strict sense in regard to pre-nuptial investigation will be treated in a later article.

Pastors in the broad sense. Canon Law recognizes the existence of certain priests, who have pastoral rights and obligations, including the right to assist at marriage and to make pre-nuptial investigation, but who are not pastors in the sense of canon 451, § 1. These priests may be divided into two general categories: (a) *quasi-pastors* and (b) *parochial vicars, who enjoy full parochial power.*[8]

A. *Quasi-pastors.* Quasi-pastors are those priests who are entrusted with the full parochial care of souls in quasi-parishes. They enjoy all the rights and are bound by all the obligations of pastors, including the right to assist at marriages and to institute pre-nuptial investigation. Quasi-parishes are distinct territorial divisions of a vicariate or prefecture apostolic. They resemble parishes by the fact that they have a church of their own to which a definite congregation is attached.[9]

B. *Parochial vicars.* Several distinct kinds of parochial vicars are enumerated in the Code:

[7] S. C. C., *Romana et aliarum,* 1 Feb., 1908, ad X—*Fontes,* n. 4344; canon 464, § 2.

[8] Canon 451, § 2, 1°, 2°.

[9] Canon 216, § 3; S. C. de Prop. Fide, instr., 28 Jul., 1920—*AAS* (1920), 331; Fanfani, *De Iure Parochorum,* pp. 10-12.

1. *Vicarii curati* or *actuales,* who were referred to previously, are those who exercise the actual care of souls in a parish entrusted to a moral person.[10]

2. *Vicarii oeconomi,* commonly called administrators, are those who are placed in charge of a parish by the local ordinary during its vacancy.[11] They enjoy the same rights and are subject to the same obligations as pastors, in as far as the care of souls is concerned. The Church, being mindful of the care of souls at all times, makes provision for the time between the occurring of the vacancy of the parish and the time at which the *vicarius oeconomus* is appointed by prescribing that before the setting up of the *vicarius oeconomus* the assistant (*vicarius cooperator*) will take care of the administration of the parish; if there are several assistants, the first or senior assistant takes charge; if all are equal, the older in office; if there are no assistants in the parish, the nearest pastor; if there is question of a parish entrusted to religious, the superior of the religious house.[12]

3. *Vicarii substituti* (vicars substitute). It is necessary here to draw attention to the different kinds of vicars substitute that the Code distinguishes: (a) the substitute priest who with the approval of the local ordinary takes charge of the parish when the pastor is to be lawfully absent from his parish for more than a week; [13] (b) the substitute priest who is designated by the ordinary to take the place of the pastor who has been removed from his benefice, but who has appealed to the Holy See; [14] (c) the priest who supplies in place of the pastor who for a grave cause was constrained to leave his parish suddenly and will not be able to return for more than a week. In an emergency of this kind the pastor must inform the ordinary by letter as soon as possible indicating the reason for his departure and the priest who is supplying for him.[15] If the local ordinary or the pastor does not limit the power of these substitutes, they enjoy full parochial authority as regards the care of souls in the parish and, therefore, can

[10] *Cf.* canons 471 and 1425.
[11] Canon 472, 1°.
[12] Canon 472, 2°.
[13] Canon 465, § 4.
[14] Canon 1923, § 2.
[15] Canon 465, § 5

assist at marriages and conduct pre-nuptial investigation. Here it may be well to mention that the power of the substitute is not delegated, but ordinary, according to the more common opinion of canonists.[16]

From the common law a vicar substitute has the right to assist at marriages and to institute pre-nuptial investigation, unless the ordinary or pastor reserves that right.[17] Approval of the vicar substitute by the ordinary is required, according to canon 465, § 4, and, if the substitute is a religious, the consent of his religious superior is also necessary. Canonists raise a question in regard to the nature of this approval by the ordinary, *viz.*, must the approval be special and explicit, or does general and implicit approval suffice to render the substitute capable of assisting lawfully at marriages? The Code does not add any qualifying phrases to the approval. No doubt special and explicit approval of a determinate substitute by the ordinary is sufficient. The difficulty arises only where general and implicit approval is concerned. A concrete case will serve to clarify the meaning of general approval. A pastor writes his bishop for permission for a month's vacation, and in his petition states that the priests of a nearby religious house will substitute for him. No particular priest is mentioned. The bishop gives his permission for the vacation and approves of the arrangements for a substitute. He mentions no particular priest. A priest is sent to the parish by the religious superior to act as substitute. The approval of the bishop is only general. It would seem that such general approval is in accordance with the requirements of the Code, for it is real, true, genuine approval, and as the Code does not call for determinate approval, reason seems to dictate that general and implicit approval is sufficient. Consequently a substitute so approved has the right to assist validly and lawfully at marriages in the parish and make pre-nuptial investigation.[18] Even if several priests from the religious

[16] Matthew a Coronata, *Institutiones Iuris Canonici Ad Usum Utriusque Cleri et Scholarum* (Taurini: Marietti, 1933), n. 490; A. De Meester, *Iuris Canonici et Iuris Canonico-Civilis Compendium* (Brugis, 1921-1928), II, n. 370; Fanfani, *De Iure Parochorum*, n. 251; Cappello, "De Vicario Substituto," *Periodica*, XIX (1930), 2*.

[17] Canon 474.

[18] Cappello, *De Sacramentis*, III, n. 650.

house act as substitutes for a specific time during the month's vacation, they can assist at marriages. It is well to bear in mind that the concession of diocesan faculties by the ordinary to all priests of a religious house or houses in a diocese for the purpose of hearing confessions is not approval in the sense of canon 465, § 5; because *per se* approval for confessions is not approval for a vicar substitute.[19] If the substitute is a religious, he can validly assist at marriages and conduct pre-nuptial investigation after the approval of the ordinary and prior to approval by the religious superior. The priest, who according to the prescriptions of canon 465, § 5, supplies the place of a pastor who is constrained by a serious cause to absent himself suddenly from his parish, can assist validly and lawfully at marriages as long as the ordinary, whom the pastor notified, did not decree to the contrary.[20] If a pastor inadvertently forgets his duty to inform the ordinary of his sudden absence and of the substitute left in charge of the parish, the substitute still can validly assist at marriages.[21] The same is true if the letter, though mailed, never reached the ordinary.[22] Even when a pastor is absent not beyond a week, it will be necessary for him to provide for the necessities of the faithful.[23] In this connection, however, the priest to whom he entrusts the care of the faithful is not recognized by the Code as a parochial vicar with full parochial authority; he does not require the approbation of the ordinary; and *per se* he has not ordinary jurisdiction in the parish and cannot validly assist at marriages and make pre-nuptial investigation, unless he is empowered to do so by the pastor or has secured delegation from some other source.

4. *Vicarii adjutores* (vicar adjutants) are those priests who are assigned in aid of a permanently disabled pastor, whose disability may have arisen from old age, mental debility, incompetence, blindness or some other permanent inability. If they supply for him in all

[19] "Approval and Delegation of a Substituted Priest," *AER,* XCV (1936), 196, 197.

[20] Pontifical Commission for the Authentic Interpretation of the Code, 14 Jul., 1922, II-IV—*AAS,* XIV (1922), 527, 528.

[21] Cappello, *De Sacramentis,* III, n. 650.

[22] Carberry, *The Juridical Form of Marriage,* p. 52.

[23] Canon 465, § 6.

pastoral duties and enjoy all pastoral rights, their parochial authority is equivalent to that of a pastor in the strict sense, and, consequently, they have the right to assist at marriages and make pre-nuptial investigation. If they supply for him only in some of his parochial work, their obligations and rights must be judged from their letters of appointment.[24]

5. *Vicarii cooperatores* (assistants) deserve mention here because they are frequently given the right to assist at marriages and to conduct pre-nuptial investigation. Assistants are those priests given by the local ordinary to a pastor who unassisted is unable to take proper care of the members of his parish, either because the congregation is very large or for some other similarly objective cause. Their rights and obligations are not determined by the Code, but are to be determined from the diocesan statutes, the letters of the ordinary and the commission of the pastor. Hence the rights and obligations of assistants in regard to assisting at marriages will vary in different places. However, unless diocesan statutes, the letters of the ordinary or the pastor himself limit them to a certain field of parochial work, it is their duty to render assistance to the pastor in all the parochial ministry.[25] When an assistant is placed in charge of a subsidiary church or chapel of ease which is remote from the parish church, it seems that he is appointed with full parochial power.[26] In this case the assistant does not enjoy the name "*pastor*," for he is still a subordinate of the pastor of the principal church and his status as assistant remains unchanged. To obviate any difficulties that may possibly arise and the better to regulate the relationship between assistant and pastor when the assistant is placed in full parochial charge of a subsidiary or mission church within the confines of the parish, a clear outlining of the assistant's authority in regard to the mission church in the letters of the local ordinary will be most valuable.

The *putative pastor* is a priest who is not an actual pastor in the strict juridical sense of the word, but one who on account of common

[24] *Cf.* canon 475.

[25] Canon 476.

[26] Gasparri, *Tractatus de Matrimonio*, n. 934; Carberry, *The Juridical Form of Marriage*, p. 54.

error or positive and probable doubt either of law or of fact is considered a pastor. The Church supplies him with jurisdiction according to the ruling of canon 209. Consequently the parochial functions or duties which he performs are juridically valid.[27] The *putative pastor* must not be confounded with the *parochus intrusus.* A *parochus intrusus* is a priest who is named and appointed as pastor without the consent of the legitimate ecclesiastical authority, *e. g.*, if the civil government without the consent of the legitimate ecclesiastical authority appoints a certain priest as pastor.[28]

The *local ordinary,* according to canon 1096, can validly assist at marriages and institute pre-nuptial investigation, and may be considered as coming under the term "pastor." The following local ordinaries are distinguished in the Code: The Roman pontiff for the whole world; in their respective territories the residential bishop, the abbot and prelate *nullius* and their vicar-generals, the administrator of a diocese, and the vicar and prefect apostolic and the vicar delegate in mission territories. Those who succeed the foregoing ordinaries during the vacancy of their offices according to the prescriptions of law or of lawfully approved constitutions are likewise local ordinaries.[29] Until a vicar capitular is appointed the residential bishop is succeeded by the cathedral chapter, unless an apostolic administrator was appointed or some other provision was made by the Holy See; [30] the abbot or prelate *nullius,* if there is question of a religious abbacy or prelacy, is succeeded by the religious chapter, unless the constitutions prescribe otherwise; if there is question of a secular abbacy or prelacy *nullius,* the chapter of canons succeeds.[31] In the United States the diocesan consultors take the place of the cathedral chapter and the administrator of a vacant diocese takes the place of the vicar capitular.[32] Here the word "administrator" does not refer to the apostolic administrator mentioned in canon 431, § 1. The re-

[27] *Cf.* Gasparri, *Tractatus Canonicus de Matrimonio,* n. 936.

[28] *Cf.* Gasparri, *Tractatus Canonicus de Matrimonio,* n. 938.

[29] Canon 198, § 1.

[30] Canon 431.

[31] Canon 327, § 1.

[32] Canon 427; *Concilii Plenarii Baltimorensis II, Acta et Decreta,* tit. II, cap. 2, n. 18.

ligious chapter, the chapter of canons and, in the United States, the diocesan consultors can assist at marriage collectively or through a delegate. The individual members of these bodies, unless delegated, cannot assist, because the jurisdiction lies in the group and not in the individual members of the group.[33] When the episcopal see is not vacant but the bishop is impeded from the exercise of his jurisdiction, those who rule the diocese according to the prescriptions of canon 429 can assist at marriages.

Vicars and prefects apostolic in mission countries are succeeded by pro-vicars and pro-prefects apostolic during the vacancy of their sees.[34]

Cardinal bishops are ordinaries and can assist at marriages and conduct pre-nuptial investigation in their own territories. All other cardinals are not ordinaries *per se* and cannot be included under the term "pastor." Previous to the constitution *Romanus Pontifex* of Innocent XII even cardinal deacons had quasi-episcopal jurisdiction over the clergy and people of their titular churches, but this ceased with the aforesaid constitution.[35] In the Code legates of the Holy See such as nuncios, internuncios and apostolic delegates are not recognized as ordinaries, and *per se* have no right to assist at marriages or make pre-nuptial investigation.

Do military chaplains come under the term "pastor" and have they the right to assist validly at marriage and make pre-nuptial investigation? The Code explicitly states that their powers are determined by the particular prescriptions of the Holy See. Hence their powers may vary considerably and the special regulations of the Holy See must be consulted for each particular case. If full parochial jurisdiction is given to them, they will have the status of personal pastors and can assist at the marriages of their subjects and conduct pre-nuptial investigation. Other chaplains, such as those placed in charge of a hospital, orphanage, school, prison, etc., or the rector of a seminary, do not enjoy the rights of a pastor according to the Code, and do not *per se* have the right to assist at the

[33] Carberry, *The Juridical Form of Marriage*, p. 56.

[34] Canon 309, § 2.

[35] Gasparri, *Tractatus Canonicus de Matrimonio*, n. 940; Carberry, *The Juridical Form of Marriage*, p. 57.

marriages of their subjects or institute pre-nuptial investigation, unless these rights accrue to them from some other source.[36] However, if in accordance with canon 464, § 2, the foregoing institutions are withdrawn from the jurisdiction of the local pastor and placed under the authority of a chaplain or a rector, it would seem that the chaplain or rector does receive the power to assist at the marriages of his subjects and to conduct pre-nuptial investigation, unless the bishop reserves these powers to himself or others.

The priest who assists at marriages in the extraordinary circumstances of canon 1098, §§ 1, 3 deserves mention here though he is not a pastor, because he has the right from the common law to assist at marriages in the said circumstances. In addition, he has the obligation to investigate the freedom of the parties to marry prior to assisting at their marriage.

Article 2. The Pastor Who Has the Right to Assist at Marriages and Conduct Pre-nuptial Investigation

The right and obligation to make pre-nuptial inquiry into the freedom to marry of the prospective bride and groom do not belong to every pastor; they are reserved by common law to the pastor who has the right to assist at the marriage. Therefore, having enumerated those who come under the term "pastor" for the purpose of pre-nuptial investigation, the question as to what pastor in particular has the right to assist at marriages naturally suggests itself. As the pastor is obligated not only to act validly, but also to act lawfully, in assisting at marriage, it is necessary for the sake of clarity to divide this article into three parts: (a) the pastor who has the right to assist validly at marriage; (b) the pastor who has the right to assist lawfully at marriage; (c) the pastor of preference when several pastors are competent to assist at the marriage.

A. *The Pastor Who Has the Right to Assist Validly*

Canon 1095 lays down the conditions that are necessary on the part of the pastor for valid assistance at marriage:

[36] Gasparri, *Tractatus Canonicus de Matrimonio*, n. 938.

Canon 1095. § 1. Parochus et loci Ordinarius valide matrimonio assistunt:

1°. A die tantummodo adeptae canonicae possessionis beneficii ad normam can. 334, § 3, 1444, § 1, vel initi officii, nisi per sententiam fuerint excommunicati vel interdicti vel suspensi ab officio aut tales declarati;

2°. Intra fines dumtaxat sui territorii; in quo matrimoniis nedum suorum subditorum, sed etiam non subditorum valide assistunt;

3°. Dummodo neque vi neque metu gravi constricti requirant excipiantque contrahentium consensum.

1. *Canonical possession of their benefices or entrance into office* is the first requirement for valid assistance at marriage by the pastor or local ordinary. Mere nomination or appointment to a benefice is not sufficient; actual canonical possession must take place. Residential bishops take canonical possession of their benefices either personally or by means of a proxy by showing the apostolic letters of appointment to the cathedral chapter in the presence of the secretary of the chapter or the chancellor of the diocesan curiae who records the matter in the acta.[37] The Code does not require any particular manner of taking canonical possession for pastors, but mentions that canonical possession will take place according to the manner prescribed by particular law or accepted by legitimate custom. The ordinary, however, may dispense in writing from the manner or ceremony of taking canonical possession.[38] In the event of a dispensation, canonical possession takes place at the moment the dispensation is given. If no dispensation is granted, one must look to the diocesan statutes or the recognized custom of the place to determine the actual time of canonical possession of the parish by the pastor. The pastor has no right to assist validly at marriages or make pre-nuptial investigation before taking canonical possession of the parish, even though he has already received his letters of appointment from his local ordinary.

Entrance into office. A passing glance at those clerics mentioned in the previous article as having the power to assist at marriages

[37] Canon 334, § 3.

[38] Canon 1444, § 1.

reveals that a number of them do not possess an ecclesiastical benefice, *e. g.*, the vicar-general, the administrator of a diocese, the vicar *oeconomus, adjutor, substitutus,* etc. However, they do hold an ecclesiastical office, and it is to them that the phrase *"initi officii"* is applied in canon 1095, § 1, 1°. Authors generally do not define the phrase *"initi officii."* [39] It seems reasonable to hold Woywod's opinion that the phrase means the beginning of the actual exercise of the duties of office by the appointees.

As long as a pastor or local ordinary retains his benefice and as long as those who come under the name of "pastor," even if they are not pastors in the strict sense, remain in office, they can assist validly at marriages and make pre-nuptial investigation. When they lose their benefice or office by renunciation, deprivation, removal, transfer, etc., according to the prescriptions of canons 183-195, their competency to assist validly at marriages and make pre-nuptial investigation ceases, unless the Church in their case supplies jurisdiction because of common error, or in view of positive and probable doubt either of law or of fact.[41]

Three additional ways by which competency to assist validly at marriages is lost are enumerated in canon 1095, § 1, 1°, namely, (a) excommunication, (b) interdict, and (c) suspension from office after a declaratory or condemnatory sentence. Until the sentence is actually handed down, however, a pastor, who has committed a delict to which a penalty of excommunication, interdict or suspension was attached, can validly assist at marriages and conduct pre-nuptial investigation. After the sentence, assistance at marriage by him would be invalid. The one exception where sentence of the pastor is not required is found in canon 2343, § 1, 1°, which states that one laying violent hands upon the person of the Roman Pontiff incurs an excommunication *latae sententiae* and is *ipso facto vitandus.* In this lone case denunciation by sentence or by decree is unnecessary according to canon 2258, § 2. Should a pastor, therefore, lay violent hands on the person of the Holy Father he is, from the very moment of the crime, incapable of assisting at marriages as long as he is under

[39] Woywod, *A Practical Commentary on the Code of Canon Law,* n. 1100.
[40] Woywod, *A Practical Commentary on the Code of Canon Law,* n. 1100.
[41] Canon 209.

excommunication. The Code does not require publicity of the punishment or of the declaratory or condemnatory sentence; but there is a strong probability that publicity will customarily ensue. In the event that the sentence imposed on the pastor remains secret, so that the general public erroneously believe the pastor can validly assist at marriages, canon 209, which supplies jurisdiction in common error and in positive and probable doubt either of law or of fact, would enter in and the putative pastor could validly assist at marriages and conduct pre-nuptial investigation.[42]

Although assistance at marriage is not an act of jurisdiction, it is closely allied to it, because the right to assist at marriages is acquired by virtue of an office and the right to assist can also be delegated like jurisdictional acts.[43] Canon 20 seems to be in accord with this view. The Rota favors this opinion by using the word "delegate" in connection with the permission to assist at marriage, a nomenclature that is used in jurisdictional matters.[44] The use of such jurisdictional terms as "delegation" and "sub-delegation" by the Pontifical Commission for the authentic interpretation of the Code is also a confirmatory argument for the view of that assistance at marriage is looked on as closely akin to an act of jurisdiction.[45]

2. *Territory as a condition for valid assistance.* Under the *Tametsi* decree there were no limitations placed on the *parochus proprius* by reason of territory. He was competent to assist validly at the marriages of his subjects everywhere, even outside the boundaries of his parish. Moreover, among pastors he alone had the right validly to assist or to delegate others to assist at marriages of his subjects.[46]

The *Tametsi* discipline was not found to be perfectly satisfactory, because in practice difficulties frequently arose as to what pastor was the *parochus proprius.* In cases where parishioners had traveled

[42] Cappello, *De Sacramentis,* III, n. 662.

[43] Cappello, *De Sacramentis,* III, n. 694; canon 1095, § 2.

[44] S. R. Rota, *in Divionensi* (Dijon), 20 Jan., 1911—*AAS,* III (1911), 285.

[45] 28 Dec., 1927 ad IV, 1 et 2—*AAS,* XX (1928), 61; *cf.* Woywod, "Delegation of Priest to Assist at Marriage," *HPR,* XXIV (1924), 957-965.

[46] De Smet, *Betrothment and Marriage,* n. 64; Carberry, *The Juridical Form of Marriage,* pp. 67, 68.

far away from the parish and desired to marry outside the parish, it was often a very grave inconvenience for other priests to get in touch with the pastor and receive from him the necessary delegation to assist at the marriage. For those reasons the *Ne temere* decree introduced the civil law practice of territorial competence by prescribing that pastors and local ordinaries could validly assist at marriages only within the limits of their territory. Furthermore, it decreed that within the limits of their territory they could assist validly not only at the marriages of their subjects, but also at the marriages of non-subjects. If the ordinary was outside his diocese or the pastor was outside his parish, he could no longer validly assist at the marriages of his subjects.[47] Time proved the practical value of this new legislation, so much so that the Code retained the law intact. Territorial limits are taken in the strict physical sense; not in the moral sense. Even a pastor who without delegation assisted at a marriage of his own subjects immediately within the limits of an adjacent parish would act invalidly.[48]

When a pastor has no independent parochial territory over which he presides solely and exclusively, that is, when he has parochial rights in a given territory cumulatively with another pastor, or even with several other pastors, have both or all these pastors the power to assist validly at all marriages taking place in this territory? This question arises where there are national parishes, military chaplains with parochial power and pastors of disparate rite, *e. g.*, if within the town there is a parish for Italians, one for Germans, one for Poles, etc., the parish of each extending to the whole town. Can, for instance, the pastor of the German church assist validly at the marriages of Italians in his territory without delegation from the pastor of the Italian church? First, it is necessary to establish whether the pastor of the German church and the pastor of the Italian church are personal pastors in the strict sense or whether they are personal pastors in the broad sense. If they are personal pastors in the broad sense, their jurisdiction is both territorial and personal, and they validly assist at the marriages of all Catholic people in their terri-

[47] S. C. C., decr., *Ne temere,* 2 Aug., 1907, art. 4, § 2—*Fontes,* n. 4340.

[48] Cappello, *De Sacramentis,* III, n. 665.

tory.[49] The pastors of national parishes in the United States have, in general, both personal and territorial jurisdiction, and hence are personal pastors in the broad sense. If pastors of national churches have jurisdiction only over their subjects and are not confined to any territory in the exercise of their jurisdiction, they are personal pastors in the strict sense. It may be mentioned here that although pastors in the broad sense assist validly at all marriages in their territory, they do not assist lawfully without the permission of the proper pastor to whom the parties are subject. Thus if a pastor of a certain national church assisted at the marriage of a member of the English-speaking parish without permission of the pastor of the English-speaking parish, his assistance would be unlawful.[50] Personal pastors in the strict sense have not exclusive jurisdiction over their subjects, *e.g.*, military chaplains who have parochial power. The pastor of the place where the subjects of the personal pastor live can validly assist at their marriages, the reason being that they are within the limits of his territory. The only exception is in the East Indies, where on account of special circumstances strictly personal pastors enjoy exclusive jurisdiction over their subjects.[51]

3. *Active assistance at marriage and freedom from force and fear* on the part of the assisting pastor or local ordinary are essential for valid assistance at marriage. The requirement of active assistance is definitely stated in canon 1095, § 1, 3°: *"Dummodo . . . requirant excipiantque contrahentium consensum."* The pastor must actually ask the bride and groom if they take each other for man and wife. Mere presence of the pastor does not suffice; he must put the interrogations to the parties. Consequently, mere negative or passive assistance would render the marriage invalid.

Even if the pastor actively assists at the marriage when constrained to do so by grave force or fear, the marriage is invalid. The words *"neque vi neque metu gravi constricti"* in canon 1095, § 1, 3° clearly imply that mere internal or intrinsic fear is not suffi-

[49] *Cf.* S. C. C., *Romana et aliarum,* 1 Feb., 1908, ad VIII—*ASS,* XLI (1908), 108-111.

[50] *Cf.* "National Parishes and Assistance at Marriages," *AER,* LXXX (1929), 88-94.

[51] S. C. de Sacramentis, 2 Jun., 1910—*AAS,* II (1910), 447.

cient to invalidate the marriage; the fear must come from some extrinsic cause.[52] The fear must be grave, either relatively or absolutely. Any shade of fear that falls short of grave fear does not invalidate the marriage. Must the fear be unjustly caused, or is just fear sufficient to invalidate the contract? It seems that the better opinion is that *just* as well as *unjust grave fear* brought to bear on the pastor assisting at marriage invalidates the marriage. The Code does not distinguish the kind of fear here mentioned. As a rule the Code singles out the fact when only an *unjust* fear stands in the way of a valid act or contract.[53] Almost invariably the fear will be unjustly inflicted.[54] Inducing a pastor to assist at marriage by deceit of one kind or another does not invalidate the pastor's assistance at marriage, unless the deceit is accompanied by grave force or fear.

B. *The Pastor Who Has the Right to Assist Lawfully*

The conditions for lawful assistance at marriage by the pastor are enumerated in canon 1097:

> Canon 1097. § 1. Parochus autem vel loci Ordinarius matrimonio licite assistunt:
>
> 1°. Constito sibi legitime de libero statu contrahentium ad norman iuris;
>
> 2°. Constito insuper de domicilio vel quasi-domicilio vel menstra commoratione aut, si de vago agatur, actuali commoratione alterutrius contrahentis in loco matrimonii;
>
> 3°. Habita, si conditiones deficiant de quibus n. 2, licentia parochi vel Ordinarii domicilii vel quasi-domicilii aut menstruae commorationis alterutrius contrahentis, nisi vel de vagis actu intinerantibus res sit, qui nullibi commorationis sedem habent, vel gravis necessitas intercedat quae a licentia petenda excuset.

[52] Vlaming, *Praelectiones Iuris Matrimonialis*, II, n. 57; Payen, *De Matrimonio*, II, n. 1774.

[53] *Cf.* canons 103, § 2; 1684, § 1; 1087, § 1; 185; 1307, § 3.

[54] *Cf.* Wouters, *De Forma . . . Celebrationis Matrimonii*, p. 19; Wernz-Vidal, *Ius Canonicum*, V, n. 537; De Becker, *De Matrimonio* (ed. nova), p. 137; Payen, *De Matrimonio*, II, 1744; Ayrinhac-Lydon, *Marriage Legislation in the New Code of Canon Law*, p. 244; Carberry, *The Juridical Form of Marriage*, p. 75.

> § 2. In quolibet casu pro regula habeatur ut matrimonium coram sponsae parocho celebretur, nisi iusta causa excuset; matrimonia autem catholicorum mixti ritus, nisi aliud particulari iure cautum sit, in ritu viri et coram eiusdem parocho sunt celebranda.

The fact that a pastor has complied with the conditions for valid assistance at marriage does not give him the right to assist lawfully; the conditions for lawful assistance must likewise be observed. To omit any of these conditions knowingly and willfully is seriously sinful for the pastor. Consequently their importance for the pastor, who investigates the parties prior to marriage, cannot be minimized.

1. Moral certainty of the *status liber* of the parties is the first requisite for lawful assistance by the pastor at marriage.

2. The pastor must also have a title to assist at marriage, arising from the fact that at least one of the parties has a domicile or quasi-domicile or a month's residence in the parish, or an actual residence in the parish in the case of *vagi*.[55]

A domicile is acquired in two ways: (a) by residence in a parish or quasi-parish or at least in a diocese or vicariate or prefecture apostolic with the intention of remaining there perpetually, if nothing calls one away, or (b) by actual residence for ten complete years.[56]

A quasi-domicile is also acquired in a twofold manner: (a) by residence in a parish, diocese, vicariate or prefecture apostolic with the intention of remaining there for the greater part of the year (*i. e.*, for over 6 months) or (b) by actual residence for the greater part of the year.[57] The domicile acquired in a parish or quasi-parish is called *parochial;* that which is acquired in a diocese, vicariate or prefecture apostolic, without being rooted simultaneously in a parish or quasi-parish, is termed *diocesan*.[58] A minor has a necessary or legal domicile with those under whose authority he is, namely, his parents or guardians, but after infancy he can acquire

[55] Carberry, *The Juridical Form of Marriage*, p. 98.

[56] Canon 92, § 1.

[57] Canon 92, § 2.

[58] Canon 92, § 3.

a quasi-domicile of his own.[59] Whether a minor shares the quasi-domicile of his parents or guardian is a disputed point. As there are authors on both sides, it may be considered a probable opinion that he does.[60]

Both domicile and quasi-domicile are lost by departure from the place of residence with the intention of not returning. The necessary domicile offers the only exception to this rule.[61] Leaving the place of domicile or quasi-domicile for the purpose of contracting marriage does not involve a loss of domicile or quasi-domicile before marriage, because when one leaves with a view to getting married, the departure is not absolute, but conditional, since it presupposes the condition that the marriage will take place.[62]

In addition to domicile and quasi-domicile, a month's residence by one of the parties immediately prior to marriage renders the pastor of the parish competent to assist lawfully at the marriage. The *Ne temere* decree declared that a month's residence in a parish by a party rendered the pastor competent to assist lawfully at the party's marriage.[63] The Code simply retained the *Ne temere* legislation. An actual and complete month, to be reckoned by the calendar according to the prescriptions of canon 33, § 3, 1°, is required. It should be spent within the pastor's territory, but it is not necessary for the party to spend every minute of the month in the parish; all that is required is a morally continuous month. An absence of a day or two does not violate this moral continuity. In the case of a convert the month's residence prior to conversion is considered as coming within the law. It must, however, immediately precede the marriage; consequently, a month's stay at any time prior to the marriage is not sufficient.[64] It is well to mention that the sojourn is judged rather by the place where the person sleeps at night than by where he is during the day.[65] It is not required that the stay be

[59] Canon 92, §§ 1, 2.

[60] Costello, *Domicile and Quasi-Domicile*, p. 177.

[61] Canon 95.

[62] Carberry, *The Juridical Form of Marriage*, p. 99; Fourneret, *Le Mariage Chrètien* (Paris, 1909), p. 146 ss.

[63] 2 Aug., 1907, Art. V, § 2—*Fontes*, 4340.

[64] S. C. de Sacramentis, 26 Jan., 1916—*AAS*, VIII (1916), 65, 66.

[65] Gasparri, *Tractatus Canonicus de Matrimonio*, n. 986.

after the manner of an inhabitant (*per modum habitantis*) of the place; any reason such as vacation, business, etc., suffices.[66]

C. *Pastor of Preference When Several Pastors Are Competent to Assist at Marriage*

It frequently happens that the prospective bride and groom have different proper pastors for marriage. This arises from the fact that they belong to different parishes, that they have different domiciles or quasi-domiciles or that they have established a month's residence in different parishes. The result is that several pastors, in accordance with canon 1097, § 1, 3°, have the right to assist at the marriage and likewise to make pre-nuptial investigation. Canon 1027, § 2 anticipates this situation when it sets up the rule that in every case the marriage should be celebrated before the pastor of the bride, unless a just cause excuses; and that in the case of marriages of mixed rite, unless particular law decrees otherwise, marriages should be celebrated in the rite of the man and before his pastor. Such a rule obviates many difficulties that otherwise would necessarily arise concerning the rights of pastors when their subjects intend to marry spouses who have a domicile, quasi-domicile or month's residence in other parishes. The rule that marriages be celebrated before the bride's pastor is to be followed in every case unless a *just* cause excuses. A serious cause therefore is unnecessary. A just cause would be any reaonable cause from the viewpoint of convenience or utility,[67] such as the fact that the bride made her First Communion in the groom's parish; the fact that her parents were married there; [68] that the convenience for the contemplated wedding-trip can thus be better served; that the church of the bridegroom offers more spacious accommodations; [69] that the pastor of the bridegroom's parish is a relative of either the bride or the groom; that the bride has to work

[66] Carberry, *The Juridical Form of Marriage*, p. 101.

[67] Woywod, *A Practical Commentary on the Code of Canon Law*, n. 1115.

[68] Ayrinhac-Lydon, *Marriage Legislation in the New Code of Canon Law*, p. 257.

[69] Carberry, *The Juridical Form of Marriage*, p. 111.

away from home and thus finds it more congenial to have the marriage guests received in the groom's parish; that the parents of the bride are unreasonably opposed to the marriage and, in consequence, might cease to attend church, either in the parish or even elsewhere, if the bride's pastor assisted at her marriage, etc. It is the pastor of the groom that has the right to adjudge the presence of a just cause. If the pastor of the bride objects within a probably reasonable sphere, the pastor of the groom will preferably, for the sake of prudence in his pastoral ministration, submit the final decision to the discretion of the diocesan ordinary.[70] The obligation of ceding the preference to the pastor of the bride is not one of grave import. The Code indicates a rule rather than a strict law; it recognizes the general fact that even the pastor of the groom has a title to assist at the marriage. It is for the sake of preventing vexatious issues from arising between pastors and for the sake of signalizing their rights in an otherwise co-ordinate sphere of power that the preferred right of assisting at marriages is accorded to the pastor of the bride.

As far as pre-nuptial inevstigation is concerned, both the pastor of the groom and the pastor of the bride have a right to institute the inquiry, but in practice the same rule will hold as for assistance at marriage, namely, the pastor of the bride will institute the pre-nuptial investigation, except a just cause connects this duty with the pastor of the groom in view of the latter's right to assist at the marriage in accordance with the permission of the law itself. Even if a pastor becomes a pastor of the bride by reason of her stay for a month in his parish, his right to assist at the marriage is preferred to that of the groom's pastor. To promote efficiency in the canonical investigation there should be a happy co-operation between both pastors. Though the pastor of the bride has the preference, he will frequently need the aid of the pastor of the groom, especially when the parties live in parishes that are a long distance from each other. In such a case it is practical that the pastor of the bride ask the pastor of the groom to investigate the free status of the groom, while he himself investigates the free

[70] "For What Reason May Marriage Be Celebrated in the Parish of the Groom?" *HPR*, XXVIII (1927-1928), 409, 410.

status of the bride. Then the groom's pastor should send the results of his inquiry to the bride's pastor. For the groom's pastor to undertake the investigation of the groom without the consent or notification from the bride's pastor or, at least his reasonably presumed consent, is hardly in accord with the spirit of the law.[71]

When both contracting parties are Catholics, the preference of the bride's pastor over the groom's pastor in regard to assistance at marriage and pre-nuptial investigation is admitted by all commentators. There is a difference of opinion as to whether the words *"coram sponsae parocho"* of canon 1097, § 2 refer also to the pastor of the bride, when the bride is a non-Catholic. One opinion maintains that the preference to assist at mixed marriages is not given to the pastor of the non-Catholic bride, because the non-Catholic bride is not a subject of the pastor of the place where she lives.[72] A second opinion holds that if the non-Catholic bride is baptized her pastor has the preference in assisting at the marriage; if she is not baptized, the pastor of the bridegroom assists at the marriage.[73] The reason urged for the view is that a non-Catholic bride who is unbaptized cannot have a proper pastor. A third opinion maintains that the phrase *"coram sponsae parocho"* refers to the pastor of the non-Catholic as well as to the pastor of the Catholic bride. One argument for this opinion is the fact that the Code makes no distinction between the non-Catholic and Catholic bride in the case, for it uses the words *"in quolibet casu,"* which apparently include the cases when the bride is non-Catholic, as well as the cases when the bride is Catholic.[74] A further argument is deduced from a decision given by the Sacred Congregation of the Sacraments which implied that a month's residence irrespective of the religion of the party gave the pastor a lawful title to assist at the marriage.[75]

[71] Gasparri, *Tractatus Canonicus de Matrimonio,* n. 129.

[72] Cronin, *New Matrimonial Legislation,* p. 298; Creagh, *A Commentary on the Decree, "Ne Temere,"* p. 50; Fanfani, *De Iure Parochorum,* n. 309; Woywod, "For What Reason May Marriage Be Celebrated in the Parish of the Groom?" *HPR,* XXVIII (1928), 410; "Coram Sponsae Parocho," *AER,* LXII (1920), 691.

[73] Payen, *De Matrimonio,* 1805.

[74] *Cf.* canon 1097, § 2.

[75] 26 Jan., 1916—*AAS,* VIII (1916), 64-66; Carberry, *The Juridical Form*

It is apparently the custom in the United States for the parties to come to the pastor of the groom when the bride is a non-Catholic, rather than to the pastor of the place where the bride lives. Some diocesan statutes require this,[76] and the fact that the bride is a non-Catholic seems to justify such procedure.[77] As the Holy See has not made any pronouncement on the matter, one cannot say that the pastor of the bridegroom is wrong if without the consent of the pastor of the non-Catholic bride he assists at the wedding; neither can a serious objection be made if the pastor of the non-Catholic bride assists at the wedding. An interpretation as to whether or not the phrase "*coram sponsae parocho*" extends to the pastor of the non-Catholic bride is desirable, but in the meantime let the ordinary be consulted when disputes about the matter arise in actual cases.

The bride may have several proper pastors as far as assistance at marriage and pre-nuptial investigation are concerned, *e. g.*, she may have a domicile in one place, a quasi-domicile in another and a month's residence in another. As a matter of fact, canonists recognize that it is possible for an individual to have a plurality of domiciles or quasi-domiciles.[78] When several pastors have the right to conduct pre-nuptial investigation, which one has the preference? The Code is silent on the subject. However, it seems in accordance with reason that the bride may select any one of the competent pastors to assist at the marriage and conduct the pre-nuptial investigation.

of Marriage, p. 109; F. Schenk, *The Matrimonial Impediments of Mixed Religion and Disparity of Cult* (The Catholic University of America, Canon Law Studies, n. 51, Washington: The Catholic University of America, 1929), p. 285; "Coram Sponsae Parocho," *AER*, LXIII (1920), 417-419; "The Pastor of the Bride Assists Lawfully Even if She Be a Non-Catholic," LXXVII (1928), 523, 524; "'The Pastor of the Bride Assists Lawfully at Marriage Even if She Be a Non-Catholic' and Diocesan Statutes," LXXX (1929), 200.

[76] Schenk, *The Matrimonial Impediments of Mixed Religion and Disparity of Cult*, p. 285.

[77] Aertnys-Damen, *Theologia Moralis* (11 ed., Turin: Marietti, 1928), n. 841.

[78] *Cf.* Costello, *Domicile and Quasi-Domicile*, pp. 151-156.

Article 3. Delegation to Institute Pre-Nuptial Investigation

Under this heading two questions of importance arise: 1. When delegation to assist at marriage is granted to a priest by the pastor or the local ordinary, are the right and the obligation to make pre-nuptial investigation concerning the freedom of the parties to marry likewise conceded? 2. Are the right and obligation of making pre-nuptial investigation so strictly personal to the pastor, who has the right to assist at the marriage, that delegation is never permissible?

As regards the first question, it seems that when another priest is delegated to assist at marriage, either by the pastor or the local ordinary, he is not thereby entrusted with the right and the obligation to make pre-nuptial investigation; apparently, the onus of the investigation still remains with the pastor. This is evidently the only conclusion warranted by canon 1096, § 2, taken in conjunction with canon 1096, § 1. Canon 1096, § 1, declares that, when delegation is given to another priest to assist at marriage in accordance with the prescriptions of canon 1095, it must be granted expressly to a determinate priest for a specified marriage, all general delegations being excluded, unless there is question of assistants (*nisi agatur de vicariis cooperatoribus*) in reference to the parish at which they are appointed; otherwise the delegation is invalid. Canon 1096, § 2, states that "*the pastor or local ordinary shall not grant permission or delegation until after all things are completed which the law requires for the proving of the free state of the parties.*" In these words the Code explicitly requires that the pastor see to it that the parties are free to marry before he gives permission or delegation to another priest to assist at the marriage. This law of the Code is a desirable one, as the pastor is usually in a better position than the delegated priest to interrogate and examine the parties. As the pastor is directly responsible for the care of souls in his territory, it seems only reasonable that he should have the right to act in a matter that is so intimately connected with the care of souls as pre-nuptial investigation, even when a delegate is to assist at the marriage. As a matter of fact a really zealous pastor well acquainted with his people and territory will as a rule be more efficient in conducting the pre-nuptial investigation than any other priest. The interpretation of commentators is also definitely in favor of the view that the right and obligation of pre-nuptial investigation remain with the pastor, and are not transferred to the delegated priest.[79] Even in the case of assistants who have general delegation to assist at marriages in the parish, it would seem that it is the pastor of the parish, and not the assistant, that has the obligation of instituting the pre-nuptial investigation; [80] because in his work in the parish the assistant acts under the direction of the pastor, and it is to the pastor that the care of souls is directly and primarily entrusted. Of course, if the assistant were entrusted with the entire care of a subsidiary church within the confines of the parish and given full parochial authority over it, the burden of the pre-nuptial investigation of members of his congregation would primarily fall on him, because of the special connection he has with the church.

The question as to whether a pastor can delegate another priest to make the pre-nuptial investigation may be answered in the affirmative. The obligation of making the pre-nuptial investigation is not an absolutely personal one; it can be fulfilled *per se* or *per alium*.[81]

In the Code there is no restrictive phrase saying that the pastor alone, and nobody else, may institute the pre-nuptial investigation. Apparently it is the intention of the law that the pastor should personally assist at the interrogation of the parties, unless reasons of necessity or some just cause urge him to depute another priest to examine the parties.[82] A pastor overburdened with parish work or one who is ill would certainly be justified in deputing another

[79] Gasparri, *Tractatus Canonicus de Matrimonio*, n. 129; Payen, *De Matrimonio*, n. 136; Cappello, *De Sacramentis*, III, n. 151; Woywod, *A Practical Commentary on the Code of Canon Law*, n. 991; Carberry, *The Juridical Form of Marriage*, pp. 81, 82.

[80] Carberry, *The Juridical Form of Marriage*, p. 54.

[81] Cappello, *De Sacramentis*, III, n. 151.

[82] Cappello, *De Sacramentis*, III, n. 151; Gougnard, *Tractatus de Matrimonio*, p. 54; Joseph P. Petrovits, *The New Church Law of Matrimony* (Philadelphia: John Joseph McVey, 1921), p. 44.

to make the investigation. In some very large parishes where the number of weddings is unusually great, it is perfectly legitimate for a pastor to depute one or more of the assistants to conduct the pre-nuptial investigation. If in a rectory there is a priest expert in Canon Law or one who had proved himself most efficient in the pre-nuptial interrogation and examination of contracting parties, there is no reason why the pastor may not delegate him, especially in the more difficult cases, to institute the pre-nuptial investigation. However, as the Code imposes the obligation of parochial investigation on the pastor, he should not for every little reason transfer the obligation to other priests.

Article 4. Gravity of the Pastor's Obligation

In order that a law may bind with a grave obligation it is necessary that at least the matter of the law be grave and that the legislator intend to oblige *sub gravi*.[83] That in virtue of his office as well as by ecclesiastical law the pastor is under a grave obligation to make pre-nuptial inquiry into the freedom of the parties to marry is beyond question. To neglect seriously this duty would be gravely sinful for the pastor. This is evidenced by the serious importance of pre-nuptial investigation and the purpose behind the law, namely, to preserve the sacredness of marriage and to prevent unlawful and invalid marriages, which, as history has proved, have wrought much evil to society, to the Church and to the individual. The words of the Fourth Lateran Council on the subject of pre-nuptial investigation by the pastor are definitely preceptive, indicating that the legislator intended to bind under penalty of serious sin. This fact is confirmed by the drastic sanctions imposed for the violation of the law.[84] The words of Benedict XIV in his several pronouncements on the subject leave no room for doubt regarding the gravity of the pastor's obligation.[85] The terminology

[83] H. Noldin, *De Principiis Theologiae Moralis* (Oeniponte: Typis et sumptibus Fel. Rauch, 10 ed., 1921), I, *De Principiis*, n. 162.

[84] IV Lateran Council (1215), c. 51—Mansi, XX, 1038.

[85] Encycl. epist., *Etsi minime*, 7 Feb., 1842, § 11—*Fontes*, n. 324; Encycl.

of the Code law likewise indicates a grave obligation on the part of the pastor, because of its preceptive character, and also because of the fact that the duty of pre-nuptial investigation is mentioned several times.[86] Were pre-nuptial inquiry not considered a really serious matter, the Code would hardly be so particularly insistent on it. Even in an extreme case like that of danger of death it cannot be neglected, but must be conducted insofar as circumstances will allow.[87] An instruction subsequent to the Code issued by the Sacred Congregation of the Sacraments dissipates all misgivings about the gravity of the pastor's obligation; for it decrees that ordinaries shall instruct their pastors that they are forbidden to marry persons under any pretext, even for the purpose of keeping the faithful from living in unlawful concubinage or of averting the scandal of a so-called civil marriage, unless they have proof that the parties are free to marry.[88] The collective interpretation and viewpoint of commentators confirm the seriousness of the pastor's duty.[89]

Even if the pastor is already certain, either from personal knowledge or from some other source, that the parties are really free to marry, he is not thereby released from the duty of making the pre-nuptial investigation. In reference to the proclamation of the banns it is the common opinion of authors that the law continues to bind, despite the pastor's certain knowledge of the parties' freedom to marry. Similarly in reference to the pre-nuptial investigation there is equal reason to hold that the law continues in force, even though the pastor feels certain that no impediment or hindrance to marriage will be detected. However, when the pastor is already

epist., *Nimiam licentiam,* 18 Maii, 1743, § 10—*Fontes,* n. 337; Encycl. litt., *Cum religiosi,* 26 Jun., 1754, § 4—*Fontes,* n. 429.

[86] Canons 1019; 1020; 1096, § 2; 1097, § 1, 1°.

[87] Canon 1019, § 2.

[88] S. C. de Sacramentis, instr., 4 Jul., 1921—*AAS,* XIII (1921), 348, 349.

[89] Gasparri, *Tractatus Canonicus de Matrimonio,* n. 130; Cappello, *De Sacramentis,* III, n. 146; Payen, *De Matrimonio,* n. 376; Woywod, *A Practical Commentary on the Code of Canon Law,* n. 991; Noldin, *Summa Theologiae Moralis,* III, n. 550; Ayrinhac-Lydon, *Marriage Legislation in the New Code of Canon Law,* p. 26.

morally certain of the freedom of the parties to marry, his interrogation may be more brief and summary, as the common law does not prescribe any definite questions to be asked of the parties.[90] Nevertheless, if diocesan statutes or the bishop's decrees prescribe a definite interrogatory, the pastor will be obliged to follow it.[91]

Article 5. Important Qualifications for the Investigating Pastor

Taking it for granted that the pastor has zeal for the good of souls, there are three qualifications in particular that may be mentioned here as requisites for sound and efficient pre-nuptial investigation:

1. Knowledge of theology and, in particular, of Canon Law;
2. Knowledge of human character;
3. Prudence and tact.

I. *Knowledge* of the revelation of God and of the teachings and laws of the Church on the Sacrament of Matrimony is a prime essential for successful pre-nuptial investigation. It is a serious and imperative duty for the pastor to possess a substantial knowledge of the marriage laws of the Church. Lack of such knowledge would frequently jeopardize the validity and the lawfulness of marriages. The obviation of this inherent danger surely constitutes for the pastor an obligation of grave and serious import. Frequent consultation of the marriage laws of the Code, the periodic perusal of approved commentators on the Code and the habitual reading of good current ecclesiastical reviews or magazines for the purpose of keeping abreast of the latest developments in the Church's laws and their official interpretation will normally suffice to ensure the requisite knowledge.

II. *Knowledge of human character* is a decided asset to the pastor in his investigation, especially for the evaluation of the testi-

[90] Gasparri, *Tractatus Canonicus de Matrimonio,* n. 130.

[91] *Cf.* canon 1020, § 3.

mony of the parties and witnesses. Though most of those who present themselves at the rectory for marriage will be well intentioned and will be anxious that the marriage they contemplate be valid and lawful, still pastoral experience proves that some will endeavor to conceal impediments and will not be very much concerned whether their marriage be valid or not. Moreover, a knowledge of character will greatly help to determine what should be the nature of the interrogations; what impediments are likely to arise; and how detailed the questions ought to be.

Nupturients do not fall into any common mould. There are the learned and the unlearned, the communicative and the uncommunicative, the responsive and the unresponsive, the bold and the timid, the aggressive and the docile, the bigoted and the tolerant, the petulant and the stolid, the attentive and the apathetic—in a word, people whose traits of personality reveal human character in all its forms of the normal and the abnormal. Pastoral experience together with observation and character study will give the pastor the happy faculty of being able to form a sound and reliable judgment of the contracting parties.

III. *Tact and prudence.* Knowledge alone of the laws of marriage and of the character of the parties will not suffice for efficient investigation. Prudence and tact in actual interrogation are most necessary. They will dictate an apposite and equitable form of procedure. With them as a guide the pastor will be kindly in his manner and display a sincere sympathy with the interests of the bridal couple. With the unlearned he will seek to converse in their own simple and unadorned manner of speech. With the timid and shy he will strive to inspire a free and generous confidence. With the aggressive, arrogant and obstinate he will season his pastoral forbearance with resolute and uncompromising firmness. With the stolid and apathetic his manner will be full of inspiration. With the bigoted and petulant his demeanor will be tolerant. He will do nothing by his criticism to wound feelings or offend sensibilities, for antagonism, regardless of its nature, destroys the hope of mutual confidence. With the scrupulous he will avoid all unsubstantial detail; with the lax he will insist on a searching interrogation. With the learned he will be courteous, with the responsive he will show deep appreciation and with the attentive he will show his genuine compliment. In his conduct of the pre-nuptial interrogation the pastor will first explore the character, temperament and disposition of the parties, if his lack of acquaintance with them makes this procedure helpful and desirable. Thereupon he can plan the method, form, and content of his interrogation. He will suit and adapt it to the needs he has ascertained. In his progress throughout there will then be reflected its supremely concentric purpose—the Church's abiding concern for the good of souls.

CHAPTER VI

GENERAL FEATURES OF PRE-NUPTIAL INVESTIGATION BY THE PASTOR

ARTICLE 1. THE SUBJECT OF PRE-NUPTIAL INVESTIGATION

As has been repeatedly stated, it is the pastor who has the right to assist at marriages that also has the right to conduct the pre-nuptial investigation of the contracting parties.[1] A pastor, therefore, has no right to investigate the free status of the parties to a forthcoming marriage unless they are his subjects by reason of his right to assist at their union. To determine who in general are subject to the pastor's pre-nuptial investigation it is sufficient to enumerate those who are required by law to contract marriage in the presence of the pastor (pastor here is used in the broad sense to include the local ordinary also). They are: (a) *persons baptized in the Catholic Church,* and (b) *converts from heresy and schism.* Even though they lapse from the Church, they are stilly bound to contract marriage in the presence of the pastor and are subject to pre-nuptial investigation by him, not only when they marry among themselves but also when they marry non-Catholics.[2] Catholics of the Oriental rites are bound by the form of marriage and by pre-nuptial investigation by the pastor when they contract marriage with members of the Latin rite.[3] Here it is well to determine who are comprehended under (a) persons baptized in the Catholic Church and (b) converts from heresy and schism.

A. *Persons Baptized in the Catholic Church.* Baptism, even if conferred by non-Catholics, is valid, if there is no defect in the matter and form of the sacrament and in the intention of the minister to perform a valid baptism. The canonical distinction between

[1] Canon 1020, § 2.

[2] Canon 1099, § 1, 1° and 2°.

[3] Canon 1099, § 1, 3°.

baptism in the Catholic Church and baptism outside it, according to authors, depends largely on three things: (a) the intention of the subject, if the subject has the use of reason; (b) the intention of the parents or guardians, if the subject has not yet reached the use of reason; (c) the intention of the minister of the sacrament in certain circumstances.[4] Here baptism in the Catholic Church has reference to the external enrolling of the person baptized in the visible society of the Catholic Church.[5] Without going into unnecessary details the following assertions may be made in regard to baptism in the Catholic Church:

1. Infants, brought by their parents or guardians to a Catholic priest for baptism, with the intention of enrolling the infant in the Catholic Church, not just internally, but externally also, are certainly baptized in the Catholic Church. The intention of the parents may be expressed or tacit.

2. Infants, baptized by a non-Catholic minister in urgent danger of death, the intention of the parents being to have them made members of the Catholic Church, are considered baptized in the Catholic Church, even though the minister may have had the intention of enrolling them in his own sect and had actually baptized them according to his own rite.

3. Infants who are born of Catholic parents, and who through error, deceit or fraud were baptized by a non-Catholic minister, whose intention was to enroll them in a non-Catholic sect, are nevertheless considered baptized in the Catholic Church, if the parents wished to enlist them in the Church's membership by baptism. It is the intention of the parents that decides the matter in the case of infants.

4. Infants born of infidel parents, and baptized in danger of death by a Catholic priest, cleric, or lay person, are considered baptized in the Catholic Church, even if the baptism took place

[4] Gasparri, *Tractatus Canonicus de Matrimonio,* nn. 569-573; Cappello, *De Sacramentis,* III, n. 411; Carberry, *The Juridical Form of Marriage,* p. 120; Schenk, *The Matrimonial Impediments of Mixed Religion and Disparity of Cult,* p. 104.

[5] Cappello, *De Sacramentis,* III, n. 4111.

against the will of the parents.[6] According to canon 751 the same is true of infants of heretics, schismatics and apostate Catholics.

5. Infants born of infidel, heretical or schismatical parents, and baptized by a Catholic minister outside of danger of death, are considered baptized in the Catholic Church, when their parents or guardians consent to the baptism and guarantee the Catholic education of the infants so baptized. If the heretical or schismatical parents (father, mother, grandfather, grandmother) or guardian of the child are dead, or if the parents or guardian lose their right to the child or cannot in any way exercise that right, such a child baptized by a Catholic minister is considered baptized in the Catholic Church.[7]

6. Infants unlawfully baptized by a non-Catholic minister contrary to the prescriptions of canons 750 and 751, and reared from infancy in the Catholic religion, are considered baptized in the Catholic Church. If they were reared from infancy in heresy, schism, or without any religion, authors are not agreed whether or not they are to be considered as baptized in the Catholic Church. Consequently the matter is doubtful.[8] In practice, as far as pre-nuptial investigation is concerned, it will not cause much difficulty, for canon 1099, § 2 exempts such persons from the canonical form of marriage and thus also from the pre-nuptial investigation by the pastor.

7. Infants who in danger of death are baptized by a Catholic minister, though their heretical or schismatical parents wish to attach them to their own sect, are nevertheless considered baptized in the Catholic Church.[9]

8. Adults who willingly ask for and receive baptism in the Catholic Church are certainly baptized in the Catholic Church.

[6] Canon 750, § 1.

[7] Canons 750, § 2; 751.

[8] *Cf.* Gasparri, *Tractatus Canonicus de Matrimonio,* n. 570; Cappello, *De Sacramentis,* III, n. 411; Carberry, *The Juridical Form of Marriage,* p. 122; Schenk, *The Matrimonial Impediments of Mixed Religion and Disparity of Cult,* p. 108.

[9] Canon 750, § 1.

9. Adults who willingly ask for baptism in the Catholic Church, but are baptized by a non-Catholic minister according to the rite of some heretical sect, the intention of the minister being to attach them to that sect, are considered baptized in the Catholic Church. It is the intention of the adult that decides the matter.

10. An adult who is baptized by a Catholic minister, but who wishes and expressly declares that he wants to be aggregated to some non-Catholic sect, is not baptized in the Catholic Church. This case is more theoretical than real, for it is difficult to imagine a priest, cleric or well instructed Catholic layman who would perform a baptism under these express conditions.

When a doubt exists as to whether a person was baptized in the Catholic Church or outside it, the presumption is that he is baptized in the Catholic Church.[10]. However, an effort must be made to dispel the doubt.

B. *Converts From Heresy and Schism.* A heretic is a baptized person who, while retaining the name "Christian," stubbornly denies or doubts a truth or truths defined by the Church as divinely revealed. Members of the Protestant Church are considered in this category, because they deny some of the defined doctrines of faith.

Apostates from the Church are also heretics, because they reject the faith entirely, while a schismatic is one who refuses to subject himself to the authority of the Supreme Pontiff or to have communication with members of the Church subject to the Pope.[11] If, therefore, a heretic rejects his errors and a schismatic returns to communion with the Church and subjects himself to the authority of the Pope by converting to the Catholic Church, both of these become subjects of canonical pre-nuptial investigation. It is well to remember that infidels who convert to the Catholic Church are not converts from heresy or schism, but are subject to pre-nuptial investigation because of baptism in the Catholic Church.

Non-Subjects of Pre-Nuptial Investigation. By reason of canon 1099, § 2 considered in conjunction with canon 1020, § 2, unconverted non-Catholics, whether *baptized,* such as heretics and schismatics, or *unbaptized,* such as infidels or pagans, are not sub-

[10] Cappello, *De Sacramentis,* III, n. 411.

[11] Canon 1325, § 2.

ject to canonical pre-nuptial investigation when they marry among themselves. It is important to keep in mind the clause, "when they marry among themselves," for if an infidel, a heretic or a schismatic desires to marry a Catholic, he becomes subject to canonical investigation indirectly.[12]

Infidels, heretics and schismatics who are under instruction, but who have not yet been received into the Catholic fold, are reckoned as non-Catholics.

It is stated in canon 1099, § 1, 1° and 2°, that all persons baptized in the Catholic Church are bound by the canonical form of marriage, both when they marry among themselves and when they marry non-Catholics. In virtue of canon 1020, § 2, they are subject also to canonical pre-nuptial investigation. It is most important, however, for the investigating pastor to note an exception to this common rule made by the second part of canon 1099, § 2, which states, that *those born of non-Catholics, although baptized in the Catholic Church, but who from their infancy were reared in heresy, schism or infidelity or without any religion, are not obliged by the canonical form of marriage when they marry non-Catholics.* They are likewise exempt from canonical pre-nuptial investigation. The *Ne temere* decree did not contain this exemption. However, prior to the Code, questions arose as to the validity of marriages entered into without the canonical form by those born of non-Catholic parents who, though baptized in the Church, were not reared in the Catholic faith. According to a reply of the Holy Office on March 31, 1911, the Holy See was to be consulted in each particular case.[13] When the Code expressly made the above exemption, it was certainly evident that when both parents were non-Catholic, the children born of them and baptized in the Catholic Church, but reared from infancy outside the Catholic Church, were exempt from the canonical form of marriage and likewise from pre-nuptial investigation by the pastor. There was a difference of opinion in regard to the children of mixed marriages. The majority of the commentators after the Code maintained that those who were born of a valid mixed marriage and were

[12] Canon 1099, § 1, 2°.

[13] *AAS,* III (1911), 163, 164.

baptized in the Catholic Church, but who were not reared from infancy in the Catholic faith, were bound by the canonical form of marriage.[14]

Three decisions of the Pontifical Commission for the Authentic Interpretation of the Code, given respectively on July 20, 1929, February 17, 1930, and July 25, 1931, clarified the meaning of the phrase *"ab acatholicis nati."*

In the first decision it was declared that among the *ab acatholicis nati* there were included also those who were born of parents of whom only one was a non-Catholic, even if at the time of marriage the *cautiones* were given in accordance with canons 1061 and 1071.[15] Therefore, the phrase *"ab acatholicis nati"* includes those who are born of valid mixed marriages. This decision was contrary to the opinion maintained by the majority of canonists.

The second decision of the Pontifical Commission declared that those who are born of apostates are likewise embraced by the phrase *"ab acatholicis nati."* Who are apostates? Canon 1325, § 2 defines an apostate as a baptized person who has entirely rejected the faith. Those who are born of such persons certainly are embraced by the decision of the Pontifical Commission. The defection from the faith, however, must be public and be capable of proof in the external forum.[16] Commentators extend the term "apostate" not only to those who have totally rejected the faith, but also to those who have definitely withdrawn from the Catholic Church.[17] If a Catholic joins a heretical or schismatical sect or joins a sect that professedly teaches or inculcates atheism or some doctrine which involves a departure from the Church, he may be regarded as an apostate. If he has not joined some such sect or organization, the matter must be judged according to the circumstances. If the external circumstances indicate a defection from the

[14] Schaaf, "An Exemption from the Canonical Form of Marriage," *AER*, LXXXIII (1930), 184-195.

[15] Pont. Comm. Interp. Cod., 20 Jul., 1929—*AAS*, XXI (1929), 573.

[16] Gasparri, *Tractatus Canonicus de Matrimonio*, n. 1023; Cappello, *De Sacramentis*, III, n. 702.

[17] *Periodica*, XIX (1930), 268, 269; Carberry, *The Juridical Form of Marriage*, p. 132; Schaaf, "An Exemption From the Canonical Form of Marriage," *AER*, LXXXIII (1930), 495.

faith, he will also be presumed to have defected internally,[18] and in the external forum he will be regarded as an apostate until the contrary is evident. However, one must distinguish between the children of apostate Catholics and the children of careless Catholics. Careless and negligent Catholics are by no means apostates, as is indicated by the fact that in times of trouble or in danger of death many of them return to the practice of their faith, and attribute the non-fulfillment of their duties to mere negligence. Children of careless Catholics are not included under the phrase *"ab acatholicis nati,"* and are subject to the canonical form of marriage and canonical pre-nuptial investigation.

If one parent is an apostate and the other a Catholic, are their children subject to the canonical form of marriage and to pre-nuptial investigation by the pastor? Arguing by analogy from the decision of the Pontifical Commission which declared that *"ab acatholicis nati"* included those born of mixed and disparate marriages, it would seem that children born of parents of whom only one is an apostate, likewise come within the phrase *"ab acatholicis nati."*

In reference to the time element connected with the apostasy of parents, it is evident of course that children who are born after the apostasy of their parents are *ab acatholicis nati.* It would seem also that if the parents apostatized at any time during the infancy of their children, these could still be considered as *ab acatholicis nati.*[19] There seems to be no valid reason for maintaining the contrary, because if the parents apostatized during the infancy of their children, and these children were reared outside the Church from that time on, it can yet be truly said that these children are the children of apostate parents and were reared from infancy outside the faith. Canon 1099, § 2 does not say that the rearing of children outside the faith from the beginning of their infancy is necessary in order to consider them exempt from the canonical form of matrimony.

The third decision of the Pontifical Commission declared that the interpretation of canon 1099, § 2, as given on July 20, 1929,

[18] Cappello, *De Sacramentis,* III, n. 702.

[19] Carberry, *The Juridical Form of Marriage,* p. 153.

was declarative,[20] *i.e.*, that it was simply a declaration which pointed to the words of the law as being clear in themselves. Hence it did not require a new promulgation of the law and moreover was retroactive.[21] Although it has not been expressly stated by the Pontifical Commission that the decision handed down on February 17, 1930 concerning the children of apostates was declarative, it seems that it was, because the Pontifical Commission has no power to give extensive interpretations of law.[22]

Article 2. Time and Place of Pre-Nuptial Investigation

A. *Time*. In a general way canon 1019, § 1 specifies the time of pre-nuptial investigation by stating that it should take place prior to the celebration of the marriage. Canon 1020, § 1 is more determinate and states that the examination of the parties should take place at an *opportune* or suitable time before the marriage (*opportuno antea tempore*). The Code does not explicitly state what is meant by the phrase "*opportuno antea tempore*." Perhaps the variety of circumstances, which makes the opportune time for different cases variable, supplies the reason for this lack of clearer specification by the Code. It would hardly be in accordance with intelligently adopted procedure to set up an inflexible standard from which a departure would never be conceded. In order to establish some kind of general rule regarding the time of the investigation, cases may be reasonably divided into two categories, *ordinary* and *extraordinary*.

1. *Ordinary Cases*. In ordinary cases it is not necessary that the investigation precede betrothal, for common law merely states that it should be conducted prior to the celebration of the marriage. Hence, despite the fact that before betrothal investigation of the freedom of the parties to marry may be of great utility, it is not required. The proper time for pre-nuptial investigation when both parties are Catholic is before the first publication of the banns.[23]

20 *AAS*, XXIII (1931), 388.

21 Canon 17, § 2.

22 *Cf.* Benedict XV, motu proprio, *Cum iuris canonici*, 17 Sept., 1917—*AAS*, IX (1917), 483.

23 Gasparri, *Tractatus Canonicus de Matrimonio*, n. 134; Wernz-Vidal, *Ius Canonicum*, V, n. 115; Cappello, *De Sacramentis*, III, n. 151.

Such was the prescription of Benedict XIV in his encyclical epistle *Nimiam licentiam.*[24] Previous to the time of Benedict XIV, Pope Innocent XII and Clement XI decreed that the banns of marriage were not to be published in church by the pastor until he had found out that the parties were sufficiently instructed in the rudiments of their religion.[25] The view that pre-nuptial investigation should precede the banns of marriage is indicated by the order of the Code, which treats of pre-nuptial investigation immediately prior to the publication of the banns. It is also in accord iwth canon 1031, § 2, 2°, which implicitly presumes that pre-nuptial investigation takes place antecedently to the publication of the banns, when it states: "In the event of the detection of a public impediment before the publication of the banns is begun, the pastor shall not announce the banns until the impediment is removed, even though he may be aware that a dispensation from the impediment—but one for the forum of conscience only—has in the meantime been obtained." A further confirmation of the foregoing view is found in the former discipline, which required that the juridical examination of witnesses for the purpose of proving the *status liber* of the parties should precede the publication of the banns.[26] It may be concluded then that the *tempus opportunum* ends at the moment of the first publication of the banns.[27] The actual time, therefore, that should normally elapse between pre-nuptial investigation and the wedding ceremony will depend on whether the proclamation of the banns is oral [28] or written.[29] If oral, a period of about three weeks or a month is required. If the ordinary permits a written publication of the banns as a substitute for the oral, a period of approximately two weeks is necessary. In case a dispensation from some impediment is required, the time must be extended. The time requisite for the obtaining of dispensations from the episcopal curia will extend from a few days to a week, or even longer. The interval of time that must be allowed will depend not only on the factor of distance be-

[24] 18 Maii, 1743, § 10—*Fontes*, n. 337.

[25] *Cf. Bullarium Clementis XI* (Romaé, 1723), n. 11, p. 376.

[26] *Cf.* S. C. S. decr., *Cum alias,* 21 Aug., 1670—*Fontes*, n. 742.

[27] Petrovits, J., *The New Church Law on Matrimony,* n. 88.

[28] Canon 1024.

[29] Canon 1025.

tween the parish and the diocesan curia but also on the frequency of the mail delivery. The length of time required for receiving dispensations from the Holy See will depend on the distance of the petitioner from Rome and on the nature of the dispensation required. For the United States of America the obtaining of a dispensation in ordinary cases will require an interval of time ranging from three weeks to two months. Common law insists that the dispensation be obtained before the publication of the banns.[80] When the pastor is certain that a dispensation from the Holy See is not necessary, pre-nuptial investigation a month before the marriage is a safe rule. Usually the parties will not have any day set for the wedding before they approach their pastor on the matter, and if they actually have a day set for the wedding, they commonly announce their intention to the pastor two or three months ahead of time.

When the publication of the banns is omitted as in mixed marriages [81] or also, as is the custom in some places, in the marriage of Catholics, an opportune time would be a month before the marriage. A pastor could hardly be censured if, in certain instances, he postpones the pre-nuptial investigation to a few days before the celebration of the marriage, when he is most certain that there is no impediment to the marriage.[82] However, this should not be made a practice.

2. *Extraordinary Cases.* Under certain extraordinary circumstances the opportune time for pre-nuptial investigation will be considerably less than a month. In danger of death of one or both contracting parties the time for investigation will depend on the seriousness of the danger. If death is very imminent, investigation will have to be made immediately and the marriage should immediately follow. If the danger of death is more remote, *e. g.*, in the case of a party with a lingering illness that will certainly end in death, more time can be permitted. Prudence and experience will guide the pastor as to the time he should permit to elapse between the investigation and the marriage. Consultation with the physician will likewise be an aid. Deathbed marriages, however, are not so very frequent, ex-

[80] Canon 1031, § 2, 2°.

[81] Canon 1026.

[82] Payen, *De Matrimonio,* n. 377.

cept in the case of those who desire to have their marriages convalidated. Having obtained the moral certainty of the parties' freedom to marry, it is best in this instance, for the sake of the peace of conscience of the parties and for the legitimation of any children that may be born of their invalid union, to celebrate the marriage as soon as possible after the investigation.

Apart from the danger of death, other circumstances may arise that call for a limitation of the average time that should elapse between pre-nuptial inquiry and the wedding ceremony. To enumerate all the posible urgent cases that might arise is really impracticable, but the following reasons may be mentioned in illustration of cases which would justify a limitation of the usual time: the safeguarding the parties' reputations, the needed protection for a pregnant bride, the convalidation of an attempted marriage, the obviation of a state of concubinage. Even the fact that the marriage invitations have been sent out or that the marriage date has been publicly announced, or also the fact that one of the parties must suddenly depart for distant parts without being able to return soon would constitute an acceptable reason for shortening the interval between the pre-nuptial inquiry and the marriage. It is well to bear in mind that a limitation of the time between investigation and marriage does not exempt the pastor from the duty of definitely ascertaining that the parties are free to marry, for even the danger of death, the convalidation of an attempted marriage, and the rectification of a status of concubinage, etc., do not in any way jointly or separately excuse the pastor from making the investigation and establishing the freedom of the parties to marry.

B. *Place of Investigation.* Under this heading there is question of the proximate place where the interrogations should be addressed to the parties. The Code does not specify any particular place. The seriousness and sacredness of the investigation suggest that the interrogation should be made in some respectable place. The reception room or parlor of the rectory, the pastor's office, library or study are the most suitable places. The sacristy is also a becoming place. Interrogation of the parties in their private homes is less desirable and should be discouraged, except in a case of necessity.

ARTICLE 3. MANNER OF INTERROGATION OF NUPTURIENTS

The manner of interrogating the prospective bride and groom is expressly stated in canon 1020, § 2: *"Tum sponsum tum sponsam etiam seorsum et caute interroget. . . ."* Both the groom and the bride must be interviewed. Therefore, to examine the bride and not the groom, or to examine the groom and not the bride, is contrary to the law. The practice that existed in some dioceses of interrogating the groom and the parents or guardians of the bride, but not the bride herself, is also contrary to the law and cannot be upheld. [33] While interrogation of the parents of the bride may be useful, the Code calls for personal interrogation of the bride and rightly so, because the bride should have the right to express herself freely on the matter. Usually she is also more competent to testify, especially concerning her freedom of consent. Moreover, she is thus given full opportunity of revealing any coercion or duress to which she might perchance be subjected. Such revelation would at least possibly, if not probably, be concealed if she were not questioned personally. The personal interrogation is the safest means for ensuring the bride's absolute freedom to marry the man of her choice, and not the one whom her parents or others may have selected for her against her wishes.

Physical presence of the bride and bridegroom before the investigating pastor is necessary. Presence by proxy is insufficient except in a case of necessity. Interrogation of the parties over the telephone is likewise insufficient. It may be permitted in a case of necessity, but even then it would hardly be of obligation, because telephonic conversation is not always absolutely private, while interrogation of the contracting parties is really a private matter. Oral interrogations and oral responses are required. An exception must be made for those who are deaf and dumb. In their case the questions and responses may be written. If the nupturient is deaf but not dumb, the interrogations can then be written out and the responses may be received orally. If the party is dumb but not deaf, the interrogations can be made orally and the responses may be received in writing. Should it ever occur that a person who is deaf, dumb and

[33] Gasparri, *Tractatus Canonicus de Matrimonio,* n. 131; De Smet, *Betrothment and Marriage,* n. 332.

blind intends to marry, interrogation will be practically impossible except with the aid of the Braille system of writing. The interrogation of parties under the influence of intoxicating drink or drugs should be postponed until they have fully recovered the normal and full use of their reason.

It sometimes occurs that parties who do not speak the pastor's language present themselves for pre-nuptial investigation. In such a case it will be necessary to secure the services of a priest who speaks their language or to use an interpreter. As interrogation by means of an interpreter is sometimes unsatisfactory and necessarily slow, it is preferable to assign the duty of investigation to a priest acquainted with the language of the parties.

A twofold examination of the contracting parties is indicated in canon 1020, § 2, namely, interrogation of both parties *together* and interrogation of each party *separately*. It is customary in the United States of America for both parties to come with each other for the examination. Not infrequently they are accompanied by relatives or friends. The examination of both parties simultaneously and in the presence of each other may be conducted on the occasion of their first visit to the pastor, when they signify to him their intention of getting married. It will chiefly concern the identification of the parties, names, addresses, age, religion, parish or parishes they belong to; whether or not they are subjects of the inquiring pastor as far as marriage is concerned. Having satisfied himself that he can validly and lawfully assist at their marriage, the pastor will question the parties concerning public impediments and those impediments which imply no wrongdoing or shame,[34] such as consanguinity, affinity, spiritual relationship, etc. The relatives and friends of the parties may remain in the room during this interrogation.[35]

Separate interrogation of the bride and groom is also required by the Code. This provision of law is not new, for separate interroga-

[34] Chelodi, *Ius Matrimoniale*, n. 21; P. Nicolaus Farrugia, *De Matrimonio et Causis Matrimonialibus* (Taurini-Romae, 1924), n. 117; Gougnard, *Tractatus de Matrimonio*, p. 57.

[35] John F. Turner, "Preliminary Arrangements for Marriage," *AER*, LXXIV (1926), 489-495.

tion of the parties was previously prescribed by the encyclical epistle *Nimiam licentiam* of Benedict XIV.[86] Apparently it is the intention of the Code that the pastor first interrogate the man and then the woman, for canon 1020, § 2 places the word "sponsum" before the word "sponsam." However, it does not make very much material difference which one is interrogated first; what the canon chiefly wants to stress is the separate interrogation of the parties. This separate interrogation of the nupturients may immediately follow the interrogation of both together, or may be postponed to another occasion. As a matter of fact, the separate interrogation may be conducted on different days, on one day for the man and on another day for the woman, but to prevent any collusion on the part of the parties it is best that the questioning of the one immediately succeed the interrogation of the other. Inquiry concerning the existence of any occult impediments, *e. g.*, vows or impediments that carry with them a certain amount of shame or personal guilt as, for example, crime, public propriety, etc., will form the chief content of this separate inquiry; also the matter of freedom of consent, their instruction in Christian doctrine and the obligations of the married state.[87] Should any suspicion remain that the parties, when being interrogated in each other's presence, concealed certain impediments, they ought to be further questioned on these points in the separate examination. Usually parties are more frank in the separate interrogation and are more apt to confide in the pastor.

Diligent investigation is prescribed by canon 1020, § 1. Diligence implies care and precision in the inquiry. Thoroughness in accordance with the circumstances of the case should characterize the interrogation. The questions should not be too general, nor too few, and should not be asked in a careless, lackadaisical fashion, as if they were unimportant or a mere matter of course. The meaning of the questions should be clear. Freedom to marry must not be taken for granted simply because the parties have a good reputation in the community or because they are well known to the pastor. Doubts and suspicions about impediments and freedom of consent

[86] 18 Maii, 1743, § 10—*Fontes*, n. 337.

[87] Gasparri, *Tractatus Canonicus de Matrimonio*, n. 131; Cappello, *De Sacramentis*, III, n. 153; Vermeersch, *Epitome Iuris Canonici*, II, n. 287.

should be accurately investigated and dispelled. When documents are required by the law in proof of certain points, the pastor should see to it that they are obtained and, having obtained them, should carefully scrutinize them to establish their authenticity. The diligent investigator will not immediately refuse difficult cases of investigation, simply because the obtaining of the desired information is difficult, though not impossible. Rather he will first exhaust the means of obtaining the information and then decide on what course he should follow.

Careful investigation. The law requires that the diligence employed in examining the parties be regulated by carefulness and caution.[38]

Therefore, the pastor must take into account the character, disposition and temperament of the parties and observe all that has been said above under the heading of prudence and tact.[39] He will be careful not to injure the rightful sensibilities of the parties; not to be prudish in matters that must be plain-spoken; not to be jocose about the amenities of married life. Not only will he avoid giving any offense but he will also furnish motives for an exalted mutual respect. He will use care to employ a demeanor that seals their confidence; to be modest when dealing with delicate questions; to be earnest in his treatment of marital duties. In a word he will strive to make the interrogation a model of conscientious, circumspect and edifying inquiry.[40]

When dealing with impediments that may involve sin or shame, carefulness and prudence will dictate in certain instances that the interrogation be indirect rather than direct. Instead of putting the questions in interrogative fashion, the pastor may propose the impediments by saying: "This is the teaching of the Catholic Church on this point" (giving the name of the impediment), and then proceed to inform the party of the law on the point. With people who are sincere this is the better practice, for if they discover from the words of the pastor that there is an impediment to their marriage,

[38] Canon 1020, § 2.

[39] See pp. 85-87.

[40] *Cf. Catechismus ex Decreti Concilii Tridentini* (Augustae Taurinorum, 1890), n. 33.

their conscience will prompt them to reveal it.[41] If the ordinary has prescribed any special regulations for the interrogation of the parties, the pastor will not measure up to his duty of careful investigation unless he observes those regulations.

Carefulness and caution must accompany both the time and place of the pre-nuptial interrogation. The interrogation of the parties, and especially of the bride, should be conducted in a respectable place or situation and always at an acceptable time or hour so that no suspicion of scandal may ever arise.[42] The Council of Milan (1576) prescribed the precautionary measure that the woman be questioned in the sight of friends yet at such a distance from them, that they could not overhear her responses and that she would not be deterred by her sense of modesty from freely expressing her mind to the pastor.[43]

While this is an admirable precaution to allay any suspicion of scandal and is certainly consonant with canon 1020, § 2, it is not necessary that the phrase "in the sight of friends" be taken in the very strict and literal sense. The important point is that no suspicion of scandal may arise. The average person takes no scandal from the fact that a pastor is alone in his study or reception room with a prospective bride for the purpose of interrogating her concerning her *status liber*. However, there are the few who may take scandal from it, and hence it is well for the pastor to be cautious lest the suspicion of scandal arise. Such precautionary measures as leaving the door of the room open or ajar help to preclude the possibility of scandal. Some pastors have rendered this unnecessary by having the door of the reception room fitted with glass. The latter arrangement is probably the most satisfactory, for many rectories lack the spaciousness and solidity of construction which would prevent the sound of the human voice from carrying to other parts of the house, if the door of a room were left open or ajar.

On the completion of the examination, the careful pastor will not neglect to forewarn the parties to mention their forthcoming

[41] Gougnard, *Tractatus de Matrimonio*, p. 57; Vermeersch-Creusen, *Epitome*, II, n. 287.

[42] De Smet, *Betrothment and Marriage*, n. 332.

[43] C. 9—Mansi, XXXIV A, 315, 316.

marriage to their confessor and to manifest to him any difficulties they may labor under in regard to marriage.[44]

Article 4. Obligation of Parties to Reveal Impediments

Just as the pastor has the right and grave obligation to institute pre-nuptial inquiry, so also have the contracting parties a corresponding obligation to reveal matrimonial impediments which affect the lawfulness or validity of their marriage.[45] The reason is obvious. To enter into an unlawful or invalid marriage is a serious evil spiritually and has serious consequences materially. To be responsible for causing another to enter into a forbidden marriage is also seriously sinful. And that is exactly what one party does to the other when, on interrogation concerning his freedom to marry, he willfully conceals an impediment that renders marriage either unlawful or invalid. If both parties know of the impediment and knowingly conceal it, both are guilty of grave sin.

What impediments are the parties obliged to reveal, and to whom are they obliged to reveal them? The nupturients have the grave obligation to enter into a valid and licit marriage. As the revelation of occult or secret impediments is just as important as the revelation of public impediments for the attaining of that end, it cannot be gainsaid that they are obliged to reveal secret impediments as well as public impediments. Even if the secret impediment is the result of sin on their part or carried with it a certain shame or moral turpitude, there is no good reason for not manifesting it. Public impediments belong to the sphere of the external forum and consequently should be revealed to the investigating pastor. The pastor is acting perfectly within his rights when he asks necessary questions concerning public impediments, even when these impediments carry with them a certain shame or moral turpitude. Has the pastor a right to interrogate the patries concerning purely occult impediments? Purely occult impediments belong to the sphere of the internal forum. The internal forum is both sacramental and extra-sacramental. In

[44] Ayrinhac-Lydon, *Marriage Legislation in the New Code of Canon Law*, p. 27.

[45] Wernz, *Ius Decretalium*, IV, n. 130.

the confessional or on its occasion the pastor certainly has the right to question the parties concerning occult impediments. But has he the right to interrogate the parties concerning occult impediments in the internal extra-sacramental forum, *e. g.*, in the separate interrogation of the parties? It would seem that he has, and apparently the nupturients have a corresponding obligation to reveal such impediments. However, if the occult impediments are in any way connected with sin or wrongdoing, it is proper to leave their investigation to the confessor. If the parties have already obtained a dispensation from occult impediments in the internal forum or will certainly receive a dispensation prior to the marriage, there is no obligation on the parties to reveal the occult impediments. The reason is, they have already satisfied their obligation of preventing an invalid or unlawful marriage.[46] If the occult impediment becomes public in the meantime, it will be necessary to get a dispensation from it in the external forum; for a dispensation in the internal forum does not suffice for the external forum.[47] As the nupturients are not as a rule well versed in the law and are not acquainted with the meaning of dispensations given in the internal forum and granted in the external forum, they will usually, if they are sincere, manifest occult impediments quite readily and even spontaneously. If perchance on account of a false modesty or from a sense of shame the responses of the parties are given hesitatingly and betray some suspicion of the concealment of existing impediments, it is well to exhort them to manifest to their confessor their intention of getting married, and to inform him of any doubts they may have about their freedom from impediments. An admonition of this kind is all the more necessary, if the pastor was not too particular about the investigation of the occult impediments or if he proposed the impediments by way of instruction[48] A brief preliminary instruction on the parties' obligation to enter a lawful and valid marriage and on their obligation to reveal any exisiting impediments is commendable. Even if the pastor through a lapse of memory failed to ask them about certain impediments, it is the duty of the parties to reveal them spon-

[46] Payen, *De Matrimonio,* n. 385.
[47] Canon 202, § 1.
[48] Payen, *De Matrimonio,* n. 385.

taneously. If they knowingly failed to reveal them, they would have the bad will of receiving the Sacrament of Matrimony either invalidly or illicitly.[49]

Article 5. Moral Certitude of the Free Status of the Contracting Parties Required

In order that a pastor may declare that the contracting parties are free to marry, he must be *certain* that there are no obstacles to the valid and lawful celebration of the marriage.[50] Certainty or certitude is the firm assent or adherence of the mind to a truth without any prudent fear of error.[51] The certitude required by the Code for the freedom of the parties to marry is moral certitude. In moral certitude all prudent fear though not all absolute fear of error is excluded. The arguments in favor of the free status of the nupturients must be such as to convince the average normal prudent man. Merely negative arguments and conjectures alone do not suffice to produce moral certitude, *e. g.*, the fact that the pastor never heard that a party was married before does not give him moral certainty that the party is free from the impediment or *ligamen*. Some positive evidence must be forthcoming.[52]

The testimony of the parties themselves, the word of sworn witnesses, the statements of reliable documents as well as adminicular and circumstantial evidence are the materials from which the pastor will have to judge whether there is moral certainty of the parties' freedom to marry. Consideration will be given to these in later articles.

Article 6. Interrogation of Witnesses and Parties Under Oath in Doubts About the Existence of Impediments

As long as there is a prudent doubt about the existence of an impediment there is no moral certainty of the parties' freedom to

[49] Eduardus Genicot, *Institutiones Theologiae Moralis* (8. ed., Bruxellis, 1927), n. 448.

[50] Canons 1019 and 1097, § 1, 1°.

[51] P. Coffey, *The Science of Logic,* II, *Method, Science and Certitude,* (London: Longmans, Green & Co., 1918), p. 211.

[52] Cappello, *De Sacramentis,* III, n. 145.

marry. In order that the necessary moral certainty be established, canon 1031, § 1, 1° states that, when a doubt arises about the existence of an impediment, the pastor will investigate the matter more accurately and will interrogate under oath at least two witnesses, provided there is not question of an impediment that would bring disgrace or dishonor on the parties. Furthermore, the same canon states that, if necessity requires it, the pastor may interrogate under oath the parties themselves.

When there is a doubt about the existence of a matrimonial impediment, the judgment of the mind is withheld or suspended on account of the presence of two contradictory propositions, the one that an impediment is present, the other that it is absent. The doubt may be positive or negative. A positive doubt is one in which there are some reasons both for and against the existence of the impediment. A negative doubt is one that is not based on reasons or one based on weak or negligible reasons. There is question here only of the positively doubtful existence of an impediment. The doubt must be objective, *i. e.*, existing outside the mind and having some basis in fact. Furthermore, the doubt in question is a factual doubt (*dubium facti*). If it were a doubt concerned with the meaning or import of the law (*dubium iuris*), further investigation would not be necessary, since in the case of such a doubt the law has no intention to bind its subjects.[53]

As the pastor is obliged to make certain that there are no impediments of any kind hindering the valid and lawful celebration of the marriage, it seems that the word "impediment" in canon 1021, § 1, 1° is to be taken in the broad sense, and therefore it includes not only those impediments which the Code classifies as prohibitive and diriment and which are impediments *ex parte personae*, but also every other obstacle to marriage such as defect of consent, force or fear, defect of form, etc., which may hinder the valid or lawful celebration of the marriage.

The doubt may arise before, during or after the publication of the banns. If it arises before the publication of the banns, the pastor should proceed with the publication; and if it arises during the publi-

[53] Canon 15.

cation of the banns, he should continue the publication in the hope that the banns may aid in dispelling the doubt.[54]

To clear up the doubt, a more accurate investigation of the possible existence of the impediment is required. Two methods of dispelling the doubt are mentioned in canon 1031, § 1, 1°: (a) the interrogation of witnesses under oath, which is the ordinary method, and (b) the interrogation of the parties themselves under oath, if necessity requires it. Other means are apparently permissible, especially when witnesses cannot be produced, or when they are excused from testifying, or when they refuse to appear. The Code, however, considers the interrogation of witnesses as the most practical and ordinary means.[55]

A. *Interrogation of Witnesses.* Common law requires that at least two witnesses testify in a doubt about the existence of an impediment. More than two are permissible. Sometimes more than two witnesses will be obligatory, *e. g.*, when the two first witnesses give testimony that is contradictory, or when they testify to something altogether different (for instance, if one says there is an impediment of age present and another contends that there is an impediment or consanguinity), or when the testimony of one does not sufficiently complement the testimony of the other to produce moral certitude.

No detailed norms governing the use of witnesses are given in the canons dealing with pastoral pre-nuptial investigation. The manifold and diverse factors involved in the interrogation of witnesses do not permit the formulation of uniform and infallible rules. However, it does seem to be in accord with reason to invoke the aid of canons 1754 and 1791, which concern judicial witnesses. These canons are the result of experience and reason; they aim at producing reliable testimony and hence, with some modifications, can be applied to the testimony of witnesses in the pre-nuptial investigation of doubtful impediments. The use of the directive norms of the pre-Code discipline on the interrogation of witnesses for the purpose of proving the *status liber* of the contracting parties will likewise prove helpful.

Various classes of witnesses are distinguished. The principal kinds

[54] Canon 1031, § 1, 2°.

[55] Cappello, *De Sacramentis,* III, n. 175.

are: Simple witnesses; expert witnesses; authorized witnesses; witnesses of personal experience, such as those who have been eye-witnesses and ear-witnesses to events and happenings they have personally observed; quasi ear-witnesses, who at an unsuspected time received from others information of an original event or fact; hearsay witnesses, who have heard of the existence of a certain impediment to the marriage of the parties from a witness of personal experience; witnesses of the notoriety of an impediment; witnesses who testify to the rumor of an impediment; opinion witnesses, who simply express their own opinion on the matter; and character witnesses.[56]

Not all witnesses are equally reliable in their testimony. As a matter of fact, some are definitely unreliable. The Code considers some witnesses as unqualified (*non idonei*), suspected (*suspecti*) and disqualified (*incapaces*). The *unqualified* witnesses include those under the age of puberty and the mentally weak.[57] A girl is considered as having reached the age of puberty when she has completed the twelfth year; a boy after he has completed the fourteenth year.[58] Though those who have reached the use of reason are naturally capable of testifying, their judgment before the age of puberty is considered rather immature and hence they are considered as unqualified. After puberty they may be accepted as qualified witnesses, even for events that occurred before puberty. Among those suffering from weakness of mind are idiots, imbeciles, morons, the mentally deranged, monomaniacs, those who are afflicted with visual and auditory hallucinations, the feeble-minded and the senile. Those under the influence of intoxicating drink or drugs are more or less mentally handicapped for the time being. The dumb, the blind and deaf, while frequently very capable of acting as reliable witnesses, may err in their observation of facts and events because of their handicaps and consequently will sometimes become unqualified as witnesses.[59] The *suspected* wit-

[56] Payen, *De Matrimonio*, nn. 402-404; Wanenmacher, *Canonical Evidence in Marriage Cases*, nn. 187-189.

[57] Canon 1757, § 1.

[58] Canon 88, § 2.

[59] Donald Whalen, *The Value of Testimonial Evidence in Matrimonial Procedure* (The Catholic University of America, Canon Law Studies, n. 99, Washington: The Catholic University of America, 1935), pp. 111, 112.

nesses are: (a) Excommunicates, perjurers and the infamous who have been declared as such by a condemnatory or declaratory sentence.[60] Prior to the condemnatory or declaratory sentence they are not suspected. (b) Those who are so low and perverse in morals that they cannot be considered worthy of credence, for instance, robbers, thieves, prostitutes, habitual drunkards, inveterate drug addicts, notorious criminals of various kinds. (c) Public and bitter enemies of the party concerned.[61] *Disqualified* for giving testimony are confessors who have received knowledge concerning the existence of impediments to marriage either from the parties themselves or from others in the confessional. The same holds true of interpreters for a party in confession or anyone who accidentally or intentionally overhears [62] or reads the confession of another.[63] If a confessor has extra-confessional knowledge of an impediment or is permitted by the penitent to reveal the impediment outside the confessional, strictly speaking he could be permitted to testify concerning the impediment, provided no scandal arose from his so doing. However, prudence may dictate that he be excluded from testifying.

Those to whom knowledge of an impediment has been committed while acting in their professional capacity may be considered exempt from testifying in a doubt about the existence of that impediment, *e. g.*, doctors, physicians, obstetricians, priests, government officials, advocates, notaries, lawyers, nurses,[64] psychiatrists and psychoanalysts. Confidence of the public in them would otherwise suffer injury. However, they should urge their clients to reveal the impediment. Professional people are not excluded from acting as witnesses in regard to impediments they have learned from sources other than their profession. Those who have been entrusted with natural and promised secrets are not excused from testifying. When the law requires professional men to testify, they are obliged to do so.[65]

[60] Canon 1775, § 2, 1°.

[61] Canon 1757, § 2, 3°.

[62] Canon 1757, § 3, 2°.

[63] Whalen, *The Value of Testimonial Evidence in Matrimonial Procedure*, p. 129.

[64] Canon 1755, § 2, 1°; Wanenmacher, *Canonical Evidence in Marriage Cases*, n. 210.

[65] Canons 1978 and 1982.

Unqualified and suspected witnesses may be admitted by the pastor if he prudently judges that despite their handicaps they are reliable.

Relatives of the contracting parties, and especially close relatives, such as parents, brothers, sisters, uncles, aunts and cousins, as well as close friends of the party in society or business are usually the most suitable witnesses whenever a doubt about the existence of an impediment is concerned. They are usually better informed than others.[66] Otherwise they would not be so frequently mentioned in Rota cases.[67] Servants and dependents of the contracting parties may be admitted as witnesses by the pastor, due care being taken that they do not unduly favor the parties on account of their dependence on them. Non-Catholics as well as Catholics, women as well as men, may be permitted to act as witnesses provided they are trustworthy.[68]

Canon 1031, § 1, 1° requires that the testimony be given under oath. Obviously the oath here mentioned is the oath to tell the truth (*de veritate dicenda*). It should be tendered by the pastor to the parties personally prior to the interrogation.[69] It is important to impress on the witness beforehand the sacredness of the oath. It should be tendered with dignity and respect and without the undue and uncalled for haste that often characterizes the tendering of the oath in civil affairs. A priest witness taking the oath places his hand on

[66] Canon 1974; S. C. S. Off., resp., 24 Feb., 1847—*Fontes*, n. 900; S. C. S. Off. instr., *Matrimonii vinculo*, 12 Maii, 1868—*Coll.*, n. 1321; S. C. S. Off., resp., Vic. Apost. Constantinop., 2 Apr., 1873—*Fontes*, n. 1025.

[67] *S. R. R., Parisien., Nullit. Matrim.*, 26 Apr., 1916, *Coram R. P. D., Gulielmo Sebastianelli*, dec. XII, n. 8—*Decisiones*, VIII (1916), 138, 139; *S. R. R., Trinomalien., Nullit. Matrim.*, 1 Feb., 1913, *Coram R. P. D., Aloisio Sincero*, dec. VIII, n. 2—*Decisiones*, V (1913), 84; *S. R. R., Nullit. Matrim., Vic. Apost. Tonkin. Orientalis*, 18 Aug., 1921, *Coram R. P. D., Friderico Cattani Amadori*, dec. XXVI, n. 2—*Decisiones*, XIII (1921), 252; *S. R. R. Nullit. Matrim.*, 9 Jan., 1922, *Coram Iosepho Florczak*, dec. I, n. 13—*Decisiones*, XIV (1922), 6; *S. S. R., Camenecen., Nullit. Matrim.*, 17 Maii, 1922, *Coram R. P. D., Ioanne Prior*, dec. XVI, n. 6—*Decisiones*, XIV (1922), 149.

[68] S. C. S. Off., decr., *Cum alias*, 21 Aug., 1670—*Fontes*, n. 742.

[69] Eugene James Moriarty, *Oaths in Ecclesiastical Courts* (The Catholic University of America, Canon Law Studies, n. 110, Washington: The Catholic University of America, 1937), pp. 42, 43; canon 1746.

his breast; a layman puts his hand on the book of the Gospels.[70] The oath may be omitted if the witnesses are considered unqualified or suspected.[71] Though the decree *Cum alias* did not desire that the oath be generally tendered to non-Catholics, it did not forbid it.[72] Today, there seems to be no good reason why non-Catholics who believe in God should not be tendered the oath, as the oath strengthens their testimony, unless there is some cause that persuades otherwise. If a non-Catholic should refuse to take the oath, the pastor should not insist on it.

The witnesses should be interrogated separately; [73] for if interrogated in each other's presence, they will naturally be more reserved in imparting information. It is advisable, though not essential, that the witnesses be examined immediately after each other in order to prevent collusion. The interrogation should be oral, unless oral interrogation becomes morally impossible, *e. g.*, in the case of the deaf and of those who on account of a grave inconvenience cannot appear. In such cases it may be in writing.

A prepared interrogatory by the pastor is not required by the common law but it is helpful, particularly if the questions are manifold. It serves as an aid to the memory. Being an extra-judicial interrogation, the testimony of the witnesses need not be written down. However, consigning the testimony to writing has many advantages, not only for the purpose of comparing the testimonies of the two witnesses to see if they are conformative and complementary, but also for future reference, should the marriage be questioned. Some pastors use a special book or card file for the purpose of preserving such testimony.

No place in particular is prescribed for the interrogation of the witness. Any respectable place suffices. The usual place is the rectory. The sacristy is also a suitable place. Even a private home may be used; but sometimes it is not so satisfactory and ordinarily is not to be recommended.

The first questions addressed to the witness should be general: full

[70] Canon 1622, § 1.

[71] Canons 1767, § 1; 1758; 1757, §§ 1, 2.

[72] S. C. S. Off., 21 Aug., 1670—*Fontes*, n. 742.

[73] Canon 1772, § 1.

name, age, religion, occupation or profession, place of residence, whether the witness is a relative of the party or not, how long he has known him.[74] These general questions, especially concerning the age, religion, profession and relationship with the contracting party give some indication of the credibility of the witness.

The particular questions concern the existence of the particular doubtful impediment, *e. g.*, consanguinity, affinity, age, *ligamen*, etc. In this connection it is well to keep the prescriptions of canon 1775 in mind. The questions should be simple, brief and clear so that the witness may grasp their meaning without too much intellectual effort. It is best to have only one point in each question, for a question containing too many points is confusing to the average mind. If a witness has knowledge of some impediment, he should be asked the source of his knowledge; when he received the information; in what circumstances; who were present, etc. Moreover, the questions should be courteous; should not suggest the answer; should pertain to the point at issue and should not be communicated to the witness prior to the interrogation.[75] The investigation should be an accurate one; [76] attention must be paid to details. However, the actual degree of accuracy required will vary with the nature of the case, and the circumstances affecting it.

If the pastor prudently judges that it is necessary, the oaths *de veritate dictorum* and *de secreto servando* may be tendered to the witnesses at the conclusion of the interrogation, but ordinarily they will not be necessary.

Excluded from the interrogation are those impediments which bring disgrace on the parties,[77] the reason being that the contracting parties have a right to their good name and reputation as long as there is a doubt about the existence of an impediment which implies dishonor. To enumerate all the impediments which bring disgrace is impossible; for they vary according to the circumstances of places and persons. However, there are some impediments that bring disgrace generally, *e. g.*, the impediments of crime, of public propriety, of abduction, of

[74] *Cf.* canon 1774.
[75] Canon 1776, § 1.
[76] Canon 1030, § 1, 1°.
[77] Canon 1031, § 1, 1°.

the use of violence, force and fear to induce unwilling patries to marry, of consanguinity that has arisen from illicit relations between the father of the groom and mother and of the bride or *vice versa,* of a previous secret marriage with another, especially if the latter was far below the station of the former, of impotency arising from some cause considered disgraceful, such as sex perversion, a private immoral life, etc.

B. *Interrogation of the Parties Themselves Under Oath.* The second method mentioned in canon 1031, § 1, 1° for dispelling doubts about the existence of impediments is the interrogation under oath of the parties themselves. The oath in this instance is known as the suppletory oath. This method should be employed, according to the Code, if necessity requires it. Necessity will exist if documents and witnesses are wanting to prove the existence or non-existence of the doubtful impediment. Likewise, it is present when there is question of impediments that bring disgrace on the parties and, in many cases of danger of death, when there is no time to obtain documentary evidence or the testimony of witnesses.

This further interrogation of the parties under oath will run along much the same lines as the interrogation of the witnesses just treated above. Hence, what has been said about the interrogation of the witnesses concerning the tendering of the oath, the questions, etc., equally applies to the interrogation of the parties themselves.

Article 7. Evaluation of the Testimony of Nupturients and Witnesses

No norms for the evaluation of the truth of the responses given by nupturients and witnesses are given in the canons dealing with pre-nuptial investigation. As a matter of fact, to formulate uniform and unerring regulations that would invariably guarantee moral certainty of the reliability of the responses of nupturients and witnesses is impossible, because too many diverse factors are involved. Pastoral prudence and experience will have to be employed in forming judgments in each individual case. However, there are some factors that generally help to estimate the probative value of the testimony of nupturients and witnesses, and which deserve consideration here.

A. *Evaluation of the Testimony of Nupturients.* The age, religion, rank and dignity of the contracting parties occupy some place in the appraisal of their testimony. All things considered, the party of more mature age may generally be depended on to give more truthful information than one who is younger. There are, however, numerous exceptions. The average Catholic about to marry is usually conscientious in answering the questions of the pastor, because of his appreciation of the sacredness of marriage and the seriousness of the evil of an unlawful or invalid union. The careless and negligent Catholic is less reliable. Non-Catholics are often less reliable than Catholics since they have a lesser appreciation of the sacredness of the marriage bond (*e. g.*, many believe in absolute divorce), and may falsely consider many of the interrogations of the pastor as a mere matter of form. The devout non-Catholic is generally more dependable than the careless one. Those professing some religion are usually more reliable than those professing none. Though rank and dignity are by no means sure signs of the credibility of parties, it can perhaps with safety be said that those of higher rank and dignity and station in life are frequently more reliable than those of lower status.[78] Those who occupy positions of trust, where reputation in the community is an important qualification for success and prestige, can generally be relied on to give more truthful information. However, God-fearing persons of lower status are usually sincere and truthful, and frequently surpass those of higher rank in credibility.

Knowledge on the part of the contracting parties is an item that cannot be overlooked in the appraisal of their testimony. Two kinds of knowledge may be distinguished here: (1) doctrinal knowledge concerning the matrimonial laws of God and the Church, especially the laws on marriage impediments; (2) personal knowledge of the parties themselves concerning the fact of their freedom or lack of freedom from marriage impediments.

The conscientious bride and groom who are well versed in the marriage laws of the Church may be considered reliable in their testimony, and will most probably reveal any impediments affecting their union, even though the pastor may fail to question them regarding these impediments. When the bride and groom are poorly versed in the marriage legislation of the Church, the outcome of the pastor's

[78] Canon 1789, 1°.

investigation will depend very much on the thoroughness of his interrogation.

Personal knowledge of the parties themselves as to their actual freedom or lack of freedom from marriage impediments will not be equal in all nupturients. As a rule, the party will know about the substantial factors connected with his age, his baptism, confirmation or ordination, his religious profession, his private vows, his legal adoption, his previous marriage and the associated fact of his partner's death, his relationship to his contemplated spouse, etc. He will be able to testify to the presence or absence of such factors as the foregoing, either from personal experience or from knowledge gained from others, particularly his parents. In exceptional cases a party may be unable to testify to the presence or absence of certain impediments. For example, a party whose parents died while he was young may not know what his age is; whether or not he was baptized; who his relations are; who his sponsors in baptism were. The same may be true if the party was a foundling. As a rule, a foundling also will be unable to testify concerning the impediments of affinity and consanguinity. In such cases the pastor will have to have recourse to other sources, such as documents or witnesses or circumstances, to establish the party's freedom or want of freedom to marry.

The character and personality of the party are also decidedly important in the appraisal of his testimony. Normally people desire to tell the truth, unless there is some advantage to be gained by telling an untruth. Despite the fact, however, that the truth may be disadvantageous from certain viewpoints, a person of good moral caliber is likely to be truthful. Mere knowledge in a party of the existence of impediments, if it is not reinforced with a background of good moral qualities of character, and especially with the virtue of truthfulness, will mean little, if anything, for the reliability of the responses made by him. As a matter of fact, his doctrinal knowledge of the number and nature of the various matrimonial impediments may impede, rather than promote a satisfactory pre-nuptial investigation; for, if he wishes to do so, he can all the better and more efficiently conceal the existing impediments to his marriage. Hence, the pastor should make sure that the nupturients are truthful. If a party has a reputation for being a notorious liar or perjurer, little credence can be placed in his assertions. If a man normally possesses good moral qualities, he will be presumed to be truthful. Even though a man has several bad habits and immoral qualities, yet withal enjoys a reputation for veracity, his testimony may be presumed to be truthful.

Qualities of personality frequently affect the credibility of a party. For example, it is more likely for a reticent, shy and bashful individual to conceal impediments that bring disgrace than for a person who is frank and open-minded. The bashful individual is prone, for instance, to conceal the fact that a certain amount of unjust force or fear has been brought to bear on him. On the other hand, the aggressive, optimistic and forceful type of person, who goes to extremes to assure the pastor of his freedom to marry, may be using these traits of personality to conceal impediments that he is aware of. Emotions and feelings should likewise be taken into account, as they have a tendency to distort truth. The influence they have on the assertions of the party should be noted by the pastor. The manner, attitude, facial expressions and conduct of the party during the interrogation may furnish some clue as to his credibility. If he is constant, stable, firm, cool, calm and collected in his manner, the chances are that his testimony is true. If he is unstable, variable, hesitating, doubting and contradictory,[79] there may be some reason to be suspicious of his truthfulness. However, there are many people who are naturally of a nervous, highly strung and variable disposition, which is sometimes accentuated by the presence of the investigating priest. Such nervousness does not proceed from the desire to conceal an impediment, but from other causes. With nervous and excitable witnesses an effort should be made to discover the causes of the nervousness.[80] The party who during the interrogation deliberately makes every effort to turn the attention of the pastor from the point at issue by interposing some interesting things foreign to the subject of marriage may be suspected of using a psychological trick to conceal an impediment. The same may be said of the lackadaisical individual who does not co-operate with the pastor in the investigation, or co-operates only in a half-hearted way. When a party desires

[79] Canon 1789, 4°.

[80] Reiffenstuel, *Ius Canonicum Universum*, lib. II, tit. XX, nn. 318-320.

unduly to hurry the celebration of a marriage and gives no really good reason for it, there may likewise be a suspicion that an effort is being made to hide some impediment.

B. *Evaluation of the Testimony of Witnesses.* The reliability of the testimony of a witness concerning the freedom of a contracting party from matrimonial impediments depends on his knowledge of the party, the accuracy and extent of his perception and observation, his memory of facts and events and his truthfulness in reporting what he observed.[81]

Knowledge of the Parties. The general questions addressed to the witnesses concerning their age, religion, occupation or profession, whether they are related to the parties, how long they have known them, under what circumstances they met them, and the frequency of their association give the pastor some clue as to the competency of the witnesses in regard to knowledge. The longer they know them, the more closely they are associated with them, and the closer their relationship, the more efficacious will be their testimony, all things considered.

Immediate witnesses of events, facts and happenings connected with the nupturients, provided their sense of perception is accurate and their memories normally good, are more reliable than mediate witnesses. The reason is because they are witnesses of personal experience, who have perceived the facts and events with their senses and are testifying from first-hand knowledge. Consequently, from the point of view of knowledge, the eye-witness and the ear-witness, who have personally observed facts relating to the parties, are the most reliable. The more accurate and keen their observations, the greater will be their credibility. Quasi ear-witnesses, who heard information regarding the parties *tempore non suspecto, i. e.,* at a time when they were unaware of the present intended marriage of the parties, are quite valuable. The reliability of the testimony of hearsay witnesses will depend on how reliable the original witnesses were; how they got their knowledge; how truthful they are; how tenacious the memories of the hearsay witnesses are; how credible they are.

[81] Sylvester J. Hartman, *A Textbook of Logic* (New York: American Book Co., 1936), p. 349; Wanenmacher, *Canonical Evidence in Marriage Cases,* nn. 193, 254, 256

The information supplied by those with well trained and tenacious memories surpasses in trustworthiness the information of those whose memories are poor. The credulity of the hearsay witness must likewise be taken into account. Some men and women are very credulous; they readily believe almost everything they hear, are apt to draw unwarranted conclusions from insufficient data, and consider presumptions as certainties.[82] Such people are very unreliable. It is necessary to examine the sources of their information before passing judgment on it. Excessive incredulity is the exact opposite of excessive credulity, and will affect the testimony of the witness by preventing him from giving evidence that a person of normal credulity would consider as certain and would not hesitate to give.

The mere fact that a certain impediment to the marriage of the parties is declared by a witness to be a matter of common knowledge or rumor in the community does not mean that the impediment is certainly present. An effort should be made to determine if there is foundation in fact for the notoriety or rumor of the impediment.[83]

The more notorious and widespread the knowledge or rumor of the impediment, the greater will be the suspicion that the impediment is present. If those who propagated and those who testified to the current rumor are truthful, conservative and well-balanced, the presumption that the impediment is present is increased. If a witness testifies from personal knowledge of the rumor, and not from what he heard others say, the presumption of the presence of the impediment is even greater.[84] Frequently rumors of impediments may be circulated about contracting parties for reasons of hate, jealousy, prejudice and revenge, and if they cannot be traced to some reliable source and have not any reasonable factual evidence to support them,

[82] P. Josephus Noval, *Commentarium Codicis Iuris Canonici,* lib. IV, *De Processibus,* Pars I, *De Iudiciis* (Augustae Taurinorum, Romae: Marietti, 1920), n. 510, p. 351; Whalen, *The Value of Testimonial Evidence in Matrimonial Procedure,* p. 214.

[83] *Cf.* Reiffenstuel, *Ius Canonicum Universum,* lib. II, tit. XX, nn. 384, 392; Whalen, *The Value of Testimonial Evidence in Matrimonial Procedure,* 215-217.

[84] *Cf.* Eduard Eichmann, *Das Prozessrecht des Codex Iuris Canonici* (Paderborn: Ferdinand Schöningh, 1921), p. 150.

the impediment may be considered as non-existent by the pastor.[85]

What has been said above in regard to the character, truthfulness, emotions, constancy or inconstancy, steadfastness or vacillation, certainty or uncertainty, and general attitude and manner of the parties during their interrogation by the pastor applies with equal force to the evaluation of the testimony of the witnesses.

Two reliable witnesses testifying under oath from personal knowledge to the presence of an impediment, provided they are concordant in their testimony, give moral certitude of the existence of the impediment. If two witnesses are concordant, but agree in every little point and detail, there may be a suspicion of collusion, which is deleterious to their testimony. The testimony of one qualified witness gives full proof concerning those things which appertain to his office.[86] The testimony of one simple witness who is above all suspicion, who testifies from his own personal knowledge and who is supported by sufficient adminicular proof is capable of proving with moral certainty that the parties are free to marry. Even the testimony of one witness may sufficiently complement the testimony of another to produce full proof.[87] Two reliable witnesses testifying about the common hearsay or rumor of an impediment, while not capable of producing full proof, will give moral certainty, if there is sufficient adminicular or circumstantial evidence supporting their assertions. Testimony, being a very human thing, is subject to the weaknesses of human nature, and the pastor will be the judge whether in given instances it produces moral certitude.

Article 8. The Use of Documents in Pre-Nuptial Investigation

Documents have been employed in the Church for centuries for the purpose of proving facts of one kind or another, and are today used extensively. In pastoral pre-nuptial investigation, next to

[85] *Cf.* Wernz-Vidal, VI, *De Processibus*, n. 484, pp. 425, 426.

[86] Canon 1791.

[87] Schmalzgrueber, lib. III, tit. XIX, n. 17; James Austin Hughes, *Witnesses in Criminal Trials of Clerics* (The Catholic University of America, Canon Law Studies, n. 106, Washington: The Catholic University of America, 1937), p. 115.

interrogation of the contracting parties themselves, there is perhaps no means more commonly and successfully employed to establish the free status of the nupturients than the use of documents. As a matter of fact, the written word not only supports the spoken word, but very frequently surpasses it in probative value.

In its canons dealing with pre-nuptial investigation, the Code does not go into many details in regard to documents. Perhaps the reason is that it does not desire to be too strict in requesting documentary evidence, if other evidence, especially oral evidence, is forthcoming. Morover, if rigid documentary testimony were required in each particular case, it would render pre-nuptial investigation cumbersome and perhaps very inconvenient, especially for people whose cultural and educational level is below the average. Nevertheless, there are in the Code some explicit references to the use of documents in pre-nuptial investigation. Canon 1029 states that if another pastor conducts the pre-nuptial investigation and announces the banns, the pastor who is to assist at the marriage should not do so until he has been informed by ***authentic document*** about the outcome of the investigation and the publication of the banns. Canon 1031, § 1 decrees that after the investigation and the publication of the banns have been completed, the pastor shall not assist at the marriage unless he has received all the ***necessary documents.*** The Code, therefore, admits that documents may be used to establish the freedom to marry of the contracting parties, and seems to encourage their use by insisting on certain written records of matters pertaining to marriage, *e. g.*, by requiring that canonical betrothal be in writing,[88] that marriages be recorded,[89] that a proxy for a contracting party be appointed in writing[90] and that the *cautiones* given in mixed marriages should regularly be given in writing.[91] Mention of documents concerning the free status of the parties is also made in the instruction of the Congregation of the Sacraments issued on July 4, 1921.[92]

[88] Canon 1017, §§ 1, 2.

[89] Canons 1046; 1047; 1103, §§ 1, 2; 1107.

[90] Canon 1089, §§ 1, 2.

[91] Canon 1061, § 2.

[92] *AAS,* XIII (1921), 348.

Admission of documentary testimony to prove the *status liber* of the parties is nothing new. Prior to the Code, the instruction *Cum alias* of the Sacred Congregation of the Holy Office required that letters of freedom to marry had to be obtained from the proper ordinary of the parties.[93] The instruction *Matrimonii vinculo* of the same Congregation[94] insisted that documentary evidence was the first testimony to be sought after in establishing the death of a former spouse.

Particular law and custom as well as the *praxis* of the Roman Curia have made extensive use of documents in pre-nuptial investigation. Without attempting to be exhaustive the following list of documents, more or less commonly used according to diverse circumstances in establishing the *status liber* of contracting parties, is indicative of the trend towards the recognized value of documents in pre-nuptial investigation: birth certificates to establish the age of the parties; certificates of Baptism, First Holy Communion, and Confirmation to confirm the reception of these sacraments; rescripts of the Holy See and the episcopal curia containing dispensations from various impediments, *e. g.*, disparity of cult, mixed religion, consanguinity, affinity, etc., and sanations *in radice*; certificates of attendance at a Catholic school to prove sufficiency of religious knowledge; declarations of nullity of attempted marriages; sentences of the nullity of religious profession; letters certifying that the banns were published; documents attesting the reduction to the lay state of clerics in major Orders and their release from sacerdotal celibacy;[95] certificates of death taken from parochial death records or from civil records; civil marriage licenses and civil decrees of divorce and separation; legal documents giving testimony of guardianship; medical certificates of insanity and impotency; legally written pre-nuptial agreements; affidavits on various points of the *status liber* sworn before a notary public or ecclesiastical official, etc.

When documentary testimony is produced to prove the parties' *status liber*, satisfactory pre-nuptial investigation demands that the testimony be reliable and trustworthy. Untrustworthy testimony is

[93] 21 Aug., 1670—*Fontes*, n. 742.

[94] 13 Maii, 1868—*Coll.*, m. 1321.

[95] Canon 214, § 1.

not productive of moral certainty of the *status liber* of the parties. The canons treating of pre-nuptial investigation by the pastor do not mention any rules for establishing the reliability of documents, but there is no reason why the regulations of canons 1812-1819 dealing with proof through the medium of instruments cannot be invoked as a guide. Space does not permit here a thorough treatment of proof through documents; hence the intention is to emphasize only some important points to which the pastor should give due consideration.[96]

Produced documents, whether civil or ecclesiastical,[97] original or copies of originals, public or private,[98] should be carefully scrutinized by the pastor. He will first satisfy himself as to the authenticity and genuineness of the document, *i. e.*, he will find out if it was written or drawn up by an individual legitimately appointed for that purpose and that the solemnities called for by Canon Law in the case of ecclesiastical documents and by the civil law in the case of civil documents have been observed, such as signature, seal, date, etc. He should make certain that the document is not a forgery; that the signature is not falsified; that suspicious erasures, changes, additions and subtractions in the text of the documents are subjected to critical scrutiny. Not all erasures, changes, additions and subtractions are made by forgers; some may be made by the author of the document to correct errors he has made in drawing up the document. However, public documents, *i. e.*, documents written and signed by a public official in his official capacity are presumed to be authentic until the contrary is evident.[99] Hence, if there are slight erasures and changes in a public document, the presumption will be that they are authoritatively made by the public official who drew up the document and do not interfere with the value of the document. In a case of doubt, it is best to make sure by consulting or writing the official. As the Code does not presume the genuineness of private documents, *i. e.*, docu-

[96] For a more thorough discussion of documentary proof see Wanenmacher, *Canonical Evidence in Marriage Cases*, nn. 334-381.

[97] *Cf.* canon 1813.

[98] Canon 1812.

[99] Canon 1815.

ments written by private individuals or by public officials acting in a private capacity, the pastor will have to be on his guard for forgeries.

Usually the documents produced are copies of the originals, *e. g.*, baptismal certificates, confirmation certificates, copies of divorce decrees, death certificates, etc. The reliability of copies of originals will depend on the carefulness of the person who transcribed them from the original records and on the accurate knowledge contained in the originals. Not infrequently does it happen, for instance, that in entering the baptisms in the baptismal registers, the priest who baptizes the party may enter the baptism incorrectly, especially when names have the same pronunciation but a different spelling. In such a case one may verify the baptism from the other items mentioned in the records, the date of birth, the names of the parents, godmothers, etc. The same is true of other records, and consequently more careful investigation as well as prudence will dictate the course to follow. Again it is sometimes very difficult to distinguish the writing in very old registers, especially if the entries are not plainly written, and thus the copyist is liable to spell names wrongly. Consequently, a pastor should not too hastily conclude that a document or certificate is unauthentic and not genuine, simply because a name is misspelled or a date is slightly erroneous, for, in transcribing from a baptismal register the copyist might inadvertantly put the date of baptism in the place of the date of birth, or *vice versa.*

Public documents give full proof concerning those things which are directly and principally affirmed in them,[100] *e. g.*, baptismal records give full proof of such facts as the date, place, sponsors and name of the baptized person. They do not give full proof of the date of birth. A death record gives full proof of the facts concerning death, but not of other facts perchance mentioned therein, such as whether the party was married or single and the date of the party's birth. However, mention of secondary information in records is proof that can be accepted by the pastor in the absence of direct and primary proof.[101]

[100] Canon 1816.

[101] *Cf.* Wanenmacher, *Canonical Evidence in Marriage Cases,* n. 369.

It will be necessary for the investigating pastor not only to establish the authenticity, genuineness and accuracy of a document, but also to interpret the document properly. As many of the documents produced will be rescripts from the Holy See or the local ordinary, they must be interpreted according to the proper signification of the words and the common usage of the language, and they must not be extended to cases outside of those expressed.[102]

Rescripts, in cases of doubt, should be interpreted according to canon 50. Private documents should be interpreted according to the proper sense of the words used.[103] It is well to scrutinize the words carefully in their text and context. As the meanings of certain words sometimes differ in different places, it is important to take into account the circumstances of place and the time when the document was issued. Civil public documents must be interpreted in their proper sense and according to the civil regulations on the matter.

Article 9. The Regulations of the Local Ordinary on Pre-nuptial Investigation

Common law gives very few specific regulations concerning the pre-nuptial examination of the contracting parties. For the most part the canons on pre-nuptial investigation enunciate general principles. It is not surprising that the Code did not particularize to a greater extent; for if it attempted to give detailed regulations on pre-nuptial investigation, many inconveniences would arise for both pastor and parties in the effort to put the same detailed universal rules into practice in all places and among all peoples. Therefore, the Code in canon 1021, § 3 wisely authorizes the ordinary (who is better acquainted with local circumstances) to prescribe according to his prudent judgment special regulations for the examination of those who desire to contract marriage.[104] Consequently, the right and also the duty of formulating special rules for pre-nuptial

[102] Canon 49.

[103] Wanenmacher, *Canonical Evidence in Marriage Cases*, n. 366.

[104] Gasparri, *Tractatus Canonicus de Matrimonio*, n. 136; Cerato, *Matrimonium*, p. 26; Cappello, *De Sacramentis*, III, n. 153.

investigation within his territory belongs to the local ordinary and not to the individual pastor.[105]

A very suitable time for the formulation of such rules is the time of the diocesan synod, when they can be placed in the diocesan statutes. The advantage of having them in the diocesan statutes is that they can be easily consulted by pastors and will be more readily put into effect. The regulations bind only in the territory of the local ordinary; not outside his territory.

In drawing up particular norms on pre-nuptial investigation, the local ordinary must be careful not to run counter to the marriage laws of the Code. His decrees may be either *secundum ius* or *praeter ius* but not *contra ius*.[106] If, therefore, a local ordinary issues decrees on pre-nuptial investigation that are contrary to the marriage prescriptions of the Code, they have not the force of law and pastors are not bound to observe them. If they are according to the Code or outside of the Code, pastors are obliged to follow them.[107] It may be asked here, can local ordinaries prescribe in *ordinary* cases that witnesses be juridically examined under oath to prove the free status of the parties? This practice was formerly decreed by the instruction *Cum alias*,[108] but may now be considered abrogated, as the Code makes no mention of it except for the case of the doubtful existence of a matrimonial impediment.[109] In reply it is necessary to mention that the prescription of the instruction *Cum alias* was observed only in the papal states and in a few other places, particularly in central Italy.[110] Where the practice was customary for the space of one hundred years, or from time immemorial, the local ordinary may tolerate the custom if, taking into account the circumstances of person and place, he judges that the examination of witnesses cannot be prudently abolished.[111] However, if it never was customary in his territory, he cannot introduce the prac-

[105] Ayrinhac-Lydon, *Marriage Legislation in the New Code of Canon Law*, p. 29.

[106] Canon 6, 1°.

[107] Cappello, *De Sacramentis*, III, n. 153.

[108] S. C. S. Off., 21 Aug., 1670—*Fontes*, n. 742.

[109] Canon 1031, § 1.

[110] Cappello, *De Sacramentis*, III, n. 158.

[111] Canon 5.

tice because it is opposed to the general law of the Code. To put it into practice would be to restore an abrogated law, which is beyond the power of the ordinary to do.[112] There is apparently no evidence showing that the juridical examination of witnesses to prove the *status liber* of the parties was ever in vogue in the United States. Consequently local ordinaries in the United States cannot now introduce the practice for ordinary cases by statute or precept. However, a just cause may arise in individual cases that will justify the local ordinary to demand interrogation of witnesses concerning the *status liber* and to reserve to himself the right to examine and pass on the results of the investigation before permitting the pastor to proceed with the marriage.[113] Such a just cause would exist, for example, in the case of a pastor who is notorious for declaring contracting parties free to marry on very flimsy grounds, and who has, as a result, assisted at many invalid and illicit marriages.

The particular regulations of the local ordinary must be formulated according to prudent judgment. There must be some good reasons for his action, *e. g.*, reasons of necessity or utility, such as the frequency of invalid and illicit marriages, the fact that a number of the pastors in the diocese are somewhat lax about interrogating parties on their freedom to marry, the fact that parties are employing false means of one kind or other to establish their free status, etc. Therefore, the ordinary must take into account circumstances of person, place and time, and not proceed to draw up a number of arbitrary regulations that have no value.

The following may be cited as examples of particular regulations by the ordinary: that the pre-nuptial examination take place at a definite time, for instance, a month or three weeks before the marriage; that detailed questionnaires issued by the curia be carefully filled in by the pastor during the interrogation of the parties and be returned to the curia for filing; that specific blank forms be filled in when petitioning for a dispensation, and not forms drawn up by the pastor himself; that authentic certificates of baptism, confirmation and death be demanded from the parties; that in the case of mixed marriages the *cautiones* be given in the particular form de-

[112] Gasparri, *Tractatus Canonicus de Matrimonio*, n. 135.

[113] Cappello, *De Sacramentis*, III, n. 158.

sired by the local ordinary; that strangers and people from outside be not permitted to marriage until they have produced written testimonials of their pastor testifying to the fact that they are free to marry, even though it may be otherwise evident that they are free to marry; that letters of freedom to marry be obtained from the pastors of all places where the parties have lived for a period of six months after attaining puberty. The ordinary may also draw up rules which he prudently judges will produce moral certitude of freedom to marry, rules for solving doubts, rules regarding the admission of witnesses when there is a doubt about the existence of an impediment, rules relating to the form of the oath to be taken, and regulations that the testimony of parties and witnesses be written down in a special book, etc. Should a pastor fail to observe the particular prescriptions of the ordinary, the investigation is not invalid; for at most these rules are required for lawfulness.

Article 10. When the Ordinary is to be Consulted

Not all couples who come to arrange with the pastor concerning their intended marriage can be declared free to marry by the pastor acting on his own initiative. Some cases which demand more caution and consideration in investigation must for prudential or other reasons be referred to the local ordinary before the pastor may proceed with the marriage. Most of these cases involve more than ordinary difficulty in investigation or possibly also some danger to faith or morals. Hence in solicitude for the sacredness of marriage the Church adds the legal safeguard of consulting the higher authority of the ordinary.

The following are the cases in which the pastor is obligated to refer the matter to the ordinary:

1. (a) *If a party after attaining the age of puberty dwelt for six months in a place other than his own proper parish or parishes;* (b) *if a party after attaining the age of puberty dwelt in a place for less than six months, when there is some suspicion that he contracted an impediment to marriage.*[114] If in the latter case there is no suspicion that he contracted an impediment, the pastor need not refer the matter to the ordinary.

[114] Canon 1023, §§ 2 and 3.

It is implied that when a party dwells in a place for a period of six months after reaching the age of puberty, there is a possibility that he may have contracted a matrimonial impediment. Even though the pastor is aware that there was not any impediment contracted during that time, he is still obligated to consult the ordinary. The ordinary may demand publication of the banns or prescribe that further proofs of the free status of the parties be obtained.[115] What the further proofs mentioned in canon 1023, § 2 will be depends altogether on the will of the ordinary. He may request letters of freedom from the pastor of the place, interrogation of witnesses who know the party, etc.

2. *When parties entering a marriage with a dispensation from mixed religion or disparity of cult wish, contrary to the common practice, to have the banns of marriage announced.* In this case the local ordinary may grant permission to publish the banns, provided, (a) scandal is removed, (b) a dispensation from the impediment of mixed religion or disparity of cult has been obtained, and (c) no mention is made of the religion of the non-Catholic party.[116]

3. *If, after investigation by the pastor, a prudent doubt about the existence of an impediment remains.*[117] The pastor, however, should have exhausted the means at his disposal for solving the doubt before he refers the matter to the ordinary. If the pastor can solve the doubt himself, he need not consult the ordinary.

4. *When vagi intend to marry, outside a case of necessity, the pastor before assisting at the marriage must refer the matter to the ordinary or to a priest delegated by him to receive permission to assist at the marriage.*[118] It is important to note that the marriages of workingmen who have recently come from distant countries may not, as a rule, be celebrated without consulting the local ordinary, because these workingmen are either *vagi* or, if they are not *vagi*, they are not sufficiently known. Consequently in many cases there is no sufficient certainty that they are free to marry. The Sacred Congregation of the Sacraments in an instruction issued on July 4,

[115] Canon 1023, § 2.
[116] Canon 1026.
[117] Canon 1031, § 1, 3°.
[118] Canons 1032 and 90.

1921 forbids pastors to assist at these marriages without consulting the local ordinary, except in a case of necessity or rather in danger of death.[119]

5. *When minors, despite the exhortation of their pastor to the contrary, insist on entering marriage without the knowledge or against the reasonable will of their parents.*[120]

When parents are unreasonably unwilling to consent to the marriage of their minor children, the pastor is not obliged to submit the matter to the ordinary.[121]

6. *When the pastor knows with moral certainty that the parties have either per se or by proxy exchanged matrimonial consent or intend to renew matrimonial consent before a non-Catholic minister acting in his religious capacity.* Because such procedure on the part of the Catholic is *communicatio in sacris* in a non-Catholic religious service and because there is reason to doubt the sincerity of the *cautiones* given by the non-Catholic party, the pastor is not permitted to proceed with the marriage without consulting the local ordinary.[122]

7. *When the faithful cannot be deterred from contracting marriage with those who have notoriously left the Catholic faith* (although they have not joined a non-Catholic sect), *or with those who belong to societies condemned by the Church.*[123] In both instances the fact of disassociating themselves from the Church must be notorious. The reason for the regulation is the proximate danger of the perversion of the faithful Catholic party and the children that might be born of the union. Experience has proved that very frequently the bitterest and most active enemies of the Church are those who have definitely and notoriously left the faith.

8. *In the case of public sinners who refuse to go to sacramental confession, and also in the case of notoriously censured persons who refuse to be reconciled to the Church.* The pastor cannot assist at

[119] *AAS*, XIII (1921), 348.

[120] Canon 1034.

[121] See pp. 249-251.

[122] Canon 1063, §§ 1, 2.

[123] Canon 1065, §§ 1, 2.

such marriages, unless there is a grave and urgent reason, concerning the existence of which the ordinary is the judge.[124]

9. *When some religious ceremonial is requested by the parties to a mixed marriage.*[125]

10. *When the nupturients desire to enter into a marriage of conscience.*[126]

11. *When a party wishes to receive the nuptial blessing within the forbidden times, i. e.,* from the first Sunday in Advent to the Feast of the Nativity of Our Lord (Dec. 25) inclusive, and from Ash Wednesday to Easter Sunday inclusive.[127]

12. *When Catholic parties wish to celebrate marriage in private homes or in the churches or oratories of seminaries or religious women.*[128]

13. *When the parties to a mixed marriage desire to be married in the Church.*[129]

Consultation with the ordinary by the pastor in the foregoing cases is not required for the validity of the marriage; it is required only for lawfulness. In each case the signification of the words of the canons indicate that the consultation is merely preceptive. Therefore, should a pastor fail, even intentionally, to consult the ordinary in the given cases, he would act sinfully, but the marriage would be valid, unless an invalidating impediment interfered. Cases of moral impossibility, necessity or urgency will occur at times and will constitute a proportionate reason of sufficient gravity to excuse the pastor from referring the matter to the ordinary.[130]

It may be mentioned here that when certain public but dispensable impediments to a marriage are discovered by the pastor, he will usually refer them to his own local ordinary, if the ordinary has the power to grant them. If they are impediments for which a dispensation from from the Holy See is necessary, he could petition the

[124] Canon 1066.

[125] Canon 1102, § 2.

[126] Canons 1104-1107.

[127] Canon 1108, §§ 2, 3.

[128] Canon 1109, §§ 1, 2.

[129] Canon 1109, § 3.

[130] *Cf.* Cappello, *De Sacramentis,* III, nn. 186, 317, 331, 332.

Holy See directly, but the *praxis Curiae Romanae* is that they be referred to the Holy See through the local ordinary.

Article 11. Referring Cases to the Curia for Solution by Ecclesiastical Trial or Process

It is not infrequent for parties unhappily married, separated or divorced, and who have inclinations of marrying again, to approach their pastor for the purpose of discovering whether or not it is possible to have their previous marriage declared null or to have it dissolved. Sometimes such marriages do actually prove to have been contracted invalidly or there is a possibility of a dissolution of the bond of marriage. Assuming that the pastor has made a sincere but unsuccessful effort to effect a reconciliation of the parties, or a convalidation of the invalid union, or that the case is such that reconciliation is impossible, the pastor cannot there and then declare on his own initiative that the union is invalid or that the marriage is dissolved. It will be necessary for him to refer the matter to the proper curia for adjudication.

In handling such cases pastors should act prudently. They should not forward to the curia cases that are hopeless and devoid of proof. They should not definitely assure the parties that a favorable decision is inevitable and that it will be obtained within a certain specific time. The case may involve unforeseen difficulties and may take an unexpected length of time. Besides, there is the danger of imbuing the parties with false hopes, which may encourage them to prepare prematurely for another wedding.

The marriage cases to be referred to the curia may be divided into four classes: (a) those requiring administrative procedure; (b) those requiring the informative process;[131] (c) those requiring the summary marriage process;[132] (d) those requiring the formal judicial process.[133]

[131] Matthew Ramstein, *The Pastor and Marriage Cases* (New York: Benziger, 1936), p. 109.

[132] Edwin Joseph Kennedy, *The Special Matrimonial Process in Cases of Evident Nullity* (The Catholic University of America, Canon Law Studies, n. 93; Washington: The Catholic University of America, 1935), pp. 51-76.

[133] Thomas Henry Kay, *Competence in Matrimonial Procedure* (The Cath-

A. *Cases Requiring Administrative Procedure.* Under this heading come the following: I. Clandestinity cases. II. Pauline privilege cases. III. Cases where the dissolution of the previous bond of marriage cannot be proved by an authentic death certificate.

I. *Clandestinity Cases.* Under this heading there will come for adjudication those marriage cases in which it is contended that the marriage or marriages in question are invalid because the parties concerned, though bound by the canonical form of marriage, did not celebrate their marriage with due observance of the prescribed canonical form of marriage. In this connection the Pontifical Commission for the Authentic Interpretation of the Code declared that there are three cases of clandestinity which can be settled by the ordinary himself, or by the pastor after consultation with the ordinary in the preliminary investigation prior to the celebration of the marriage (canon 1019). These three cases do not require a judicial process nor the intervention of the *defensor vinculi.* The cases are: (a) When two Catholics in a place subject to the decree *Tametsi,* or after the decree *Ne temere,* entered into a civil marriage only, without any ecclesiastical rite, afterwards obtained a divorce and now wish to contract a new marriage in the Church. (b) When a Catholic, having contracted marriage with a non-Catholic in a Protestant church, either in a place subject to the decree *Tametsi* to which the Benedictine declaration had not been extended, or after the decree *Ne temere,* and having obtained a civil divorce, now wishes to contract a new marriage with a Catholic in the Church. (c) When apostates from the Catholic faith were married civilly or in a non-Catholic rite and later, having obtained a civil divorce, returned to the faith and now wish to contract a new marriage with a Catholic in the Church.[134]

Before a pastor sends a clandestinity case to the curia for adjudication he should investigate whether or not the parties were actually bound by the canonical form of marriage. If after investigation he is in doubt as to whether the party or parties were bound by the canonical form, he should not neglect to refer the matter to the curia.

olic University of America, Canon Law Studies, n. 53; Washington: The Catholic University of America, 1929), pp. 88-108.

[134] 16 Oct., 1919—*AAS,* XI (1919), 479.

II. *Pauline Privilege Cases.* In virtue of the Pauline privilege, the valid marriage of two unbaptized persons, though consummated, can be dissolved in favor of the faith on the fulfillment of certain conditions.[135] The following conditions are required for the use of the privilege: (a) The marriage must have been entered into during the infidelity of both parties, *i. e.*, when both parties were still unbaptized. (b) The valid baptism of one party must have actually taken place. One under instruction prior to baptism cannot use the privilege.[136] According to the more common opinion of canonists even the valid baptism of a party in a non-Catholic Christian sect suffices.[137] (c) Departure of the unbaptized party must have occurred. The departure may be *physical* (*e. g.*, in case of desertion, separation, divorce, marriage to another) or moral (*e. g.*, when the unbaptized party does not live peacefully with the baptized, provokes quarrels, makes homelife very unhappy, refuses to have the children baptized or educated in the Catholic faith, is blasphemous, makes efforts to lead the baptized party into sins against conjugal chastity).[138] (d) The interpellation of the unconverted party is necessary, unless a dispensation from the interpellations had been obtained. The interpellations must extend to the following points: (1) whether the unconverted party wishes to be converted and receive baptism, and (2) whether he is willing at least to live peaceably with the baptized party without any offense to the Creator.[139] As the interpellations should ordinarily be made under the authority of the ordinary of the converted party,[140] it is proper for the pastor not to make the interpellations prior to referring the matter to the curia. Having ascertained, therefore, that the marriage was entered into in infidelity and that one party was validly baptized and that the unbaptized party has departed, the pastor should refer the matter to the curia.

135 St. Paul, 1 Cor., vii, 12-15; Canon 1120.

136 S. C. de Prop. Fide, resp., 16 Jan., 1803—*Coll.* n. 665; S. C. S. Off., 15 Mart., 1901—*AAS*, XXXIII (1900, 1901), 549, 550.

137 Cappello, *De Sacramentis*, III, n. 768.

138 Cappello, *De Sacramentis*, III, n. 770.

139 Canon 1121, § 1.

140 Canon 1122, § 1.

III. *Cases where the dissolution of the previous bond of marriage by presumed death cannot be proved by an authentic death certificate.* In the absence of such a document, the pastor should collect all the suitable evidence he can, such as the testimony of witnesses, especially that testimony which was given *tempore non suspecto,* as well as the circumstantial and adminicular evidence, and forward it to the curia.

B. *Cases Requiring the Informative Process.* Two cases come under this heading: I. *Matrimonium ratum et non-consummatum.* II. *The dissolution of the natural bond of marriage.*

I. *Matrimonium Ratum et Non-consummatum.* According to canon 1119 an unconsummated marriage of two baptized persons, or of a baptized person and one not baptized, is dissolved *ipso iure* by solemn religious profession, or by a dispensation granted by the Apostolic See. A just cause, however, is required before the dispensation may be obtained. The dispensation may be petitioned by both parties, or by one party, even though the other is unwilling. When the parties approach the pastor in regard to obtaining the dispensation, the pastor should inquire judiciously (a) whether the marriage was consummated by marital intercourse and (b) whether there is a reasonable cause for seeking the dissolution of the union, *e. g.,* a suspicion of impotency, venereal disease in a partner, personal hatred of one for the other without hope of true reconciliation, civil divorce, great unhappiness in marriage, etc.[141] An instruction outlining the procedure to be followed in *ratum et non-consummatum* cases was issued by the Sacred Congregation of the Sacraments on May 7, 1923.[142] As the parties who present cases of this kind to the pastor are often under the impression that the matter can be decided within a very short space of time and with little procedure, it is only reasonable for the pastor to indicate to them that the adjudication of these cases is reserved to the Holy See (to the Congregation of the Sacraments when both parties in the case are Catholic; to the Holy Office when one of the parties is a non-Catholic); that the ordinary must petition the Holy See to initiate the process; that the parties themselves and witnesses *septimae manus* will be interro-

[141] Cappello, *De Sacramentis,* III, 762.

[142] *AAS,* XV (1923), 389.

gated; that the woman will be submitted to a medical examination, unless from the facts of the case such examination would prove useless. The imparting of those items of information will obviate any complaints from the party or parties to the effect, that they were falsely led to believe that the case would be decided within a short period of time and that there was very little inconvenience involved, and that if they had been acquainted beforehand in regard to the inconveniences involved, they would never have pursued the matter to a conclusion. However, the pastor should not exaggerate the difficulties involved so as to deter worthy parties from pursuing such cases. Rather, he should lend his aid to the party concerned in drawing up the introductory petition, a specimen copy of which is to be found in the instruction of the Sacred Congregation of the Sacraments.[143]

II. *Dissolution of the Natural Bond of Marriage.* Petitions have been sent to the Sacred Congregation of the Holy Office asking from the Supreme Pontiff a dissolution in favor of the faith of certain marriages contracted between baptized non-Catholics and non-baptized non-Catholics. Dispensations have been granted in some cases, even though the marriages were consummated.[144] Two conclusions may be drawn from the fact that such dispensations have been granted: (a) that the Supreme Pontiff has the power to dissolve such marriages; and (b) that such marriages are not sacramental, as the Pope has not the power to dissolve a consummated sacramental marriage.[145]

Before the Holy See will grant such a dispensation it will have to be proved (a) that one party remained unbaptized during the whole period of conjugal life between the parties; (b) that after the baptism of the unbaptized non-Catholic there was not any use of marriage; (c) that the restoration of conjugal life is morally impossible; (d) that the conversion of the party to the Catholic faith was sincere and based on grave reasons; (e) that if the dispensa-

[143] S. C. de Sacramentis, instr., 7 Maii, 1923, Appendix I—*AAS,* XV (1923), 389.

[144] *Cf.* T. Lincoln Bouscaren, *Canon Law Digest,* I (Milwaukee: Bruce, 1934), pp. 552-554.

[145] Canon 1118.

tion is granted, no scandal will result. It will, therefore, be necessary for a pastor to make inquiries on these points before he aids the convert to draw up his petition for the dispensation. The ordinary, on receipt of the petition, will appoint the officials required for the process, and the information therein received together with the necessary documents (*e. g.*, a copy of the marriage record, a copy of the divorce decree, baptismal certificate of the convert, the recommendation of the convert's petition by the ordinary, etc.) will be sent to the Sacred Congregation of the Holy Office for a decision.

C. *The Summary Marriage Process.* Mention of this process is made in canon 1990, which states: "When an impediment of disparity of cult, orders, solemn vow of chastity, valid bond of marriage, consanguinity, affinity, or spiritual relationship rendered a marriage invalid, and the existence of the impediment can be proved from a certain and authentic document which cannot be contradicted and is subject to no exception, and at the same time there is the same certainty that no dispensation from these impediments has been granted, the formalities for a regular trial need not be observed. The ordinary may declare the nullity of the marriage after summoning the witnesses and consulting the *defensor vinculi.*" [146]

The pastor, having assured himself that the marriage is invalid on account of one of the above-quoted impediments and that no dispensation from the impediment was obtained, prepares the petition, giving all the facts of the case, the names and the addresses of the witnesses. The petition should be signed by the party and the pastor, and should be properly dated and sealed. The necessary documents (those proving the existence of the impediment, the marriage certificate, the decree of divorce, etc.) should accompany the petition.[147]

D. *The Formal Trial.* With the exception of the cases mentioned above as requiring either administrative procedure, the informative process, or the summary marriage process, it may be said that all cases involving the invalidity of the bond of marriage are recognized as demanding the regular marriage trial. This

[146] Canon 1990.

[147] *Cf.* Kennedy; *The Special Matrimonial Process in Cases of Evident Nullity*, pp. 77-146.

trial will be conducted according to the formalities mentioned in canons 1552-1924 and in accordance with the instructions issued by the Sacred Congregation of the Sacraments on August 15, 1936.[148] Having satisfied himself that the party has a case that merits the attention of the tribunal, the pastor should aid the party to draw up the introductory petition according to the prescriptions of canons 1706-1710, and send it to the tribunal together with the necessary documents (which will vary with the nature of the case).

Article 12. Investigation of the Causes for Matrimonial Dispensations

Matrimonial impediments are either *dispensable* or *indispensable.* *Dispensable* impediments are those from which the Church can and *de facto* does dispense. *Indispensable* impediments are those from which the Church cannot dispense, or at least, does not dispense.[149] The legislator who established the impediments, his successor, his superior, and those to whom the faculty of dispensing has been granted, have the power to dispense.[150] As several matrimonial impediments are of ecclesiastical origin, the Roman Pontiff can dispense from them and can concede to others the power of dispensing from them. He actually grants this power to others under certain restrictions as mentioned in the Code, and he grants it frequently by means of particular indults. However, the Roman Pontiff is not accustomed to dispense from certain impediments of ecclesiastical law. He never dispenses from an impediment concerning which there is a controversy as to whether it arises directly from the natural law or merely from positive ecclesiastical law. Such a controversy exists in regard to the first degree of consanguinity in the collateral line. He never dispenses from the impediment of sacred orders in a bishop, nor from the impediment of public crime occasioned by conjugicide except in danger of death. Very rarely does he dispense from the impediment arising from the first degree of affinity in the direct line when the marriage has been consum-

[148] *AAS,* XXVIII (1936), 315-361.

[149] Cappello, *De Sacramentis,* III, n. 196.

[150] Canon 80.

mated, or from the impediment of abduction, or from that of the sacred order of the priesthood.[151]

It is most important for the pastor to note that the Roman Pontiff requires a just and reasonable cause in order to dispense lawfully from a matrimonial impediment. If the dispensation is granted by an inferior, *e. g.*, by the local ordinary, a just and reasonable cause is required not only for the lawfulness, but also for the validity of the dispensation. In a doubt about the sufficiency of the cause the dispensation can be lawfully requested and can also be lawfully and validly granted.[152]

Various causes for dispensations are distinguished:

1. *Motivating* and *Impulsive*. A motivating cause is one which in itself is sufficient to move or induce the proper authority to grant the dispensation. An impulsive cause is one which simply impels or urges the proper authority to grant the dispensation.[153]

2. *Canonical* and *Non-Canonical*. Canonical reasons are those which are expressly and generally admitted in accordance with the prevalent formularies, customary usage and habitual practice (*stylus et praxis*) of the Roman Curia. All other causes are non-canonical.[154] The Roman Curia does not confine itself to the acceptance of canonical causes only; it also admits non-canonical causes, if they are of sufficient force.

3. *Honorable* and *disparaging (honestae et inhonestae)*. Honorable causes are those that carry with them no trace of infamy; disparaging reasons are those that contain some element of disgrace.

[151] Cappello, *De Sacramentis,* III, n. 224.

[152] Canon 84, §§ 1, 2; Gommarus Michiels, *Normae Generales Iuris Canonici,* Lublin, 1929, II, pp. 499, 500.

[153] Reiffenstuel, *Ius Canonicum Universum,* lib. I, tit. 3, n. 194; Sanchez, *De Matrimonio,* lib. VIII, disp. 21, n. 41; Vincentius De Justis, *De Dispensationibus Matrimonialibus,* Lucae, 1726, lib. III, c. I, n. 46; Payen, *De Matrimonio,* III, n. 727; William A. O'Mara, *Canonical Causes for Matrimonial Dispensations* (The Catholic University of America, Canon Law Studies, n. 97, Washington: The Catholic University of America, 1935), pp. 43, 44.

[154] Cappello, *De Sacramentis,* III, 257; Gasparri, *Tractatus Canonicus de Matrimonio,* n. 297; O'Mara, *Canonical Causes for Matrimonial Dispensations,* pp. 44, 45.

A list of the more common and more potent canonical causes for dispensations was issued by the Sacred Congregation of the Propagation of the Faith on May 9, 1877, in which were enumerated the following sixteen causes: (1) *The woman's limited prospects of marriage (angustia loci),* (2) *her super-marriageable age (aetas superadulta),* (3) *her lack or insufficiency of dowry,* (4) *the issue of legal litigation,* (5) *the poverty of a widow,* (6) *the advantage of peace,* (7) *excessive, suspected and dangerous familiarity (nimia, suspecta, periculosa familiaritas),* (8) *previous sexual intercourse between the parties,* (9) *the evil repute of the woman,* (10) *the convalidation of an invalid marriage,* (11) *the danger of a mixed marriage or of the celebration of the marriage before a non-Catholic minister,* (12) *the danger of incestuous concubinage,* (13) *the danger of a civil marriage,* (14) *the removal of grave scandals,* (15) *the cessation of notorious concubinage,* (16) *excellence of merits.*[155] A further list of 28 ordinary causes for matrimonial dispensations was issued by the Apostolic Datary in the year 1901. A comparison with the list of the Sacred Congregation for the Propagation of the Faith indicates that many of them are mentioned in both lists. Several of those in the list of the Apostolic Datary are not considered as motivating causes. When many are taken conjointly, or when one individual cause is taken in conjunction with other causes not mentioned in the list, they may be sufficiently convincing to induce the proper authority to grant a dispensation. The 28 causes are: (1) *limited prospect for marriage in one locality,* (2) *limited prospect for marriage in several localities,* (3) *limitation of prospect along with insufficiency of dowry outside the present locality of the woman,* (4) *insufficiency of dowry,* (5) *increase of dowry by the prospective husband,* (6) *total lack of dowry,* (7) *increase of dowry by some extraneous person,* (8) *abatement of hatreds,* (9) *the attainment of peace or its consolidation between kings and princes,* (10) *the settling of lawsuits concerning the succession to property,* (11) *the ending of lawsuits over questions affecting the dowry,* (12) *legal settlements involving things of great value,* (13) *the burden of children resting upon a widow or the fact that she is bereft of parents,* (14) *woman's age if it exceeds 24 years,* (15) *a man's*

[155] *Coll.,* n. 1470.

difficulty in coming to a place for the purpose of contracting marriage with one of its inhabitants, (16) *the safeguarding of religion for a contracting party and the avoidance of the danger of a mixed marriage,* (17) *the hope of the conversion of the non-Catholic party to the Catholic faith,* (18) *the retention of property or temporal goods within a given family,* (19) *the perpetuation of a noble family or the preservation of a royal heir,* (20) *excellence of merits,* (21) *the maintenance of a family's honor,* (22) *the allaying of infamy and scandal,* (23) *the act of sinful congress (copula); the crime of abduction,* (24) *the avoidance of civil marriage,* (25) *previous marriage before a Protestant minister,* (26) *the convalidation of marriage,* (27) *the presence of certain reasonable causes,* (28) *special reasons affecting the petitioners known to the Holy See, e. g.,* illicit relations or dishonorable conduct, the explicit detailing of which is not expedient in view of the parties' station in life or dignity.[156]

The final judge of the justness, equity and reasonableness of causes alleged for a dispensation from a matrimonial impediment is the one who grants the dispensation. He is the one on whom the duty is placed of determining if the cause is really and truly just, equitable and reasonable. However, as the one dispensing is usually not acquainted with the petitioners and as a rule resides at a long distance from them, he will ultimately have to depend in practically all cases on the judgment of the investigating pastor for the objective presence and truth of the causes alleged. Consequently, the pastor is gravely obligated to investigate the presence and truth of the causes mentioned in the petition for the dispensation. While the lists of causes issued by the Sacred Congregation for the Propagation of the Faith and the Apostolic Datary are merely illustrative, rather than exhaustive, they will serve as a guide to the pastor in seeking the presence of sufficient causes for dispensations. If the pastor in the petition mentions any one of these causes, he should be certain that the meaning he attaches to them is the approved meaning. The pastor is not obligated to confine his reasons for the dispensations to the above-mentioned causes. Other causes may also be alleged, *e. g.*, the fact of deformity or infirmity in a party; the fact that a girl has already been deprived of her virginity by

[156] *ASS*, XXXIV, pp. 34, 35.

another; the fact that a certain man and woman need each other's aid to run a business or a home; the fact that everything is prepared for the wedding; the fact that it is widely rumored that a certain couple will be married; the fact of good morals in both parties; the fact that a marriage proves suitable for the parties; the fact that a party is a great public benefactor; the fact that the father or mother of a party needs some helper; the fact of mutual help in old age.[157]

It is important that the investigating pastor keep in mind what is meant by a just, equitable and reasonable cause. In this connection attention should be paid to canon 84, § 1: "*A lege ecclesiastica ne dispensetur sine iusta et rationabili causa, habita ratione gravitatis legis a qua dispensetur, . . .*" The words "*habita ratione gravitatis legis a qua dispensetur*" indicate that the phrase "just and reasonable cause" is not to be accepted in the absolute sense, but rather in the relative sense, *i. e.*, in proportion to the gravity of the law. It implies that laws are of varying importance. The same is true of matrimonial impediments. Some are more important and contribute more to the public good of the faithful than others.[158] Hence the gravity of the impediment must be taken into account in weighing the justness, equity and reasonableness of the cause. Thus, the just and reasonable cause for a dispensation from the impediment of disparity of cult would have to be more serious than would a reasonable cause for a dispensation from the impediment of legal relationship. Moreover, among the causes themselves even the canonical causes are not all of equal value, *e. g.*, the danger that the parties will celebrate marriage before a non-Catholic minister is a more serious cause than the super-marriageable age of a prospective bride. Another point that should not be lost sight of is the fact that what is a serious cause in one place may not at all be so in another place, *e. g.*, in certain places in Europe the lack of a dowry is a serious matter, while here in the United States it is not generally looked upon as of importance. In the petition for a dispensation it is advisable for the pastor to mention more than one cause, if more than one cause is really present. With additional causes mentioned, the reasons for granting the dispensation will be more

[157] Gasparri, *Tractatus Canonicus de Matrimonio*, n. 319.

[158] *Cf.* O'Mara, *Canonical Causes for Matrimonial Dispensations*, pp. 46, 47.

convincing and the probability of obtaining the dispensation will be greater.

Though the Roman Pontiff can dispense validly from ecclesiastical matrimonial impediments even apart from a just cause, he cannot do so lawfully. However, he is evidently not wont to dispense without a just and reasonable cause.[159] This furnishes a further reason for care by the pastor in investigating the cause of matrimonial dispensations.[160] A dispensation granted without a sufficient cause by an inferior to the Pope, *e. g.*, by the residential bishop, is necessarily invalid.[161]

A further cause for diligence on the part of the pastor in the investigation of the truth and presence of the causes for matrimonial dispensations lies in that fact that the customary manner of granting dispensations is by rescript. Consequently, if the rescript is invalid, the dispensation is not granted. All rescripts are considered as given on the condition—always implied when it is left unstated—that the petition be truthful. Canons 45 and 1054 offer the only exceptions to this universal norm.[162] Consequently, if on discovering an impediment to a marriage a pastor simply glanced at the list of canonical causes and without any investigation as to their objective truth or presence wrote into the petition for a dispensation such cause or causes that appeal to him at the moment, he would be guilty of running the risk of obtaining an invalid dispensation. The same may be said of a pastor who, irrespective of the impediment involved and without any investigation, always writes down the same causes in the petition. More guilty still is the pastor who deliberately alleges false causes, for he definitely places an act that will invalidate the dispensation.

Physical certainty of the presence of a cause is not required in

[159] *Cf.* Conc. Trident., sess. XXIV, *de ref. matrim.*, c. 5; Benedictus XIV, *De Synodo Dioecesana*, lib. XIII, c. 5, n. 7; S. C. de Prop. Fide, litt. encycl., 11 Mart., 1868—*Coll.*, n. 1234; S. C. de Prop. Fide, instr., 9 Maii, 1877—*Coll.*, n. 1470.

[160] Giovine, *De Dispensationibus Matrimonialibus*, c. IV, § 69; Sanchez, *De Matrimonio*, lib. VIII, disp. 17, n. 17.

[161] Canon 84.

[162] Canon 40.

order that such a cause may be alleged. Moral certainty suffices. To attain moral certainty the pastor will frequently have to question either the parties themselves or outside witnesses. He may also have to consult documents. He may possibly even have to rely for his moral certainty on his deductions from circumstantial evidence. At any rate, he must not rely on mere guesswork or unconfirmed rumor.

CHAPTER VII

PARTICULAR INVESTIGATION OF A CATHOLIC BRIDE AND GROOM

When a couple present themselves to the pastor and declare to him their intention of entering marriage, his first duty will be to identify them, unless he is already well acquainted with them. Complete identification will include the following items: their full names, their parents' names (maiden name of mother), their religion, occupation, residence and age. Equipped with this information concerning the parties before him, the pastor will have a starting point from which to draw up his plans for the interrogation of the parties on their freedom to marry.

In regard to the names of the parties and their parents, it is a good practice to consign them to writing, asking the parties to spell the names, if the actual manner of spelling them is not clear to the pastor. Many names distinct in spelling have a similar pronunciation (*e. g.*, Donahue, Donohue, Donoghue), and for identification purposes it is necessary to obtain them correctly, especially if there are several people of the same name in the locality. Moreover, the names of the parties and of their parents may suggest a suspicion of consanguinity or affinity, which is an added reason for correctness in spelling them.

The preliminary questions on religion, occupation and age are no less important than the questions concerning the names of the parties; for differences in the religion, occupation and age of the nupturients demand certain variations in the pastor's interrogatory.

The present chapter will be devoted to the investigation of the *status liber* of Catholic couples of the Latin rite. However, many of the remarks made herein will apply with equal force to mixed marriages and marriages of Latin Catholics with Oriental Catholics.

Article 1. Residence of the Parties

The interrogations concerning the residence of the parties ought to be somewhat extensive and particular, especially if the parties are not well known to the pastor. They should be asked where they actually reside (place, street and street number); the name of the parish; how long they have lived at their present addresses; whether they have lived in other parishes; when they left these parishes and whether they left them with the intention of not returning. It is also well to ask them if they have more than one home; whether they reside in different places during certain seasons of the year (*e.g.*, some may have a winter home and a summer home); how long they reside in these respective places; whether the occupations of the parties are such that they must necessarily reside in different places during the year. They should be asked, in addition, whether their present addresses are only temporary; whether they lived at them after the manner of inhabitants or whether they have assumed these addresses simply for a brief period, *e.g.*, for reasons of business, vacation, convalescence, etc. Furthermore, the pastor should question them as to the various places in which they have lived since they attained the age of puberty; how long they resided in these places and in what parishes they resided. The importance of these interrogations will be seen presently.

The major reason for interrogating the parties concerning their place or places of residence is to determine if the pastor himself is competent to conduct their pre-nuptial investigation. If he himself is not competent, the responses of the parties to his questions will establish what pastor is competent. Should another pastor be competent, the pastor whom they approached will refer them to their own proper pastor or obtain from him the necessary permission to assist at the marriage. To establish his competency the pastor must have the assurance that the parties have either a domicile, a quasi-domicile or a month's residence in his parish. Any one of these three titles is sufficient. If the parties are *vagi,* he must be morally certain that they have actual residence in his parish.[1]

As the marriages of *vagi* will be treated later, the competency of the pastor in regard to them will not be treated here.

During his interrogation in regard to the residence of the parties, the pastor must be mindful of the conditions necessary to acquire a domicile, a quasi-domicile or a month's residence in the parish.[2]

[1] Canon 1097, § 1, 2°.

[2] See pp. 75-77.

Not only should the pastor have in mind the conditions necessary for acquiring a domicile and quasi-domicile, but also he will have to be attentive to the manner by which a domicile and a quasi-domicile are lost, and plan his questions accordingly. Both a domicile and a quasi-domicile are lost by the departure of the party from his place of residence with the intention of not returning, the necessary domicile being the only exception.[3] The establishing of the party's intention not to return will frequently cause much difficulty. If a party leaves a place with all his household effects, etc., he may be regarded as having the intention of not returning, unless there is some special reason to indicate the contrary. However, it must be borne in mind that departure from the place of domicile or quasi-domicile for the purpose of contracting marriage does not involve loss of domicile or quasi-domicile before marriage, because when one leaves with the intention or in view of getting married, his departure is not absolute. It is really conditioned on the fact that marriage will take place.[4]

When the parties have acquired a domicile by reason of ten years' residence in a parish, or a quasi-domicile by reason of six months' residence, or when they have a title to marriage in a given parish even by reason of a month's residence there prior to the marriage, the competency of the pastor to assist at their marriage is manifest. The pastor's difficulty in the investigation of his competence arises when the parties have just newly arrived in the parish and have not yet completed the month's residence. His duty then will be to determine their intention regarding residence, *i. e.*, do the parties intend to live in the parish for over six months? If so, they have acquired a quasi-domicile. *A fortiori* the pastor is competent if they intend to live there perpetually. Frequently their intention to stay for six months will be established by circumstances, *e. g.*, the fact they have bought a home, that their occupations necessitate their remaining there, etc. If the parties declare that they do not intend to remain for six months, the postponement of the marriage for a

[3] Canon 95.

[4] Carberry, *The Juridical Form of Marriage*, p. 99; Fourneret, *Le Mariage Chrètien* (Paris, 1909), pp. 146 ss.

month will render the pastor competent to assist at their marriage, *i. e.*, if they continue to live in *his* parish for the month.

When the pastor has determined his own competence to assist at the marriage, or has gotten the necessary permission to assist (if he is not already competent), he must then question the parties as to whether they have acquired a domicile or quasi-domicile in other parishes. The reason is that the banns of marriage must be published by the various proper pastors of the parties, unless a dispensation from their publication has been obtained; [5] and the duty of informing the various proper pastors of the parties concerning the contemplated marriage will usually fall on the investigating pastor.

It is also necessary to question the nupturients regarding their places of residence since they attained the age of puberty. Canon 1023, §§ 2, 3 furnishes the reason: "If one of the parties has lived in another place (outside of his own parish or parishes) for six months after reaching the age of puberty, the matter shall be submitted to the ordinary, who, according to his prudent judgment, will either demand that the publications be made in that place, or require that other proofs be obtained to prove the free status of the parties. If there is some suspicion that an impediment was contracted, the pastor shall, even for a shorter residence, consult the ordinary, who is forbidden to permit the marriage until the suspicion is lawfully removed."

Article 2. Investigation of Baptism and Confirmation

A. *Baptism.* Baptism is the door and foundation of all the other sacraments.[6] Hence, it is important that the investigating pastor inquire whether those who intend to receive the Sacrament of Matrimony are validly baptized. The law definitely prescribes that, unless baptism was conferred in his own territory, the pastor is obliged to demand testimony of baptism from both contracting parties, or from the Catholic party only if there is question of parties who contract marriage with a dispensation from the impediment of disparity of cult.[7]

[5] Canon 1023, § 1; Roberts, *The Banns of Marriage*, p. 70.
[6] Canon 737, § 1.
[7] Canon 1021, § 1.

In regard to requesting testimony of baptism, a distinction is to be made between those nupturients who were baptized in the pastor's territory and those baptized outside of it. Territory here obviously refers to the parish, not to the diocese to which the pastor belongs.

If the parties were baptized in the pastor's parish, the law does not require him to demand testimony from them concerning their baptism. Apparently the reason is because he can ascertain the necessary testimony from the parochial baptismal register, of which he is the custodian. If he has been pastor of the parish for a number of years, he probably knows well from his own personal knowledge whether the party is baptized. In these circumstances there is ordinarily no reason for asking the parties for testimony of their baptism, and the law exempts the pastor from that duty.[8] However, if the party asserts that he was baptized in the parish and if there is no record of the baptism in the parochial baptismal register or if the pastor cannot recall baptizing him, then reliable testimony of baptism must be produced before the pastor can proceed with the marriage.

When the parties were baptized outside the parish, the pastor must request testimony of their baptism. The investigating pastor in that case has not easy access to the baptismal records of the place of the parties' baptism and, as a rule, has no personal knowledge of their baptism. His obligation to demand testimony of their baptism is seriously binding in conscience unless he certainly knows from some other source that baptism was conferred.[9] What is the meaning of the phrase "*testimonium baptismi*" in canon 1021, § 1? Apparently it does not necessarily mean an authentic certificate of baptism copied from the baptismal register, but extends also to other reliable means of proof of baptism, *e. g.*, the testimony of two trustworthy witnesses, or even of one absolutely trustworthy witness when the rights of third parties are not concerned. If the party was baptized in adult age, his assertion under oath that he was validly baptized is sufficient proof.[10] However, it seems reason-

[8] Canon 1021, § 1.

[9] Payen, *De Matrimonio*, n. 417; Cappello, *De Sacramentis*, III, n. 149.

[10] Canon 779; Woywod, *A Practical Commentary on the Code of Canon Law*, n. 993.

able to state that ordinarily an authentic baptismal certificate should be requested from the parties, if it can conveniently be obtained.[11] Cappello is somewhat strict in his interpretation of *testimonium baptismi* when he states that other proof of baptism should not be admitted for marriage, if an authentic baptismal certificate can be had.[12] The reason why an authentic baptismal certificate should be ordinarily required is not so much because it furnishes proof of baptism, but because it also furnishes proof of the freedom of the parties from certain matrimonial impediments, in virtue of the provisions of canons 470, § 2, 1103, §§ 1-3, and 1988. The contents of these canons prove how valuable the baptismal certificate is to the investigating pastor. Canon 470, § 2 prescribes that a proper notation should be made in the baptismal book, when the baptized party has received confirmation, when he has contracted marriage (provided it was not a marriage of conscience), when he has received the order of sub-diaconate, or when he has made solemn religious profession. Furthermore, the same canon states that these items should be mentioned by the pastor when issuing baptismal certificates. Marriages of conscience are not recorded in the regular baptismal book, but rather in a special book to be kept in the secret archives of the curia.[13]

Canon 1103, §§ 1-3 states: "After the celebration of the marriage, the pastor, or the priest who takes his place, shall as soon as possible enter in the marriage register the names of the married persons and of the witnesses, the place and the date of the marriage, and other particulars prescribed by the ritual and by the proper ordinary. Furthermore, the pastor shall, in accordance with canon 470, § 2, note in the baptismal register that the parties contracted marriage in his parish on such a day. If one or both parties were baptized elsewhere, the pastor of the parish where the marriage took place shall send notice of the contracted marriage to the pastor of the place where the parties were baptized, either *per se* or through the episcopal curia. Whenever marriage is contracted according to the prescriptions of canon 1098, the priest,

[11] Gasparri, *Tractatus Canonicus de Matrimonio*, n. 140.

[12] Cappello, *De Sacramentis*, III, n. 148.

[13] Canon 1107; *cf.* also canon 379.

if one happens to be present, otherwise the witnesses, are bound *in solidum* together with the contracting parties to see that a notation of the marriage is entered in the prescribed registers as soon as possible."

Canon 1968 adds another precaution: "The local ordinary has the duty to see that mention of the decree of nullity of the marriage be made in the baptismal and matrimonial registers where the fact of the celebration of the marriage is recorded."

If the foregoing precautions are accurately observed, the baptismal register or recent baptismal certificate will supply most valuable information regarding the freedom of the nupturients from the impediments of *ligamen,* age, solemn vow of chastity and sacred orders. Furthermore, a comparison of the names on the baptismal certificates of the parties may reveal indications of the possible presence of the impediments of consanguinity, affinity, and spiritual relationship. For these reasons it seems perfectly legitimate to conclude that ordinarily the investigating pastor should request baptismal certificates from the parties. This view is also supported by the insistence of the Sacred Congregation of the Sacraments on the obligation of the pastors to send without delay notice of the marriages at which they have assisted to the parish of the parties' baptism.[14] If pastors do not fulfill this duty of sending the notice of the marriage to the pastor of the place of baptism, the value of a baptismal certificate as an aid towards proving the *status liber* of the contracting parties is lessened. It was expressly stated in the instruction of the Congregation of the Sacraments that many pastors were negligent of this duty. Consequently, the investigating pastor must not come to the hasty conclusion that a party is perfectly free to marry, if the baptismal register or baptismal certificate does not contain annotations regarding matrimonial impediments. Even when a pastor records and sends the information, it must be remembered that there are several impediments a party might contract, which cannot possibly be proved from a baptismal register or certificate.

The investigating pastor should examine the baptismal certificate to see if it was issued by the pastor of the place of baptism or by

[14] 4 Jul., 1921—*AAS,* XIII (1921), 348.

someone acting on his authority. The seal and signature will sufficiently attest this point. The certificate ought to be recent, which fact can be ascertained from its date. The more recent it is, the more valuable it will be as an aid to proving the *status liber* of the parties. It is also well to find out, if possible, whether the pastor who wrote the certificate knew that the party was about to get married; for if the certificate was gotten for some other reason, the pastor may have failed to mention facts in regard to marriage that may, perchance, have been noted in the baptismal register.

No particular form for baptismal certificates is mentioned in the Code. Diocesan statutes, the decrees of the local ordinary, or perhaps local custom may prescribe a particular form and, if so, it should be followed. However, the usual certificate forms frequently do not leave space for the mention of facts in regard to the reception of Confirmation, Sacred Orders, previous bond of marriage, etc. Hence, should any annotations on these points be made in the baptismal register, it will be necessary for the pastor of the place of baptism to transcribe them on a separate sheet of paper. It is not necessary that the facts regarding baptism and the annotations in the baptismal register be transcribed word for word. Transcription of the substantial points will be sufficient, but in the absence of a special form for the certificate a word for word transcription is more valuable to the investigating pastor and more commendable.[15] The usual points to be mentioned in a baptismal certificate are the full name of the baptized party, the full names of the parents and sponsors, the date of birth and of baptism and the place of baptism.

As far as the investigating pastor is concerned, it makes no difference whether the baptismal certificate is sent directly to him or transmitted to him through and with the approval of the diocesan curia. However, transmission through and with the approval of the diocesan curia is recommended when the place of baptism and the contemplataed place of marriage are situated in different dioceses or countries.[16]

[15] Cappello, *De Sacramentis,* III, n. 148.

[16] S. C. de Sacramentis, instr., 4 Jul., 1921, § 5—*AAS,* XIII (1921), 348; Cappello, *De Sacramentis,* III, n. 149.

The investigating pastor satisfies his obligation if he personally calls on the pastor of the place of baptism and with the latter's permission inspects the matter in the baptismal register. Likewise it is permissible for the investigating pastor to call the pastor of the place of baptism by telephone and have him read to him the record of the baptism. However, employment of this method, except in a case of haste, should be discouraged.

If the baptismal records were burned, destroyed or lost, other means must be employed to prove the baptism of the parties, *e. g.*, the reliable testimony of two witnesses or of one absolutely reliable witness (*e. g.*, a sponsor, the minister of the sacrament or one of the parents of the party), or the sworn affirmation of the party, if the party was baptized in adult age. In danger of death the sworn affirmation of the party that he was baptized is sufficient in the absence of other proof.[17] Equivalent proofs taken, for instance, from certificates of Holy Communion or confirmation are acceptable.[18] The fact that parents were zealous and careful about having their children baptized may furnish moral certitude of the baptism, unless some unusual circumstances intervened in their habitual mode of life. However, if time permits, the pastor should refer the matter to the ordinary whenever doubts remain after the pastor himself has exhausted all the available means at his disposal for dispelling them.[19] If time does not permit, he should baptize the person *sub conditione.*[20]

B. *Confirmation.* The Code does not expressly mention the testimony of Confirmation as being required for marriage. However, the Code does state that Catholics who have not received the Sacrament of Confirmation should receive it before they are to be admitted to marriage, if it can be received without a grave inconvenience.[21] The obligation would seem to be a grave one on the part of the nupturients.[22] Although the obligation immediately

[17] Canon 1019.
[18] Cappello, *De Sacramentis,* III, n. 148.
[19] Canon 1031, § 1, 3°.
[20] Cappello, *De Sacramentis,* III, n. 148.
[21] Canon 1021, § 2.
[22] Gasparri, *Tractatus Canonicus de Matrimonio,* n. 139.

binds the nupturients, the pastor in virtue of canon 787 has an obligation to see that the faithful receive Confirmation at an opportune time. And it is certainly opportune that the sacrament be received prior to marriage.

There is a good reason why the Code is silent about the requirement of the testimony of Confirmation from the parties. The testimony seems to be sufficiently taken care of by the inspection of the baptismal register or by the obtaining of the baptismal certificate, which will incorporate a notation of the fact of Confirmation whenever the baptismal register has been properly kept, that is, in accordance with the rules stated in canon 470, § 2. In the absence of a notation of the fact of Confirmation in the baptismal register or baptismal certificate, inspection of the confirmation register, a confirmation certificate, the testimony of a really reliable witness or the oath of the confirmed party (unless the party was confirmed in infancy) will suffice to establish the desired proof of Confirmation.[28]

If the pastor discovers that a nupturient has not received Confirmation, he must investigate if it is a *grave incommodum* for him to receive Confirmation prior to the celebration of the marriage. The *grave incommodum* may arise from many causes. Usually it will arise from the fact that the next confirmation trip of the bishop to the party's parish is at a time that is gravely inconvenient for the party. When the pastor has satisfied himself that a *grave incommodum* prevails, regardless of its cause, he may permit the marriage.

Article 3. Consent of Parents

Regarding the investigation of the consent of the parents to the marriages of their children, a distinction must be made between those nupturients still in their minority and those who have reached their majority.

1. *Nupturients who are still in their minority.* Minors can marry validly without any consent of their parents. However, they cannot marry licitly without their parents' consent or in opposition

[28] Canon 800.

to their reasonable will. Apparently the reason is that without parental guidance minors are oftentimes prone to reflect imprudence in their selection of a partner for marriage. As long as they are minors, children are under *patriapotestas.* Consequently, their duties of filial love, respect and obedience will rightfully prompt them not to enter marriage against the reasonable wishes and mature judgment of their parents. The prescriptions of canon 1034 concern minors only. Hence those who have completed their twenty-first year are not strictly bound to ask and receive the consent of their parents. It would seem that in the matter of requiring consent from their parents all lawfully emancipated minors may be considered equal to those who have reached their majority.

The investigating pastor, having established that the nupturients are minors and not lawfully emancipated, should interrogate them as to whether their parents know of the marriage and give their consent to it. It is understood that the consent of the parents of both parties should be requested, if both parties are minors. No difficulty arises when the parents give their consent. However, should the pastor have a positive suspicion that the parties falsely assert that they have obtained the necessary parental consent, he should consult the parents, if they live in the parish. If the parties come from some other parish, the pastor may consider parental consent as being sufficiently established by the letters of their freedom to marry presented by their proper pastor.

If the parties asked the consent of their parents, but were refused, it is the duty of the pastor to find out if the unwillingness of the parents is reasonable. If the parents are definitely unreasonable, the pastor may proceed with the marriage without consulting the local ordinary.[24] The unreasonableness must be judged from the circumstances and by prudently weighing the reasons for and against the marriage. Mere avarice of the parents, their social and business ambitions for their children, their unreasonable hatred for the party selected by their child, and the fact that they desire a certain marriage that the child definitely dislikes are certainly unjustifiable reasons for the refusal of consent by the parents. If parents indeed have grave reasons for opposing the marriage, but

[24] De Smet, *Betrothment and Marriage,* n. 332; *cf.* canon 1034.

their child, which is a minor, has even more serious reasons for entering marriage, it would seem that the parents in such cases would act unreasonably if they refused their consent. Sometimes children who are minors have no good reason for entering marriage, while their parents may have perfectly justifiable reasons for refusing their consent, *e. g.*, if the marriage would lead to family disgrace, scandal, dissension; if the prospective partner selected by their child is a notorious drunkard, is immoral, is in poor health, incapable, lazy, incompetent to support a wife or family, of inferior status, etc.[25] When the parents are reasonable in their opposition, the investigating pastor is gravely obliged to dissuade the parties from marriage. If the parties insist on marriage, he must refer the matter to the ordinary.[26]

If the pastor considers that there are proportionately serious reasons why the parties should get married, such as grave spiritual danger, the danger of incontinence, concubinage, scandal, etc., it would seem that the pastor is justified in permitting the marriage, in spite of the opposition of the parents and without recourse to the local ordinary. In such a case, opposition from the parents would be unreasonable, because of the serious spiritual danger involved.[27] Likewise, there is no necessity to have recourse to the ordinary when it is impossible to ask parental consent.[28]

Should the nupturients desire to conceal the matter of their forthcoming marriage from their parents for some grave reason, the investigating pastor should inquire what the reason is, and refer the matter to the ordinary.

If only one parent opposes the union and the other consents to it, the pastor may permit the marriage, if the parent who consents is the father. The reason is that the father is the head of the home. If the father dissents while the mother consents, the ordinary should be consulted. However, when the father is dead, the mother's consent suffices.[29] In the event that both parents are dead, it

[25] Gougnard, *Tractatus de Matrimonio*, p. 28.

[26] Canon 1034.

[27] *Cf.* De Smet, *Betrothment and Marriage*, n. 332.

[28] Gougnard, *Tractatus de Matrimonio*, p. 28.

[29] Cappello, *De Sacramentis*, III, n. 191.

seems that it is not necessary that the guardians or nearest relatives of the party be asked for their consent to the marriage. Canon 1034 simply requires that the parents' consent be had. However, the pastor should, for the purpose of avoiding dissension and quarrels, urge the nupturients to consult their guardians or near relatives on the matter.

2. *Nupturients who have reached their majority.* Canon Law does not require those who are over the age of twenty-one to obtain the consent of their parents. However, the natural law should prompt nupturients to seek the wiser and more experienced counsel of their parents in a matter of such very serious importance as marriage. Therefore, the pastor should seek to induce unwilling nupturients to let their parents know of their marriage and seek their advice and counsel. Reasons sometimes arise that will justify the pastor in not urging the parties to seek parental counsel, *e. g.*, when he knows definitely that the parents are unreasonably opposed to the intended marriage.[30]

Article 4. Classification of Matrimonial Impediments

Before giving consideration to the investigation of the matrimonial impediments individually, it is opportune to set forth the various classifications into which these impediments are divided. The very general division of impediments into impediments *in the strict sense* and impediments *in the comprehensive sense* has been referred to above. Impediments in the strict sense are the matrimonial impediments properly so called. The present article will concern matrimonial impediments in the strict sense, *i. e.*, those which are impediments *ex parte personae.* They are classified as follows:

1. *By reason of origin or source* impediments are either of the *natural law,* the *divine positive law,* the *ecclesiastical law* or the *civil law,* depending respectively on whether they have proceeded from the law of nature, from the revealed law of God, from the positive law of the Church or from the law of civil authority.

2. *By reason of extension* impediments are classified as *absolute*

[30] *Cf.* Cappello, *De Sacramentis,* III, n. 191.

and *relative.* An absolute impediment hinders a person from marrying anyone, *e.g.*, lack of the required age is an unqualified and unconditional bar to marriage. A relative impediment forbids a person from marrying certain determinate persons,[31] *e.g.*, consanguinity bars marriage with certain blood relations, but not with all blood relations, nor with persons not related by blood.

3. *By reason of duration* impediments are *perpetual* and *temporary.* Perpetual are those which are of such a nature that they will last always, *e.g.*, spiritual relationship. Temporal are those which of their nature last only for a certain time, *e.g.*, age.[32]

4. *By reason of the possibility of dispensation* impediments are *dispensable* and *indispensable,* depending on whether a dispensation from them can or cannot be obtained. From some impediments the Church cannot dispense, *e.g.*, from *ligamen,* when a baptized married couple have consummated their marriage. From some impediments the Church can but does not dispense, *e.g.*, from the public impediment of crime arising from conjugicide. From other impediments the Church can and does dispense, *e.g.*, from mixed religion.[33]

5. *By reason of degree* impediments are *minor* and *major.* The minor impediments are those enumerated in canon 1042, § 2. All others are considered major impediments.

6. *By reason of their outward disclosure* impediments are *public* and *occult.* Public impediments are those which can be proved in the external forum. Occult are those which do not yield to proof in the external form.[34] Impediments are *public by nature* when the fact on which they are founded is of its own nature public, for instance, the facts of religious profession and sacred orders. An impediment is occult by nature when the fact on which it is founded is of its nature occult, for instance, the fact of a private vow of chastity. It is possible that an impediment *public by nature* may be *de facto occult,* and that an impediment *occult by nature* may be-

[31] De Smet, *Betrothment and Marriage,* n. 235.

[32] Bernardus Culver Alford, *Ius Matrimoniale Comparatum* (Romae: Anonima Libraria Cattolica Italiana, 1938), p. 42.

[33] Cappello, *De Sacramentis,* III, n. 196.

[34] Canon 1037.

come *de facto public*. An impediment is said to be *altogether occult* when it is known to nobody except to the parties and to the confessor. It is *simply occult* when it is known only to a few prudent people who will not divulge it.[85] If the fact on which the impediment is based is known, but it is not known that an impediment arises from *that* fact, the impediment is *materially public* but *formally occult*. However, to constitute a public impediment in the sense of canon 1037, it is sufficient that the fact alone on which the impediment is based be public.[86] Consequently an impediment *materially public* but *formally occult* is really a public impediment because it is provable in the external form.

7. *By reason of the degree of evidence for them* impediments are *certain* or *doubtful*. *Certain impediments* are those which the mind affirms to be present without prudent fear of error. *Doubtful impediments* are those whose presence the mind neither denies nor affirms, but in relation to which it sees some reasons both for affirming and denying their existence. The doubtful impediment may be one of fact (*dubium facti*), one of law (*dubium iuris*), or one of both law and fact (*dubium iuris et facti*). In a doubtful impediment of fact one is certain in his knowledge of the law that an impediment arises from some specific, particular fact, but at the same time is doubtful in his perception of whether that fact really exists. For instance, a pastor knows the law that second cousins are hindered from marrying, but is doubtful whether the couple he is interrogating are really second cousins. In a doubtful impediment of law one has certain knowledge of a given fact, but is doubtful whether an impediment arises from that fact. For instance, a pastor knows for certain that two particular infidel parties are brother and sister, but there is doubt whether the natural law forbids the marriage of brother and sister. In a doubtful impediment of both law and fact there is simply a conjunction of both issues.[87]

8. *By reason of effect* impediments are *prohibitive* and *diriment*. Prohibitive impediments are those which render marriage unlawful.

[85] Cappello, *De Sacramentis*, III, n. 200.

[86] Pont. Comm. Interp. Cod., 25 Jun., 1932—*AAS*, XXIV (1932), 284.

[87] *Cf.* Gasparri, *Tractatus Canonicus de Matrimonio*, n. 222.

Diriment impediments are those which render marriage invalid as well as unlawful. [38]

In the articles immediately following, attention will be given to the investigation of the prohibitive and diriment impediments that may possibly arise in the case of Catholic couples intending marriage.

Article 5. The Impediment of Simple Vow

The simple vow of virginity, of perfect chastity, of not marrying, of taking sacred orders or also of embracing the religious state, renders marriage *unlawful*. No simple vow invalidates marriage except by special prescription of the Holy See.[39]

An example of a simple vow that invalidates marriage by special prescription of the Holy See is that taken by the scholastics of the Society of Jesus.[40]

Ordinarily the investigating pastor may omit to question nupturients on the impediment of the simple vow; for outside of those professed in religious communities the number of persons who take or make vows is small, if not almost negligible. However, if a nupturient formerly belonged to a religious community, or spent time in a seminary studying for the priesthood, or even lived a very pious and self-sacrificing life in the world, there is a possibility that he may have made one of the five above-mentioned vows, at least privately. Such persons should be questioned carefully on the impediment of the simple vow.[41]

It is well to confine the investigation of the impediment of the simple vow to the separate examination of the nupturients, because the impediment is frequently occult. Moreover, those who have left or were dismissed from religious communities and those who may have made private vows do not, as a rule, desire to discuss the matter before others.

When a nupturient asserts that he made one of the simple vows mentioned above, the pastor should not immediately conclude that

[38] Canon 1036.

[39] Canon 1058, §§ 1, 2.

[40] Cappello, *De Sacramentis*, III, n. 292.

[41] *Cf.* De Smet, *Betrothment and Marriage*, n. 332.

the impediment of the simple vow is present. Many people, especially scrupulous people, tend to consider simple promises made to God as real vows. It will be necessary, therefore, for the pastor to make sure that the conditions for a real vow were present; namely, (a) that the promise of virginity, of perfect chastity, of taking sacred orders, of not marrying, or of embracing the religious state was actually made to God, not to the Blessed Virgin or to a saint; (b) that the party intended not only to make a promise but also to bind himself by means of the virtue of religion; (c) that the promise was made with perfect deliberation; (d) that there was no substantial error; (e) that the party was perfectly free in making the promise; (f) that the matter of the vow was morally possible for him.[42]

The five vows mentioned in canon 1058, § 1 are distinct from each other.

1. *The vow of viriginity* is the vow to abstain from the first carnal consummated act by which virginity is lost materially, formally and irreparably.[43] Virginity is lost materially, formally and irreparably by the first voluntary act of complete sexual satisfaction.[44] The one who violates this vow sins indeed but thereafter can no longer be bound by this particular matrimonial impediment of simple vow.

2. *The vow of perfect chastity* is the vow to abstain from all sexual pleasure, both internal and external, lawful and unlawful.[45] This vow differs from the vow of virginity, because it can be made by one who has already lost his virginity both materially and formally. If one with a vow of perfect chastity violates his vow or contracts marriage, the impediment of the vow still remains.

[42] Noldin, *Summa Theologia Moralis*, II, *De Praeceptis*, nn. 207-213.

[43] Cappello, *De Sacramentis*, III, n. 298; Gasparri, *Tractatus Canonicus de Matrimonio*, n. 427; Payen, *De Matrimonio*, n. 825; *cf. etiam*, A. Vermeersch, *De Castitate* (Romae: Università Gregoriana, 1919), nn. 139-143; A. R. D. Eschbach, *Disputationes Physiologico-theologicae* (2. ed., Romae, 1901), 48, c. 2, n. 4.

[44] Ayrinhac-Lydon, *Marriage Legislation in the New Code of Canon Law*, p. 96.

[45] Gasparri, *Tractatus Canonicus de Matrimonio*, n. 428.

Consequently if his partner in marriage died, he still is forbidden to marry.

3. *The vow of receiving sacred orders* is the vow to receive the sub-diaconate, diaconate or priesthood.[46] If one bound by this vow marries, he commits sin. Even after the marriage the vow itself does not cease to exist.

4. *The vow of embracing the religious state* is the vow to enter a religious institute, *i. e.*, an order or a religious congregation.[47] Like the vow of receiving sacred orders, this vow remains after marriage, unless the party was legitimately released from it.

5. *The vow of not marrying* is simply the vow to refrain from contracting marriage. This vow ceases, if the party who made it marries.

When the pastor has satisfied himself that the nupturient has made one of the above vows, he must inquire whether or not the vow has ceased. Canon 1311 states the various ways a vow ceases: (a) *By lapse of time, e. g.*, if the vow was made for a specific time and that time is now completed. (b) *By a substantial change in the matter promised,* so that the vow becomes morally impossible. (c) *By failure of a condition, e. g.*, if the vow was made subject to a condition and the condition was not verified. (d) *By cessation of the final cause of the vow, i. e.,* if the very motive or dominant purpose of the vow ceases. This is the case when one with a vow of virginity has lost virginity materially and formally by a completed act of sexual satisfaction. (e) *By annulment.* (f) *By dispensation.* (g) *By commutation* (canon 1314). The pastor must have sufficient evidence from the party to produce moral certainty that the vow has ceased.

Being an impediment of ecclesiastical origin, the impediment of simple vow is subject to dispensation. Consequently, if the vow has not already ceased, the pastor should aid the parties in petitioning the competent authority for the dispensation. In this connection it is in order to mention that vows are *reserved* or *non-reserved.* A *reserved* vow is one from which the Holy See alone can grant a dispensation. All others are *non-reserved.* Only two private vows are

[46] Canon 949.

[47] *Cf.* canons 487 and 488.

reserved to the Holy See: (1) the vow of perfect and perpetual chastity and (a) the vow of entering a religious institute with solemn vows. Their reservation obtains only when they were made absolutely and after the party had completed the eighteenth year.[48] In regard to public vows, it will be necessary to consult the constitutions of the particular religious institute to which the nupturient belonged in order to find out whether the vow he made while in the institute was reserved or non-reserved. If on investigation the pastor finds out that a nupturient is bound by a reserved vow, the petition for a dispensation from it must be submitted to the Holy See. If the vow is not reserved, the petition should be referred to the proper competent authority. According to canon 1313 non-reserved vows may be dispensed for a just cause, provided the dispensation does not injure the acquired rights of others, (1) by the local ordinary, who may dispense his own subjects anywhere and non-subjects sojourning in his territory, (2) by the religious superior of an exempt clerical religious institute, who may dispense professed members and the novices of his institute and also such others who stay day and night at the religious house for the purpose of service or education, or because of sickness, or even for the sake of hospitality, (3) by those who have delegated power to dispense.[49]

Article 6. The Impediment of Legal Relationship

Two canons of the Code deal with the impediment of legal relationship: canon 1059 and canon 1080. Canon 1059 states: "In those regions where the relationship arising from legal adoption renders marriage unlawful according to the civil law, marriage is also unlawful in Canon Law." According to canon 1080, "Those who by civil law are incapable of marrying each other on account of legal adoption are also incapable of contracting a valid marriage in Canon Law."

The impediment of legal relationship arising from adoption is, therefore, a *prohibitive* impediment to marriage in those countries

[48] Canon 1309.

[49] Woywod, *A Practical Commentary on the Code of Canon Law,* n. 1333.

wherever the civil law recognizes it to be such. It is a *diriment* impediment in those countries where the civil law recognizes it to be a diriment impediment. In other words, the Canon Law simply canonizes the civil law on the subject.[50]

For the investigation of this impediment the pastor will have to consult the civil law of the country or state wherein the marriage is to take place. He will have to find out if the civil law recognizes the impediment of legal relationship and, if so, whether it renders marriage only unlawful, or whether it renders marriage both unlawful and invalid. It will also be necessary for the pastor to find out what is the extent of the impediment and how long it lasts, what its effects are and what are the various conditions under which it may militate against the validity or lawfulness of marriage. The nature, conditions and effects of this impediment vary considerably in different countries. There is no perfect uniformity of legislation concerning it.

In the United States the impediment of legal relationship will not cause much difficulty to the investigating pastor; for, although legal adoption is recognized in some states, it does not constitute an impediment to marriage except in Puerto Rico. In Puerto Rico legal adoption is considered a diriment impediment to marriage. It exists between:

1. the adoptive father or mother and the person adopted;
2. the person adopted and the surviving husband or wife of the adopter;
3. the adopter and the surviving husband or wife of the adopted;
4. the legitimate descendants of the adopter and the adopted person during the time the adoption exists.[51]

Ordinarily, pastors in the United States need not question the nupturients on the impediment of legal adoption. If the nupturients have come from other countries where the impediment of legal rela-

[50] *Cf.* Ayrinhac-Lydon, *Marriage Legislation in the New Code of Canon Law*, p. 97.

[51] Civil Code of Puerto Rico, 1911-1913, n. 3205, nn. 3, 4; Alford, *Ius Matrimoniale Comparatum*, n. 163; John J. Carberry, "Legal Relationship as an Impediment to Marriage in the United States," *AER*, XC (1934), 394-403.

tionship exists, it is necessary to make a distinction in regard to the investigation of the impediment. If they have left their domicile in the foreign country and intend to reside in the United States, they have lost their former domicile and the law of their mother country concerning legal adoption no longer binds them.[52] If they have not given up their domicile in the mother country, but just came to stay in the United States for a while, they are still bound by the impediment of legal adoption that exists in their mother country. When such a case arises, it is expedient for the pastor not to rely on his personal knowledge of the civil law in regard to legal adoption, but to consult a civil lawyer on the matter.

Should a pastor discover that the parties are bound by the impediment of legal relationship, he cannot admit them to marriage unless a dispensation has been obtained according to the ecclesiastical law. A dispensation from the impediment in the civil law alone does not suffice, for the binding force of the impediment of legal relationship comes from the Canon Law; not from the civil law.[53] Nevertheless, the pastor should conform also with the prescriptions of the civil law in regard to getting a civil release from the civil impediment of legal relationship, in order to avoid conflict with the civil authorities.

Article 7. The Impediment of Age

A boy who has not completed his sixteenth year and a girl who has not completed her fourteenth year cannot validly marry.[54] The investigating pastor, therefore, is obliged to make sure that the nupturients have reached these legal ages before admitting them to marriage.

The fourteenth year in the case of the girl and the sixteenth year in the case of the boy must be physically complete. Moreover, they must be solar years.[55] It is not enough if the years be morally

[52] *Cf.* Woywod, *A Practical Commentary on the Code of Canon Law*, n. 1037; canon 95.

[53] Chelodi, *Ius Matrimoniale*, n. 57.

[54] Canon 1067, § 1.

[55] Payen, *De Matrimonio*, n. 941; Ayrinhac-Lydon, *Marriage Legislation in the New Code of Canon Law*, p. 125.

complete only. Nor is it allowable to reckon in lunar years. A party who is short of the legal age even by a single day cannot marry validly as long as a dispensation is not granted.[56]

The pastor must compute the years according to the calendar. As the birth of a party scarcely ever coincides with the beginning of the day, the ages of the parties must be computed according to the prescription of canon 34, § 3, 3°. Consequently the first day will not be counted. A boy, therefore, will have reached the legal age after the sixteenth anniversary of his birthday and a girl after the fourteenth anniversary of her birthday. Thus a male child born on June 13, 1924, cannot validly marry until June 14, 1940; a female child born on the same day cannot validly marry until June 14, 1938.

All the points in the foregoing paragraphs must be kept in mind by the investigating pastor. Usually the observant pastor will be able to declare from a glance at the parties whether they have reached the legal age for marriage. However, he should not rely too much on his observation of the parties, for many persons are actually younger and others are actually older than their appearance indicates.

While in most cases the pastor can rely on the assertions of the nupturients concerning their ages, he should not too readily accept as true the statement of every nupturient concerning his age. If the pastor is suspicious that the parties are not telling the truth in regard to their ages, he should ascertain their true ages from some other source, *e. g.*, from their baptismal certificate, birth certificate, school records, or from a reliable witness such as a parent, sponsor at baptism, a school mate, a close associate, or, as a last resort, from the suppletory oath of the parties themselves. Pastoral experience has proved that nupturients sometimes misrepresent their ages when petitioning for a marriage license, especially when they are below the legal civil age for marriage, which is usually more advanced than the legal canonical age. Hence in the absence of adminicular proof of the ages of the parties, the marriage license should not be invariably accepted as furnishing their correct ages.

[56] Cappello, *De Sacramentis,* III, b. 335.

Though the Code recognizes as valid the marriage of a boy after completing the age of sixteen and the marriage of a girl after completing the age of fourteen, it does not encourage marriage at a very early age. Rather, it prescribes that pastors should persuade youthful nupturients from marrying at an earlier age than the one made acceptable by the custom of the locality.[57] Therefore, pastors must take into account local circumstances when investigating the ages of the parties. It may be regarded as a general rule, subject to some exceptions, that in countries and regions where boys and girls reach natural puberty at an early age, the customary age for marriage is early. Natural puberty is hastened or retarded by such factors as climate, temperature, race, country, urban or rural environment, etc. In warmer climates it occurs earlier than in the temperate and frigid zones. Marrying at an earlier age than is customary in a locality is undesirable, especially from a social viewpoint. Besides, very young people are immature physically, mentally, emotionally and morally for marriage and are apt to enter into unwise unions.[58] While the pastor should dissuade young people from marrying below the local customary age, he would not be acting in accordance with the spirit of the law if he refused to assist at the marriage, when there are grave reasons why a young couple should be married. Such reasons, for instance, would be the fact that the parties are living in concubinage, that they are habituated in the sin of fornication, that there is need to legitimize their offspring, that one or both parties are seriously exposed to the danger of incontinence or that the stigma of disgrace must be removed from the girl. The younger the boy or girl, the graver also the reasons required.

As it is the desire of the Church, when it is legitimately possible, to avoid conflict with the state, the pastor should investigate whether the parties observe the state laws in regard to the required age. Several states forbid marriage below a certain age. That age varies considerably in the United States, the most usual age being the age of eighteen for men and sixteen for women.[59] Each pastor, therefore,

[57] Canon 1067, § 2.

[58] *Cf.* Cappello, *De Sacramentis,* III, n. 335; Wernz, *Ius Decretalium,* IV, n. 311.

[59] Woywod, *A Practical Commentary on the Code of Canon Law,* n. 1047.

must acquaint himself with the local civil statutes on the matter and investigate whether nupturients observe them.

Very seldom is a dispensation from the impediment of age granted by the Church. It is never granted if the party or parties have not attained the use of reason. In such a case marriage is forbidden by the natural law, from which the Church cannot dispense. Usually dispensations from the impediment of age are granted only in countries where early marriage is common, as among certain primitives in missionary countries. As the customary age in the United States is well above the age of sixteen for the boy and fourteen for the girl, there will seldom be a request for a dispensation from nonage. If a request should be made by the parties, it should be forwarded to the competent authority only for grave reasons.

Article 8. The Impediment of Impotency

Antecedent and perpetual impotency, whether on the part of the man or on the part of the woman, whether known to the other party or not, whether absolute or relative, invalidates marriage by the law of nature. If the impediment is doubtful, either by a doubt of law or by a doubt of fact, marriage is not to be prohibited. Sterility, however, neither invalidates nor prohibits marriage.[60]

The impediment of impotency is one of the most difficult impediments to investigate satisfactorily. Three important reasons may be alleged for this difficulty: (1) because society looks upon impotency as a serious human misfortune, due frequently to causes suggestive of sin, and as a result a nupturient may resent being interrogated on the subject or, if interrogated, may answer untruthfully; (2) because there is much ignorance concerning the fact that a diriment impediment of impotency exists and (3) because very frequently a party cannot assert with certainty before marriage that he is or is not impotent.

It is, perhaps, safe to assert that the impediment of impotency is not an infrequent occurrence. However, when impotency is present, the party no doubt is often unaware of it. On that account, it seems perfectly legitimate for a pastor ordinarily to omit interrogation of the nupturients on the impediment of impotency, unless there

[60] Canon 1068.

is some positive indication or suspicion of its presence. Some grounds for suspecting the presence of the impediment are present when a man has undergone the operation of double vasectomy with a view to sterilizing him; when a previous marriage of a nupturient was declared invalid because of impotency; and when one of the reasons alleged for the dissolution of a nupturient's previous ratified and non-consummated marriage was impotency. The Rota occasionally adds a *vetitum* in its *sententia,* which *vetitum* prohibits the impotent party from entering into a new marriage or marrying without consulting the Holy See.[61] If a party who was given such a *vetitum* presents himself before a pastor for marriage, the pastor should act in accordance with the contents of the *vetitum.* The fact that a nupturient is known in the community to be a sexual pervert or invert may likewise give sufficient grounds for investigation of the impediment of impotency. When a diocesan regulation or a prescribed questionnaire has formulated questions on the impediment of impotency, the pastor should not hesitate to address them in a tactful manner to the parties intending marriage.

It has been pointed out that prudence should characterize prenuptial investigation. In connection with the impediment of impotency prudence frequently dictates that the matter be proposed not in the form of interrogation, but in the form of instruction. Moreover, as the impediment is usually occult, when it does occur, any investigation to be made concerning it should be confined to the internal form. Should a party freely assert that he has serious reasons for doubting his potency, he should be directed to consult a physician qualified to give an opinion on the case from the point of view not only of scientific knowledge but also of Christian probity. If the physician declares without the shadow of a doubt that the party is impotent, incurably and perpetually, the pastor cannot admit him to marriage. If any doubt remains in the physician's mind, the nupturi-

[61] *Cf. S. R. R., Nullit. matrim.,* 4 Aug., 1927, *Coram R. P. D., Maximo Massimi,* dec. XLII, n. 11—*Decisiones,* XIX (1927), 368; *S. R. R., Nullit. matrim.,* 1 Mart., 1926, *Coram R. P. D., Maximo Massimi,* dec., VIII, n. 9—*Decisiones,* XVIII (1926), 61; *S. R. R., Nullit. matrim. et disp. super rato,* 20 Mart., 1926, dec., XI, n. 34—*Decisiones,* XVIII (1926), 92; *S. R. R., Nullit. matrim.,* 10 Mart., 1925, *Coram R. P. D., Ubaldo Manucci,* dec., XVII, n. 6—*Decisiones,* XVII (1925), 129.

ent may be admitted to marriage.[62] It is best to request the *written* opinion of the physician, for then the pastor will be better able to judge whether the opinion is in accordance with the requirements of the Code for the impediment.

In order that the pastor may be equipped with sufficient knowledge to investigate the presence of the impediment, the reading of some good author or authors on the subject is advisable.[63] Here only a brief survey of the principal features of the subject can be presented.

Authors distinguish two kinds of impotency, *impotentia generandi* and *impotentia coeundi.* According to the best authors *impotentia coeundi* is the only impotency that invalidates marriage; not so the *impotentia generandi.* Another name for *impotentia generandi* is sterility.[64]

Impotentia coeundi may be defined as the inability or incapacity of a man or a woman to perform the conjugal or sexual act by which true male semen is deposited in a natural manner in the female vagina. It is the act by which the parties become one flesh, and is commonly and variously termed, *copula, copula perfecta, coitus,* marital congress, the marital act, the act of coition.

In order that a man be considered capable of performing the marital act, there are required on his part (1) at least one testicle capable of producing true male semen; (2) a male member capable of intromission into the female vagina in a natural manner and capable of emitting the semen therein.[65] It is not necessary for potency that the semen be fecund. Infecund semen, *i. e.,* true semen which is devoid of spermatozoids, is sufficient.[66]

[62] Canon 1068, § 2.

[63] The following authors are offered by way of suggestion: Vermeersch, *De Castitate,* nn. 57-88; Gasparri, *Tractatus Canonicus de Matrimonio,* nn. 502-550; Cappello, *De Sacramentis,* III, nn. 340-389; I. Rossi, *De Impedimento Impotentiae* (Romae, 1910); Eschbach, *Casus de feminae impotentia* (Romae, 1899); O'Malley-Walsh, *Essays in Pastoral Medicine* (New York: Longmans, Green & Co., 1925), pp. 326-344.

[64] De Smet, *Betrothment and Marriage,* n. 276; Vermeersch, *De Castitate,* n. 58.

[65] Cappello, *De Sacramentis,* III, n. 342.

[66] *S. R. R., Nullit. matrim.,* 14 Jun., 1923, *R. P. D., Coram Maximo Massimi,* dec., XII, n. 6—*decisiones,* XV (1923), 104.

In order that a woman be considered capable of performing the marital act, a vagina capable of receiving the male member is necessary. Therefore, even though the vagina be present, but for some reason or other (*e. g.*, incurable vaginismus or excessive narrowness) it is incapable of receiving the male member, she is impotent.[67] A controversy exists as to whether a woman who is deprived of her womb and ovaries is or is not impotent. One opinion holds that she is impotent.[68] The other opinion maintains that she is not impotent.[69] The latter opinion seems to be supported by several decisions of the Holy See.[70] According to a declaration of the Holy Office issued on January 16, 1895, cases of the kind under discussion should be referred individually to the Holy See.[71]

For impotency to invalidate marriage, the following conditions are necessary: (1) it must be *antecedent to the marriage, i. e.*, it must precede the mutual exchange of matrimonial consent by the spouses; (2) it must be certain, *i. e.*, all prudent fear of doubt about the person's incapacity must be excluded; (3) it must be *perpetual, i. e.*, it must be incurable by lawful means or by such means as do not involve serious danger to life.[72]

Provided the conditions mentioned in the preceding paragraph are fulfilled, the impediment is present, irrespective of whether the impotency is natural or accidental, known or unknown to one or both parties, absolute or relative. A party is absolutely impotent when he is incapable of marital congress with any member of the other sex.

[67] Cappello, *De Sacramentis*, III, n. 342.

[68] I. Antonelli, *Medicina Pastoralis* (Romae, 1932), n. 536 ss; *De Conceptu Impotentiae et Sterilitatis Relate ad Matrimonium* (Romae, 1900), p. 10 ss; Bucceroni, *Institutiones Theologiae Moralis*, IV, *De Matrimonio* (Romae, 1915), n. 958 cum nota, pp. 487-490; Santi-Leitner, *Praelectiones Iuris Canonici*, lib. IV, tit. 15, n. 1, in nota; Augustinus Lehmkuhl, *Theologia Moralis*, II, n. 975; Noldin, *Theologia Moralis*, III, *De Sacramentis*, n. 571.

[69] Gasparri, *Tractatus Canonicus de Matrimonio*, nn. 523-538; Josephus Cardinalis D'Annibale, *Summula Theologiae Moralis* (3. ed.), III, n. 413, nota 6; A. Ballerini, *Opus Theologiae Moralis*, VI, *De Matrimonio* (Prati, 1900), n. 865; Cappello, *De Sacramentis*, III, n. 358.

[70] *Cf.* Vermeersch, *De Castitate*, n. 59.

[71] *Coll.* n. 1907, footnote 2.

[72] Gasparri, *Tractatus Canonicus de Matrimonio*, nn. 539-543.

He is relatively impotent when he is similarly incapable in reference to a certain member or even several members of the other sex.[73] Absolute impotency, therefore, hinders the party from marrying anyone. Relative impotency forbids marriage only with a certain person or several designated persons.

From the viewpoint of its immediate cause, impotency may be classified as (1) *organic,* (2) *functional* and (3) *psychic.*

Organic impotency, also called mechanical or instrumental,[74] arises from congenital or acquired absence, malformations, distortions and deficiencies of the genital organs, by which the act of coition is rendered impossible. In functional impotency the genital organs are anatomically sound, but due to some disease, functional fault or pathological cause, the party is rendered incapable of performing the conjugal act. Psychic impotency proceeds from some psychic or mental cause such as fear, joy, repugnance, hatred, aversion, but is usually curable. It is often due to perversions of the sex impulse such as sadism, masochism, fetishism and sex inversion.[75]

It has previously been noted that sterility or *impotentia generandi* does not constitute a diriment impediment to marriage. Sterility means the incapacity of procreating children despite the unquestioned possibility of an act of perfect conjugal union between the parties.[76]

In connection with sterility there arises the question of sterilization for eugenic purposes, which is legalized today in many countries and states. In America there are quite a number of sterilized criminals and defectives. As the propaganda for sterilization is growing, there is a possibility that some sterilized parties may present themselves to the pastor for marriage. The question is, does eugenical sterilization ever cause impotency and constitute a diriment impediment to marriage? In answering that question a few words on the operation for sterilization are necessary. The sterilization operation in women

[73] Vermeersch, *De Castitate,* n. 70.

[74] *S. R. R., Nullit. matrim.,* 29 Jul., 1920, *Coram R. P. D., Petro Rossetti,* dec., XXIII, n. 3—*Decisiones,* XII (1920), 215-226.

[75] *Cf.* O'Malley-Walsh, *Essays in Pastoral Medicine,* pp. 331-334; De Smet, *Betrothment and Marriage,* n. 276.

[76] *S. R. R. nullit. matrim.,* 20 Mart., 1926, *Coram R. P. D., Iulio Grazioli,* dec., XI, n. 6—*Decisiones,* XVIII (1926), 79; *Cf. etiam* Meaker, *Human Sterility* (Baltimore: Williams & Wilkins Co., 1934), p. 3.

is called *fallectomy*; in men *vasectomy*. Sometimes X-rays are used for sterilization purposes. Mere sterilization in women does not render them impotent. In men the operation called vasectomy can be of two kinds: *Simple vasectomy* and *double vasectomy*. In *simple vasectomy* only one of the canals or ducts that convey the male semen, which has been produced in the testicles, is cut or ligated, the other canal remaining intact. In *double vasectomy* both these canals or ducts are cut or ligated, so that emission of the semen in the female vagina becomes impossible if the operation has been performed effectively. If, then, the operation called double vasectomy is so effectively performed that there is no possibility for the male semen to be deposited in the female vagina in a natural manner, and the results of the operation cannot be cured without an operation that would endanger the life of the man, all the conditions for the impediment of impotency are present. It seems certain that the pastor could not admit such a one to marriage. However, each individual case must be thoroughly investigated, and a medical examination by medical experts is necessary to determine the matter finally, for in regard to double vasectomy in general medical men are not agreed as to whether its effects are incurable.[77]

In regard to hermaphroditism the general principles of impotence also hold. If hermaphrodites are capable of the *actus coeundi* they must be admitted to marriage: if they are definitely incapable thereof, because of an insufficiency of organs and that condition is incurable without a serious operation that would endanger life, the pastor cannot permit the marriage. Cases of true hermaphroditism are rare. Some cases of hermaphroditism have occurred in which the true sex of the party remained scientifically undetermined after medical examination. Most hermaphrodites on examination prove to be pseudohermaphrodites. One sex or the other predominates.[78]

[77] Gasparri, *Tractatus Canonicus de Matrimonio,* II, Appendix, *De Vasectomia,* pp. 467-471; De Smet, *Betrothment and Marriage,* n. 276; P. Joannes Ferreres, *De Vasectomia Duplici necnon de Matrimonio Mulieris Excisae* (ed. altera, Madrid, 1913), pp. 55-58, 100-107; *cf.* Arend, "De Genuina Ratione Impedimenti Impotentiae," *ETL,* IX (1932), 28-69.

[78] Hugh Hampton Young, *Genital Abnormalities, Hermaphroditism and Related Adrenal Diseases* (Baltimore: Williams & Wilkins Co., 1937), pp. 46-206.

Very rarely will it occur that a hermaphrodite will present himself to the pastor with a view to marriage. However, should it happen that one manifests his condition to the pastor and desires to marry, the pastor should refer him to an expert physician who may determine the predominant sex and decide whether or not the party is impotent.

Since antecendent and perpetual impotency is an impediment to marriage which is rooted in and sanctioned by the very law of nature, the parties cannot obtain a dispensation from it.

Article 9. The Impediment of Ligamen

One who is bound by a valid bond of marriage, even though this marriage is not consummated, cannot validly contract a second marriage as long as the existing marriage bond remains intact. The solitary exception to this otherwise universal rule consists in the marriage made possible by the operation of the *privilegium fidei*. Though the first marriage be invalid and dissolved for some cause, it is not lawful to contract another marriage before it is certainly and legally evident that the former marriage was invalid or dissolved.[79]

The impediment of previous bond of marriage, also called *ligamen*, constitutes a diriment impediment to marriage. It excludes bigamous and polygamous unions, whether simultaneous or successive.[80]

Before the impediment of *ligamen* can arise it is necessary that a valid marriage actually exist. The existence of such a valid marriage, in virtue of its creation of the impediment of *ligamen*, precludes throughout its duration the possibility of a new marriage. The only exception to this law as above mentioned is provided by the operation of the case known as the *privilegium fidei*. This case embraces the use of the Pauline privilege and also the dissolution in favor of the faith and under specifically restricted conditions of the natural non-sacramental bond of marriage as effected through

[79] Canon 1069, §§ 1, 2.

[80] Gasparri, *Tractatus Canonicus de Matrimonio*, n. 552.

the plenitude of the Roman Pontiff's ministerial power.[81] In cases where the use of the Pauline privilege has been legitimately permitted, the first marriage is dissolved at the moment the second is contracted.[82] When a previous marriage has been contracted invalidly or, as a valid marriage, admits of dissolution, neither of the parties involved can proceed to new nuptials unless there is evidence that a declaration of nullity has been given or that a dissolution of the marriage has been obtained by due process of ecclesiastical law.

Today the investigation of nupturients on the impediment of *ligamen* merits the particular attention of the pastor. Civil divorce with the right to remarry has become deeply rooted in the civilization and culture of many lands, including the United States.[83] Although the evil of remarriage after civil divorce has affected chiefly the non-Catholic population, there are instances where Catholics have actually sought to remarry during the lifetime of an earlier or first spouse. This fact is emphasized by the Sacred Congregation of the Sacraments in regard to emigrants from Europe, who have been able in their deception of pastors to get married again while their previous spouses were living in Europe.[84] The concentration of the greater part of the population in large cities, the mobility of the population, the frequent changes in residence and the fact that the past history of one nupturient is very frequently unknown to the other contribute to make the task of investigating the impediment difficult, and demand more vigilance and care on the part of the pastor.

Interrogation of the nupturients on the impediment of *ligamen* may take place in the examination of both parties together. If the pastor has any suspicion that one party or both are concealing the truth, it is well to repeat the questions in the separate examination

[81] *Cf.* Ayrinhac-Lydon, *Marriage Legislation in the New Code of Canon Law*, pp. 325, 326.

[82] Ayrinhac-Lydon, *Marriage Legislation in the New Code of Canon Law*, p. 131.

[83] Edgar Schmiedeler, *An Introductory Study of the Family* (New York: The Century Co., 1930), p. 279.

[84] 4 Jul., 1921—*AAS*, XIII (1921), 348.

of the parties. If the suspicion still remains, the pastor will have to have recourse to other means such as the interrogation of capable and trustworthy witnesses or the consultation of reliable records. At what precise time during the interrogation the questions regarding *ligamen* should be asked is not mentioned in the Code. However, it would seem that the most opportune time is immediately after the general questions on the identification of the parties. The reason is this: if the parties should happen to be bound by the impediment of *ligamen,* the pastor will be saved the trouble of examining the parties in the other impediments.

The interrogation of the parties should be more intensive, when they are unknown personally to the pastor, when they have traveled extensively, when they have lived since the age of puberty in places other than the pastor's parish, when their occupations are such that their residence has not been stable and when they actually belong to other parishes. The possibility of such persons having been married previously is not so remote as it is in the case of those who live a life of stability in one parish.

When the parties are well known to the pastor, the interrogation need not be so intensive. Nevertheless, the pastor should not presume that because the parties are well known to him, they are free from the impediment of *ligamen.* It is a strange fact that some apparently conscientious Catholics, blinded perhaps by love, have all too frequently succeeded in concealing from pastors the fact of their previous marriage, and thereupon entered marriage a second time with a church ceremony—but invalidly of course—while their lawful partners were yet living.

Careful scrutiny of the records of the baptisms of the parties, or of authentic and recent baptismal certificates will valuably aid the pastor in ascertaining the freedom of the parties from the impediment of *ligamen*; because since the time of the promulgation of the *Ne temere* decree, pastors who assist at marriages are obliged to take care that the fact of marriage be entered in the *baptismal* as well as in the matrimonial register.[85] The Code has a similar provision, except for marriages of conscience, and requires that the fact be noted when baptismal certificates are is-

[85] S. C. C. decr., *Ne temere,* 2 Aug., 1907, III—*Fontes,* n. 4340.

sued.[86] However, absolute reliance cannot be placed on baptismal records or on baptismal certificates, because some pastors have been negligent apparently in their duty of entering the fact of marriage in the baptismal book, or of sending notice of the marriage to the pastor of the parties' place of baptism.[87] A faithful adherence to the laws on the banns of marriage aids considerably in detecting the impediment of *ligamen,* if it be present. When the banns are published according to provision of law in the other proper parishes of the parties, the investigating pastor should await the letters of these other pastors concerning the outcome of the banns.[88]

As many divorced persons consider themselves single, although their lawful spouses are still living, it is not advisable to put the question on *ligamen* in the form, "Are you single?" or "Are you unmarried?" It is altogether likely that such persons will answer these questions in the affirmative. It is better to put the question in some such form as this, "Were you ever married previously?" or, "Have you been married before?" or, "Have you ever been married before and received a divorce?"

Careful inspection of the civil marriage license previous to the marriage is to be much recommended. The fact of previous marriage and divorce is usually mentioned in the license, if the party on interrogation manifested that fact to the civil official who issued the license. Some pastors in the rush and hurry that often precedes the wedding ceremony are tempted not to inspect the marriage license before the wedding. Instances, therefore, have occurred where the pastor discovered from the civil marriage license immediately after the wedding that a nupturient was previously married and divorced.

Parties should be questioned not only as to whether they were previously married at a Catholic ceremony, but also as to whether they were married at a civil or non-Catholic ceremony. If it be revealed that they were married before a civil official or a non-

[86] Canon 470, § 2.

[87] *Cf.* S. C. de Sacramentis, instr., 6 Mart., 1911—*AAS,* III (1911), 102; instr., 4 Jul., 1921—*AAS,* XIII (1921), 348.

[88] Canon 1029.

Catholic minister, a few questions as to whether or not the circumstances of canon 1098 were present are in order.

When a party asserts that he was married previously, but that he obtained through the proper legal and canonical channels a declaration of nullity of the marriage or a dissolution of his marriage in virtue of the privilege of the faith, or a dispensation either from a ratified and non-consummated marriage or from the natural bond of marriage, the pastor cannot rely solely on the word of the party. He must have concrete evidence, preferably in the form of an authentic document, that the declaration of nullity of the marriage, the decree of dissolution of the marriage or the dispensation from the ratified non-consummated marriage was obtained by due process of law.[89] In this connection the record of the party's baptism or an authentic recent baptismal certificate will prove helpful.[90]

The most common means by which marriage is dissolved is death. Because it is the Church's desire to guard most carefully the indissolubility of marriage, she has been very definite and particular in her demand for establishing with at least moral certainty the death of a previous spouse before permitting the surviving partner to enter a new marriage. The Church's insistence in this regard is especially noticeable whenever there is question of a presumed death.[91] Various replies and responses have been issued by the Holy See which indicate that the utmost diligence should be employed in the matter of establishing the fact of death.[92] The

[89] See pp. 135-138.

[90] Canon 1988.

[91] C. 19, X, *de sponsalibus et matrimonio,* IV, 1; c. 2, X, *de secundis nuptiis,* IV, 21.

[92] S. C. S. Off., instr., *Ingentes bellorum clades,* 22 Jun., 1822—Feije, *De Impedimentis et Dispensationibus Matrimonialibus,* pp. 816-818; S. C. S. Off., decr., *Cum alias,* 21 Aug., 1670—*Fontes,* n. 742; S. C. S. Off., resp. ad Vic. Apost. Transvaal, 23 Jun., 1671—*Fontes,* n. 745; S. C. de Prop. Fide, instr. (ad Pro-Vic. Apost. Tonkin., Occid.), 1792—*Fontes,* n. 4632; S. C. S. Off., resp., Nank., 22 Mart., 1865— *Fontes,* n. 982; S. C. S. Off., resp. ad Vic. Apost., Corea, 12 Sept., 1855—*Fontes,* n. 934; S. C. S. Off., resp. ad Vic. Apost. Pondicherry, 28 Jun., 1865 —*Fontes,* n. 984; S. C. S. Off., resp. Tchely, Meridio-Occid., 21 Nov., 1866—*Fontes,* n. 997; S. C. de Sacramentis, resp. (Messanen.-Rhegienen.), 12 Mart., 1910—*AAS,* II (1910), 196-199; resp. (Mohilovien.), 16 Dec., 1910—*AAS,* III (1911), 26-29; resp., 1914—*AAS,* VII (1915), 40; resp. 1915—*AAS,* VII (1915),

most complete and most important of all these documents was the instruction *Matrimonii vinculo,* issued by the Holy Office on May 13, 1868. As frequent reference has been made to it in the more recent replies of the Holy See, its directions may be employed today in establishing the death of a previous spouse.[93]

The full text of the instruction *Matrimonii vinculo* is to be found in the Appendix.[94] Here only the important points will be noted.

When the nupturient contends that his former spouse is deceased, the pastor cannot accept his word alone as constituting full proof of death. It would seem resonable, however, to maintain that the pastor need not hesitate about permitting the marriage, when he has personal knowledge of the former spouse's death or when it is a matter of more or less common knowledge in the neighborhood.

When the pastor does not know personally of the spouse's death and the neighbors are not aware of it, direct proof of death should be obtained, if available. Documentary proof (*e. g.*, an authentic certificate of death issued by the pastor, hospital, army, navy, or the civil government of the place) is preferable. In the absence of documentary evidence, the testimony of two reliable witnesses should be sought. If their testimony is concordant and circumstances point to the truth of their statements that the former spouse is dead, their testimony may be considered sufficient. Close relatives, friends and associates of the spouse are perhaps the most desirable and reliable as witnesses. Even the testimony of one witness who is above all suspicion may be accepted as furnishing moral certainty of death, if it is supported by adminicular evidence.

The testimony of one witness, if, *tempore non suspecto,* he heard from some reliable source that the former spouse was deceased, will also aid in establishing moral certainty of death when circumstances point to the fact of death.

As documentary proof and the concordant testimony of two witnesses produce full legal proof of death, the pastor may in view

235, 236; resp., 1915—*AAS,* VII (1915), 476-479; resp., 25 Feb., 1916—*AAS,* VIII (1916), 151-153; resp., 19 Jan., 1917—*AAS,* IX (1917), 120; resp., 18 Nov., 1920—*AAS,* XIV (1922), 96.

[93] *AAS,* XIV (1922), 96, 97.

[94] See pp. 289-292.

of such proof proceed with the marriage without consulting the ordinary. When only one direct witness [95] (whether he be a witness of personal knowledge or a witness who *tempore non suspecto* heard from others of the death of the spouse) is available, it would seem more prudent for the pastor to refer the matter to the ordinary.

When a spouse has disappeared and there is no direct evidence, either testimonial or documentary, of his death, the problem of establishing moral certainty of his death becomes more difficult. Mere absence or disappearance of a spouse, regardless of the length of time that has elapsed since his departure, does not constitute proof of death.[96] In the absence of documents and witnesses proof of death must be sought from reasonable conjectures, legal or factual presumptions, plausible indications and significant circumstances. The pastor, therefore, should gather and send to the ordinary all the possible information he can obtain concerning the disappearance of the spouse. The relatives, friends, neighbors and associates of the spouse should be questioned about his moral character, whether he lived piously and religiously, whether he loved his wife, whether he had a reason for disappearing, whether he had property or expected to receive some. The following questions should also be asked: Did he go away with the consent of his wife and relatives? What was the condition of his health, and how old was he? Did he write? When did he write? How often? Did he mention that he would return as soon as possible? Was there any reason for his absence?

If he left on a military expedition, was he in any battle? Was he captured? Did he desert? Did he enter dangerous places? Did he travel in perilous territory? [97]

If the party went away for business reasons, at what time did he leave? What was his destination? Was there any danger in-

[95] Gasparri, *Tractatus Canonicus de Matrimonio*, n. 562.

[96] "Proof of Death of Husband or Wife," *AER*, LXXXIX (1933), 284; S. C. S. Off., instr., *Matrimonii vinculo*, 13 Maii, 1868—*Coll.*, n. 1321.

[97] *Cf.* L. Kaas, *Kriegsverschollenheit und Wiederverheiratung nach staatlichem und kirchlichem Recht* (Paderborn: Ferdinand Schöningh, 1919), pp. 7-122; *cf. etiam*, W. Ursprung, *Verschollenheit und Todeserklärung* (Aarau: H. R. Saurlander & Co., 1918).

volved? Was he alone or accompanied? Was it to a country where there was internal trouble, war, famine, plague, etc.?

If he went on an ocean voyage, from what port did he embark? Who were his companions? What was his destination? What was the name of the ship? Who was the captain of the ship? Did he suffer shipwreck?

Was there any rumor of his death? What was the nature of the rumor? It is expedient for the pastor to have two trustworthy witnesses testify to the rumor, if there was one. The rumor should be traced to its originator, if possible. The pastor might also have recourse to advertising in the newspaper, if he thinks it useful and prudent.[98]

Whatever information the pastor may have obtained in regard to the foregoing points and any additional information that would help to decide whether the absent party is living or dead should be transferred to the ordinary. Until he has received a favorable decision from the ordinary, the pastor should not admit the surviving spouse to remarriage.

Article 10. The Impediment of Sacred Orders

A marriage is invalid if attempted by clerics in sacred orders.[99]

By sacred or major orders are understood the priesthood, the diaconate and the sub-diaconate. The minor orders of acolyte, exorcist, lector and porter are not designated by law as *sacred orders* and do not constitute a diriment impediment to marriage.[100]

Very rarely will it occur today that a person who has received a sacred order in the Latin Church will seek to enter marriage. For that reason the pastor may ordinarily omit questioning the prospective bridegroom on the impediment of sacred orders. However, if there are some grounds for suspecting that a prospective bridegroom has received a sacred order, the pastor should not hesitate to interrogate him on the point. A suspicion may be present if a

[98] "Proof of Death of Husband or Wife," *AER,* LXXXIX (1933), 284, 285; S. C. S. Off., instr., *Matrimonii vinculo,* 13 Maii, 1868—*Coll.,* n. 1321.

[99] Canon 1072.

[100] Canon 949.

man spent some time in a religious institute or in a seminary. Such a person should be questioned as to whether he received sacred orders. If the party answers in the negative and the pastor suspects he is not telling the truth, consultation of the record of the party's baptism or the receipt of a recent authentic certificate of his baptism will serve to clarify the matter.[101] If a record of his baptism cannot be had because the baptismal register perished in a fire or otherwise, a letter from the rector of the seminary is perhaps the most convenient means of proving the party's freedom from the impediment of sacred orders. The testimony of a reliable companion or classmate in the seminary is likewise very satisfactory.

If the party asserts that he received sacred orders, but was dispensed from the impediment by the Roman Pontiff, the pastor should request the rescript of the dispensation and have the ordinary pass on its authenticity and genuineness. Sometimes the Holy See does grant dispensations from sacred orders to deacons and subdeacons It never grants them to bishops. At the present time the same apparently holds true, at least in the external forum, in the case of priests, though in the past dispensations have been granted from the sacred order of priesthood.[102]

It is well for the pastor to bear in mind that a cleric who has received a major order through grave fear may be reduced to the lay state by sentence of an ecclesiastical judge, provided he can prove that he has not, at least tacitly, ratified the ordination afterwards by the exercise of the order. This reduction to the lay state will release him from the obligation of celibacy and the Divine Office. However, the grave fear and the non-ratification of the sacred order must be proved after the manner set forth in canons 1993-1998,[103] and in the instruction issued by the Sacred Congregation of the Sacraments on June 9, 1931.[104]

If a party asserts that he obtained this sentence of reduction

[101] *Cf.* canon 471, § 2.

[102] Gasparri, *Tractatus Canonicus de Matrimonio,* n. 619; Cappello, *De Sacramentis,* III, n. 443; S. Poenit., decr., 19 Apr., 1936—*AAS,* XXVIII (1936), 586-588.

[103] Canon 214.

[104] *AAS,* XXIII (1931), 457-492.

to the lay state, the investigating pastor must request that he produce authentic proof of the sentence, *e. g.*, an authentic copy of the sentence. Likewise, if a nupturient claims that he has secured a definitive sentence of the invalidity of his ordination on the grounds of a substantial defect in the sacred rite, the pastor must ask authentic proof of this definitive sentence.[105]

Two comparatively recent instructions from the Holy See, if carefully observed, now render remote the probability of a candidate being constrained to receive sacred orders through grave fear or force. The first was issued on December 27, 1930, by the Sacred Congregation of the Sacraments for the purpose of testing in seminaries the candidates for sacred orders.[106] The second was issued on December 1, 1931, by the Sacred Congregation of Religious for the testing of religious candidates for sacred orders.[107] Both instructions are somewhat similar and require that the candidate swear that he is not urged by any compulsion, force or fear to receive sacred orders.

Article 11. The Impediment of Solemn Vow

Marriage is invalid when attempted by religious with solemn vows, or by religious whose simple vows have the power of annulling marriage by special prescriptions of the Holy See.[108]

The diriment impediment of vow, therefore, affects only two classes of persons: (1) those who have made solemn religious profession and (2) those who have taken simple vows to which the Holy See by special disposition of law has attached an invalidating effect upon marriage. The only present day example of a simple vow that invalidates marriage is the vow taken by the Jesuit scholastics on the completion of their two years' novitiate.[109]

Solemn vows are taken only in religious orders of men and women.[110] Consequently, women as well as men can incur the

[105] *Cf.* canon 1933, § 2.
[106] *AAS*, XXIII (1931), 120.
[107] *AAS*, XXIV (1932), 74.
[108] Canon 1073; Conc. Trident., sess. XXIV, *de matrimonio*, c. 9.
[109] Cappello, *De Sacramentis*, III, n. 447.
[110] Canon 488, 2°.

diriment impediment of vow. In the case of solemnly professed men, it is not necessary for the incurring of the impediment that they be in sacred orders. It is also to be noted that simple profession, whether in a religious order or in a religious congregation, does not invalidate marriage, though it does render it unlawful.[111]

Solemn vows are always perpetual and cannot be taken before the completion of the age of twenty-one years.[112] Consequently, unless it is proved in a case that the nupturient was a Jesuit scholastic, he need not be questioned on the diriment impediment of vow if he has not completed his twenty-first year of age.

Very few pastors will meet with nupturients who were solemnly professed, for comparatively few solemnly professed religious depart or are dismissed from their institutes. The number that is secularized is also small. However, if on investigation or from the baptismal record or certificate[113] or by any other means, the pastor discovers that a nupturient was solemnly professed, the nupturient should be interrogated as to whether he was released from his vow. In this connection it is worthy of remembrance that a religious who has received an indult granting secularization (*saecularizatio*) is thereby liberated from his religious vows, and in consequence, from the impediment of vow,[114] but that a religious who has obtained an indult conceding to him only exclaustration (*exclaustratio*) nevertheless remains subject to his religious vows in as far as their observance can be kept in his secular mode of life, in particular to his vow of perfect and perpetual chastity.[115] For a secularized or exclaustrated religious who is in sacred orders the diriment impediment of sacred orders remains, unless a separate and distinct dispensation was granted for its removal. The secularization or exclaustration of a solemnly professed religious is ordinarily

[111] Ayrinhac-Lydon, *Marriage Legislation in the New Code of Canon Law*, pp. 155, 156.

[112] Timotheus P. Schäfer, *Compendium de Religiosis ad normam Codicis Iuris* (Münster i. Westf., Ex Typographia Aschendorff, 1931), 273; canon 573.

[113] Canons 576, § 2, and 470, § 2.

[114] Canon 640, § 1, 2°.

[115] Canon 639.

proved by the production of an authentic copy of the corresponding indult. If the nupturient is an apostate or a fugitive from his order, he is not liberated thereby from the obligations of his vows.[116] A religious professed with perpetual vows when dismissed from his institute remains bound by his vows even after his dismissal, unless he has been released from these obligations either by the constitutions of his religious institute or by an indult of the Holy See.[117] The diriment impediment of vow ceases when a solemnly professed religious with permission of the Holy See passes to a religious congregation in which there is only simple profession.[118] In this case, however, the investigating pastor cannot there and then permit the marriage of the one thus transferred, because simple profession constitutes a prohibitive impediment to marriage. Jesuit scholastics can be dispensed from their vows not only by the Holy See, but also by the General of the Society of Jesus. Legitimate dismissal also releases them from their vows, and they can marry validly and lawfully.[119] When there are serious arguments for the invalidity of a party's solemn profession, or even when its invalidity is certain, the pastor cannot proceed with the marriage of the party until the matter has been referred to the Holy See in accordance with canon 586, § 3, and a decision in favor of its invalidity has been obtained. A party solemnly professed may also get a release from his vow by means of a dispensation, for it is in the power of the Roman Pontiff to grant such a dispensation.[120]

If a solemnly professed religious has been released from the impediment of vow in any of the above-mentioned ways, the pastor should demand an authentic copy or certificate of his release. If the party himself is not in personal possession of such a document, and asserts that he is free from the impediment, it will be necessary for the pastor preferably through the curia to write to the superior of the religious community and await his reply before proceeding further. It is well to obtain, if possible, a copy of the rescript

[116] Canons 644 and 645, § 1.

[117] Canon 669, § 1.

[118] *Cf.* canon 636.

[119] Cappello, *De Sacramentis,* III, n. 454.

[120] Gasparri, *Tractatus Canonicus de Matrimonio,* n. 629.

certifying the release of the party from his vow, and to have the ordinary carefully scrutinize its contents and adjudge its authenticity.

If the party is still obliged by his vow, and wishes to marry, petition may be made for a dispensation. However, as a rule, it should not be made unless there is a grave and urgent cause, either public or private, for making the petition.[121]

Article 12. The Impediment of Abduction

Between the abductor and the woman he abducted for the purpose of marriage there can be no marriage as long as the abducted woman is in the abductor's power. If the abducted woman, after having been separated from her abductor and restored to a safe and free place, consents to marry her abductor, the impediment ceases. As far as the nullity of marriage is concerned, the violent detention of a woman is considered equivalent to abduction; namely, when a man for the purpose of marriage detains her forcibly in the place where she resides or to which she came of her own accord.[122]

Abduction constitutes a diriment impediment to marriage. The pastor investigating its existence in nupturients must keep in mind the conditions necessary for the impediment. They are: (1) The removal of the woman from one place to another, or violent detention of a woman in the place where she resides or in a place to which she came of her own free will. (2) The abduction or retention must be the abduction or retention of a woman by a man. Consequently, the abduction or forcible retention of a man by a woman does not come under the impediment of abduction. The impediment arises whether the man abducts the woman himself or employs an agent or agents to do so. The agent of the abductor may be a man or a woman. (3) The abduction or retention must take place with a view to marriage. If the abduction or retention is carried out for some other purpose, *e. g.*, for revenge, for the sake of concubinage, with a view to white slavery, for the purpose of extorting money, etc., then no impediment of abduction arises. (4) The abduction

[121] Cappello, *De Sacramentis,* III, n. 453.

[122] Canon 1074, §§ 1-3; Ayrinhac-Lydon, *Marriage Legislation in the New Code of Canon Law,* pp. 158, 159.

or retention must be violent. It may be violent physically (*e. g.*, if physical force is used to remove the woman from one place to another or to detain her in a given place) or morally (*e. g.*, if the abduction or retention is effected by threats or by grave fear). Therefore, seduction by promises, by gifts, by the spell of suave argument or convincing conversation, etc., does not constitute the impediment of abduction. Elopement, where the woman consents both to run away with a man and to marry him, does not come under the impediment of abduction. However, if the woman runs away with a man not with the intention of marrying him while the man has the intention of marriage, the impediment of abduction is present.[123] The impediment lasts only as long as the woman is in the power of the man. Once she is released from his power by separation from his influence or that of his agents, and restored to a safe place, the impediment ceases. She is then free to marry the one who abducted her.[124]

Today the average pastor meets very seldom, if at all, with nupturients hindered from marriage by the impediment of abduction. Undoubtedly, the growing independence of the modern woman is not favorable to the abduction of women by men. Nevertheless, abduction does still occur sometimes, and consequently when a suspicion of the impediment comes to the notice of the pastor, he should not neglect to make prudent inquiries concerning it. It is best to confine the inquiries to the separate interrogation of the parties. The man from a sense of guilt and the woman from that of fear may not be willing to reveal it in the examination of both parties together. Prudent inquiry (without revealing the reasons for the inquiry) among some trustworthy members of the congregation concerning the history and background of the woman and man concerned will frequently be useful and decidedly helpful when the pastor has a grave doubt about the existence of the impediment.

If the prospective bride shows from her attitude, manner and conversation that she is not interested in the marriage, that she has

[123] Woywod, *A Practical Commentary on the Code of Canon Law*, n. 1061; Cappello, *De Sacramentis*, III, nn. 459-469; Ayrinhac-Lydon, *Marriage Legislation in the New Code of Canon Law*, pp. 159-161.

[124] Payen, *De Matrimonio*, n. 1285.

aversion for her prospective husband, and is rather dejected than cheerful, there may be a suspicion of the impediment of abduction. Hence it may be advisable for the pastor to question her prudently about the impediment of abduction, or at least to find occasion to give some instruction on matrimonial impediments, laying emphasis on abduction. If the pastor gains her confidence, she will probably pour out her story of abduction, if it really occurred.

When circumstances point to the fact that a girl is marrying a man to get out of some serious difficulty and there are some indications that he endeavored to keep her in that difficulty at the same time proposing marriage to her, the pastor might suspect abduction. Such cases may more readily happen when a girl is away from home, when she is out of work and penniless, especially if the girl is young and orphaned, has none or few friends, and particularly, if she came from some rural district to the city. Interrogation on the impediment of abduction is not out of place in such circumstances. A few questions from the pastor as to how long the girl has known her prospective husband, in what circumstances they met each other, whether there was a period of engagement and how long it lasted, whether she really loves her prospective husband, whether there was any influence used to prevail upon her to marry, such as threats from parents, relatives or the prospective husband himself, will help to clear up the matter. If her answers clearly suggest the presence of the impediment of abduction, the pastor's subsequent questions should make sure if all the above-mentioned conditions for the impediment are fulfilled.

When the pastor has satisfied himself that the impediment is really present, he should endeavor to have the girl removed to a safe place where she will be free from the influence of her abductor. If, after complete separation from his influence, she still wants to marry him, the pastor may permit the marriage. If separation of the girl from the influence of her abductor cannot be accomplished and the girl wishes to marry her abductor, a dispensation may be requested provided it is morally certain that coercion is absent. As such dispensations are rarely given, it should be petitioned only when very serious reasons are present.[125]

[125] Cappello, *De Sacramentis,* III, n. 474.

ARTICLE 13. THE IMPEDIMENT OF CRIME

There can be no valid marriage between:

1. those who during the same lawful marriage have committed adultery and mutually promised to marry each other or actually attempted marriage, even by a mere civil act;

2. those who during the same legitimate marriage have committed adultery if, in addition, one of them committed conjugicide;

3. those who by mutual physical or moral co-operation, even without adultery, committed conjugicide.[126]

The impediment of crime enunciated above is a diriment impediment to marriage. There are three distinct species of it: (1) adultery together with a promise of marriage, or adultery along with an attempted marriage; (2) adultery with conjugicide; (3) conjugicide alone.[127]

Ordinarily investigation of the impediment of crime should be confined to the confessional or to the separate interrogation of the nupturients on account of its illicit and infamous nature, unless the impediment has become public.[128]

A. *Adultery Together with a Promise of Marriage or Along with an Attempted Marriage*

This is the most common species of the impediment of crime with which pastors meet. It is twofold: (a) adultery together with a promise of marriage; (b) adultery along with an attempted marriage.

I. *Adultery together with a promise of marriage.* When there are rumors in the neighborhood that the nupturients have been accomplices in the crime of adultery, together with a promise of marriage, the pastor should not hesitate to investigate prudently the foundations of these rumors. Furthermore, in the absence of rumors

[126] Canon 1075, 1°-3°.

[127] John F. Donohue, *The Impediment of Crime* (The Catholic University of America, Canon Law Studies, n. 69, Washington: The Catholic University of America, 1931), p. 37.

[128] Eduard Weigl, *Das Kirchliche Brautexamen* (München: G. J. Manz, 1932), p. 13.

the pastor should investigate the presence of the impediment, if circumstances point to it. Such suspicion may be aroused if a man arranged for a new marriage shortly after the death of his wife or when the woman he intends to marry is one who has been living in the house with him during his wife's illness,[129] (*e. g.*, in the capacity of a servant, nurse, housekeeper, etc.), and there is no legitimate reason for such early remarriage. Even if the woman he intends to marry has dwelt elsewhere, but has been more than usually familiar with him during his wife's illness, especially if the illness was a lingering one, investigation of the impediment of crime is not out of place. The fact that a man displayed by his manner of acting that he did not love his wife, that he had a reputation of being unfaithful to her, that he had been seen frequently with other women at entertainments, shows, night clubs, etc., and showed more than ordinary interest in them, strengthens the suspicion. Some suspicion may also be present if the occupation of a man took him away from his wife a great deal and he is known to have been on very intimate terms with the woman he now proposes to marry.

However, caution must be displayed in interrogating parties on the impediment of crime, for the fact that there is such an impediment is not, as a rule, well known among the laity. Besides, many parties are hesitant in admitting their guilt when face to face with their pastor. Consequently, proposing the impediment by means of instruction is often advisable. If the parties do not admit their guilt to the pastor there and then, there is the hope they will admit it to their confessor prior to the wedding. However, should the pastor deem it necessary or prudent to ask the parties direct questions on the matter, his preliminary questions on the subject might be very general, and then he may gradually particularize, *e. g.*, he might first ask them how long they have known each other, when they first met, the circumstances of their meeting, whether there was an engagement, whether they were on friendly terms during the lifetime of the first lawful spouse, whether they promised marriage to each other before the spouse died. If the answers to the questions indicate the existence of the impediment, the vital question as to whether they had sexual intercourse or committed adultery while

[129] *Cf.* De Smet, *Betrothment and Marriage*, n. 332.

the lawful spouse was alive is in order. If in response to this question the parties make an admission, the pastor will seek in the remaining interrogation to establish specifically if all the conditions in connection with the promise of marriage and the act of adultery which are requisite for inducing the impediment were actually and unmistakably present. These conditions are:

1. Adultery and the promise of marriage must exist conjointly. Adultery without a promise of marriage or a promise of marriage without adultery is not sufficient to constitute the impediment.

2. The adultery and the promise must both have been effected during the same valid marriage and prior to its dissolution. The promise may precede the adultery or *vice versa*. However, if the promise preceded the adultery, but is then revoked prior to the adultery, there is no impediment of crime. It is necessary that the revocation be expressed in words or signs. If a promise preceded the adultery, but was revoked only after the adultery had occurred, the impediment exists.[130]

3. The adultery itself must meet certain qualifications. (a) As a material act it must be *complete (perfectum), i. e.,* it must be a natural act of consummated sexual congress between the accomplices. Consequently, if mechanical contraceptives were used which prevent the male semen from being deposited in a natural way in the female vagina, or if intercourse was a *coitus interruptus,* there was no complete and perfect sexual union and therefore no adultery. (b) In its objective basis it must be *true, i. e.,* it must be an act between accomplices of whom at least one is validly married. In this sense the act cannot be designated as adultery if performed by accomplices of whom one is a putative husband or wife or of whom even both are putative spouses.[131] (c) In its moral aspect the adultery must be such that it can be disignated as *formal.* Both accomplices must be aware of their sin as a sin of adultery, *i. e.,* they must mutually know that at least one of them is a validly married person. If this mutual knowledge supervenes only upon the completion of the material act of adultery, then the act was devoid of the formal element

[130] Donohue, *The Impediment of Crime,* pp. 37-39.

[131] Sanchez, *De Sancto Matrimonii Sacramento Disputationum,* lib. VII, disp. LXXXIX, n. 30.

necessary to designate it as adultery in the sense of the law governing the impediment of crime.[132]

4. The promise of marriage must also meet certain qualifications. It must be: (a) *True, i. e.,* it must be a genuine promise, not a mere thought, desire or suggestion of marriage. A simple promise without any oath or legal formality suffices. (b) *Serious, i. e.,* it must be made with a sense of obligation to contract the contemplated marriage. It is the common opinion of canonists that a false or fictitious promise does not suffice. (c) *Free, i. e.,* it must be made without being extorted by force, grave fear or fraud. (d) *External, i. e.,* it must be expressed in words, in signs or in writing. (e) *Mutual, i. e.,* it must consist of a promise and a re-promise. (f) *Absolute, i. e,.* it must be free of conditions. (g) *Matrimonial, i. e.,* it must be made with a view to a future marriage after the dissolution of the present one. (h) *Made with a knowledge of the existing lawful marriage, i. e.,* it must be entered into by accomplices who at the time of their promise are fully cognizant of the existing bond of marriage on the part of one or both of them.[133]

If the pastor, after close questioning of the party on all the foregoing items, finds that any one of the conditions is absent, there is no impedient of crime and he may proceed with the marriage, if no other impediment stands in the way.

II. *Adultery along with an attempted marriage.* There are many zealous pastors who will frankly admit that interrogation on this kind of crime escaped their notice inadvertently, even when the evidence for its presence was perfectly manifest. Consequently, the pastor should be on his guard to prevent even the inadvertent omission of it from his interrogations. This species of the impediment of crime arises when, during the same legitimate marriage, two parties commit adultery and attempt to enter marriage. It is not necessary that the adultery precede the attempted marriage. However, both the adultery and the attempted marriage must take place during the same legitimate marriage of at least one of the parties.

[132] Cappello, *De Sacramentis,* III, n. 481.

[133] Donohue, *The Impediment of Crime,* pp. 42-53.

Usually the case occurs when, during a valid marriage, a husband leaves his wife, or is divorced or separated from her, becomes acquainted with another woman and attempts marriage with her, either before a non-Catholic minister or a civil official. Then on the dissolution of the marriage, he approaches a priest to have his attempted marriage convalidated, as the impediment of *ligamen* has been removed. What has just been said in regard to the husband applies equally to the wife, if she is the one that committed the crime. In every case, therefore, where parties in the above circumstances want to have their attempted marriage convalidated in the Church, interrogation of the parties on the impediment of crime arising out of adultery along with an attempted marriage is imperative.

The points on which the pastor should concentrate his questions are: Was there an attempted marriage and was adultery committed? If the parties have only attempted marriage but have not yet had adulterous intercourse, there is no impediment of crime. However, once the marriage has been attempted and cohabitation has ensued, the presumption will be that they also have committed adultery.

The adultery must meet all the qualifications mentioned above, *i. e.*, it must be complete, true, and formal. Moreover, the attempt at marriage must be a real, true and genuine attempt.[134]

Attempted marriage before a priest and two witnesses is not necessary; an attempted marriage before a civil judge, a non-Catholic minister or even an attempted common law marriage suffices. Mere concubinage, however, does not suffice.[135]

Should the pastor discover from his inquiries that the adultery lacked any of the requirements necessary for a complete, true and formal adultery, or if the adultery has indeed met all these conditions necessitated by the law but the apparently attempted marriage was nothing more than concubinage, then there is no impediment of crime.[136]

[134] See. . . .

[135] *Cf.* Cappello, *De Sacramentis,* III, n. 486.

[136] Cappello, *De Sacramentis,* III, n. 486.

B. *Adultery Together with Conjugicide*

This species of crime is more heinous than the preceding one and does not occur as frequently. It differs from the preceding one by the fact that it requires the additional sin of conjugicide. However, it does not require a promise of marriage nor an attempted marriage by the accomplices in order to become an impediment. To be incurred as an impediment the following conditions are necessary:

1. The adultery and the conjugicide must occur during the same existing marriage of at least one of the accomplices.

2. The adultery must be a complete, true and formal adultery, which must occur before the death of the lawful spouse is actually effected by the murderous attack.

3. The conjugicide must be committed by one or the other of the accomplices. It may be committed physically and personally by one of the accomplices, or it may be effected by the evildoer through the agency of another.

4. The innocent party who is murdered must be the lawful spouse of one of the accomplices in the adultery.

5. The murderous attack must be *intentional,* must end in *death,* and must be committed with a *view to entering marriage* with the accomplice in adultery. It is not necessary that both adulterers have the intention of entering marriage.[137] The pastor will have to proceed very cautiously and prudently in the investigation of this species of the impediment of crime. Unless a nupturient has been definitely proved guilty of spouse-murder which is obviously accompanied with the intention of remarriage, the pastor should omit direct interrogation about it. The nupturient, if innocent, may look upon direct interrogation as a definite accusation of the crime in question. Consequently, it is more prudent to leave any direct interrogation on the matter to the confessor. There is no reason, however, why the pastor should not mention the impediment in his instructions before marriage, pointing out its invalidating effects, and then leave the matter of disclosing the crime, if the crime is present, to the conscience of the nupturients.

[137] Cappello, *De Sacramentis,* III, nn. 489-492.

C. *Conjugicide by Conspired Effort*

This last species of the impediment of crime arises between two parties who have not committed adultery, but who have mutually co-operated either physically or morally in killing the lawful spouse of one of them in order that they may marry each other.

What has been said above in regard to the prudent investigation of the murder of the spouse holds equally true in regard to this species of the impediment. If the nupturients reveal or admit their conspiracy to kill the lawful spouse in a marriage by which one or the other was bound, the subsequent investigation will extend to establishing whether or not all the conditions for the incurring of the impediment were present. The conditions are: (a) The murderous attack upon the lawful spouse must be real, true, intentional and end in death. (b) The accomplices must have mutually and efficaciously conspired either physically or morally to bring about the death of the innocent spouse. (c) The accomplices must have had the intention of marrying each other after the death of the lawful spouse.[138]

Should the investigation of the nupturients reveal that their marriage is hindered by the impediment of crime, the pastor will be mindful of the attitude of the Holy See towards dispensations from the respective classifications of the impediment. Dispensations are not granted when *public* conjugicide is committed, irrespective of whether the conjugicide was committed by one or both nupturients. If the conjugicide is *occult,* dispensations are granted only for very grave causes. As the impediment of crime arising from adultery together with a promise of marriage or along with an attempted marriage is an impediment of minor degree,[139] the Holy See is more liberal in dispensing from it than from the two other classifications. However, a more serious cause it required for granting a dispensation when the facts of adultery and of the promised or attempted marriage are public than when they are occult.[140]

[138] Donohue, *The Impediment of Crime,* pp. 66-72.

[139] Canon 1042, § 2.

[140] Cappello, *De Sacramentis,* III, n. 504.

Article 14. The Impediment of Consanguinity

Consanguinity means relationship by blood. In the direct line of consanguinity marriage is invalid between all ascendants and descendants, whether legitimate or natural. In the collateral line marriage is invalid between blood relations to the third degree inclusively, but the impediment becomes multiple only when there is a multiple common stock. However, marriage is never to be permitted when a doubt exists as to whether the parties are related in any degree of the direct line, or in the first degree of the collateral line.[141]

In the *direct* line the impediment of consanguinity renders the marriages of all ascendants and descendants invalid. Therefore, mother and son, father and daughter, grandmother and grandson, grandfather and granddaughter are hindered from marriage.

In the *collateral* line the marriage of blood-relations is forbidden to the third degree inclusively. Therefore, brother and sister, and among themselves both first cousins and second cousins are hindered from marriage; also uncle and niece, great-uncle and grandniece, aunt and nephew, great-aunt and grandnephew.

Unless a pastor is well acquainted with the families and genealogy of the nupturients, it is well to inquire from them as to whether they are related by blood. It is especially necessary for the pastor to make careful inquiry concerning consanguinity when the nupturients come from the same or practically the same locality. Inquiry is all the more necessary when the family life of the place is very fixed and stable; when there has been considerable intermarriage; when every family or practically every family boasts of a large number of relations in and about the locality.

In many isolated villages where the descendants have remained close to the family homestead of their ancestors, it is not unusual to find a large percentage of the inhabitants interrelated by some tie of blood.

As many nupturients are not well acquainted with their genealogy, it is also advisable to consult their parents or the older members of their family about the presence of consanguinity. When the baptismal records or certificates of the nupturients contain a similarity

[141] Canon 1076, §§ 1-3.

of names, accurate investigation of consanguinity is imperative. On the discovery of a bond of consanguinity between the nupturients, it is advisable for the sake of accuracy to draw up a diagram or chart of the genealogical trees of the nupturients and compare them to see if the blood-relationship comes within the forbidden degrees.[142] The investigating pastor should be on the alert, not only for simple consanguineous relationship between the parties, but also for multiple blood-relationship. Here again a tracing of the genealogical tree of the nupturients is desirable. According to the present discipline, multiple relationship is possible only when the common ancestry from which persons descend is a multiple one. This multiple relationship can occur (a) when two blood-relations marry and have descendants; (b) when two brothers of one family marry two sisters of another family and have descendants; (c) when a man successively marries two persons who are sisters or cousins, or a woman successively marries two persons who are brothers or cousins, and begets children.[143]

As the impediment embraces illegitimate as well as legitimate blood-relationship, the pastor should watch for traces of blood-relationship in the case of nupturients who are illegitimate. A prudent endeavor should be made to trace who their parents were. If a nupturient was a foundling, it will usually be impossible to determine who his parents were. If he was not a foundling, his mother will usually be known but considerable difficulty may be encountered in finding out who was his father.

When the grandmother or mother of a nupturient is known to have had illicit intercourse with one of the male ancestors of the other nupturient, so that some suspicion may be entertained as to the existence of the impediment of blood-relationship between the nupturients, investigation should be made in as far as prudence will allow. Circumstances of place, of time and of person should be given due consideration. If the investigation discloses that illicit intercourse did take place, which gives rise to a conjecture that the parties about to marry may be brother and sister, marriage cannot

142 *Cf.* De Smet, *Betrothment and Marriage,* n. 332.

143 Ayrinhac-Lydon, *Marriage Legislation in the New Code of Canon Law,* p. 172.

be permitted, for canon 1076, § 3 states that marriage shall never be permitted when there is doubt whether the parties are related in the first degree of the collateral line. If the man who wants to marry had illicit relations with the mother of the prospective bride at such a time that it is possible that he might be the father of the girl, then doubtful consanguinity arises and, as the doubt concerns relationship in the direct line, the pastor cannot admit them to marriage.[144] Should the doubtful relationship concern the second or the third degree of collateral line, then marriage is permissible, provided a dispensation has been obtained in accordance with the norm of canon 15.

Dispensations from the impediment of consanguinity are not granted in any degree of the direct line or in the first degree of the collateral line. The Holy See is also very reluctant to grant dispensations for marriages of uncle and niece, aunt and nephew, as is indicated by an instruction issued by the Sacred Congregation of the Sacraments on August 1, 1931. The instruction points out the evils attached to such marriages and urges that the abuse of asking frequent dispensations from them be checked. However, it states that should occasions arise for the petitioning of such dispensations, bishops should regard as justly and proportionately grave only such causes as are held legitimate in view of the canonical provisions and the constant and long continued practice of the Holy See, such as the prevention of notable scandal, the settlement of important questions affecting the succession of property, or the relief of involved and very distressing family conditions. The instruction considered as insufficient such causes as the limited prospect for marriage, the super-marriageable age of the woman, the want of a dowry and others of the same kind, except in cases where these, although individually insufficient, yet when cumulatively taken constitute so grave a reason as to make the dispensation advisable. Moreover, the instruction required that special commendatory letters of the bishop should accompany the petition for the dispensation.[145] The Holy See grants dispensations from consanguinity in the second and

[144] Canon 1076, § 3; Pont. Comm. Interp. Cod., resp., 3 Jun., 1918—*AAS*, X (1918), 346.

[145] *AAS*, XXIII (1931), 413; Bouscaren, *The Canon Law Digest*, I, 514-516.

third degrees of the collateral line for proportionately grave causes.[146]

When preparing a petition for a dispensation, the pastor will do well to draw up a chart (such as may be found in almost all textbooks dealing with consanguinity), which indicates exactly the nature of the impediment. The value of the chart is that it prevents errors in petitioning for dispensations. If an error is actually made in asking for a dispensation and the dispensation is granted, it is valid if the degree of consaguinity actually existing is inferior to the one mentioned in the rescript of the dispensation.[147] *A fortiori*, an error in the cause assigned in the petition for the dispensation will not invalidate the dispensation, if the impediment is one of only minor degree.

Article 15. The Impediment of Affinity

Affinity in the direct line invalidates marriage in every degree; in the collateral line it invalidates marriage to the second degree inclusively. Affinity is multiplied wherever the impediment of consanguinity from which it proceeds is multiplied, and also by successive marriage with a blood-relation of the deceased spouse.[148]

The basis of affinity in the Code discipline differs from that of the pre-Code law. In the pre-Code law the basis of affinity was carnal intercourse, whether licit or illicit. In the present discipline affinity arises only from a valid marriage, whether ratified only or ratified and consummated. It exists between the man and the blood-relations of the woman and between the woman and the blood-relations of the man. Consequently, it does not exist between the blood-relations of the woman and the blood-relations of the man.[149]

The computation of the relationships in affinity is determined according to the relationships in consanguinity. Affinity is so computed that the blood-relations of the man are related to the woman by affinity in the same line and degree in which they are related to the man by consanguinity and *vice versa*.[150] Thus, for instance, a wife is related to her husband's father in the first degree of affinity

146 *Cf.* Cappello, *De Sacramentis*, III, n. 525; canon 1042, § 2, 1°.
147 Canon 1052.
148 Canon 1077, §§ 1, 2, 1°, 2°.
149 Canon 97, §§ 1, 2.
150 Canon 97, § 3.

in the direct line, and to his grandfather in the second degree of the direct line. She is related to her husband's brother in the first degree of the collateral line, to her husband's first cousin in the second degree.

In the direct line affinity hinders the woman, even after the dissolution of the marriage, to marry her husband's grandfather, father, son or grandson. It hinders the man from marrying his wife's grandmother, mother, daughter or granddaughter.

In the collateral line, affinity hinders a woman from marrying her husband's brother, uncle, nephew or first cousin. It hinders the man from marrying his wife's sister, aunt, niece or first cousin.

The pastor investigating affinity will have to keep in mind that affinity arises only from a valid marriage, whether consummated or not. Consequently, it does not arise when the previous marriage of a nupturient was invalid either from lack of form, from defect of consent, or from a diriment impediment. Therefore, if from his investigation of the impediment of *ligamen* the pastor discovers that neither nupturient was ever married before, no questions on the impediment of affinity should be addressed to him. Likewise no interrogations on the impediment are necessary if a nupturient, who had contracted an invalid marriage previously, produces authentic proof that he had obtained a decree of nullity of his marriage by due process of ecclesiastical law.

Affinity and consanguinity are closely related to each other and usually when a pastor asks if the nupturients are related, or questions their parents or the older members of their family on it, they will in all probability manifest to the pastor the impediment of affinity, if it exists.

As affinity is an impediment of ecclesiastical origin in all of its degrees, the Holy See can dispense from it. *De facto,* however, the Holy See is not wont to dispense from it in any degree of the direct line when the marriage has been consummated, though in some instances dispensations have been given.[151] Dispensations from affinity in the collateral line are granted for a proportionately grave cause, whether public or private. In petitioning for a dispensation

[151] Cappello, *De Sacramentis,* III, n. 539; S. Poenit., 2 Dec., 1911—*Periodica,* XI (1914), 593.

the pastor should note the causes for the dispensation, the degree to be dispensed from, and it is proper also that a chart showing the relationship accompany the petition.

ARTICLE 16. THE IMPEDIMENT OF PUBLIC PROPRIETY

The impediment of public propriety arises from an invalid marriage, whether consummated or not, and from public and notorious concubinage; it invalidates marriage in the first and second degree of the direct line between the man and the blood-relations of the woman or *vice versa*.[152]

The impediment of public propriety differs from the impediment of affinity by reason of the basis on which it is founded. Affinity arises from a *valid* marriage, while public propriety arises from an *invalid* marriage and from *public* or *notorious concubinage*.

The basis for public propriety in the Code law differs from its basis in the pre-Code law. According to the pre-Code discipline public propriety arose from valid betrothal and from an unconsummated marriage, whether valid or not, whereas according to the present discipline, as noted above, the basis for the impediment is an invalid marriage or public or notorious concubinage.[153]

The extent of the impediment of public propriety is much more restricted than the impediments of consanguinity and affinity. It extends only to the first and second degrees of the direct line. A man, therefore, is hindered from marrying the mother, grandmother, daughter and granddaughter of the woman with whom he contracted an invalid marriage, or with whom he lived in public or notorious concubinage. A woman is hindered from marrying the father, grandfather, son and grandson of the man with whom she contracted an invalid marriage or with whom she lived in public or notorious concubinage. The man or the woman in the case is not hindered from marrying collateral blood-relations of the one with whom he or she contracted an invalid marriage or lived in public or notorious concubinage.[154]

[152] Canon 1078.

[153] Gasparri, *Tractatus Canonicus de Matrimonio*, n. 728.

[154] Ayrinhac-Lydon, *Marriage Legislation in the New Code of Canon Law*, p. 182.

As the impediment of public propriety is opposed to natural decency and carries with it a certain amount of infamy or disgrace, the pastor should confine interrogation regarding it to the separate interrogation of the nupturients or to the confessional. When circumstances, especially the manner of living of a nupturient, or rumors point to a solid suspicion of the impediment of public propriety, the pastor should not hesitate in making investigation concerning it. Prudence dictates that his first investigations should aim at finding out if there are certain general indications of the impediment and then, when its existence becomes more apparent, the pastor's questions may become more specific.

The interrogation of the nupturients on the impediment of *ligamen* will usually bring to light whether one of the parties had contracted an invalid marriage with a person related to the other nupturient in the first or second degree of the direct line. Authentic proof, however, of the declaration of the invalidity of this former marriage must be produced. Even a marriage invalid from defect of matrimonial consent or from defect of form, or a marriage that is invalid on account of some diriment impediment is sufficient to constitute the impediment of public propriety, provided it has the appearance of marriage.[155] As merely civil marriage is not recognized as having the appearance of marriage, the impediment of public propriety does not arise from it, unless cohabitation has taken place.[156] However, if public or notorious cohabitation follows the civil marriage of the parties, the impediment of public propriety arises by reason of concubinage.

When investigating the impediment of public propriety which arises from public or notorious concubinage, the pastor must be mindful of all the conditions necessary for the impediment and question the parties accordingly. The following are the necessary conditions:

1. *The concubinage must be real, true concubinage.* True concubinage implies a somewhat fixed or permanent cohabitation of an unmarried man and woman, during which sexual intercourse is habitually intended and exercised, somewhat as in marriage, but

[155] Gasparri, *Tractatus Canonicus de Matrimonio,* nn. 732, 733.

[156] Pont. Comm. Interp. Cod., 12 Mart., 1929 ad II—*AAS,* XXI (1929), 170.

without marital intent or apart from the appearance of marriage. The man and woman may live in the same place or in different places. There is concubinage, for instance, when a man keeps and supports a mistress in a separate apartment, or even in her own home.[157] A certain continuity of sexual relationship between the man and woman is necessary for concubinage. Mere isolated acts of fornication, even though repeated several times with the same person, do not constitute concubinage as long as the intention of protracting sexual life is absent.[158] A certain degree of exclusiveness in carnal relations is also necessary, *i. e.*, the practice of intercourse with one and the same person.[159]

2. *The concubinage must be public or notorious.* Concubinage is public, if it has already been divulged or if it is exercised in such circumstances that it can and must be prudently judged that it will easily be divulged. Concubinage may be notorious by *notoriety of law* or *notoriety of fact.* It is notorious by notoriety of law (a) after the sentence of a competent judge which has become irrevocable, or (b) after judicial confession of one of the guilty parties in court. It is notorious by notoriety of fact if it is publicly known and also when it is exercised under such circumstances that it cannot be concealed by any subterfuge nor excused by any legal excuse.[160]

The impediment of public propriety is a perpetual one and does not end with the dissolution of the invalid marriage or the cessation of the public and notorious concubinage. Hence, before a pastor can admit to marriage one bound by the impediment, a dispensation from it must be obtained. A dispensation can be obtained from the impediment in both forbidden degrees, as the impediment of public propriety is solely a matter of ecclesiastical law. Before asking for the dispensation, the pastor should make sure that the woman whom the man intends to marry is undoubtedly *not* the man's own natural daughter by the woman to whom he had been invalidly married or with whom he lived in public or notorious concubinage.

[157] Cappello, *De Sacramentis,* III, n. 544; Gasparri, *Tractatus Canonicus de Matrimonio,* n. 737.

[158] Payen, *De Matrimonio,* n. 1540.

[159] Cappello, *De Sacramentis,* III, n. 554.

[160] Canons 2197, 1°-3°, and 1750.

Article 17. The Impediment of Spiritual Relationship

According to the present discipline the matrimonial impediment of spiritual relationship arises only from Baptism, whether solemn or private. It invalidates marriage (a) between the person who baptizes and the one baptized and (b) between the sponsors and the one baptized.[161] It arises when the minister and sponsor are of the sex other than that of the one baptized. Spiritual relationship arising from Confirmation[162] does not constitute an impediment to marriage since the promulgation of the Code.[163]

Today, pastors do not frequently meet with nupturients whose marriage is hindered by the diriment impediment of spiritual relationship. This is due, perhaps, in a large measure to the restricted character of the impediment. However, occasional cases of the presence of this impediment may manifest themselves in pre-nuptial investigation. Unless the pastor is vigilant, he may neglect to make inquiry regarding the impediment of spiritual relationship because of its infrequency. Moreover, many Catholics are not aware of the existence of such an impediment in the law and, hence, spontaneous revelation of it to the pastor is not probable. Consequently, when there are any grounds for suspecting the presence of the impediment, the pastor should readily investigate the matter further.

When both nupturients were baptized in infancy, it will not be necessary for the pastor to question them on the impediment of spiritual relationship, if they are approximately of the same age. However, if there is a considerable disparity in their ages, and particularly if one or both of the parties were baptized in late infancy, interrogation on the impediment of spiritual relationship is in order. Inquiry is all the more expedient if the parties are relatives, or if a close bond of friendship exists between their families, for sponsors are usually selected from relatives or close acquaintances of the parents. Suspicion of the impediment of spiritual relationship may also be present when a nupturient asserts he was baptized in a case of necessity, *e.g.*, when a friend was

[161] Canons 1079 and 768.

[162] Canon 797.

[163] Gasparri, *Tractatus Canonicus de Matrimonio*, n. 749.

called in to do the baptizing, or when the nupturient is marrying an interne of the hospital where she was baptized in danger of death, and he is known to have administered Baptism in cases of necessity, etc.

When nupturients were baptized in adult age, particular care must be exercised by the investigating pastor in regard to the impediment in question. Very often the sponsor in such baptisms is a close personal friend of the baptized and a member of the other sex. In such instances the possibility of a proposal of marriage to a sponsor by the baptized party, or by a sponsor to the baptized party, is not altogether a remote contingency.

Inquiries in regard to the impediment of spiritual relationship when a nupturient is a convert to the Church are desirable; for not infrequently has it occurred that the sponsor selected for a convert's Baptism was the convert's prospective partner in marriage.

The most suitable means of ascertaining whether or not the impediment of spiritual relationship hinders a certain marriage is a careful perusal of the baptismal record of the parties' baptisms or of an authentic certificate of their baptisms.

If the pastor discovers from his inquiries and investigations that the impediment of spiritual relationship was really contracted, his next step will be to aid the parties in preparing a petition for the necessary dispensation. A dispensation from the impediment of spiritual relationship is easily obtainable, as the impediment is one of minor degree.[164] In the petition for the dispensation any reasonable cause which has the approval of the Holy See will suffice.[165]

Article 18. The Investigation of the Freedom of the Parties' Consent

According to canon 1020, § 2, the pastor who has the right to assist at the marriage is obliged to inquire, not only whether the parties are free from matrimonial impediments, but also whether the parties, especially the woman, are consenting freely to the marriage.

There are many factors which can interfere with the matrimonial

[164] Canon 1042, § 2, 4°.

[165] Gasparri, *Tractatus Canonicus de Matrimonio,* n. 761.

consent of parties, namely, force and fear, defect of the use of reason, defect of sufficient knowledge, error, simulated consent, conditional consent. However, canon 1020, § 2 in obliging the pastor to inquire whether the parties are freely consenting to the marriage seems to have specifically in view the factors of force and fear. The reason is that the canon lays special stress on the examination of the woman as to her liberty in consenting to the marriage. Woman is of a gentler and less aggressive nature than man. Hence she is more likely than man to have her liberty of consent interfered with by the influence of force or fear. The other influences mentioned above as affecting matrimonial consent seem to affect equally both men and women. For instance, defect of the use of reason or defect of sufficient knowledge will have more or less the same effects in the case of a man as in the case of a woman. Consequently it may be accepted that the freedom of consent referred to in canon 1020, § 2 specifically refers to freedom from the factors of force and fear.

Nevertheless any influence that interferes with matrimonial consent claims the attention of the pastor in the scheme of pre-nuptial investigation. For that reason upon considering the investigation of the freedom of the parties from the influence of force and fear, consideration will be given to the pastor's obligation of examining the nupturients as to their freedom from the following influences: defect of the use of reason, defect of sufficient knowledge, error, simulated consent and conditional consent.

1. *Force and Fear*

Force is usually defined as an impetus of greater degree than can be resisted. Fear is the perturbation of the mind as effected by some imminent danger. Though the terms "force" and "fear" differ from each other, they are sometimes used synonymously.[166]

It is important for the investigating pastor to remember that marriage is invalid if contracted under the influence of force or grave fear caused unjustly by some external agent with the result that a person is forced to choose marriage to free himself from the force or

[166] Joseph V. Sangmeister, *Force and Fear as Precluding Matrimonial Consent* (The Catholic University of America, Canon Law Studies, n. 80, Washington: The Catholic University of America, 1932), pp. 5-10.

fear.[167] Absolute physical violence destroys all freedom of consent, and consequently a marriage contracted under its influence would be invalid. In order that fear may be considered as invalidating marriage the following conditions are required: (a) it must be external, *i. e.*, it must proceed from some outside agent; (b) it must be grave either absolutely or relatively; (c) it must be unjust either in itself or in the manner in which it is inflicted; (d) it is necessary that the affected party have the persuasion that he cannot liberate himself from the fear unless he enters marriage. Therefore it is not necessary that the fear be inflicted for the explicit purpose of forcing a party to marry.[168]

The pastor should confine his interrogations on the parties' liberty of consent to the separate interrogation of the nupturients. If the man and woman intending marriage are interrogated in the presence of each other as to their freedom of consent, they are not likely to admit the presence of any such existing influence as force or fear or at least will be very reluctant to do so.

If it is evident to the pastor that the parties have positive aversion or repugnance for each other or that their parents or relatives are urging a hasty marriage for no good reasons, interrogation of the parties as to whether any pressure is being brought to bear on them to marry is perfectly in order. If, in addition, the man or the woman is known to be definitely in love with somebody else, there may be a very strong suspicion of the presence of force or fear, and the pastor should not hesitate to make due inquiry into the matter.

In accordance with the prescriptions of the Code, the pastor should be particularly alert in watching out for the presence of force or fear in regard to the woman. In certain circumstances, he ought to pursue his inquiries with more than usual diligence, *e. g.*, when the girl comes from a home where the parents do all the arranging for marriages, when the parents are cruel to the girl, or when they rule the home with an iron discipline, and are definitely unreasonable in the undue submission they demand of their children. While mere reverential fear does not invalidate marriage, there may be circumstances

[167] Canon 1087, § 1.

[168] *Cf.* Gasparri, *Tractatus Canonicus de Matrimonio,* nn. 852-856; Cappello, *De Sacramentis,* III, n. 606; Sangmeister, *Force and Fear,* pp. 86-126.

associated with it that are sufficiently strong to induce a girl to marry against her will. For instance, it may be accompanied by threats of disinheritance, of death, of suicide and of physical punishment. These factors may in given cases be sufficiently potent so as to influence a person of weak character and sometimes even a person of stronger character to choose marriage rather than face the outcome of these threats.[169]

Even though canon 1021, § 2 lays emphasis on the interrogation of the woman as to her freedom of consent, it does not in any way imply that the interrogation of the man in this matter should be slighted or executed carelessly. The pastor should not refrain from prudently and tactfully interrogating the man as to whether any pressure to marry has been exercised on him when he has been responsible for the seduction of the girl; when he has been the cause of her pregnancy; when he is reputed to be the father of an illegitimate child born to her, and in such like cases. In these circumstances, there is a possibility that some external pressure to marry the girl may have been brought to bear on him by the girl's parents, relatives or friends.

If a pastor discovers definite manifestations of force or fear either from the admissions of the parties themselves or from some other source, his next step should be to determine whether the force or fear has been unjustly thrust upon the parties, and whether it fulfills all the other conditions mentioned above as necessary for invalidating the marriage. If these conditions are present, he should refuse absolutely to assist at the marriage. If some force or fear is definitely present but is insufficient to invalidate the marriage, he should dis-

[169] *S. R. R., Nullit. Matrim.*, 21 Jul., 1910, *Coram R. P. D., Gulielmus Sebastianelli*, dec. XXVIII—*Decisiones*, II (1910), 288-294; *S. R. R., Nullit. Matrim.*, 7 Jul., 1911, *Coram R. P. D., Francisco Heiner*, dec. XXX—*Decisiones*, III (1911), 332-340; *S. R. R., Nullit. Matrim.*, 2 Jun., 1911, *Coram R. P. D., Michaele Lega*, dec. XXI—*Decisiones*, III (1911), 224-236; *S. R. R., Nullit. Matrim.*, 10 Maii, 1918—*Coram R. P. D., Gulielmus Sebastianelli*, dec. V—*Decisiones*, X (1918), 36-40; *S. R. R., Nullit. Matrim.*, 9 Jan., 1922, *Coram R. P. D., Josepho Florczak*, dec. 1—*Decisiones*, XIV (1922), 1-12; *S. R. R., Nullit. Matrim.*, 17 Maii, 1922, *Coram R. P. D., Ioanne Prior*, dec. XVI—*Decisiones*, XIV (1922), 147-154; *S. R. R., Nullit. Matrim.*, 11 Feb., 1925, *Coram R. P. D., Andreas Iullien*, dec. IX—*Decisiones*, XVII (1925), 67-73.

courage the parties from marriage and thus anticipate any unhappiness that might arise from such a matrimonial venture. In discouraging the marriage he will be acting in accordance with the mind of the Church, which is solicitous that a person be perfectly free and unhampered in choosing a partner for marriage.

2. *Defect of the Use of Reason*

The investigating pastor should see to it that nupturients have sufficient use of reason so as to be capable of giving proper consent to the marriage.[170]

Insanity is one influence that interferes in a greater or lesser degree with the use of reason. The degree of its influence on reason will depend on the nature, character and extent of the insanity. *Amentes,* who are those who are insane in all matters, are certainly incapable of matrimonial consent. *Dementes* or monomaniacs are those who are insane on some particular point or points. If their dementia concerns marriage, they are absolutely incapable of marriage as long as they remain in that state. Even when the dementia concerns other matters, there are psychiatrists who consider them incapable of the deliberation necessary for contracting a valid marriage. However, if they actually are capable of sufficient deliberation, they can enter a valid marriage contract. Idiots lack sufficient discretion to enter a valid marriage. The same is often true of imbeciles and lunatics. Morons will generally have sufficient knowledge to give proper matrimonial consent.[171] As mental disorders are quite prevalent today, the pastor should look out for them in nupturients, especially when he knows or when he has heard that the nupturients were confined at one time or other to institutions for the insane, or suffered from shellshock. Should a pastor notice or learn that a nupturient's behavior has been peculiar and bizarre, that he has been subject to illusions, hallucinations, very strange emotional reactions, delusions, outbreaks of violence, ecstatic moods, hysteria, obsessions, strange peculiarities of speech, etc., he will have reason to doubt the person's sanity. When a serious doubt about the sanity

[170] *Cf.* canon 1081.

[171] *Cf.* Gasparri, *Tractatus Canonicus de Matrimonio,* n. 785.

of a nupturient arises, it is expedient to refer such a one to some expert on mental disorders. If an expert in mental disorders declares that the nupturient has not sufficient discretion to give matrimonial consent, the pastor should not admit him to marriage.[172]

Not infrequently parties partially under the influence of intoxicating drink present themselves before pastors and signify to them their intention of contracting marriage, or after actually going through a civil marriage ceremony they approach the pastor for the purpose of having their civil marriage convalidated. Furthermore, cases have occurred where two parties under the influence of drink have presented themselves before the pastor for the purpose of contracting marriage simply because one of their friends dared them to marry. In cases such as these pastors should realize that the minds of the parties are somewhat befuddled by intoxicating drink and that their reasoning powers are not perfectly clear. Moreover, there is a strong possibility, if not a probability, that the same parties would never think of contracting marriage were they in their sober senses. Pastors should refrain from instituting pre-nuptial investigation in such cases until the parties are perfectly sober. Even if the pastor knows that the parties will go through a marriage ceremony before a civil magistrate or non-Catholic minister if he himself refuses to assist at the marriage, it is best for the parties concerned and for the Church that the pastor refuse to assist at the union. Should the intoxicated parties have already gone through a marriage ceremony either before a civil magistrate or a non-Catholic minister, the pastor should not permit the pleadings of the parties to induce him to convalidate their marriage until the full use of their reasoning powers have been completely restored.

[172] *Cf. S. R. R., Nullit. Matrim.*, 7 Jan., 1918, *Coram R. P. D., Gulielmus Sebastianelli*, dec. I, nn. 2-6—*Decisiones*, X (1918), 3-6; *S. R. R., Nullit. Matrim.*, 23 Dec., 1918, *Coram R. P. D., Aloisio Sincero*, dec. XVIII, nn. 2-6—*Decisiones*, X (1918), 143-149; *S. R. R., Nullit. Matrim.*, 3 Jun., 1922, *Coram R. P. D., Pietro Rossetti*, dec. XXIII—*Decisiones*, XIV (1922), 223-227; *S. R. R., Nullit. Matrim.*, 25 Jun., 1926, *Coram R. P. D., Iulio Grazioli*, dec. XXVII, nn. 3-22—*Decisiones*, XVIII (1925), 214-220; *S. R. R., Nullit. Matrim.*, 29 Oct., 1934, *Coram R. P. D., Maximo Massimi*, dec. XLI, nn. 2-4—*Decisiones*, XVI (1924), 372-376; *S. R. R., Nullit. Matrim.*, 25 Jun., 1928, dec. XXVIII, nn. 2-7—*Decisiones*, XX (1928), 258-265.

3. *Defect of Sufficient Knowledge*

In order that matrimonial consent can be had it is necessary at least that the contracting parties be not ignorant of the fact that marriage is a permanent society of a man and a woman for the procreation of children.[173] Ignorance of this minimum of knowledge is not presumed after the parties have attained puberty. As a rule the pastor need not question the parties as to the sufficiency of their knowledge for marriage. Very rarely will it occur that parties are ignorant of the necessary minimum of knowledge. However, if the pastor has suspicion that the parties lack the necessary knowledge, prudence and tact dictate that he instruct them on the nature of marriage and on their marital obligations rather than directly interrogate them as to their knowledge.

4. *Error*

Very rarely, if ever, will the present day pastor have occasion to interrogate nupturients in regard to the factor of error. In the event that an exceptional case might occur some remarks in regard to the different classes of error and their effects on matrimonial consent are not out of place.

The Code mentions three kinds of error that invalidate matrimonial consent: (a) error regarding a person's identity; (b) error regarding a person's qualities, when it so overflows its normal channels that it approximates *error in personam;* (c) error regarding a person's basic status in life, which is had when a free person marries a slave whom he thinks and believes to be free.[174] Error regarding a person's identity is also known as substantial error.[175]

To differentiate the two kinds of error listed under (a) and (b), the use of examples by way of illustration may serve the purpose best.

[173] Canon 1082, § 1.

[174] Canon 1083.

[175] Herbert Theodore Rimlinger, *Error Invalidating Matrimonial Consent* (The Catholic University of America, Canon Law Studies, n. 82, Washington: The Catholic University of America, 1932), p. 30.

If John, desiring to contract marriage with Mary, falsely thinks because of the darkness of the church that the girl in his presence is the person of his love, but in reality this girl is Anna, who had been substituted by her parents in place of Mary, then there is present a case of *error in personam*. Such a marriage would be invalid. In practice, error of this kind will hardly ever occur.[176] Hence when both parties meet each other face to face for investigation by the pastor, there is no necessity of questioning them concerning their freedom from *error in personam*.

Suppose that Mary wants to marry John, simply because he is the first-born son and is heir to his father's estate, and she definitely wants to marry no other son. The second son, Hugh, however, is substituted for John, Mary believing that he is the first-born son. Here there is present a case of error *qualitatis redundans in errorem personae*. In general practice the pastor may omit interrogation about such error, unless he suspects from the conversation of a nupturient that one party has deceived the other by alleging false qualities which when truthfully accepted and intensely believed might become the basis for error approximating *error in personam*.

The third kind of error where one contracts marriage with a person whom he believes to be free, whereas in reality that person is a slave, is not of any practical importance in the United States, because slavery properly so-called has been abolished here. However, interrogation on this species of error should not be ommitted in countries where slavery still flourishes.

Simple error concerning the unity, indissolubility or sacramental dignity of marriage, even though it is the cause of the contract, does not vitiate matrimonial consent.[177] Simple error is error which is purely mental or intellectual. It remains in the intellect and does not influence the will in giving matrimonial consent. The error is simple, for instance, if a spouse contracts marriage erroneously believing that marriage can be terminated by divorce, but does not permit this false idea to interfere with his matrimonial consent. The

[176] *S. R. R., Nullit. Matrim.*, 16 Apr., 1913, *Coram R. P. D., Francisco Heiner*, dec. XXI, nn. 2-6—*Decisiones*, V (1913), 243-247; *cf.* Rimlinger, *Error Invalidating Matrimonial Consent*, pp. 31, 32.

[177] Canon 1084.

man who falsely thinks that venereal disease, epilepsy, adultery, etc. on the part of a married spouse is sufficient reason for invalidating a marriage is subject to a simple error and his marriage is valid even though his spouse is afflicted with these diseases or is guilty of adultery, provided he does not make these matters a condition of marriage.

However, if the pastor discovers that a certain party is subject to a simple error in regard to the properties of marriage, he should dispel the error on account of the many difficulties that such an error might afterwards create.

5. *Simulated or Fictitious Consent*

Simulated or fictitious consent takes place when a party pronounces the words of matrimonial consent or signifies by signs that he consents to the marriage in the form prescribed by law, but gives no internal consent.[178]

In order to establish that there will be no simulation of matrimonial consent, the pastor should interrogate each party in the separate examination as to whether they really and truly wish to give internal consent to the marriage. Detailed questioning on the subject is not necessary when it is evident to the pastor that they really and truly love each other. However, the interrogation ought to be intensive when motives enter in that suggest simulation of consent, *e. g.*, when one party is madly in love with someone else; when one party has aversion for the other or manifests that he is little interested in marriage; when a girl is penniless and indications show that she is marrying simply because marriage will offer her a home and financial security; when a girl is pregnant and marriage is necessary to save her own reputation as well as that of her family; when a girl's parents are cruel and there are indications that she turns to marriage as an escape from them; when a girl has a large dowry and the man seems more interested in the dowry than in the girl; when a girl has strong tendencies towards fortune-hunting and social climbing and the man is blessed with considerable money

[178] Gasparri, *Tractatus Canonicus de Matrimonio,* n. 814.

and a high social rank; when an illegitimate child has been born to a girl and the civil court decides to give the reputed father of the child the alternative to marry the girl or support the child.[179]

To treat thoroughly of the various kinds of simulation of consent is impossible here. The pastor will find them discussed extensively in any of the better textbooks on the Canon Law of marriage. A perusal of any of these works will furnish him with the necessary knowledge for formulating his interrogatory for cases in which he suspects simulation of consent.

6. *Conditional Consent*

Since matrimonial consent should be unconditional, the pastor must as a rule not fail to ask the parties if they are qualifying their consent with the stipulation of any conditions, prerequisites, reservations, provisos, exceptions, restrictions, limitations, modifications or other like considerations. Conditionally contracted marriage is contrary to the wishes of the Church and should not be permitted except for some grave reason and with the permission of the local ordinary.[180]

If the pastor, therefore, discovers that a betrothed bride wants to enter marriage under certain stipulated conditions, *e. g.*, that the fiance be free from disease, that he be a man of influence and wealth, that he prove faithful to his marriage vows, that he is not a gambler or a drunkard, that he will laudably practice his newly found religion upon his conversion to the faith, etc., then the pastor should decline to assist at her marriage until she has rectified her vacillating or possibly even self-centered attitude and intent.

If the pastor finds that the affianced groom seeks to enter a

[179] *S. R. R., Nullit. Matrim.*, 30 Aug., 1911, *Coram R. P. D., Michaele Lega,* dec. XL, nn. 4-24—*Decisiones,* III (1911), 461-472; *S. R. R., Nullit. Matrim.*, 1 Jul., 1911, *Coram R. P. D., Gulielmus Sebastianelli,* dec. XXIX, n. 2-8—*Decisiones,* III (1911), 326-336; *S. R. R., Nullit. Matrim.*, 18 Jul., 1911, *Coram R. P. D., Ioanne Prior,* dec. XXXII—*Decisiones,* III (1911), 346-352; *S. R. R., Nullit. Matrim.*, 9 Jul., 1911—*Coram R. P. D., Ioanne Prior,* dec. XXII—*Decisiones,* III (1911), 236-244.

[180] Cappello, *De Sacramentis,* III,, n. 626.

marriage with certain reservations, *e. g.*, that the bride be a virgin, that she will keep her plighted troth, that she be suited for motherhood, that she be frugal in the management of the home, that she be self-sacrificing in her service to him, that she offer him the joy of sympathy and companionship, that she be a compatible wife, etc., then the pastor should similarly refuse to allow his marriage until he has discarded all these restrictions from his matrimonial consent. The pastor should seek to have the parties retract such stipulations. If they insist on harboring certain prerequisites, he will point to the need of abiding their fulfillment before marriage shall follow.

Article 19. The Investigation of the Religious Instruction of the Parties

It is expressly stated in canon 1020, § 2 that the pastor should interrogate the prospective bride and groom on the sufficiency of their instruction in Christian doctrine. However, the same canon permits an exception from this interrogation, if the pastor knows that it would be superfluous in view of the praiseworthy qualifications of the parties. The phrase "*personarum qualitatem*" in the canon refers to their qualifications from the viewpoint of religious knowledge rather than from the viewpoint of their rank or station in life. It is true that those of high rank and dignity are frequently well instructed in the Christion religion, but it is equally true that there is much ignorance of Christian truths among many of them. Hence the pastor should not too easily conclude that those of rank and dignity are sufficiently instructed in Christian doctrine.

What may be considered as sufficient instruction for the nupturients? The Code does not give any information on the point. Authors consider that the parties should be acquainted with those truths which are necessary for salvation by necessity of means and necessity of precept, namely, God's creation of all things, His punishment of the wicked and His reward of the good, the truths contained in the Apostles' Creed, the Ten Commandments of God, the Six Precepts of the Church, the Our Father, the Hail Mary, the acts of Faith, Hope, Charity and Contrition, the Seven Sacraments.

Especially should they be acquainted with the rights and obligations of the conjugal state.[181]

A few discreet questions concerning the extent of the parties' religious education will usually enable the pastor to judge whether the parties are sufficiently versed in Christian doctrine, *e.g.*, what schools they attended (name of grade school, high school, college, university); whether these schools were Catholic or non-Catholic; how long they attended them. If the parties spent considerable time in a Catholic school, it may be concluded that they have a fairly good knowledge of the rudiments of their faith. If they never attended the Catholic schools or if they attended them for only a very short time and received no religious instruction in the state or undenominational schools at which they attended, it seems necessary to ask them what provisions were made for their religious instruction, *e.g.*, whether they attended Sunday School, religious vacation school, Catholic study clubs, lectures on Catholic faith, or whether they received instruction from their parents and, if so, what was the extent of the instruction. It is the duty of the pastor to judge from the replies he receives whether the parties did receive sufficient instruction.

A formal and direct examination, *i.e.*, asking the nupturients specific questions on the principal truths and obligations of the Christian life and requesting that they recite the prayers usually known by Catholics is perhaps the most thorough means of determining the extent of their religious knowledge. However, unless a practice of this kind has been customary in the parish, nupturients, especially those who are more advanced in age, may consider such direct questioning as puerile in purpose and humiliating in its effect, and therefore may resent it. Hence, if the investigating pastor suspects that the parties are poorly versed in their religion, it seems that he satisfactorily fulfills his obligation of investigating the religous knowledge of the parties by simply taking occasion to instruct them in the rudiments of their faith and the duties of the state

[181] A. Tanquerey, *Synopsis Theologiae Moralis*, I: *De Poenitentia, de Matrimonio et de Ordine* (Romae, 1920), n. 878; Wernz, *Ius Decretalium*, IV, n. 131; Ayrinhac-Lydon, *Marriage Legislation in the New Code of Canon Law*, p. 28; Cappello, *De Sacramentis*, III, n. 152.

in life that they are about to enter. This manner of procedure will usually be acceptable to the parties, is more prudent and saves the parties the humiliation of admitting their ignorance of the fundamentals of their religion.[182] Moreover, it accomplishes the object of the inquiry into the parties' religious knowledge, *i. e.*, to make sure that they are properly instructed for the important task of living a Christian married and family life. If the parties refuse to take the instructions, they are not to be looked upon as public sinners, and the pastor should not for that reason refuse to assist at their marriage.[183] Neither should the pastor refuse to permit the marriage of those who are so dull of intellect that they cannot acquire much religious knowledge.[184]

Though canon 1033 deals, not with interrogation regarding religious instruction, but with the imparting of instruction to the parties, it merits some mention here; because it has a close connection with the interrogation concerning religious instruction. It states: "The pastor shall not omit to instruct the spouses, according to their different conditions, on the sanctity of marriage, their mutual obligations, and the obligations of parents to children; he shall also earnestly exhort them before marriage diligently to confess their sins and piously to receive Holy Communion." There is reference here to the private instruction of the parties by the pastor. Though many couples will have sufficient instruction on the points mentioned in the canon, there is today a serious need for such instruction. If the pastor discovers from his interrogation that the parties are ignorant of the nature, dignity, ends and properties of Christian marriage, instruction on these points is of obligation. In imparting the instruction he should accomodate himself to the mentality, education and condition of the nupturients. It is well to stress such points as mutual love, mutual fidelity, mutual respect; the sinfulness of divorce and adultery; the obligation of parents to love, rear, feed and clothe their children and to train and educate them physically, intellectually, morally, religiously and spiritually; the duty of administering and the manner of con-

182 *Cf.* Payen, *De Matrimonio*, n. 413.

183 Pont. Comm. Interp. Cod., 2, 3, Jun., 1918, IV, 3—*AAS*, X (1918), 345.

184 Benedictus XIV, *De Synodo Dioecesana*, lib. III, c. 4, n. 6.

ferring baptism in a case of necessity; the need of giving good example at home as well as abroad and the Christian joy of reaping the fruits of a virtuous life. These instructions may be given immediately after the interrogation of the parties, or they may be postponed to a later occasion.[185]

Because of the many erroneous teachings that are disseminated today regarding the use of marriage, some instruction on that point is necessary. It is best to postpone this instruction to a few days before the marriage. First of all proper stress should be paid on the lawfulness of the conjugal act. Then also it should be emphasized that husband and wife are bound to render the *debitum* whenever they are reasonably requested to do so. Finally they should be reminded of the duty of moderation in the use of marriage, which duty on certain occasions, in view of the consideration of health or other reasons, may comprise even the obligation of complete continence in wedded life. In certain cases the pastor may have to resort to explicit instruction on the points which married parties are bound to respect in strict justice, in Christian charity, in mutual good will or as a matter of merely optional accomodation. Such instruction, of course, will offer ready opportunity for the pastor to indicate, not only what is indefensible, but also what is laudably permissible to partners in married life. If from the words of the parties or the demeanor of the parties the pastor should discover that they are ignorant of what is implied by the use of marriage, he will either himself give them the necessary enlightenment or refer them to their parents for the needed instruction. Still another and frequently most helpful way to impart this knowledge would be the giving to them of some book on marriage that covers the desired points of information. In this latter event, the pastor will make sure that the book which he gives them is written in accordance with Catholic principles of morality.[186]

In speaking of the use of marriage the pastor must be modest and prudent in his language. Because of the prevalence today of the evil of artificial birth-prevention, abortion and onanistic *copula*, some words of warning on the seriousness of those sins should be

[185] Cappello, *De Sacramentis,* III, n. 184.

[186] *Cf.* De Smet, *Betrothment and Marriage,* n. 335.

imparted to nupturients. Here the practical question arises as to what should be the attitude of the investigating pastor towards the practice of married parties confining the use of marriage to the sterile period in family life. Not infrequently nupturients ask about the legitimacy of the practice. In reply it may be stated that the general attitude of the Church towards the practice is one of definite disfavor, because it is a deviation from the ideal and is likely to promote selfishness, which is the source of many evils in married and family life. The large family is in accordance with the purpose of God. A reply of the Sacred Penitentiary on the subject of natural birth prevention declared that a confessor can suggest with *caution* birth control by natural means to those married people whom he has sought in vain to deter from the sin of onanism.[187]

This reply, however, has direct reference to a period after the celebration of marriage; not to the time of pre-marital instruction. If nupturients allege that for definitely serious reasons they should refrain from having children or having only a restricted number of them, and the pastor is aware of the presence of these grave reasons, he may by way of instruction mention that for these reasons the practice of birth control by natural means is permissible, yet he should earnestly and with telling arguments counsel the parties against it and impress upon them the ideal of God—the normal unrestricted family. Very often the reasons of the parties for birth control by natural means are more imaginary than real. And unless a reasonable cause for the practice exists, birth control by natural means is sinful.[188]

Article 20. The Banns of Marriage

The pastor's obligation in pre-nuptial investigation is not fully satisfied when he has concluded the interrogation of the parties concerning their freedom from matrimonial impediments, their freedom of consent and their knowledge of Christian doctrine. He still

[187] S. Poenit., resp., 16 Jul., 1880—*Decisiones Sanctae Sedis de Usu et Abusu Matrimonii,* collegit P. Hartmann Batzill (Taurini: Marietti, 1937), p. 21.

[188] Coucke-Walsh, *The Sterile Period in Family Life* (New York: Wagner, 1933), p. 13.

has the obligation of making sure that the banns of marriage are published and of examining what was the outcome of their publication.

Realizing that the personal investigation by the pastor of the parties' freedom to marry suffers from certain handicaps, the Church has added the additional safeguard of the banns of marriage to promote more efficient pre-nuptial investigation, and to endeavor to bring to light latent impediments that might perchance have escaped the attention of the pastor. The institution of the banns, which is closely allied to personal investigation of the parties by the pastor, has the further value of deterring the parties from concealing or denying the existence of impediments.

It is necessary here to state briefly the doctrine on the banns of marriage and to point out the pastor's obligation in regard to them.

The law requires that the banns of marriage be published by the proper pastor of the parties,[189] *i. e.*, by the pastor of the place where the parties have a domicile or quasi-domicile, and in the case of *vagi* where these at the time maintain their actual residence. It would seem that among the *vagi,* as here considered, there must also be included those who have only a diocesan domicile, quasi-domicile or month's residence.[190] In practice, if there is only one proper pastor and he is the one who investigates the *status liber* of the parties, he alone will have the obligation of announcing the banns. Very frequently there are several proper pastors. In that case the investigating pastor (as he is usually the only one acquainted with the intended marriage of the parties) will have the duty of notifying the various proper pastors of the parties concerning their contemplated marriage. He should send them all the necessary data, the names of the parties, the names of their parents, the date of birth, the names of their proper parishes, etc., and request them to publish the banns in the manner prescribed by law and diocesan custom. He also might mention in his request to these proper pastors that on the completion of their publication of the banns they send him notice concerning the outcome of the publica-

[189] Canon 1023, § 1.

[190] Roberts, *The Banns of Marriage,* p. 70.

tion and inform him of their findings in respect of the *status liber* of the parties.

If after attaining the age of puberty, the parties lived for a period of six months in a place or parish other than their present proper parish or parishes, the investigating pastor will refer the matter to the ordinary,[191] and abide by his instructions. If there be some suspicion of the contraction of an impediment by the parties when they lived elsewhere for a period of even less than six months, the pastor should likewise consult the ordinary. The contemplated marriage should not be permitted by the ordinary until all suspicion has been removed, either by a publication of the banns in the respective parish or by such other means as may be necessary in the case to guarantee the *status liber* of the parties.[192]

The faithful are bound to reveal to the pastor or the local ordinary prior to the celebration of the marriage any impediments of which they know in reference to the parties whose intention of marriage is published or proclaimed.[193] The obligation is a grave one. Exempted from this obligation are confessors who have obtained knowledge of impediments in the confessional, and professional men who have obtained knowledge of impediments in the discharge of their professional duties. However, they must warn the parties themselves to reveal the impediments.[194]

Should the pastor recognize that there is a legitimate cause for a dispensation from the banns, he may petition the proper local ordinary for a dispensation. In this connection, if there is only one proper ordinary, the pastor will petition him. If there are several proper ordinaries, he will petition the one in whose diocese the marriage takes place. If the marriage is celebrated outside of the territories of the various proper ordinaries, he may petition any one of them for the dispensation. In the petition, according to the circumstances, he may ask for a total dispensation, *i. e.*, a dispensation from all the publications, or for a partial dispensation, *i. e.*, a dispensation from one or two publications of the banns.[195] Not any and

[191] Canon 1023, § 2.

[192] Canon 1023, § 3.

[193] Canon 1027.

[194] Roberts, *The Banns of Marriage*, p. 112.

[195] Canon 1028, §§ 1, 2; Roberts, *The Banns of Marriage*, pp. 99-105.

every cause will justify the pastor to seek for a dispensation. The cause should be legitimate and reasonable, as, for instance, scandal, infamy, great disparity in age and rank of the parties, etc.[196] Should the pastor, however, suspect that any impediments hinder the marriage, he should be reluctant, rather than enthusiastic, about asking the proper local ordinary for a dispensation from the banns.

Article 21. The Pastor's Obligation After the Publication of the Banns

The pastor's obligation after the publication of the banns will depend largely on what the outcome of the publication is.

Should a doubt arise about the existence of any impediment to marriage, he will be obliged to investigate the matter more accurately by interrogating under oath at least two trustworthy witnesses, provided there is not question of an impediment which, if known, would bring disgrace on the parties. If necessary, he may interrogate the parties themselves under oath.[197]

If the publication of the banns gives rise to the certified existence of some impediment which is *indispensable,* the pastor must inform the parties of the matter and refuse to assist at their marriage. If the impediment is a dispensable one, it will be either *occult* or *public.* If *occult,* he should refer the matter to the local ordinary or to the Sacred Penitentiary for a dispensation, mentioning the causes for the dispensation, but concealing the *true* names of the parties in the petition for the dispensation. If the dispensable impediment is a *public* one, he may petition the local ordinary or the Holy See for a dispensation, mentioning the actual names of the parties and the causes for the dispensation. Until the dispensation is granted, he cannot assist at the marriage of the parties. If the publication of the banns did not reveal the existence of an impediment, he may proceed with the marriage after he has obtained all the necessary documents required by law, and has assured himself with moral certainty that no impediment stands in the way of a licit and valid marriage.

196 Roberts, *The Banns of Marriage,* p. 107.

197 Canon 1031, § 1: see p.

A problem sometimes arises when the other proper pastors refuse to publish the banns, or when they neglect to do so; or if they publish them, when they neglect to send the results of the publication to the investigating pastor. This creates a practical difficulty. After waiting a reasonable length of time for a reply from the other proper pastors, it appears that the most prudent procedure for the investigating pastor is to lay the matter before the ordinary and follow his instructions. However, if the pastor is really certain that the parties are free to marry, he can hardly be censured if he goes ahead with the celebration of the marriage without consulting the ordinary.

CHAPTER VIII

PRE-NUPTIAL INVESTIGATION IN MIXED MARRIAGES

Upon discussion of the pre-nuptial investigation of Catholic couples, it is quite logical to give some special consideration to pre-nuptial investigation in mixed marriages. Many of the interrogations and inquiries discussed in the preceding chapter in regard to Catholic marriages will apply with equal force to mixed marriages. However, some variations and additions in the pre-nuptial investigation of couples intending to enter a mixed marriage will be necessary, as there are several decided dissimilarities between mixed marriages and purely Catholic unions. In this chapter it will not be necessary to treat anew those points in pre-nuptial investigation that are common to both Catholic and mixed marriages; it will be sufficient to refer to the articles in which they were treated in the preceding chapter. Consequently the present chapter will principally consider those features of pre-nuptial investigation which are peculiar to mixed marriages and which are not found in distinctly Catholic unions.

Article 1. Attitude of the Church Towards Mixed Marriages

In investigating the free status of couples intending to enter a mixed marriage, the pastor should not neglect to keep in mind the attitude of the Church towards such marriages. The Church's attitude towards them should be also the pastor's attitude. As a general policy the attitude of the Church towards Catholics contracting mixed marriages is one of reasonable opposition and disfavor. Ordinaries and pastors of souls are obliged to deter the faithful from entering such unions in as far as this may be possible. If they cannot prevent these marriages, they must take care that they be contracted in accordance with the laws of God and the Church.[1] The Church

[1] Canon 1064, 1°, 2°.

seeks by legislation to deter Catholics from entering mixed unions. She has made mixed religion [2] and disparity of cult [3] impediments to marriage. She requires that mixed marriages be celebrated with less solemnity than Catholic marriages by prescribing that they be celebrated outside the church, unless the ordinary according to his prudent judgment and in order to avoid more serious evils grants a dispensation to celebrate them in the church.[4] All sacred rites are prohibited in the mixed marriage ceremony. Nevertheless, if the ordinary foresees that more serious evils will arise from such a prohibition, he can permit some of the customary ecclesiastical ceremonies, provided he always excludes the celebration of the nuptial Mass.[5]

The severe attitude of the Church towards mixed unions is nothing modern. It existed from the days of early Christianity and was particularly rigorous during the Middle Ages.[6] Popes and ecclesiastical councils have frequently expressed in no uncertain terms their opposition to Catholics entering such marriages.[7] After the so-called reformation the rigorous discipline of the Church on mixed marriages was somewhat relaxed, but strict opposition to the contracting of such unions still prevails.

This strict attitude of the Church towards mixed marriages is not only justifiable but very reasonable. Its purpose is the protection of Catholic faith and morals. Experience has proved that mixed marriages in many cases have constituted a grave danger to the faith and morals of the Catholic spouse and the children born of such unions. While in some cases this danger is removed or rendered remote, the general danger of perversion cannot be minimized. The stern facts of statistics demonstrate that mixed marriages have frequently been responsible for apostasy, heresy and indifferentism to religion on the part of the Catholic partner, for

[2] Canon 1060.

[3] Canon 1070.

[4] Canon 1109, § 3.

[5] Canon 1102, § 2.

[6] *Cf.* Schenk, *Mixed Religion and Disparity of Cult,* nn. 28-113.

[7] Francis Ter Haar, *Mixed Marriages and Their Remedies,* translation by Aloysius Walter (New York: Pustet, 1933), pp. 3-13.

the jeopardizing of the Catholic education of the children, for the practice of artificial birth-prevention, for divorce and for religious tensions in the home. Nor are such evils to be wondered at. When there is no harmony and compatibility of minds and hearts on religious matters in the home, when parents do not pray and worship together, when each has a separate code of morality, when there is considerable intermingling with the non-Catholic associates, relatives and friends of the non-Catholic married partner, it is easy to visualize how great is the danger of perversion of the Catholic partner and children. This danger of perversion is accentuated when the Catholic party is weak in faith and religious knowledge and is ready to make compromises when matters of faith and morals are at stake.[8] If the non-Catholic is personally convinced of the truth of his own beliefs, and especially if he is of a strong-willed or obstinate character, the danger of perversion is more proximate.

The natural law and the divine law prohibit mixed marriages as long as the danger of perversion to the Catholic party or to the offspring continues to exist.[9] When the danger of perversion is removed, the prohibition of the natural and divine law ceases, but the ecclesiastical prohibition forbidding mixed unions remains. The Church, however, has the power to grant a dispensation from her own law on the impediments of mixed religion and disparity of cult. Realizing that mixed unions are practically inevitable, especially in regions where a large percentage of the population is non-Catholic and where the opportunities for men and women entering suitable Catholic marriages are limited, the Church today frequently grants dispensations from the impediments of mixed religion and disparity of cult. However, she grants them reluctantly and only after she has obtained moral certainty in regard to the three following points: (a) that there are proportionately just and grave causes for the dispensation; (b) that the non-Catholic party has given guarantees that the danger of perversion for the Catholic party will be removed and that both parties promise that all the children will be baptized and educated in the Catholic faith; (c) that there is moral certainty that the promises will be fulfilled.

[8] *Cf.* Ter Haar, *Mixed Marriages and Their Remedies*, pp. 13-56.
[9] *Cf.* canon 1070.

Article 2. The Impediment of Mixed Religion

The impediment of mixed religion is aptly enunciated in canon 1060: "The Church most severely and everywhere forbids marriage between two baptized persons, one of whom is a Catholic and the other is a person enrolled in a heretical or schismatical sect; if danger of the perversion of the Catholic party and of the offspring exists, the marriage is forbidden also by the divine law."

It is evident from canon 1060 that the impediment of mixed religion is simply a prohibitive impediment to marriage, *i. e.*, it renders marriages unlawful, but not invalid. It binds everywhere, even in those places where custom recognized that mixed religion did not render marriage unlawful.[10]

The impediment arises only between two baptized persons, of whom one is a Catholic and the other is a person belonging to a heretical or schismatical sect. The valid baptism of both parties is necessarily presupposed. Thus mixed religion is distinguished from disparity of cult which necessarily requires that one party be unbaptized.[11]

At the time of marriage one of the parties must be a Catholic, *i. e.*, an actual member of the Church, and the other must be a person belonging to a heretical or schismatical sect.[12]

The term "Catholic" includes not only Catholics who were baptized in the Catholic Church, but also converts to it from heresy and schism. It refers not only to good Catholics but also to Catholics who are public sinners; who belong to condemned societies; and who are occult heretics, apostates or schismatics.[13] Here a question may be asked in regard to the status of those who were baptized in the Catholic Church in infancy, and reared as Catholics, but who in adult age became heretics or schismatics. Are they to be considered Catholics in the sense of canon 1060? If they join a heretical or schismatical sect, authors are unanimous in considering them bound by the impediment of disparity of cult, when they

[10] Schenk, *Mixed Religion and Disparity of Cult,* n. 126; S. C. S. Off., 3 Jan., 1871—*Coll.*, n. 1434; Wernz, *Ius Decretalium,* n. 576.

[11] Canon 1070, § 1.

[12] Woywod, *A Practical Commentary on the Code of Canon Law,* n. 1039.

[13] Schenk, *Mixed Religion and Disparity of Cult,* n. 129.

marry unbaptized non-Catholics; however, they are not considered bound by the impediment of mixed religion when they marry baptized non-Catholics.[14] In his admirable work on mixed religion and disparity of cult, Schenk maintains that Catholics who become heretics or schismatics, but do not join a heretical or schismatical sect, must be excluded from the term "Catholic" in canon 1060.[15] Although he presents good arguments for his position, one can hardly agree with him in the light of the decree issued by the Holy Office on January 30, 1867. The decree seems to favor the opposite view. In regard to a marriage between a Catholic party and one who has departed from the true faith, but did not attach himself to a false religion or sect, it declares that the pastor is bound to do his utmost to impede the marriage. If he cannot impede the marriage and he prudently fears that grave scandal or injury will be occasioned by his refusal to assist at the marriage, the decree directs that he refer the matter to the bishop. It furthermore states that the bishop can permit the pastor to assist passively at the marriage as an authorized witness, provided that the Catholic education of the offspring is safeguarded and other similar conditions complied with. Earlier in the same decree it was stated that when there was question of a marriage between a Catholic and a person who has denied the true faith to become an adherent of a false religion or sect, it was necessary to ask for the *customary dispensation.* There was no mention of a dispensation being asked for if a Catholic party wished to marry one who had departed from the true faith but who did not become a member of a false religion or sect.[16] Hence in the event that a

[14] *Cf.* S. C. S. Off., decr., 30 Jan., 1867—*Coll.,* n. 1300; Cappello, *De Sacramentis,* 111, n. 306; Gasparri, *Tractatus Canonicus de Matrimonio,* n. 438; Schenk, *Mixed Religion and Disparity of Cult,* n. 129; Ter Haar, *Mixed Marriages and Their Remedies,* p. 2; *cf. etiam* Pont. Comm. Interp. Cod., resp., 16 Oct., 1919, n. 7—*AAS,* XI (1919), 477.

[15] Schenk, *Mixed Religion and Disparity of Cult,* n. 129.

[16] *Cf.* S. C. S., Off. decr., 30 Jan., 1867—*Coll.,* n. 1300; Woywod, *A Practical Commentary on the Code of Canon Law,* n. 1039; Cappello, *De Sacramentis,* III, n. 306; Eduard Eichmann, *Das katholische Mischehenrecht nach dem Codex Iuris Canonici* (Paderborn, 1921), p. 11; De Smet, *Betrothment and Marriage,* n. 251.

Catholic wishes to marry a fallen-away Catholic who did not join a false religion or sect, the canonical impediment of mixed religion does not seem to arise; but the divine prohibition against such a marriage definitely remains until the proximate danger of the perversion of the faithful Catholic and of the offspring is removed.

It has been stated that for the impediment of mixed religion to arise *one of the baptized parties must be a member of a heretical or schismatical sect at the time of marriage.*

A schismatical sect is one whose members refuse either to subject themselves to the authority of the Supreme Pontiff or to communicate with the members of the Church subject to the Supreme Pontiff,[17] *e.g.*, the Greek Orthodox Church.

A heretical sect in the strict sense is one whose members, while still retaining the name Christian, stubbornly deny or doubt any of the truths that must be believed on divine and Catholic faith. Membership in such a heretical sect is exemplified by Lutherans, Methodists, Episcopalians, etc. However, it would seem that the phrase "heretical sect" in canon 1060 is not confined to a purely Christian heretical sect but includes any organized religious group that profess a false religion. It would not be consonant with reason to consider the marriage of a Catholic with a baptized member of a Christian sect as being hindered by the impediment of mixed religion and to look upon the marriage of a Catholic with a baptized person who has joined a non-Christian religious sect as being free from the impediment of mixed religion. Hence it is legitimate to conclude that the phrase "heretical sect" in canon 1060 includes both Christian heretical sects and non-Christian religious sects. A reply of the Pontifical Commission for the Authentic Interpretation of the Code given on July 30, 1934, declared that persons who belong or have belonged to an atheistic sect are to be considered, as regards all legal effects, even those which concern sacred ordination and marriage, the same as persons who have belonged to a non-Catholic sect.[18] In virtue of this reply the phrase "heretical sect" mentioned in canon 1060 would

[17] *Cf.* canon 1325, § 2.

[18] *AAS*, XXVI (1934), 494.

extend even to an atheistic sect. Therefore a Catholic marrying a baptized person who belongs to an atheistic sect is bound by the impediment of mixed religion.

The following may be considered as members of a heretical sect:

1. Those who were baptized in the Catholic Church, but who from the age of infancy were educated in heresy and still profess heresy.
2. Those who were baptized either in the Catholic Church or outside of it and were brought up by heretics from infancy without any Catholic education, even though their heretical parents or guardians gave them little or no education in heresy. In such a case the children apparently belong to the heretical sect of their parents, unless they formally sever relations from it.[19]
3. Those baptized children who after the age of reason have fallen into the hands of heretics and who have *formally* joined a heretical sect.
4. Those persons who were born of heretical parents and caused to be baptized by them in a heretical sect, even though the persons so born and baptized made no solemn profession of heresy or were negligent of their religious duties as members of the sect. Until they *formally* depart from the sect by a positive act of the will, they remain members of that sect.[20]
5. Those who in adult age caused themselves to be baptized in a heretical sect with the intention of enrolling themselves in that sect.

What has been said in the foregoing numbers concerning membership in a heretical sect applies equally to membership in a schis-

[19] *Cf.* S. C. S. Off., litt. (ad Ep. Harlemen.), 6 Apr., 1859—*Fontes,* n. 950; Schenk, *Mixed Religion and Disparity of Cult,* n. 135; Ayrinhac-Lydon, *Marriage Legislation in the New Code of Canon Law,* pp. 98, 99.

[20] S. C. S. Off., litt. (ad Ep. Harlemen.), 6 Apr., 1859—*Fontes,* n. 950; Schenk, *Mixed Religion and Disparity of Cult,* n. 135; Ayrinhac-Lydon, *Marriage Legislation in the New Code of Canon Law,* nn. 98, 99.

matical sect. Once baptized persons have formally joined a heretical or schismatical sect the presumption is that they still remain attached to that sect until it is definitely demonstrated that they have broken relations with it by a positive act of the will.[21]

Article 3. The Impediment of Disparity of Cult

Canon 1070, § 1 states the nature of the impediment of disparity of cult in the following words: "The marriage contracted by a non-baptized person with a person baptized in the Catholic Church or converted to it from heresy or schism is null."

From the words of the canon it is evident that disparity of cult is a diriment impediment to marriage. Two important conditions are necessary as a basis for the impediment:

(a) one party must be unbaptized;

(b) the other party must have been validly baptized in the Catholic Church or have been converted to it from heresy or schism.

It is important for the pastor to note that the law of the Code on the impediment or disparity of cult differs somewhat from the pre-Code legislation. Prior to May 19, 1918, the impediment of disparity of cult arose between any baptized person and a non-baptized person. Even valid baptism outside the Catholic Church, *e. g.*, in a heretical sect, was sufficient on the part of the baptized party.[22] In the present discipline, disparity of cult arises only between a person *baptized in the Catholic Church* or converted to it from heresy or schism and a person who is unbaptized. The baptism of the person in the Catholic Church must be a real, true, objective baptism. It is not sufficient that the nupturient *thinks* he was baptized in

[21] Ayrinhac-Lydon, *Marriage Legislation in the New Code of Canon Law*, p. 99.

[22] *Cf. Benedictus* XIV, ep. *Singulari*, 9 Feb., 1749—*Fontes*, n. 394; Simon Aichner, *Compendium Iuris Ecclesiastici* (6. ed., Brixinae, 1887), § 173, n. 4; J. Schulte, *Handbuch des katholischen Eherechts nach dem gemeinen katholischen Kirchenrechte und dem österreichischen, preussischen, französischen Particularrechte, mit Rücksichtsnahme auf noch andere Civilgesetzgebungen* (Giessen, 1875), p. 224.

the Catholic Church. Actual baptism is required. If a party was actually baptized in the Catholic Church, but is unaware of it, and desires to marry an actually unbaptized person, the marriage is hindered by the diriment impediment of disparity of cult.[23] The conversion from heresy or schism mentioned in canon 1070, § 1 must also have actually taken place for the impediment to arise. Hence an unbaptized catechumen taking instructions to enter the Catholic Church is not bound by the impediment of disparity of cult if he wants to marry a non-Catholic.

The impediment of disparity of cult does not bind baptized non-Catholics.[24] Consequently heretics and schismatics who never belonged to the Catholic Church are not bound by the impediment of disparity of cult when they marry infidels.

Defection from the Catholic faith on the part of those who were baptized in the Catholic Church or converted to it from heresy or schism does not exempt them from the impediment of disparity of cult when they marry unbaptized persons. No such concession is granted by the Code to those who defect from the Catholic Church. It is true that canon 1099, § 1 exempts from the *canonical form* of marriage *those born of non-Catholics who, although they have been baptized in the Catholic Church, were raised from infancy in heresy, schism, infidelity or without any religion.* This exemption, however, extends only to the canonical form of marriage; not to the impediment of disparity of cult.

Article 4. Investigating Whether the Impediment is "Mixed Religion" or "Disparity of Cult"

When the pastor discovers from the replies to his preliminary questions on religion that one nupturient is Catholic and the other is non-Catholic, it will be his duty to establish whether the impediment affecting them is one of mixed religion or one of disparity of cult. Determination of the exact nature of the impediment is important in order that the pastor may determine what dispensation is to be petitioned by the parties.

[23] S. C. de Prop. Fide, resp., 1 Apr., 1922—*NRT,* LII (1925), 497.

[24] S. C. S. Off., resp. (ad Archiep. Friburgen.), 21 Dec., 1924—*AKKR,* CV (1925), 202; *cf. etiam ETL,* III (1925), 135.

It has been pointed out that mixed religion is a prohibitive impediment to marriage and arises between two baptized people, one of whom is a Catholic and the other a person enrolled in a heretical or schismatical sect; and that disparity of cult is a diriment impediment to marriage and arises between an unbaptized person and one baptized in the Catholic Church or converted to it from heresy or schism.

The pastor must first verify that one party is a Catholic. For that purpose it will be necessary to establish that he is a validly baptized member of the Catholic Church. In this regard the prescriptions of canon 1021 concerning the testimony of baptism should be observed.[25] It is also important to inquire as to whether he ever left the Church and whether he formally joined a heretical or schismatical sect, and, if so, whether he still belongs to it.[26]

Having established the Catholicity of the one party, the pastor should interrogate the non-Catholic party as to whether he was ever baptized. This question is of paramount importance because it is the baptism or non-baptism of the non-Catholic that really differentiates the impediment of mixed religion from the impediment of disparity of cult. If the party asserts that he is not baptized the pastor should not too readily accept his statement as absolutely true; for pastoral experience has sometimes proved that non-Catholics who claimed to be unbaptized were on investigation discovered to have been baptized. Hence, it is expedient to make some inquiries as to whether their parents had any religion or belonged to any sect in which baptism was customary. If their parents did not belong to any sect or belonged to a sect that did not believe in baptism, or if they never practised their religion, the pastor has sufficient reason, as a rule, to conclude that the nupturient is telling the truth about his non-baptism.

If the non-Catholic party asserts that he has been baptized, testimony of his baptism should be demanded.[27] Ordinarily an authentic certificate taken from the baptismal registers of the sect in which he was baptized should be requested. In the absence of such a record, or when it is impossible for some good reason to obtain the

[25] See pp. 148-153.

[26] See p. ....

[27] Canon 1021, § 1.

certificate, the testimony of reliable witnesses should be obtained. It is best to have sworn testimony. If no direct testimony can be obtained, indirect testimony should be sought. The pastor should not depend altogether on the word of the party, for some non-Catholic nupturients, believing that it is easier to obtain a dispensation from mixed religion than from disparity of cult, have not hesitated to state untruthfully that they were baptized. Moreover, it is not unusual to find that some have been misinformed concerning the fact of their baptism. Hence there is necessity for accurate inquiries concerning the baptism of the non-Catholic nupturient to a mixed marriage.

Having established the fact that the non-Catholic nupturient is baptized, the pastor should not immediately conclude that the impediment is definitely one of mixed religion. As doubt sometimes exists concerning the validity of non-Catholic baptisms, the investigating pastor should not hastily infer that testimony of the fact of baptism in a non-Catholic sect absolutely establishes the validity of the baptism. On the other hand, the pastor should not take the attitude that the validity of every non-Catholic baptism should be called into doubt. Schaaf, writing in the *American Ecclesiastical Review,*[28] clearly and with considerable attention to detail demonstrates that this attitude is wrong, and shows that the heretical views of the non-Catholic minister, the false beliefs regarding the effects of baptism that prevail in the sect and the personal intentions of the minister do not invalidate the marriage as long as the minister uses the necessary matter and form and has the general intention of doing Christ's will. Provided this general intention is present, even in an implicit or indeterminate way, there is sufficient intention for a valid baptism.[29]

[28] Valentine Schaaf, "The Invalidity of Sectarian Baptisms," *AER,* LXXV (1926), 359-370; "Are Protestant Baptisms Ordinarily Valid?," *AER,* LXXV (1926), 136-151.

[29] *Cf.* Conc. Trident., sess. VII, *de sacramentis in genere,* c. 11; S. C. S. Off., instr. (*ad Custodem Terrae Sanctae*), 30 Jan., 1833—*Fontes,* n. 871; instr. (ad Vic. Ap. Oceaniae Central.), 18 Dec., 1872—*Fontes,* n. 1024; instr. (ad Ep. Nesquallien.), 24 Jan., 1877—*Fontes,* n. 1050; Card. Robertus Bellarminus, *Opera Omnia ex Editione Veneta,* iterum edidit Justinus Fèvre (Parisiis, 1870-1874), lib. I, *de sacramentis in genere,* c. XXVII, t. III, 413.

Generalizations as to which non-Catholic sects baptize validly are impossible. The principle of the private interpretation of Sacred Scripture is so widely accepted in many non-Catholic Christian sects that it frequently happens that individual ministers within the same sect have not only different ideas about the nature and effects of baptism, but conduct the actual ceremony of baptism differently. It seems to be the desire of the Holy See that in each particular case inquiries should be made about the validity of the baptism of the non-Catholic party.[30] Consequently, in as far as this is possible, the pastor should investigate in each individual case the validity of the baptism conferred by non-Catholics. If after the investigation a doubt about the validity of the baptism still remains in the mind of the pastor, the presumption that the baptism conferred in the non-Catholic sect is valid will continue to exist until the opposite is proved.[31]

In order to investigate satisfactorily the validity of a doubtful baptism, it is necessary to find out if the minister used the proper matter and form for the sacrament and if he had the proper intention, namely, the intention of doing Christ's will.[32] The ritual of the sect would furnish information on the matter and form of the sacrament. However, it would also be necessary to make sure whether the minister followed the ritual of the sect or adopted some corruption of the ritual. Witnesses to the baptism, provided their memory of the event is good, would be in a position to attest this. Inquiry from the minister himself who did the baptizing would be necessary to discover if he had the proper intention. Circumstances will frequently render it impossible to consult the minister on the

[30] *Cf.* S. C. S. Off., litt. (ad Ep. Harlemen.), 6 Apr., 1859—*Fontes*, n. 950; instr. (ad Ep. Nesquallien.), 24 Jan., 1877—*Fontes*, n. 1050; S. C. de Prop. Fide, instr., 17 Apr., 1777—*Coll.*, n. 522; instr. (ad Vic. Ap. Myssur.), 31 Dec., 1851—*Coll.*, n. 1069; S. C. S. Off. (Ripana), 12 Dec., 1733—*Thesaurus*, VI, 178-180; (Tarvissina Baptismi), 28 Apr., 1736—*Thesaurus*, VII, 210-213; (Sutrina Baptismi), 12 Jul., 1794—*Thesaurus*, LXIII, 165-171; (Brixien. Dubia Baptismi et Matrimonii), 27 Aug., 1796—*Thesaurus*, LXV, 209-220; (Brixien. Baptismi), 11 Feb., 1707—*Thesaurus*, LXVI, 26-28.

[31] Schaaf, "The Invalidity of Sectarian Baptisms," *AER*, LXXV (1926), 358-370; S. C. S. Off., resp., 15 Maii, 1936—*Periodica*, XXV (1936), 152.

[32] Schenk, *Mixed Religion and Disparity of Cult*, n. 192.

matter, especially when the minister is prejudiced against the Catholic religion. In such a case the pastor will have to act on limited evidence. If the evidence at hand is not sufficient to produce moral certitude of the validity or invalidity of the baptism, a dispensation *mixtae religionis et ad cautelam disparitatis cultus* should be petitioned.[33] It is quite customary today for the Holy See to grant dispensations *mixtae religionis et ad cautelam disparitatis cultus.* This is a departure from the pre-Code practice, which did not favor dispensations from mixed religion granted *ad cautelam disparitatis cultus.* No doubt the reason for the present-day practice is the fact that complete investigation of the validity of non-Catholic baptisms is not always possible, or, if possible, does not always produce satisfactory results.[34] Nevertheless, if from his investigation the pastor is morally certain that the non-Catholic party to a mixed marriage is validly baptized, he should ask only for the dispensation from mixed religion. Before aiding the parties to draw up the petition for the dispensation, he should inquire whether the baptized non-Catholic belongs to a heretical or schismatical sect (in the sense above explained) at the time of the investigation; because, if by a positive act of the will he had severed relations with the heretical or schismatical sect, the marriage of a Catholic with him would not be hindered by the impediment of mixed religion.[35] When the investigation discloses that the non-Catholic party to a mixed marriage is definitely unbaptized, petition should be made for a dispensation from the impediment of disparity of cult.

Article 5. Investigation Concerning the Residence of the Parties

Assuming that the pastor has properly identified the parties, it will be necessary for him to carefully establish whether or not he is competent to assist at their marriage by reason of the fact that they have a domicile, a quasi-domicile or a month's residence in his

[33] Schenk, *Mixed Religion and Disparity of Cult,* nn. 203, 252, 253; P. Durieux, *The Busy Pastor's Book on Matrimony,* translation by Oliver Dolphin (Faribault, 1926), p. 79; Wernz-Vidal, *Ius Canonicum,* V, n. 268.

[34] Schenk, *Mixed Religion and Disparity of Cult,* n. 252.

[35] See pp. 230, 231.

parish. To determine whether or not he can assist at the marriage by reason of any of these three titles, he must question the nupturients somewhat intensively concerning their place of residence. The questions will be very like to those which have been discussed in the preceding chapter in reference to the place of residence of Catholic couples.[36] Consequently it is unnecessary to restate those questions here. However, in mixed marriages there is one question that presents a difficulty and which will affect the investigation concerning the place of residence of the parties. The question is this: Is it the bride's pastor or the bridegroom's pastor that has the preference to assist at the marriage when the bride is the non-Catholic? As already pointed out there are three different opinions regarding the answer to this question. Consequently the interrogations concerning the place of the parties, residence will depend on which opinion the investigating pastor personally maintains. In this dissertation the opinion is maintained that it is the rule that the pastor of the non-Catholic bride has the preference to assist at the marriage and conduct the pre-nuptial investigation. However, a just cause excuses from this rule.[37] It is a common practice in America for the pastor of the Catholic groom to conduct the pre-nuptial investigation and assist at mixed marriages without obtaining the permission of the pastor of the non-Catholic bride. The practice has the advantage that the pastor of the Catholic groom is usually better acquainted with the parties and is thus in a better position to conduct the pre-nuptial investigation. This seems a just cause for departure from the rule of canon 1097, § 2, when considered in conjunction with the fact that the bride is non-Catholic. Therefore it appears legitimate to hold that in a mixed marriage the pastor of the bride can assist at the marriage and conduct the pre-nuptial investigation without getting permission from the pastor of the groom, and also that the pastor of the groom, on account of the presence of a just cause, can assist at the marriage and conduct the pre-nuptial investigation without obtaining the permission of the pastor of the bride. Consequently, for the purpose of determining his competency to assist at the marriage, it will be sufficient for the pastor to establish

[36] See pp. 145-148.

[37] Canon 1097, § 2.

that either the bride or the groom has a domicile, a quasi-domicile or a month's residence in his parish. The questions concerning the residence of the parties should be formulated accordingly. However, if it happens that neither the bride nor the groom have a domicile, a quasi-domicile or a month's residence in the parish, the pastor will have to refer them to their proper pastor, or obtain from their proper pastor the necessary permission to assist at the marriage.

In the preceding chapter, where the question of domicile or residence was considered in reference to Catholic marriages, it was stated that the pastor had the obligation of interrogating the parties with a view to finding out in what various places outside of their present proper parish or parishes they ever resided since they attained puberty. Has the pastor a similar obligation in the case of parties to a mixed marriage? In reply, it is necessary to state that the obligation in regard to Catholic marriages was deduced from canon 1023 which states: "The publication of the banns of marriage must be made by the proper pastor of the parties. If a party dwelt in another place for a period of six months after attaining puberty, the pastor must refer the matter to the ordinary, who according to his prudent judgment will either demand that the publication of banns be made *there*, or prescribe that other proofs or information concerning the *status liber* of the parties be obtained. If there is any suspicion that an impediment has been contracted, the pastor should consult the ordinary, even if the stay was shorter than six months, and the ordinary cannot permit the marriage until the suspicion has been removed." The foregoing canon is one of the canons dealing with the publication of the banns of marriage. And the banns of marriage are usually not published for mixed marriages.[38] Though canon 1023 is one of the canons dealing with the publication of the banns, its ultimate purpose is to establish the parties' freedom to marry. That is the reason why it places on the pastor the obligation to inform the ordinary, if a nupturient since the time of puberty dwelt six months outside his proper parish; and likewise to inform him of a briefer stay when there is suspicion that an impediment was contracted. If this obligation of consulting the ordinary in these special circumstances holds for Catholic marriages,

[38] Canon 1026.

there seems to be even greater reason for such consultation in the case of mixed marriages. The possibility that one of the parties to a mixed marriage has contracted an impediment while dwelling outside his proper parish after the attainment of puberty is, as a general rule, more proximate than in the case of Catholic couples. Hence, it may be concluded that the pastor should likewise interrogate the parties to a mixed marriage as to whether they resided after puberty in a place or in places outside of their own proper parish.

Article 6. Investigation of the Causes for Dispensation from the Impediments of "Mixed Religion" and "Disparity of Cult"

The first prerequisite mentioned in the Code for a dispensation either from the impediment of mixed religion or from that of disparity of cult is the presence of just and grave causes.[39] The exact words which the Code uses are: *"nisi urgeant iustae ac gravae causae."* These words indicate that some urgency or necessity for the dispensation must accompany the causes.[40] Unless grave and just causes are present, a dispensation granted by the Supreme Pontiff would be illicit and if granted by one inferior in authority to the Roman Pontiff would be invalid.[41]

The final judge of the justness and gravity of the causes is the superior who grants the dispensation. However, the grantor of the dispensation does not deal immediately and directly with the nupturients. As a rule he does not even know them. Consequently, he will have to depend largely on the information furnished him by the pastor in regard to the presence of just and grave causes. Hence, it is most essential that the pastor properly appraise the causes in each given case and that he be careful to guard against an erroneous judgment. The obligation of the pastor to furnish the truth about the causes alleged for the dispensation is a grave one. The pastor should not *presume* that the causes are present; he must at least morally certify their existence.

[39] Canons 1061, § 1, 1°, and 1071.

[40] Ter Haar, *Mixed Marriages and Their Remedies,* p. 63.

[41] Canon 84, § 1.

No absolute standard of gravity can be set for forming judgments regarding the gravity of the cause. Relative standards that take into account the circumstances of time, persons and places must necessarily be employed.[42]

The Code does not furnish any list of specific causes that may be considered just and grave for dispensations from mixed marriages. However, two lists of causes recognized by the Holy See for dispensations in general have been issued by the Apostolic Datary and the Sacred Congregation for the Propagation of the Faith respectively. These lists have been given in a preceding chapter.[43] Many of the causes in those lists, *e. g.*, the limited prospects for marriage, the poverty of a widow, the lack of a dowry, the increase of dowry, the ending of a lawsuit, the super-marriageable age of the woman, etc., cannot of themselves be considered sufficiently cogent causes for dispensations from the impediments of mixed religion and disparity of cult, since they are not proportionate to the evils involved in mixed unions. However, a cumulation of several of these less cogent causes may be sufficiently strong to form a real grave reason for granting the requisite dispensation. The following enumeration is a list, but not an exhaustive list, of the more cogent causes alleged by commentators as sufficiently grave to warrant a dispensation from either the impediment of mixed religion or that of disparity of cult:

1. The public good of the Church or of the Christian State. An illustrative case is had in the desire of the non-Catholic head of the State to marry a Catholic. Of course here as elsewhere, the Church will previously insist on the *cautiones* and the moral assurance of their fulfillment.

2. The paucity of Catholics in a particular locality where non-Catholics are numerous, the Catholics being left free and safe in the exercise of their religion.

3. Grave scandal or infamy arising from pregnancy, from concubinage or from some other source, and which cannot be obviated except through the medium of a mixed marriage.

4. The serious promise of the non-Catholic party that he will embrace the Catholic faith after entering marriage.

[42] Cappello, *De Sacramentis,* III, n. 314.

[43] See pp. 140, 141.

5. The fact that a mixed marriage is the only means of guaranteeing that the children born of a former mixed marriage will be educated in the Catholic faith.

6. The fact that a mixed marriage is the only way of guaranteeing that an illegitimate child born to the parties will be educated in the Catholic faith.

7. The convalidation of a civil marriage after due repentance and reparation of scandal.

8. The danger that the marriage will be contracted before a civil magistrate or a non-Catholic minister.

9. A well-founded hope of the conversion of the non-Catholic party.

10. The grave danger that the Catholic party will apostatize, or join a heretical or schismatical sect, if he be refused a dispensation.

11. The well-founded hope that a certain family well disposed towards the Catholic Church will be converted to it by a mixed marriage.[44]

As the above list is only illustrative, other causes may be alleged. The pastor should refrain from listing in the petition any causes that are untrue, or for which there is not some evidence. The pastor need not directly interrogate the parties as to whether this or that cause is present, *e. g.*, he need not directly ask if the non-Catholic is going to become a Catholic; whether the parties are marrying because the woman is pregnant; whether they will marry outside the Church if the dispensation is refused, etc. Such direct questioning will probably do more harm than good, and is frequently imprudent, for it may provoke the parties to do what is wrong in order that they might have a sufficient cause for a dispensation. From the conversation, attitude and general knowledge of the parties, and from indirect interrogation, when it is deemed prudent, a capable investigator will be able to form his judgment as to the presence or

[44] *Cf.* Cappello, *De Sacramentis,* III, n. 314; Gasparri, *Tractatus Canonicus de Matrimonio,* n. 448; Ayrinhac-Lydon, *Marriage Legislation in the New Code of Canon Law,* pp. 103, 104; Ter Haar, *Mixed Marriages and Their Remedies,* pp. 66-68; Konings-Putzer, *Commentarium in Facultates Apostolicas* (3. ed., New York, 1893), p. 382; Zepherinus Zitelli, *De Dispensationibus Matrimonialibus* (Romae, 1887), p. 60.

absence of just and grave causes for the dispensation. In regard to the danger of civil marriage, which is one of the most frequent causes alleged for dispensations from mixed religion and disparity of cult, it is interesting to note that the Sacred Congregation for the Propagation of the Faith stated in an instruction issued on May 8, 1877, that *probable* danger of a civil marriage is sufficient.[45] However, the pastor should not make the serious mistake of assuming that this danger exists in all cases in which the dispensation is denied. There are many steadfast Catholics who would refuse to marry a non-Catholic civilly. Each individual case, therefore, must be judged on its own merits.

Article 7. Investigation Concerning the Guarantees

In addition to a just and grave cause two other conditions are necessary for dispensations from the impediments of mixed religion and disparity of cult.[46] These conditions are: (1) the giving of the guarantees by both nupturients and (2) moral certitude that the guarantees will be fulfilled. Though the grantor of the dispensation is the final judge of the presence of these conditions, he will have to depend, as a rule, on the information of the pastor when making his decision. Consequently the obligation to furnish the correct information concerning both conditions cannot be minimized or ignored by the pastor in his investigations.

A. *The Giving of the Guarantees*

The guarantees in mixed marriages are also known as *promises* and *cautiones*. Their object is to protect the Catholic party and the offspring from the danger of perversion. Hence they have a basis in the natural and the divine law, though the formalities connected with them are of ecclesiastical law.[47] The pastor is obligated to see that *both* parties give the promises. *The non-Catholic must guarantee to remove the danger of perversion from the Catholic party, and both nupturients must promise that all the children*

[45] *Coll.*, n. 1470; Chelodi, *Ius Matrimoniale*, n. 46.

[46] Canons 1060, § 1, 2°, and 1071.

[47] Schenk, *Mixed Religion and Disparity of Cult*, n. 313.

will be baptized and educated in the Catholic faith.[48] In the pre-Code discipline the Catholic nupturient was required to make the additional formal promise to do his utmost to effect the conversion of the non-Catholic party.[49] This formal promise is no longer necessary, as the Code does not refer to it. Canon 1062, however, states that the Catholic party has the charitable obligation of prudently endeavoring to procure the conversion of the non-Catholic nupturient. As the Catholic party may not be aware of this duty, the pastor should not neglect to remind him of it.

Ordinarily the pastor should demand written guarantees from the nupturients.[50] Oral guarantees or guarantees expressed by signs can be permitted in certain extraordinary circumstances, for instance, in danger of death or when it is impossible to obtain them in writing. The Code favors written guarantees as they serve to impress on the parties the serious nature of their promises. Moreover, they can be produced as evidence should the validity or integrity of the guarantees be subsequently questioned.

It is of paramount importance that the pastor secure the guarantees, because a dispensation granted without them would be invalid.[51] If without the guarantees a dispensation from the impediment of disparity of cult was granted, the marriage would be invalid; if granted from the impediment of mixed religion, the marriage would be valid but illicit.

The question as to whether the guarantees must be given sincerely for the validity of dispensations from the impediments of mixed religion and disparity of cult is a debated point among canonists. Many canonists, among whom are Toso,[52] Vromant,[53] O'Don-

[48] Canon 1061, § 1, 2°.

[49] Schenk, *Mixed Religion and Disparity of Cult,* n. 342.

[50] Canon 1061, § 2.

[51] Chelodi, *Ius Matrimoniale,* n. 50; Schenk, *Mixed Religion and Disparity of Cult,* n. 314; Francis Joseph Winslow, *Vicars and Prefects Apostolic* (The Catholic University of America, Canon Law Studies, n. 23, Washington: The Catholic University of America, 1924), pp. 106, 107; S. C. S. Off., decr., 14 Jan., 1932—*AAS,* XXIV (1932), 25.

[52] "Consultationes de Cautionibus Matrimonialibus," *Ius Pontificium,* XIII (1933), 207-214.

[53] *De Matrimonio,* n. 136.

nell,[54] De Smet[55] and Park,[56] have defended the view that sincere guarantees *are not necessary* for the validity of the requisite dispensation. Other canonists have maintained that sincere guarantees *are necessary* for the validity of the dispensation. Among them are Harrington,[57] W. H. O'Neill,[58] Nau,[59] Oesterle,[60] Petrovits,[61] Woywod,[62] White[63] and P. O'Neill.[64] As canonists are very much divided on the point, a decision from the Holy Office on the subject is desirable. The opinion maintaining that sincere *cautiones* are required for the validity of the dispensation has much in its favor. It is hard to conceive how the Church, which is so particular about the practical and objective protection of faith and morals, would grant a dispensation on insincere *cautiones*. The divine law and the natural law requires actual protection of faith and morals. If the Church permitted dispensations on the fictitious guarantees, she would not to the full extent be protecting the Catholic party and the children from danger of perversion. Moreover, it would encourage deceit and fraud by laying emphasis on external morality and not on internal morality. There is one other consideration that may be considered a partial argument for the view maintaining that sincerity in the *cautiones* is required. A dispensation from either mixed religion or disparity of cult is given usually by rescript.

[54] *IER*, XVIII (1921), 411-418.

[55] *De Sponsalibus et Matrimonio*, n. 505.

[56] "Insincere Ante-Nuptial Guarantees," *AER*, XCI (1934), 446-459.

[57] *AER*, LXV (1921), 257.

[58] *Papal Rescripts of Favor* (The Catholic University of America, Canon Law Studies, n. 57, Washington: The Catholic University of America, 1930), p. 115, n. 60.

[59] *Manual of the Marriage Laws of Canon Law* (New York: Pustet, 1933), p. 72.

[60] "De Cautionibus Matrimonialibus," *Ius Pontificium*, XIV (1934), 270-276; XV (1935), 64-81, 191-195.

[61] *The New Church Law on Matrimony* (2. ed., Philadelphia: McVey, 1926), n. 257.

[62] *A Practical Commentary on the Code of Canon Law*, n. 1056.

[63] *Canonical Ante-Nuptial Promises and the Civil Law* (The Catholic University of America, Canon Law Studies, n. 91, Washington: The Catholic University of America, 1934), p. 36.

[64] "Disparity of Worship and Fictitious Guarantees," *IER*, LXIX (1933), 630-635.

And in all rescripts, saving the prescriptions of canons 45 and 1054, the condition *"si preces veritate nitantur"* is understood.

Before requesting the guarantees the pastor should clearly explain to the parties the nature and extent of the obligations involved. The mere reading of the bare content of the guarantees is hardly sufficient, especially if the non-Catholic party is not well educated. A pastor who asks the parties to sign the document containing the guarantees without acquainting them with its contents is doing a definite wrong. Careful explanation of the seriousness and content of the guarantees is very imperative today. Many non-Catholics and some Catholics as well seem to entertain the notion that the guarantees are so much ecclesiastical "red tape," to use a popular expression, and many have apparently signed them without any realization of the grave obligations they impose. This is evidenced by the frequent violations of the guarantees that occur subsequent to the marriage ceremony. It is only just and fair that the nupturients be disillusioned of any erroneous notions they may have about the guarantees. The non-Catholic party should be instructed that the Church before granting a dispensation requires that he solemnly promise to remove from the Catholic every impediment that would in any way either directly or indirectly endanger the faith or morals of his Catholic consort. "Every impediment" implies any obstacle for which the non-Catholic himself might be responsible.[65] The pastor should inform him that the removal of every danger to faith and morals involves freedom for the Catholic party to perform all his religious duties, principally his freedom to pray, to attend Mass, to receive the sacraments, to observe ecclesiastical fast and abstinence on the appointed days and to support church and school in accordance with his means.[66] It should also be pointed out that removal of every danger to faith and morals includes refraining from any attempt to entice the Catholic party into sin, particularly the sins against Catholic marriage morality.

Both parties should receive instructions from the pastor concerning their obligation to promise to have all the children baptized

[65] Cappello, *De Sacramentis,* III, n. 310.

[66] Schenk, *Mixed Religion and Disparity of Cult,* n. 343.

and educated in the Catholic faith. Emphasis should be placed on the fact that it extends to "all children," both male and female, and that any reservation, such as an agreement that the sons will follow the religion of one parent and the daughters the religion of the other parent, is out of the question. What about the children already born? Do the guarantees extend to them? Authors are not agreed on the point. It does seem reasonable to include in the guarantees all the children born illegitimately to the parties concerned, as well as all the children born of a former mixed marriage of one or other of the parties, or of a Catholic marriage of the Catholic party.[67] Concerning the children born to the non-Catholic party from a previous and purely non-Catholic marriage it is difficult to make a definite statement. The Catholic party becomes the foster-parent of the children on his marriage to the natural parent. If the children have not reached the use of reason, they cannot do their own thinking regarding the choice of their religion. Their parents must do the thinking for them. It seems legitimate, therefore, to hold the view that when one parent is Catholic and the other non-Catholic, the preference as to the children's religion should go to the Catholic parent, even though the Catholic is only the foster-parent. If the children have already attained the use of reason, they are capable of thinking for themselves. To include such children born of a previous purely non-Catholic marriage in the *cautiones* does not seem correct. However, in such a case the non-Catholic should not be adverse to the reasonable efforts of the Catholic party to lead these children into the Church.

It should be pointed out that the promise of the parties to have all the children baptized and educated in the Catholic faith implicitly contains the promise to observe the laws of the Church in regard to the time and manner of baptism and positively to see to it that the children attend to their prayers, to Holy Mass, to the reception of the sacraments in due time and that they receive a Catholic education in accordance with the principles enunciated in canons 1372-1383. The pastor should also impress on the non-

[67] Vlaming, *Praelectiones Iuris Matrimonii*, n. 218; Schenk, *Mixed Religion and Disparity of Cult*, n. 351.

Catholic party that, should the Catholic party die, the non-Catholic's obligation to promote positively the Catholic education of the children still remains.

Having explained the content of the guarantees to the nupturients, the pastor will properly indicate the importance of sincerity in the making of the promises.

No special form for the guarantees is prescribed by the Code. It is expedient to have them drawn up in a form that will be recognized in civil law. White in his study *Canonical Ante-Nuptial Promises and the Civil Law*[68] has demonstrated that the ante-nuptial guarantees contain the essential elements of a legal contract and are really enforceable in American civil law, and should be enforced by the courts of equity. However, he also emphasizes the point that historical prejudice and mistaken legal precedents continue to form a barrier to their enforcement.[69]

B. *Moral Certainty of the Fulfillment of the Guarantees*

The giving of the guarantees alone does not suffice to obtain the necessary dispensation. Moral certitude of their fulfillment is also required,[70] *i. e.*, a certainty that excludes all grave and prudent doubt of a positive character.[71]

Experience has proved time and again that the mere giving of the promises does not *per se* offer any positive assurance of their fulfillment. Even though the giving of these promises is fully sincere, this fact in itself does not necessarily imply that the nupturients will faithfully live up to them. In determining the presence or absence of the required moral certitude, each case must be examined in the light of the circumstances that surround it then, and also of the circumstances that are likely to surround it in the future.[72] Therefore, the pastor must look not only to the present circumstances of the parties, but should also envision their future circumstances in as far as this is possible for him.

[68] Pp. 74-77.

[69] *Canonical Ante-Nuptial Promises and the Civil Law*, pp. 102 and 130.

[70] Canon 1061, § 1, 3°.

[71] Ter Haar, *Mixed Marriages and Their Remedies*, pp. 86, 87.

[72] Ter Haar, *Mixed Marriages and Their Remedies*, pp. 90, 91.

It is impossible to enumerate all the factors of which a pastor is to take cognizance in arriving at moral certainty of the future fulfillment of the promises. Diverse factors will influence the different cases. Ter Haar enumerates a number of factors that more or less enter into every case, namely, the character of both the non-Catholic and the Catholic; the sincerity of the parties at the time they give the *cautiones*; the place where the parties will reside after their marriage; the question of their dependence for a livelihood on the non-Catholic relatives or friends of the non-Catholic nupturient or even on non-Catholics generally; the factor of their proximity to or distance from the immediate family of the non-Catholic party. If the non-Catholic party previously entered a mixed marriage, his fidelity or infidelity to his duties during that union will be a fairly good criterion of how he will probably act in the marriage he now contemplates.[73]

The primary consideration, as a general rule, is the character of the parties, especially of the non-Catholic party. If he is conscientious, sincere, steadfast, stable, reliable and is generally faithful to his promises, and no contrary factors militate against these favorable indications, then the pastor may conclude that the promises or guarantees will be faithfully executed. This assurance of fidelity is strengthened if the party who makes the promises is particularly sympathetic to the Catholic Church or at least is in no way antagonistic or unfriendly towards it. However, if he is of a weak, vacillating character, easily influenced by others and negligent of the promises he ordinarily makes, the pastor cannot consider him very dependable as far as the guarantees are concerned, especially if he is prejudiced against the Church.

If he manifests a real sincerity in giving the *cautiones* and has been well instructed in their nature and extent and showed a real interest in such instructions, there is a strong indication that he will observe the guarantees. However, if his attitude is one of indifferentism, or positive dislike for any instructions in regard to the guarantees, the pastor may have reason to entertain a just suspicion about his future fidelity to his promises. Many diocesan statutes prescribe a full course of instructions on the Catholic

[73] *Mixed Marriages and Their Remedies*, pp. 91-93.

faith for the non-Catholic nupturient to a mixed marriage. The purpose of this course of instructions is to acquaint the non-Catholic with Catholic dogma and practice. The attitude of the non-Catholic towards these instructions and the traits of character he manifests during them will be a valuable asset to the pastor in foretelling with some accuracy as to whether the party will live up to his promises.

The character of the Catholic party and his devotion to his religious duties also deserve the pastor's attention. If the Catholic party is strong in faith, attentive to duty and unwavering in principle, there is every hope that the children will be properly educated in their religion. However, if the Catholic party is poorly instructed, is careless about his religious duties, assists rarely at Holy Mass and neglects the sacraments, the hope of the Catholic education of the children is very slender.

C. *The Pastor's Obligation in Regard to the Prohibition of Canon 1063*

Canon 1063 refers to three points: (1) The prohibition of the parties in a mixed marriage from attempting marriage before a non-Catholic minister when acting in his religious capacity. (2) The pastor's obligation in regard to such attempted marriages. (3) Marriage before a minister when acting in a purely civil capacity.

Even though a dispensation has been obtained from the impediment either of mixed religion or of disparity of cult, the parties are forbidden to attempt marriage before a non-Catholic minister who acts in his religious capacity. They are forbidden to go before him either prior or subsequent to their marriage before the priest. Not only are the parties prohibited from appearing personally before the non-Catholic minister, but also they are prohibited from appearing before him by proxy.[74] One obvious reason for this accurately drawn up prohibition is the manifest *communicatio in sacris* involved in such an attempted marriage. Another reason is the fact that the Catholic Church considers the marriage contract itself as being governed by its own legislation and thereby looks upon the Catholic manner of celebrating marriage as final. The prohibi-

[74] Canon 1063, § 1.

tion of canon 1063 exists only when the non-Catholic minister acts in his ministerial capacity, *i. e.*, when he receives the consent of the parties in a religious rite or ceremony. It makes no difference whether the non-Catholic minister is attached to a Christian or a non-Christian sect. Marriage before a Jewish rabbi, a pagan priest, or any minister of a false religion, if he acts in a religious capacity, is forbidden as well as marriage before a non-Catholic minister professing faith in Christ.[75]

No formal guarantee (*cautio*) of compliance with the prohibition of canon 1063 is required of the parties by the Code. Many ordinaries in the United States have, however, incorporated into the forms which contain the regular *cautiones* the promise that the parties will refrain from any and every ceremony other than the Catholic ceremony. Wherever this promise is required by diocesan regulation, the pastor has the obligation to obtain it from the nupturients. However, the pastor's non-observance of the rule to demand this promise, as required by the bishop, would not *per se* invalidate the dispensation. Even though the Code itself does not require a guarantee (*cautio*) with a view to certifying a full compliance with legal prohibition of canon 1063, the fact that the parties in a given instance contemplate violating the canonical prohibition will have some bearing on the regular guarantees mentioned in canon 1061, § 1. At least it may give rise to a suspicion that the parties were not sincere in giving the *cautiones* and may cause some doubt about their future fulfillment.[76]

As the parties will frequently be unacquainted with the prohibition of canon 1063, § 1, it will be the pastor's duty to remind them of it.

Should the pastor make definite inquiry of the parties as to whether they intend to violate the aforesaid prohibition? A response given by the Sacred Congregation of the Holy Office on January 22, 1851 definitely stated that a pastor fearing or fore-

[75] S. C. S. Off., 27 Aug., 1658—*Fontes*, n. 731; S. C. S. Off., 29 Jan., 1817—*Fontes*, n. 852; *cf.* also Schenk, *Mixed Religion and Disparity of Cult*, n. 370; Pius XI, Address, 24 Dec., 1930—*AAS*, XXII (1930), 529.

[76] *Cf.* Pius XI, Address, 24 Dec., 1930—*AAS*, XXII (1930), 529; Pius XI, *Consistorial Allocution*, 13 Maii, 1933—*AAS*, XXV (1933), 116.

seeing that the Catholic spouse will go to a non-Catholic minister is not bound to make inquiry regarding this intention.[77] Even apart from these circumstances, tact and prudence in certain instances may dictate that the pastor fulfill his obligation by reminding the party of his duty rather than by directly interrogating the party as to whether he intends to violate canon 1063, § 1.

If the pastor has received definitely *certain* information, either from the parties themselves or from some other dependable source, that they will violate the said prohibition, he is not at liberty to assist at their marriage. Assistance at such a marriage is never countenanced by the law except upon previous consultation with the local ordinary in the face of most pressing reasons and provided that the element of scandal be properly excluded from the case.[78] If there is only a suspicion of the parties' non-observance of the prohibition or a doubt about their compliance with it, the pastor may proceed with the ceremony of assisting at their marriage without consulting the ordinary.

If the parties had actually attempted marriage in the presence of the minister before calling upon the priest to assist at their marriage, they should not be admitted to marriage *coram ecclesia* until the excommunication of canon 2319, § 1, 1° is removed. The absolution from this censure is sufficient warrant for the repentance which the Church requires before the pastor may assist at the marriage.[79]

The prohibition of canon 1063, § 1 does not forbid the parties to go before a non-Catholic minister when acting in a purely civil capacity in order to give or renew matrimonial consent in his presence, if the civil law requires such a civil ceremony. However, there must be no semblance of a religious ceremony. In the absence of a religious rite there is no *communicatio in sacris*. The Church reluctantly tolerates the State's demand for a civil ceremony in order to avoid conflict with the civil law. It should be brought home to the parties that the civil ceremony has no binding effect in ecclesiastical law.

[77] Feije, *De Impedimentis et Dispensationibus*, p. 49, note 1.
[78] Canon 1063, § 2.
[79] Schenk, *Mixed Religion and Disparity of Cult*, n. 283.

ARTICLE 8. OTHER INVESTIGATIONS IN MIXED MARRIAGES

The remaining ante-nuptial investigations to be made in mixed marriages concern (a) the freedom of the nupturients from the remaining prohibitive and diriment matrimonial impediments, *i. e.*, from all those impediments outside the impediments of mixed religion and disparity of cult; (b) the freedom of the nupturients' consent to marry and (c) the sufficiency of their knowledge of Christian doctrine. These three points have been treated in the preceding chapter with regard to purely Catholic marriages. For the most part the investigation of these respective points in mixed marriages will follow along practically the same lines as those which have been indicated for Catholic marriages. However, some variations in the investigation of the above-mentioned points must be made in the case of mixed marriages because the matrimonial laws of the Code do not always apply in equal measure to Catholics and non-Catholics alike. Some remarks on these variations are in order.

A. *Investigation of Matrimonial Impediments in Mixed Marriages*

Under this heading the following two points will be given separate treatment for the sake of clarity: (a) the investigation of matrimonial impediments in those mixed marriages which are prohibited by the impediment of mixed religion; (b) the investigation of matrimonial impediments in disparate marriages, *i. e.*, in mixed marriages which are hindered by the impediment of disparity of cult.

1. *Mixed Marriages Which Are Prohibited by the Impediment of Mixed Religion*

In the case of mixed religion one party is Catholic and the other is a baptized non-Catholic. The Catholic party is bound by the matrimonial impediments of the Code. The baptized non-Catholic is likewise bound by the matrimonial impediments of the Code with the exception of the impediment of disparity of cult.[80] In the marriages under consideration the impediment of disparity of cult

[80] Canon 1070.

cannot enter in as both parties are baptized. There is, however, a possibility that the following impediments may present themselves, namely: the simple vow,[81] legal relationship,[82] age,[83] impotency,[84] *ligamen,*[85] sacred orders,[86] solemn vow,[87] abduction,[88] crime,[89] consanguinity,[90] affinity,[91] public propriety,[92] and spiritual relationship.[93]

When circumstances indicate a grave suspicion of the presence of any of these impediments, the pastor should not neglect to make further inquiries concerning them. Particular attention should be paid to the investigation of the impediment of *ligamen,* especially in connection with the non-Catholic nupturient. The reason is that many non-Catholics entertain false notions concerning the sacredness, unity and indissolubility of marriage and a goodly number enter into new unions, believing themselves to be free to do so because they have obtained a civil annulment or divorce from a previous marriage or marriages. In countries where civil divorce is legalized, interrogation of the parties on the impediment of *ligamen* is of particularly grave importance. Ordinarily the non-Catholic need not be interrogated on the impediments of the simple vow, the solemn vow, sacred orders and spiritual relationship, as these impediments are very unlikely to arise in his case.

2. *Disparate Marriages*

In disparate marriages one party is a Catholic and the other an unbaptized non-Catholic. Before mentioning in particular the matri-

[81] Canon 1058; see pp. 160-163.
[82] Canons 1059 and 1080; see pp. 163-165.
[83] Canon 1067; see pp. 165-168.
[84] Canon 1068; see pp. 168-174.
[85] Canon 1069; see pp. 174-181.
[86] Canon 1072; see pp. 181-183.
[87] Canon 1073; see pp. 183-186.
[88] Canon 1074; see pp. 186-188.
[89] Canon 1075; see pp. 189-195.
[90] Canon 1076; see pp. 196-199.
[91] Canon 1077; see pp. 199-201.
[92] Canon 1079; see pp. 201-203.
[93] Canon 1079; see pp. 204, 205.

monial impediments that can arise in such marriages, it will be useful to state a few general principles which will be helpful in determining what matrimonial impediments bind the parties in a disparate marriage. It is certain that the Catholic party is directly bound by the impediments of the natural, the divine, and the ecclesiastical law. The Catholic party is not bound by the matrimonial impediments of the civil law.[94] The unbaptized non-Catholic is not bound directly by the matrimonial impediments of purely ecclesiastical law, because he is not a subject of this law.[95] According to the better opinion an unbaptized person who is marrying a Catholic is indirectly bound by the relative impediments of the ecclesiastical law, and not by the relative impediments of the civil law. Where relative impediments of the ecclesiastical and civil law are concerned there is a clash of jurisdictions, and in the case of such a clash the religious and the sacred character of the marriage contract as well as the superior dignity of ecclesiastical law give the ecclesiastical law the preference over civil law. Moreover, to claim that civil and ecclesiastical law conjointly govern the relative impediments to marriage would lead to untold difficulties as there is often a patent contradiction between them. The practice of the Church favors the giving of the preference to ecclesiastical law in the matter of relative matrimonial impediments.

Is the unbaptized non-Catholic party bound by the absolute impediments of civil law when he marries a Catholic, as for instance would happen in connection with the impediment of age? Some maintain that the non-Catholic party is not obliged by the absolute civil impediments when he marries a Catholic. The reason is because there is a conflict between the civil and ecclesiastical law in such instances and the ecclesiastical law should prevail. Others maintain that the unbaptized non-Catholic is bound by the absolute civil impediments when he marries a Catholic. This is the more reasonable opinion. Taking it for granted that the absolute civil impediment is not contrary to the natural or divine law and is a reasonable and just impediment, the Church cannot render an unbaptized party competent to marry, if his marriage is actually impeded by such an impediment. The reason is because the Church has no jurisdic-

[94] *Cf.* canon 1016.
[95] *Cf.* canon 87.

tion over the unbaptized party. However, she can admit such a one to marriage when the absolute civil law impediment is removed by the proper civil authority.[96]

It is in order here to state briefly but specifically what matrimonial impediments may arise in disparate marriages and in what way they bind both the Catholic party and the unbaptized party. Equipped with a doctrinal knowledge of the impediments which affect both the Catholic and the unbaptized party, the pastor will have to use his prudent judgment as to what impediments may be suspected in each individual case and will interrogate the parties accordingly.

(a) *Simple vow.* The impediment of simple vow renders marriages illicit both by divine and by ecclesiastical law. In disparity of cult this impediment binds the unbaptized party by the divine law and the baptized party by both the divine and the ecclesiastical law.[97]

(b) *Legal relationship.* This impediment is of ecclesiastical law only and binds the Catholic party directly and the unbaptized party indirectly.[98]

(c) *Age.* The Catholic party, if a girl, cannot validly marry before she has completed the age of 14 years; the Catholic party if a boy, cannot validly marry before he has completed the age of 16 years. These ages are of ecclesiastical law and do not bind the unbaptized party. If the civil law has established an im-pediment of age, it is necessary for the pastor to make sure that the unbaptized non-Catholic has reached the required civil age, because the impediment of age is an absolute impediment.

(d) *Impotency.* As impotency is an impediment of the natural law it binds both the Catholic and the unbaptized party.

(e) *Ligamen,* being an impediment of the divine law, likewise binds both parties.[99]

(f) *Sacred Orders* binds the Catholic party only, not the unbaptized party, as baptism is necessary for the reception of the

[96] *Cf.* Gasparri, *Tractatus Canonicus de Matrimonio,* n. 256.

[97] See pp. 160-163.

[98] See pp. 163-165.

[99] See pp. 174-181.

sacrament of orders. Moreover, sacred orders is an impediment of the ecclesiastical law only.[100]

(g) *Solemn vow.* Solemn vows are taken only in religious orders. Consequently it may be concluded that the impediment binds only the Catholic party, as an unbaptized party is not admitted to a religious order.

(h) *Abduction* is an impediment of ecclesiastical law only. It renders marriage between a Catholic and an unbaptized person invalid because it directly affects the Catholic party and necessarily affects the unbaptized party indirectly.[101]

(i) *Crime* is an impediment of the ecclesiastical law only. The first species of crime (adultery together with a promise of marriage or along with an unbaptized marriage) renders a marriage between a Catholic and an unbaptized person invalid. It affects the Catholic party directly and the non-Catholic indirectly on account of the fact that it is a sin of complicity. If the Catholic party is a convert from infidelity, and now wishes to marry an unbaptized person with whom he committed adultery and to whom he promised marriage before his conversion to the Catholic Church, the impediment does not arise. The reason is because both parties were infidels when the adultery was committed and were not bound by ecclesiastical law. Even if the adultery was committed before conversion and the promise was made after conversion or *vice versa,* it appears that no impediment of crime is incurred, since both the adultery and the promise must take place after conversion in order to induce the impediment. The second species of crime (adultery together with conjugicide, the conjugicide having been committed by one accomplice) invalidates the marriage of a Catholic with an unbaptized person when it is the Catholic party that committed the conjugicide. The Catholic party is affected directly by the crime, the unbaptized party indirectly. If the unbaptized party commits the conjugicide no impediment arises, because he is not subject to ecclesiastical law and the Catholic party is guilty only of adultery, which of itself is not sufficient for this second species of the impediment of crime. The third species of the impediment of crime

[100] See pp. 181-183.

[101] Cappello, *De Sacramentis,* III, nn. 67 and 472; see pp. 186-188.

(where both conspired in the conjugicide) can arise in disparate marriages. It affects the Catholic party directly and the non-Catholic party indirectly.[102]

(j) *Consanguinity* will invalidate the marriage between a Catholic and an unbaptized person in the degrees mentioned in the Code. It affects both parties directly in those degrees that are of the natural law; in the degrees that are of the ecclesiastical law, it affects the Catholic party directly, and the unbaptized party indirectly.[103]

(k) *Affinity* is an impediment of ecclesiastical law and will invalidate marriage between a Catholic and an unbaptized person in the degrees mentioned in the Code. It affects the Catholic party directly; the unbaptized party indirectly.[104] However, it must be remembered that it arises only from a valid marriage regardless of whether the marriage is ratified only, or ratified and consummated.[105]

(l) *Public Propriety* may arise also in disparate marriages. It is an impediment of ecclesiastical law only and binds the Catholic party directly; the unbaptized party indirectly.[106]

(m) *Spiritual relationship* is an impediment of ecclesiastical law only and in disparate marriages can arise only when the unbaptized party baptized the Catholic party, *e. g.*, when the latter was in danger of death. It affects the Catholic party directly; the unbaptized party indirectly.

B. *Investigation of Freedom of Consent in Mixed Marriages*

The investigation of the freedom of the consent of the nupturients both in the case of mixed religion and disparity of cult will in general follow the same procedure as in Catholic marriages.[107] The pastor, however, should be particular in making sure that the non-

[102] Cappello, *De Sacramentis,* III, n. 501; see pp. 189-195.

[103] See pp. 196-199.

[104] See pp. 199-201.

[105] Canon 97, § 1.

[106] See pp. 201-203; Cappello, *De Sacramentis,* n. 549.

[107] See pp. 205-215.

Catholic party does not by a positive act of the will exclude the necessary *iur in corpus* or any essential property of marriage, especially the property of indissolubility. Because of the many loose ideas that are propagated in regard to divorce especially among non-Catholics, the pastor should ask the non-Catholic whether or not he is entering marriage with the understanding that it is an indissoluble union.

C. *Investigation Concerning the Sufficiency of the Parties' Religious Knowledge*

In mixed marriages the investigation of the religious knowledge of the Catholic party will be the same as was outlined in the preceding chapter for Catholic couples.[108] Since non-Catholics are not as a rule well acquainted with the dogmas, practices and morals of the Catholic Church, it is superfluous and imprudent formally to examine or question them as to their knowledge of Christian doctrine. It is best to take occasion to give them instructions that will enable them to know what their obligations are in regard to the Catholic party and the offspring. As diocesan statutes and regulations in many places, especially in the United States, have prescribed that the non-Catholic take a course of instructions covering the field of Catholic dogma and morality before a dispensation will be granted, there is more assurance that the non-Catholic party will enter the mixed union with such a degree of knowledge in matters of Catholic dogma and morality as will enable him, if he is well-intentioned, properly to fulfill his marital and family obligations.

The pastor may ultimately assist at the marriage ceremony only when he has made the necessary investigations and when he has obtained the necessary documents (baptismal certificates, rescripts of dispensations, etc.) and thereupon assured himself that the parties are free to marry.

[108] See pp. 215-219.

CHAPTER IX

PRE-NUPTIAL INVESTIGATION IN CERTAIN SPECIAL CASES

ARTICLE 1. MARRIAGES OF "VAGI"

Canon 1032. Matrimonio vagorum de quibus in can. 91, parochus, excepto casu necessitatis, nunquam assistat, nisi, re ad loci Ordinarium vel ad sacerdotem ab eo delegatum delata, licentiam assistendi obtinuerit.

IT is manifest from the words of this canon that the Church is very cautious about admitting *vagi* to marriage. Because of the instability of their place of residence, it is quite easy for them to conceal impediments to marriage, particularly the impediment of *ligamen*. Hence, the legislation of canon 1032 is a precaution against illicit and invalid unions, especially against bigamy and polygamy. The Sacred Congregation of the Sacraments in an instruction subsequent to the Code called attention to the pre-nuptial investigation of *vagi*. It expressly stated that European emigrants to other countries had been able to deceive pastors in those countries as to their free status and consequently were permitted to enter new nuptials while their legitimate spouses were living in Europe. Hence, the Sacred Congregation stresses the obligation of pastors to consult the local ordinary when *vagi* present themselves for marriage.[1]

The legislation of canon 1032 is not new. The Council of Trent commanded pastors not to assist at the marriages of *vagi*, or of those with no fixed abode, until pastors had first made a diligent investigation concerning them and upon referring the matter to the ordinary, had obtained from him permission to assist at the marriage.[2] The decree *Ne temere* retained substantially the discipline of the Council of Trent, but made two variations. (1) Instead of requiring the pastor to refer the matter solely to the ordinary, it required him to

[1] *Cf.* instr., 4 Jul., 1921—*AAS,* XIII (1921), 348.

[2] Sess. XXIV, *de ref. matrim.*, c. 7.

refer the matter either to the ordinary or to the priest delegated by the ordinary. (2) It did not require recourse to the ordinary or his delegate in cases of necessity. With the exception of slight changes in the wording of the law, the Code retained the *Ne temere* discipline *in toto*.[3]

Who are "vagi" according to canon 1032? This question is a practical one for the investigating pastor, as it is he who has the obligation of recourse. All commentators agree that a nupturient who has neither a domicile, nor a quasi-domicile, nor a month's residence in the territory of the ordinary or pastor is a *vagus*. The question, however, is debated among canonists as to whether a nupturient who has neither a domicile nor a quasi-domicile, but who has a month's residence in the territory of the ordinary or the pastor is also to be considered a *vagus*. Some commentators espouse the view that he is not a *vagus*.[4] The claim is made that this view is in harmony with canon 1097, § 1, 2°, because according to this canon a month's residence of a nupturient in a parish gives the pastor the right to assist at the marriage. Furthermore, it is claimed that there is no indication in the canon that a party who has the necessary month's residence must have simultaneously a domicile or quasi-domicile elsewhere in order that the pastor of the place where the nupturient has a month's residence may assist at the marriage. It is also argued that under the *Ne temere* discipline the party who had established the necessary month's residence only was not a *vagus* for matrimony. Therefore the same rule should obtain after the Code, because the Code simply restated the law of the decree *Ne temere* on the point. It is furthermore alleged that the view in question is in accordance with the mind of the legislator. O'Donnell [5] invokes the consideration of a *dubium iuris*. He looks upon the discordant opinions of authors as reflecting a definite uncertainty of law. In

[3] *Cf.* S. C. C., decr., *Ne temere,* 2 Aug., 1907, V. § 4—*Fontes,* n. 4340; canon 1032.

[4] Aertnys-Damen, *Theologia Moralis,* II, 687; L. Wouters, *De Forma Promissionis et Celebrationis Matrimonii* (5. ed., Bussum, P. Brand, 1919), p. 30; O'Donnell, "'Vagi' and a Month's Residence," *IER,* XVII (1921), 627; "The Ne temere and the Code," *ITQ,* XIV (1919), 146-148.

[5] "'Vagi' and a Month's Residence," *IER,* XVII (1921), 627.

the face of this uncertainty he appeals to the ruling of canon 6, 4°, which directs that no departure is to be made from the earlier law whenever a discrepancy between the later and earlier law remains in doubt. Basing his interpretation on this principle, he concludes that the Code law effected no change in the law of the *Ne temere* decree.[6]

The contrary opinion that the *vagi* of canon 1032 include all those who nowhere have a domicile or a quasi-domicile carries more weight. *Vagi,* therefore, include even those who have a month's residence in the territory of the ordinary or of the pastor, and who have nowhere a domicile or quasi-domicile. This view is deduced from canon 91, which states that a *vagus* is one who has nowhere a domicile or quasi-domicile. A nupturient who has only a month's residence in the territory of an ordinary or a pastor comes within the ambit of this definition. This view is definitely in accord with the mind of the legislator. The intention of the legislator is to guard against the danger of invalid marriages, especially against the danger of bigamous and polygamous marriages on the part of *vagi*. And that danger certainly continues to exist even after a *vagus* has established a month's residence in the territory of the ordinary or of the pastor. This stricter view does not imply any contradiction between canon 1032 and canon 1097, § 1, 2°, because these two canons treat of two distinctly different matters. Canon 1032 touches upon a precaution in the pre-nuptial investigation of the *status liber* of *vagi*; canon 1097, § 1, 2° deals with the *parochus proprius* for lawful assistance at marriage. The stricter view is also supported by the instruction of the Sacred Congregation of the Sacraments of July 4, 1921. Referring to the marriages of emigrant laborers, the instruction states that such marriages are to be considered as *marriages of persons who have neither a domicile nor a quasi-domicile, at which marriages according to canon 1032 the pastor should not assist without having obtained due permission from the ordinary of the place.*[7] Such a statement can only be interpreted as favoring the stricter view of the meaning of *vagi, i. e.,* the meaning defined in canon 91. To appeal to the pre-Code law for the interpretation

[6] *IER,* XVII (1921), 627.
[7] *AAS,* XIII (1921), 348.

of the word *vagi* is hardly proper as the definition of *vagus,* as given in canon 91, was not in vogue in the pre-Code discipline.[8]

Are momentary or temporary *vagi* considered as coming under canon 1032? Momentary or temporary *vagi* are those who habitually have a domicile or a quasi-domicile, but who have just left it with the intention of not returning and intend establishing a new domicile or quasi-domicile elsewhere as soon as possible. As yet they have not actually established their new domicile or quasi-domicile.[9] In the letter of the law they are *vagi.* Their proper pastor is the pastor of the place where they actually abide. However, on account of the fact that their place of residence is habitually certain, there is not present in their case the same danger of their concealing impediments to marriage as there is in the case of permanent *vagi.* Consequently there is good reason to believe that the legislator did not intend that canon 1032 refer to them. This opinion is considered as a probable opinion by some noteworthy canonists.[10] Though the opinion is by no means certain, it possesses sufficient probability to justify its practice. Hence one can hardly say that the pastor of a momentary *vagus* acts unlawfully, if he undertakes the investigation of the *status liber* of the said *vagus* without consulting the ordinary.

When the investigating pastor has satisfied himself that the parties are *vagi* in the sense intended by canon 1032, his next duty is to satisfy himself as to whether the case *is* or *is not* one of necessity. If it is not one of necessity, he is obliged to have recourse to the ordinary or his delegate. If it is one of necessity, he need not have recourse. What does canon 1032 mean by a case of necessity? Certainly danger of death to one or both nupturients is a sufficient necessity. It would seem that other cases of necessity are also admitted by canon 1032. If the Code intended that danger of death constitute the only case of necessity, undoubtedly it would, as it usually does, have expressly said so. Consequently, other cases of necessity must be admitted. As the obligation of having recourse is a grave one, the necessity excusing

[8] *Cf.* Farren, *Domicile and Quasi-Domicile,* p. 113, 114; Vermeersch, *Epitome,* II, n. 293; Payen, *De Matrimonio,* n. 498; Genicot-Salsmans, *Institutiones Theologiae Moralis,* nn. 451, 472.

[9] Wernz, *Ius Decretalium,* IV, n. 178; Payen, *De Matrimonio,* n. 497.

[10] Wernz-Vidal, *Ius Canonicum,* V, n. 133; Payen, *De Matrimonio,* n. 497.

from the law must likewise be a grave one. Any probable or certain danger of grave injury either to soul or body may be considered a grave necessity. The pastor in each individual case must judge whether this kind of necessity is verified. However, even when there is grave necessity, the pastor cannot admit the parties to marriage until he has moral certainty of their freedom to marry.[11]

If the case is not one of necessity, but the pastor is so well acquainted with the parties that he is most certain that they are free to marry, may he assist at the marriage? The answer seems to be a negative one; for the law is formulated to guard against a general danger and binds in a particular case even though the danger does not exist.[12]

The ordinary to whom the pastor must refer the matter is the ordinary of the place where the *vagus* actually tarries. This is evident from canon 94, § 2, which states that the proper ordinary of a *vagus* is the ordinary of the place where he is actually staying. Though not expressly stated, it is implied in canon 1032 that the ordinary, for the convenience of nupturients who are *vagi,* should appoint particular priests to whom the pastor may refer the cases of *vagi.* If the diocesan statutes or regulations prescribe that the *vagi* be sent in person to either the ordinary himself or to a priest delegated by him, the pastor should conform with those regulations. However, this is seldom done in practice. Ordinarily the pastor will actually conduct the investigation of the freedom of the parties to marry as outlined in canon 1021, § 1, and send in to the ordinary or his delegate the proofs he obtained concerning the *status liber* of the parties. It will be the duty of the ordinary or of his delegate to see whether or not these proofs furnish sufficient certainty of the nupturients' freedom to marry.

Until the pastor receives the necessary permission from the ordinary or his delegate, he may not admit the parties to marriage. If he admits them to marriage without referring the matter to the ordinary or awaiting the necessary permission, he acts unlawfully and is guilty of sin. The marriage, however, is valid, unless some invalidating impediment stands in the way.

[11] *Cf.* Payen, *De Matrimonio,* n. 497.
[12] Canon 21.

It is clear from canon 1032 that the pastor must refer the matter to the ordinary when both parties are *vagi*. Has he a similar obligation when only one nupturient is a *vagus*? It seems he has, because the danger of an invalid or unlawful marriage is present even when only one nupturient is a *vagus*.

Article 2. Marriages of Parties in Danger of Death

> Canon 1019, § 2. In periculo mortis, si alias probationes haberi nequeant, sufficit, nisi contraria adsint indicia, affirmatio iurata contrahentium, se baptizatos fuisse et nullo detineri impedimento.

The canon uses the phrase "*in periculo mortis*," which is not to be confounded with the phrase "*in articulo mortis*." The words "*in articulo mortis*" refer to the very moment of death or at least to the time when death is imminent. The words "*in periculo mortis*" are of wider comprehension. They refer to those circumstances in which it is reasonably probable that a person may die.[13] In estimating whether such danger of death is present, the pastor should be guided by what the average normal man would consider danger of death. While the opinion of the doctor or nurse is helpful, it is not necessary. Even when a doctor or nurse is asked about the matter and replies that there is no danger of death, the pastor cannot always rely on such a statement. Many doctors and nurses, especially if they are non-Catholic and do not understand the reason for the question, will simply state there is no danger of death in order to allay the inquirer's anxiety. The danger of death may proceed from an internal cause such as illness or disease or from some external cause such as an accident, war, the gallows, electric chair, etc.[14] The canon does not restrict the danger of death to any causes in particular. Consequently the danger of death mentioned in canon 1019, § 2 is more extensive that that required for the administration of Extreme Unction, *viz.*, danger of death arising from sickness or old age or injuries already suffered.[15] It makes no difference whether the dan-

[13] Cappello, *De Sacramentis*, III, n. 231.

[14] *Cf.* Cappello, *De Sacramentis*, III, n. 231.

[15] Canon 940.

ger exists for one or both nupturients. To require danger of death in both nupturients for the application of canon 1019 would be rather impractical, as danger of death will seldom exist simultaneously for both parties.

Two conditions are required in order that the pastor may permit the sworn affirmation of the parties alone to establish their *status liber* in danger of death. The conditions are: (1) That no other proofs of the *status liber* of the parties can be had. (2) That there are no positive indications that the parties are *not* free to marry. Both conditions must be verified in each particular case; it is not sufficient that only one of these conditions be verified.

Apparently the intention of the Code is that pre-nuptial investigation even in danger of death approximate in as far as possible the regular manner of proving the *status liber* of the parties. Consequently, if time permits, the pastor should interrogate the prospective bride and groom *together* and *separately* concerning their freedom from matrimonial impediments, their freedom of consent and the sufficiency of their instruction in Christian doctrine.[16] He should also, time permitting, obtain the necessary documents and testimonial evidence that the case may call for.[17] If time permits only a partial investigation, this partial investigation should proceed along the regular lines, and the remaining items of investigation may be covered by the sworn affirmation of the parties. If no proofs at all are available, the sworn affirmation of the parties alone that they are free to marry suffices, provided there are no positive indications to the contrary.

If other proofs of the freedom of the parties cannot be had and there are positive indications which point to a grave suspicion of a latent impediment or a positive doubt about their freedom to marry, the sworn affirmation of the parties does *not* of itself suffice.[18] Investigation of the grave suspicion and of the positive serious doubt is necessary. Otherwise there is not the requisite moral certitude of the *status liber* of the parties. If after the pastor's investigation the

[16] Canon 1020, § 1.

[17] *Cf.* canons 1021 and 1029.

[18] Payen, *De Matrimonio*, n. 369.

doubt still persists, the ordinary should be consulted.[19] If the doubt is a mere negative one, the pastor may ignore it. If the doubt is positive, but the reasons for it are rather weak, and there is not time for investigation, it would seem that the pastor is justified in proceeding with the marriage on the sworn affirmation of the parties concerning their *status liber.*[20]

If the parties affirm that they are free to marry, but will not swear to it, may the pastor proceed with the marriage? If apart from the oath there is moral certitude that the nupturients are free to marry, it is reasonable to conclude that the marriage may be permitted. If there is not moral certitude, the strict wording of the law does not permit the marriage. It is difficult, to imagine a Catholic or anyone believing in God refusing to make the necessary sworn affirmation in those extreme circumstances, and hence the question is more theoretical than practical. However, if a person refused to take the oath because he did not believe in God, but otherwise is a man of good reputation and is known to be truthful, it would seem that his word may be accepted as true. For such a person the oath would have no real meaning. Besides, when danger of death intervenes, natural virtue prompts a man to tell the truth, unless his conscience has been seriously blunted.

The suppletory oath should be requested from both nupturients, even though only one is in danger of death. It is just as important for the lawfulness and validity of the marriage to obtain the sworn affirmation of the healthy party as it is to obtain it from the party whose life is endangered.

The pastor need not require the oath to be taken in the presence of witnesses or in writing. Moral certainty that the oath has been given orally or by signs suffices. It is not even necessary that the oath be given in the presence of the pastor, since the Code does not require it. The sworn affirmation made in the presence of any other reliable person is sufficient. Nevertheless it is wise procedure that the pastor personally tender the oath to the parties and obtain it either in writing or in the presence of two witnesses. This will furnish legal proof of the sworn affirmation, should questions later

[19] Canon 1031, § 1, 3°.

[20] Payen, *De Matrimonio,* n. 369.

arise in connection with the marriage.[21] Once the parties have been admitted to marriage in danger of death on the strength of the suppletory oath, there is no necessity to institute any investigation of their *status liber* subsequent to the marriage. The reason is that the law considers the suppletory oath by itself as capable of establishing the moral certitude of the free status of the parties in the circumstances in question.

Canon 1019, § 2 refers to mixed marriages as well as Catholic marriages, since no distinction is made as to the kind of marriages to which it applies. In mixed marriages, however, the question arises whether it is necessary for the pastor to obtain the usual *cautiones* for the validity of the dispensation. Commentators are not agreed on the question. Many have maintained that the *cautiones* are not required for the validity of the dispensation in danger of death, *e. g.*, Cappello,[22] Petrovits,[23] Motry,[24] Kelly,[25] Vermeersch-Creusen,[26] Ayrinhac-Lydon,[27] Pighi,[28] Kubelbeck,[29] King,[30] and O'Keeffe.[31] Others have espoused the view that the *cautiones* are required for the

[21] Cappello, *De Sacramentis,* III, n. 157.

[22] *De Sacramentis,* III (Turin: Marietti, 1927), n. 310.

[23] *The New Church Law on Matrimony,* n. 160.

[24] Hubert Louis Motry, *Diocesan Faculties According to the Code of Canon Law* (The Catholic University of America, Canon Law Studies, n. 16, Washington: The Catholic University of America, 1922), pp. 133, 134.

[25] James Patrick Kelly, *The Jurisdiction of the Simple Confessor* (The Catholic University of America, Canon Law Studies, n. 43, Washington: The Catholic University of America, 1927), p. 185.

[26] *Epitome Iuris Canonici,* II, n. 306.

[27] *Marriage Legislation in the New Code of Canon Law,* p. 69.

[28] Jo. Bapta Pighi, *De Sacramento Matrimonii Tractatio Canonico-Moralis* (2. ed., Veronae, 1921), n. 90.

[29] William J. Kubelbeck, *The Sacred Penitentiaria and Its Relation to the Faculties of Ordinaries and Priests* (The Catholic University of America, Canon Law Studies, n. 5, Washington: The Catholic University of America, 1918), p. 64.

[30] James Ignatius King, *The Administration of the Sacraments to Dying Non-Catholics* (The Catholic University of America, Canon Law Studies, n. 23, Washington: The Catholic University of America, 1924), pp. 123-131.

[31] Gerald Michael O'Keeffe, *Matrimonial Dispensations, Powers of Bishops, Priests and Confessors* (The Catholic University of America, Canon Law Studies, n. 45, Washington: The Catholic University of America, 1927), pp. 85-92.

validity of the dispensation even in danger of death, *e. g.*, Woywod,[32] Augustine,[33] Vlaming,[34] De Smet,[35] Harrington,[36] and White.[37] A decree of the Sacred Congregation of the Holy Office issued on January 4, 1932 definitely favors the latter view. It deals specifically with the guarantees in mixed marriages and warns all bishops as well as all pastors and other persons mentioned in canon 1044, who have the power to dispense from the impediments of mixed religion and the disparity of cult, *never* to grant dispensations from these impediments without the necessary guarantees. Otherwise the dispensation is to be considered entirely null and void.[38] The explicit reference to canon 1044 (which concerns the dispensatory powers of the pastor, of the priest, who assists at marriage in the circumstances of canon 1098, 2°, and of the confessor in cases of danger of death when it is impossible to approach the ordinary indicated in canon 1043) clearly shows that the *cautiones* are required for the validity of the dispensation from disparity of cult or mixed religion *even in danger of death.* It is interesting to note that the eminent canonist Cappello espoused the contrary view in a previous edition of his work on the sacraments,[39] while in the recent edition of his work on the sacraments he maintains this same view in one place,[40] but in another place he has changed his view to correspond with the decree of 1932.[41] In virtue of the decree of 1932 it is reasonable to hold that the investigating pastor must demand the guarantees for the validity of the dispensation even in danger of death. It is not absolutely necessary that they be in writing; it is sufficient for validity that they be given by words or signs. However, because of the legal value of written guarantees, it is preferable that they be obtained in writing.

[32] *A Practical Commentary on the Code of Canon Law*, n. 1011.
[33] *A Commentary on the New Code of Canon Law*, V, 101, 102.
[34] *Praelectiones Iuris Canonici*, n. 218.
[35] *De Sponsalibus et Matrimonio* (4. ed.), n. 505.
[36] *AER*, LXV (1921), 259.
[37] *Ante-Nuptial Promises and the Civil Law*, p. 21.
[38] *AAS*, XXIV (1932), 25; *Ius Pontificium*, XII (1932), 69.
[39] *De Sacramentis*, III (Romae: Marietti, 1927), n. 310.
[40] *De Sacramentis*, III (Romae: Marietti, 1932), n. 310.
[41] *De Sacramentis*, III, n. 231.

Article 3. Marriages of Unworthy Catholics

Canon 1065, § 1. Absterreantur quoque fideles a matrimonio contrahendo cum iis qui notorie aut catholicam fidem abiecerunt, etsi ad sectam acatholicam non transierint, aut societatibus ab Ecclesia damnatis adscripti sunt.

§ 2. Parochus praedictis nuptiis ne assistat, nisi consulto Ordinario, qui, inspectis omnibus rei adiunctis, ei permittere poterit ut matrimonio intersit, dummodo urgeat gravis causa et pro suo prudenti arbitrio Ordinarius iudicet satis cautum esse catholicae educationi universae prolis et remotioni periculi perversionis alterius coniugis.

Canon 1066. Si publicus peccator aut censura notorie innodatus prius ad sacramentalem confessionem accedere aut cum Ecclesia reconciliari recusaverit, parochus eius matrimonio ne assistat, nisi gravis urgeat causa, de qua, si fieri possit, consulat Ordinarium.

Unworthy Catholics may be classified into two broad categories: (1) Those who have notoriously left the faith, although they have not joined a non-Catholic sect, and those who belong to societies condemned by the Church. (2) Public sinners who refuse to go to sacramental confession and those who, when they are notoriously under censure, refuse to be reconciled with the Church before marriage.

Though canons 1065 and 1066, which mention these two classes of unworthy Catholics, form part of the chapter of the Code on the prohibitive impediments, the restrictions of which these two canons treat do not, according to the better opinion of canonists, constitute any matrimonial impediments in the strictly canonical sense. Matrimonial impediments in the strictly canonical sense directly affect marriage in its contractual nature and only indirectly in its sacramental character.[42] Unworthiness is primarily the result of sin. But sin and the unworthiness consequent upon it immediately and directly militate against marriage only in so far as the contraction of marriage simultaneously constitutes the reception of a sacrament of the living. Thus unworthiness has only an indirect effect on marriage as a contract. Hence, it cannot be considered

[42] Schenk, *Mixed Religion and Disparity of Cult,* n. 144.

a canonical impediment in the proper acceptation of that term. Furthermore impediments in a strictly canonical sense are removed by dispensation, whereas unworthiness does not admit of removal by way of dispensation.[43] However, in a comprehensive and moral sense unworthiness must be considered as an impediment or bar to Christian marriage. Therefore it claims the earnest attention of the investigating pastor.

Sometimes the investigating pastor will know from common report that certain nupturients are unworthy Catholics, *viz.*, apostates or renegades from the faith, members of condemned societies, public sinners who will not go to sacramental confession or persons notoriously under censure who refuse to be reconciled with the Church. At other times he will have only suspicions of their unworthiness. When such suspicions arise, he should examine the matter more closely to determine the parties' true status. Having discovered that they belong to one or the other of the above-mentioned categories of unworthy Catholics, he will also make sure that they do not belong to heretical or schismatical sects. If an unworthy Catholic belongs to such a sect, a Catholic is prohibited from contracting marriage with him by reason of the impediment of mixed religion.[44] When the pastor discovers that the parties are simply unworthy Catholics, he must carry out the prescriptions of canons 1065 and 1066 in conformity with the particular category of unworthy Catholics to which the parties belong.

There is a definite reason why the precautions of canons 1065 and 1066 must be taken into account in the marriages of the faithful with unworthy Catholics. Many unworthy Catholics not only give scandal to others by their bad example, but also are a menace to the faith and morals of the good Catholic party and the future progeny. Pastoral experience has proved that unworthy Catholics have frequently interfered with the good Catholic spouse in the practice of his or her faith and have prevented the Catholic education of the children. It is true that the danger of perversion does

[43] Wernz-Vidal, *Ius Canonicum,* V, n. 200; Joseph A. M. Quigley, *Condemned Societies* (The Catholic University of America, Canon Law Studies, n. 46, Washington: The Catholic University of America, 1927), pp. 99, 100.

[44] *Cf.* canon 1060.

not exist in every particular case, yet the danger is sufficiently common to warrant the precautions of canons 1065 and 1066. With all other factors existing on a parity basis, it would appear that the class of unworthy Catholics described in canon 1065 is a more serious menace to the faith and morals of the good Catholic spouse and the children than the class depicted in canon 1066. The actions of those who belong to the former class indicate a certain rejection of the Catholic faith as such, while the obstinate attitude of the latter does not necessarily imply a definite breaking away from the Church. In view of this premise a separate consideration of canons 1065 and 1066 would seem indicated.

A. *Marriages of the Faithful With the Unworthy Catholics of Canon 1065*

According to canon 1065 the faithful of both sexes are to be deterred from contracting marriage with those who have notoriously left the Catholic faith, although they have not joined a non-Catholic sect, and with those who belong to societies condemned by the Church. The duty of deterring the faithful from such marriages will fall chiefly on ordinaries and pastors. The most favorable manner of fulfilling this duty is by suitable instruction of the Catholic youth during adolescence, or during the early courtship period. As a general rule, it will be impossible for the pastor to deter the faithful from such a contemplated marriage at the time they approach the pastor to arrange for the wedding. The persuasions of the pastor at that particular time will not have very much influence on the Catholic party, if he is deeply in love with the unworthy Catholic. Should a pastor be convinced that his efforts to deter the Catholic from such a marriage will prove fruitless, prudence will dictate that he rather concentrate his efforts on ensuring the celebration of the marriage in accordance with the laws of God and the Church, and with due precautions against the danger of perversion.

It is in order here to give some enumeration of those who may be considered as having defected from the Catholic faith, and also of the various societies condemned by the Church.

(a) *Catholics who have notoriously defected from the faith comprise* apostates and heretics, whose defection from the Church is notorious either by notoriety of law or of fact.[45] An apostate in the strict sense is one who has totally receded from the Catholic faith. A heretic is one who, while retaining the name "Christian," stubbornly denies or doubts a truth or truths that are to be believed on divine and Catholic faith.[46] In general, one may enumerate among those who have notoriously defected from the faith all those who by word, writing or action publicly attack or ridicule the Catholic faith as well as those who publicly deny their Catholicity. More specifically they are those Catholics who have become atheists, deists, materialists, rationalists, modernists, pantheists, and professed indifferentists.[47] Schenk also lists among those who have defected from the faith those baptized non-Catholics who have left the non-Catholic sect to which they belonged and thereupon are detached from every sect.

(b) *Catholics who have joined condemned societies.* Condemned societies may be generally divided into anti-social, bible, cremation, secret and theosophical societies.[48] Some of the societies condemned by the Church are condemned under pain of censure; others are condemned without censure. Both kinds are included under the prescriptions of canon 1065, § 1, as the canon makes no distinction. Specifically the known condemned societies are: Freemasons, Carbonari, Fenians, Odd Fellows, Independent Order of Good Templars, Knights of Pythias, Sons of Temperance, Nihilists, Anarchists, Extreme Socialists, Communists, Clerico-Liberalists.[49] The ladies' auxiliaries and youth organizations of these societies may likewise be considered as condemned. The Carbonari, Fenians, and Clerico-Liberalists no longer exist. Cappello lists the Y. M. C. A. as a condemned society,[50] but Quigley denies that it is

[45] Canon 2197, 2°, 3°; Schenk, *Mixed Religion and Disparity of Cult,* n. 330.

[46] Canon 1325, § 2.

[47] Gougnard, *Tractatus Canonicus de Matrimonio,* p. 134; Schenk, *Mixed Religion and Disparity of Cult,* n. 138; Cappello, *De Sacramentis,* III, n. 330.

[48] Quigley, *Condemned Societies,* pp. 7-10.

[49] *Cf.* Quigley, *Condemned Societies,* pp. 11-28, 66-68.

[50] *De Sacramentis,* III, n. 330.

condemned.[51] A letter issued by the Sacred Congregation of the Holy Office to local ordinaries on November 5, 1920, definitely indicates that the Y. M. C. A. is injurious to the faith, and consequently it requested local ordinaries to guard young people from the contagion of this and similar societies.[52] While this letter does not directly condemn the Y. M. C. A., it certainly demonstrates that the Church is adverse to Catholics joining it.

When a pastor knows or discovers from his investigation that a nupturient is a notorious renegade from the faith or a notorious member of a condemned society, he will be obliged not only to make the ordinary pre-nuptial investigations, but also to refer the matter to the ordinary. Furthermore, the pastor may not assist at the marriage until he has received the ordinary's permission to do so. Before the ordinary may give permission, he has the duty of inquiring into all the circumstances of the case; he must have moral certainty that there is a just cause for the marriage and that the education of all the children as well as the removal of every grave danger of perversion from the faithful Catholic party is guaranteed.[53] As the ordinary does not as a rule deal directly with the parties, he will have to depend for his information on the report of the investigating pastor. Consequently the pastor cannot neglect to investigate whether there is a grave cause for the marriage; also whether there is the necessary moral certitude that the danger of perversion is removed from the faithful Catholic spouse and that the children will be educated in the Catholic faith. The gravity of the cause should be estimated morally according to the merits of the case. It should be proportionate to the amount of evil that will in all probability flow from the union. Though the Code requires moral certainty that the faith and morals of the good Catholic party and of the children be protected, it does not prescribe any formal guarantees as it does for mixed marriages. Nevertheless, the pastor will have to address some questions to the parties to find out if the danger of perversion will be removed, taking into account at the same time the character of the parties and their present and

[51] *Condemned Societies,* p. 63.
[52] *AAS,* XII (1920), 595.
[53] Canon 1065, § 2.

future circumstances. If the diocesan statutes or episcopal regulations require that the *cautiones* be given in writing or in some formal manner, the pastor must comply with these regulations. Having collected all the necessary information on the matter, he should forward his findings to the ordinary and await and follow his instructions.

The ordinary to whom the pastor should have recourse is the ordinary of the place where the marriage is to be celebrated.

If grave necessity urges and there is not sufficient time for recourse to the ordinary by ordinary means, the pastor may assist at the marriage without consulting the ordinary.[54] However, he must be morally certain that the parties are free to marry; that there is a grave cause for permitting the marriage; that the danger of perversion is removed from the faithful Catholic and that all the children will be educated in the Catholic faith.

B. *Marriages of the Faithful With the Unworthy Catholics of Canon 1066*

According to canon 1066 Catholics who are public sinners and those notoriously censured are classed as unworthy Catholics. Public sinners are those who have reputations in the community for having committed grave sins or who have committed serious sins in such circumstances that they will certainly be divulged. A nupturient who seriously neglects the duties of the Christian life and whose negligence is publicly known may be considered as a public sinner, *e.g.*, one who does not fulfill the obligation of annually going to sacramental confession and Holy Communion.[55]

A notoriously censured person is one who is excommunicated or who is under personal interdict, and the censure is so public that it cannot be concealed by any legal subterfuge or excuse.[56] A person notoriously under excommunication or personal interdict is also a public sinner. However, not every public sinner is necessarily under censure.

[54] Cappello, *De Sacramentis,* III, n. 332.

[55] Cappello, *De Sacramentis,* III, n. 332.

[56] *Cf.* canon 2197, 2°, 3°.

When the pastor knows or discovers that a nupturient is a public sinner who refuses to go to confession, or that a nupturient is notoriously under censure and refuses to be reconciled with the Church, he cannot lawfully admit such a person to marriage except for a grave cause, concerning which he must consult the ordinary if it is morally possible.[57] The ordinary will have to depend on the information of the pastor for the forming of his judgment concerning the gravity of the cause. Consequently, the pastor has the duty of determining what the cause is and of correctly informing the ordinary. A graver cause is required when the nupturient is both a public sinner and also notoriously under censure. As the Code does not demand any guarantees to be given concerning the Catholic education of the children, it will not be necessary for the pastor to exact them. The divine law, however, requires that the Catholic education of the children be properly protected. Hence, the pastor should weigh the circumstances of each individual case to determine if their Catholic education is insured.

If a nupturient who is a public sinner goes to confession or seriously promises to do so before the marriage, it is not necessary to refer the case to the ordinary. The public act of approaching confession will remove the scandal caused by the past sins of the nupturient. Likewise a nupturient who is notoriously under censure is not to be referred to the ordinary, if the censure has been absolved, or if the party seriously intends to be reconciled with the Church before the marriage. If the sins of the nupturient are occult or if the censures are not notorious, the pastor need not refer the matter to the ordinary except in as far as this may be necessary to enable the pastor to absolve from the censure. However, the pastor must have moral certainty of the parties' freedom from matrimonial impediments, of their freedom of consent to the marriage and of the sufficiency of their instruction in Christian doctrine.

Article 4. Marriages Requiring an Act of Convalidation

The convalidation of an invalid marriage calls for some special attention. An invalid marriage is no marriage in the canonical sense

[57] Canon 1066.

Hence the investigation that must ncessarily precede its convalidation is truly pre-nuptial. The invalidity of a marriage may be due either to the presence of a diriment impediment or to a defect in consent or to a defect in canonical form.

When a party or parties approach the pastor for the purpose of having their marriage convalidated, the pastor's first duty will be to investigate whether or not the existing union is really invalid. For that purpose, a close questioning of the parties concerning the causes for its invalidity is necessary. Sometimes other reliable persons may have to be interrogated and documents may have to be produced to definitely decide whether the marriage is invalid or not. Having found out that the marriage is invalid on the grounds either of a diriment impediment or a defective consent or a defective canonical form, the pastor will next establish whether or not the invalidity can be remedied. If the impediment which invalidates the earlier union is one of natural or divine law and still persists, the situation cannot be remedied until the cessation of the existing impediment. However, if such an impediment has ceased in the meantime, the invalidity of the marriage becomes remediable. The union can likewise be validated if the existing impediment is one of ecclesiastical law from which the Church regularly dispenses. A marriage that is invalid on account of some substantial defect in the consent of one or both parties can be validated by the removal of the defect through a positive and canonical expression of valid consent. A marriage made null by the lack of canonical form is also remediable, since the requirement of the canonical form is purely a demand of simple ecclesiastical law.

Two kinds of convalidation are distinguished in the Code: *Simple convalidation,* which is the ordinary method of convalidation, and *sanatio in radice,* which is the extraordinary manner of convalidation.[58] *Simple convalidation* is that legal act by which an invalid marriage, after the cause of the invalidity has been removed, is rendered valid by the proper renewal of matrimonial consent,

[58] James H. Brennan, *The Simple Convalidation of Marriage* (The Catholic University of America, Canon Law Studies, n. 102, Washington: The Catholic University of America, 1937), p. 2.

given by at least that party who is conscious of the impediment.[59] This renewal of consent is required for the validity of the marriage, even though in the beginning the parties gave full consent and did not afterwards revoke it.[60] The renewal of consent must be a new act of the will.[61] *Sanatio in radice* is defined as that convalidation of marriage which implies besides a dispensation from the existing impediment or a cessation of the impediment originally present, a dispensation from the law which requires a renewal of consent and, by a fiction of the law incorporates an operation of retroactive force in respect of the canonical effects which follow upon any valid marriage. The convalidation is effected as soon as the concession of the *sanatio* is made. The accompanying retroactive effect extends to the very beginning of the marriage, unless contrary provision is expressly made.[62] There are some important differences between the simple convalidation of marriage and *sanatio in radice*. For the simple convalidation of marriage renewal of consent is necessary; for the *sanatio in radice* it is not necessary. The canonical effects of the simple convalidation begin with the renewal of the consent; the canonical effects of the *sanatio* become operative at the time the *sanatio* is actually granted. The simple convalidation is merely prospective in its effect; the *sanatio in radice* is retrospective as well as prospective.[63] It is important for the investigating pastor to note that ordinarily the simple manner of convalidation of marriage must be employed. Only when simple convalidation is impossible on account of circumstances, or when grave danger or inconveniience would result from attempting to employ it, should a *sanatio in radice* be requested for the purpose of convalidating the marriage.

A. *Simple Convalidation*

The investigation to be made antecedent to the simple convalidation of marriage must establish two points: (1) That it is possible to convalidate the marriage; (2) that the parties are free from

[59] Canon 1133, § 1.

[60] Canon 1133, § 2.

[61] Canon 1134.

[62] Canon 1138; Ayrinhac-Lydon, *Marriage Legislation in the New Code of Canon Law*, pp. 342, 343.

[63] *Cf.* Brennan, *The Simple Convalidation of Marriage*, pp. 3, 4.

every other matrimonial impediment to the marriage (*i. e.*, every other impediment besides the impediment or impediments that were responsible for invalidating the marriage), that the parties are freely consenting to the convalidation of the marriage and that they are sufficiently instructed in Christian doctrine. The second point needs no elaboration here as it has been repeatedly referred to in previous chapters. It is important, however, that the pastor have definite proof that the cause of the invalidity of the marriage is either already removed or is at least subject to removal, and that the party conscious of the existing invalidating impediment desires to renew consent. If the impediment be of such a nature that it cannot cease at all (*e. g.*, antecedent and perpetual impotency), then the parties must be informed of it and may not be admitted to marriage. Some impediments can cease by their very nature, *e. g.*, age, the previous bond of marriage. Others cease by the will of the nupturients, *e. g.*, disparity of cult, if the non-Catholic receives baptism; curable impotency; abduction, when the person abducted is freed from the power of the abductor and placed in a safe place. Some impediments, in as far as they are impediments of ecclesiastical law, can cease by dispensation, *e. g.*, disparity of cult, age, sacred orders, solemn vow, crime, consanguinity, affinity, public propriety, spiritual and legal relationship. However, it is the Church's practice not to dispense from some of these, *e. g.*, the impediment of the sacred order of priesthood, the impediment of consanguinity in the first degree of the collateral line, the impediment of crime arising from adultery and public conjugicide committed by one party, the impediment of crime arising from public conjugicide committed by both parties.

Besides achieving moral certainty that the original invalidating impediment has ceased or that a proper dispensation has been obtained for it, the pastor is also obliged to inquire whether the impediment was public or occult, and if occult whether it was known to both or only to one of the nupturients. Through properly obtained information on these points the pastor will know whether the consent of the parties should be renewed publicly or privately, and if privately, whether by both parties or by one alone.[64]

[64] *Cf.* canon 1135.

Should it happen that the marriage was invalid on account of defect of consent, *e. g.*, on account of force or fear, insanity, simulation of consent, substantial error, or a condition invalidating consent, the pastor in his investigations must inquire as to whether the parties are freely and properly renewing matrimonial consent. Interrogation of the parties as to whether the defect in their consent was internal or external, public or occult, whether on the part of one or both of the nupturients, is important in order to determine whether the renewal of consent should be internal or external, public or private, on the part of one or both of the nupturients.

If it is contended that the marriage is invalid from defect of canonical form, the pastor must inquire and make sure that the canonical form was actually not observed, *i. e.*, that the marriage was not celebrated in the presence of an authorized priest and two witnesses. In this connection an inquiry as to whether the circumstances of canon 1098 prevailed at the time of the giving of the consent is in order. If the circumstances of canon 1098 prevailed, the parties should be questioned as to whether they observed the extraordinary canonical form mentioned in that canon.

B. *Sanatio in Radice*

Before petitioning for a *sanatio in radice* the pastor must make sure from his investigation that the following points are verified: (1) That the marriage is invalid from some defect or impediment that can be remedied, if it has not already entirely ceased; (2) that the matrimonial consent previously given as adequate in its nature and innately sufficient still perseveres; (3) that there is a proportionately grave cause for the *sanatio in radice*.[65] If there is not a proportionately grave cause for the granting of the *sanatio*, the simple method of convalidating marriage must be employed. The danger of grave injury or scandal if the ordinary means of convalidation were employed seems to be a sufficiently grave cause for asking for a *sanatio;* likewise the refusal by one party to convalidate

[65] Ayrinhac-Lydon, *Marriage Legislation in the New Code of Canon Law*, pp. 346, 347.

the marriage in the ordinary way, wishing nevertheless to continue marriage relations. This happens more frequently in the case of disparate marriages than in the case of Catholic unions. It may be noted here that the ordinaries of the United States have the power in virtue of their present quinquennial faculties to grant a *sanatio in radice* for the impediments of mixed religion and disparity of cult, provided that the matrimonial consent of both parties continues to exist, and that the same cannot be legitimately renewed, either because the non-Catholic party cannot be informed of the invalidity of the existing union without danger of grave damage or inconvenience to the Catholic party, or because the non-Catholic party can by no means be induced to renew consent before the Church or to give the promises required by canon 1061, § 2; except in cases, (1) where the non-Catholic party is opposed to the baptism or to the Catholic education of the children of both sexes already born or to be born; (2) where before the attempted marriage, whether that was private or public, the parties bound themselves to the non-Catholic education of the children as above stated; provided further that there be no other diriment impediment for which the ordinary has not the power to dispense or grant a *sanatio*.[66]

Article 5. Marriages of Latin Catholics With Oriental Catholics

Pre-supposing that the pastor has determined from his preliminary questions that one nupturient is a Latin Catholic and the other a Catholic of a certain Oriental rite, the law requires him to establish the following points:

1. that he is competent to assist at the marriage;
2. that the nupturients are free from any matrimonial impediments which would affect the lawfulness and validity of the marriage;
3. that they are freely consenting to the marriage;
4. that they are sufficiently instructed in Christian doctrine.

[66] Bouscaren, *Canon Law Digest*, II, 8.

In regard to the competency of the pastor to assist at the marriage, it is necessary to keep in mind the prescriptions of the second part of canon 1097, § 2: "*Matrimonia autem catholicorum mixti ritus, nisi aliud particulari iure cautum sit, in ritu viri et coram eiusdem parocho sunt celebranda.*" Therefore the pastor will have to investigate whether or not there is any particular law governing the competency of the pastor who is to assist at the marriage of a Latin Catholic with the Oriental in question. If no particular law exists, the proper pastor of the man has the preference to assist at the marriage. If the pastor whom the parties approached is not the proper pastor of the man, he must either refer the parties to the pastor of the man or obtain from him the necessary permission to assist at the marriage. It is necessary to remark here that in the United States marriages between Greek-Ruthenians and the faithful of the Latin rite must be blessed in the rite of the woman and by the woman's pastor.[67]

The investigation of the freedom of the nupturients from matrimonial impediments will probably cause more difficulty than any other phase of pre-nuptial investigation. The Oriental party is bound directly by those impediments found in the matrimonial legislation of the rite to which he belongs. The Latin party is directly bound by the impediments found in the Code. In general the matrimonial impediments for the various rites of the Oriental Church correspond to those in force in the Latin Church before the Code. The words "in general" are used advisedly because there are some variations to be found in the different rites. The pastor will therefore have to acquaint himself with the impediments of the Oriental rite to which the Oriental Catholic belongs. If he is not acquainted with these impediments or has not at hand any authors that treat of them, it may become imperative to refer the matter to the curia or ask therefrom information on the matter.

It is impossible to give in one article all the *minutiae* concerning the extent of the various impediments in each rite of the Oriental Church. Such an undertaking would require a special and

[67] S. C. pro Eccl. Orient. decr., 1 Mart., 1929, c. IV, art. 39—*AAS*, XXI (1929), 152.

separate study. However, a general outline of the impediments that exist in the Oriental Church will help to guide the pastor.

The Oriental Church recognizes prohibitive and diriment impediments as does the Latin Church. However, the Oriental prohibitive impediments are more numerous than those in the Latin Church. They include solemn *sponsalia,* the forbidden time, the prohibition of the Church, mixed religion and the simple vow of chastity or religion. The diriment impediments are age, *ligamen,* impotency, disparity of cult, sacred orders, solemn profession, abduction, crime, consanguinity, affinity, public propriety and spiritual relationship. In particular cases the pastor will have to use his prudent judgment as to what impediments he should investigate and as to how he should investigate them. A few words about the more involved of these impediments is in order.

Solemn *sponsalia* or espousals include not only the espousals of those who have reached the age of puberty, but also the espousals contracted by the father or guardian of the child in the name of the child while it is yet below the age of puberty. In the espousals of *impuberes* contracted by the father or guardian of the child, it is understood that when the child reaches the age of puberty he can confirm or rescind the espousals, unless a consummated act of sexual union between the espoused parties has already taken place.[68]

The age required for a valid marriage in the Oriental rites is the completed fourteenth year for the boy and the completed twelfth year for the girl. However, if indications prove the presence of physiological puberty prior to that time, the parties can be validly married (*malitia supplet aetatem*). Age is a diriment impediment for all the Oriental rites except the Maronites, who look upon it as a prohibitive impediment.[69] Impotency and *ligamen,* being impediments of the natural and divine law respectively, are the same as in the Latin Church. The sub-diaconate, diaconate and priesthood render marriage invalid for the Italo-Greeks, Roumanians and Armenians. The diaconate and priesthood render marriage invalid for the Maronites, Syrians, Copts, Chaldeans and Malabars.[70] The

[68] Cappello, *De Sacramentis,* III, 895.

[69] Synod of Mount Lebanon (1736), P. II, n. 9—*Coll. Lac.,* II, 169.

[70] Cicognani, *Canon Law,* III, p. 451.

sacred order of priesthood renders marriage invalid among the Ruthenians.[71] Solemn profession exists as a diriment impediment for all Orientals. The impediments of abduction, consanguinity, crime and affinity exist in all rites with some variations in particular rites. The impediment of affinity arises, as it did in the pre-Code law for the Latin Church, from *copula licita* as well as *copula illicita*. Public propriety and spiritual relationship likewise correspond to the Latin pre-Code legislation on these impediments, *i. e.*, public propriety arises from valid espousals and from a ratified and non-consummated marriage and spiritual relationship arises from both baptism and confirmation.[72] The foregoing brief summary of matrimonial impediments that generally exist in the Oriental Uniate Church will give the pastor some idea of what impediments he should watch for in the Oriental Catholic party. No doubt the local curia will be able to furnish him with information concerning the extent of the impediments for the nupturients of individual rites. The lack of uniformity concerning the extent of matrimonial impediments existing in the Oriental Church among the various rites causes considerable difficulty and doubt at times as to whether a particular Oriental is or is not free to marry. When such doubts arise the pastor must not hesitate to refer the matter to the ordinary.

The investigation of the parties' freedom of consent as well as inquiry into the sufficiency of their knowledge of Christian doctrine will be similar to that required for couples of the Latin rite.[73]

Summary of the Commentary

Canon 1020, § 2 places the duty of instituting the pre-nuptial investigation of nupturients on the pastor who has the right to assist at the marriage. The term "pastor" includes not only those who are pastors in the strict sense, but also those who are pastors in the broad sense. In order that a pastor may have the right to assist at the marriage and institute pre-nuptial investigation, it is

[71] Cappello, *De Sacramentis,* III, n. 908.

[72] Cappello, *De Sacramentis,* III, nn. 918-920; Cicognani, *Canon Law,* p. 142.

[73] See pp. 205-215.

necessary that the conditions for valid assistance at marriage, as set forth in canon 1095, and that the conditions for lawful assistance at marriage, as stated in canon 1097, be fulfilled. Though the pastor may satisfy his obligation by delegating another to conduct the pre-nuptial investigation, the Code seems to favor the practice of personal investigation of the nupturients by the pastor himself. Hence it is expedient for the pastor personally to conduct the pre-nuptial investigation, unless there is a just reason for deputing another to do so.

To conduct pre-nuptial investigation efficiently, the following qualifications are important in the investigating pastor: (1) a knowledge of theology and in particular of Canon Law; (2) a knowledge of human character, (3) prudence and tact in dealing with nupturients.

Pre-nuptial investigation should take place at an opportune time before the marriage. This opportune time will vary with circumstances. Ordinarily pre-nuptial investigation of nupturients should be conducted approximately a month prior to the marriage. In extraordinary circumstances the interval of time between the pre-nuptial investigation and the marriage may be considerably less than a month. The Code is silent as to the proximate place where the pre-nuptial investigation should be conducted. The rectory is the usual and preferable place.

A twofold interrogation of both parties together is indicated in the Code, namely, the interrogation of both parties together and the interrogation of each party separately. The inquiry should be conducted diligently and tactfully. Should doubts arise about the existence of impediments to marriage, the pastor will investigate the matter accurately, interrogating under oath at least two witnesses, provided there is not question of an impediment that would bring disgrace on the parties. The pastor should not admit witnesses whom the Code considers as suspected, unqualified and disqualified. If necessity requires it, the pastor may interrogate the parties themselves under oath, when a doubt about the existence of an impediment arises.

When questioning the nupturients and the witnesses, a prepared interrogatory is helpful, though not obligatory as far as the general law of the Church is concerned. It is also commendable to consign the responses of the nupturients and witnesses to writing. In evaluating the testimony of the parties and witnesses, the pastor should take into account their character, knowledge, age, dignity and rank, as well as any other circumstances that may be considered as having an influence on their credibility. When documents are introduced in proof of certain points, they should be carefully scrutinized for the purpose of establishing their authenticity and genuineness.

Any specific regulations laid down by the local ordinary for pre-nuptial investigation should be carefully observed, unless they are contrary to the prescriptions of the Code. In those special instances where the Code calls for consultation with the ordinary prior to admitting nupturients to marriage, the pastor should observe the regulations of the Code. The pastor should refrain from personally deciding cases that require the intervention of an ecclesiastical trial or process. He should refer such cases to the curia. In petitioning for dispensations the pastor should see that the causes presented in the petition are true, as the authority who grants the dispensations must depend to a great extent on the information in the petition.

Passing from the more general features of pre-nuptial investigation to the particular investigation of nupturients, it may be said that the first duty of the investigating pastor is to identify the parties. For that purpose it it necessary to interrogate them as tc their names, their parents' names, their age, residence, religion and occupation. It is also necessary for the pastor to establish whether he is competent to assist at the marriage. His succeeding questions will seek to establish whether or not the lawfulness or validity of the contemplated marriage is hindered by any matrimonial impediment; whether the parties are freely consenting to the marriage and whether they are sufficiently instructed in Christian doctrine. In planning his questions he must take into account the various circumstances that surround each particular case. No uniform planned interrogatory can be drawn up to suit each particular case. However, when there are suspicions or indications that the parties are hindered from marriage by a specific impediment, the pastor should all the more earnestly pursue his inquiries and clear up any existing suspicions or doubts in regard to the free status of the nupturients. Impediments which entail sin, such as crime, abduction, public propriety, etc., should be proposed with great prudence. Discretion will frequently dictate that such impediments be proposed after the manner of an instruction rather than after the manner of an interrogation. Ordinarily the investigation of the free status of couples contemplating a mixed marriage should be more intensive than that of couples who contemplate a purely Catholic union. In the case of all nupturients the investigation of the impediment of *ligamen* should receive special attention. When parties contemplate a mixed marriage, the pastor should make sure that there are grave and reasonable causes for the union; that the parties give the requisite guarantees sincerely; and that there is moral certainty of the fulfillment of these guarantees.

When *vagi* present themselves for marriage, the pastor in accordance with the prescriptions of the Code should consult the ordinary.

When one or both nupturients are in danger of death, it is sufficient for the pastor to obtain from them the sworn affirmation that they are baptized and that they are free from every matrimonial impediment, unless there are positive indications that they are not free to marry. When there are definite indications or suspicions that they are not free to marry, the pastor should make further inquiries.

Should an unworthy Catholic appear before the pastor and declare to him his intention of contracting marriage, the pastor should proceed with consummate care and caution. He should refer the marriage to the bishop and follow his instructions.

In investigating the *status liber* of nupturients, of whom one is a Catholic of the Latin rite and the other a Catholic of an Oriental rite, the pastor must remember the variations in the matrimonial impediments of the respective rites in question. If he is not well acquainted with the matrimonial impediments of the Oriental rite, the proper procedure is to refer the case to the curia and await its instructions.

CONCLUSIONS

1. There is no trace of juridical pre-nuptial investigation in the sources of Roman Law.

2. In a letter of St. Ignatius to Polycarp there is some evidence of at least cursory pre-nuptial investigation made by the bishop, but it was not juridical.

3. The first definite trace of juridical pre-nuptial investigation is found in particular legislation and dates from the time of Charlemagne. It concerned the investigation of the impediment of consanguinity.

4. The Fourth Council of the Lateran (1215) furnishes the first universal legislation on the pastor's obligation in pre-nuptial investigation.

5. Particular councils subsequent to the Council of the Lateran and the Council of Trent stressed the pre-nuptial investigation of *peregrini, ignoti* and *vagi.*

6. There are no evidences that the decree *Cum alias,* which required that two witnesses be interrogated under oath as to the free status of each nupturient, was ever observed in the United States.

7. The pastor who has the right to institute pre-nuptial investigation is the pastor who has the right to assist at the marriage both lawfully and validly.

8. Physical presence of the prospective bride and groom before the investigating pastor is required, unless necessity renders it impossible.

9. There is no legislation requiring that the responses of the nupturients or of the witnesses be consigned to writing, but written responses are commendable.

10. Though the Code seldom calls expressly for documentary proof of the parties' *status liber,* it does seem to encourage such proof.

11. It seems reasonable to maintain that when the Code calls for the suppletory oath from the nupturients or witnesses, it should be administered even to a non-Catholic nupturient or witness, unless the non-Catholic does not believe in God.

12. No special rules for the evaluation of the testimony given by nupturients and witnesses are found in the Code. Consequently it appears consonant with canon 20 to invoke the aid of canons 1789-1791 in as far as the rules of these canons can be applied.

APPENDIX I

SACRA CONGREGATIO S. OFFICII

INSTRUCTIO AD PROBANDAM MORTEM CONIUGIS (AN. 1868)

MATRIMONII vinculo duos tantummodo, Christo ita docente, copulari et coniungi posse; alterutro vero coniuge vita functo, secundas, imo et ulteriores nuptias, licitas esse, dogmatica Ecclesiae catholicae doctrina est.

Verum ad secundas et ulteriores nuptias quod attinet, cum de re agatur quae difficultatibus ac fraudibus haud raro est obnoxia, hinc S. Sedes sedulo curavit, modo constitutionibus generalibus, saepius autem responsis in casibus particularibus datis, ut libertas novas nuptias ineundi ita cuique salva esset, ut praedicta matrimonii unitas in discrimen non adduceretur.

Inde constituta sacrorum canonum, quibus, ut quis possit licite ad alia vota transire, exigitur quod de morte coniugis certo constet, uti cap. *Dominus, De secundis nuptiis,* vel quod de ipsa morte recipiatur certum nuntium, uti cap. *In praesentia, De sponsalibus et matrimoniis.* Inde etiam ea quae explanatius traduntur in instructione *Cum alias,* 21 augusti 1670, a Clemente X sancita, et in bullario Romano inserta, super examine testium pro matrimoniis contrahendis, in curia Emi Vicarii Urbis et ceterorum Ordinariorum. Maxime vero quae proprius ad rem facientia ibi habentur, n. 12 ct 13.

Et haec quidem abunde sufficerent, si in ciusmodi causis peragendis omnimoda et absoluta certitudo de alterius coniugis obitu haberi semper posset: sed cum id non sinant casuum propemodum infinitae vices (quod sapienter animadversum est in laudata instructione his verbis: *Si tamen huiusmodi testimonia haberi non possunt, S. C. non intendit excludere alias probationes, quae de iure communi possunt admitti, dummodo legitimae sint et sufficientes*), sequitur, quod stantibus licet principiis generalibus praestitutis, haud raro casus eveniunt, in quibus ecclesiasticorum praesidum iudicia haerere solent in vera iustaque probatione dignoscenda ac statuenda; imo, pro summa illa facilitate quae aetate nostra facta est remotissimas quasque regiones adeundi, in omnes fere orbis partes homines divagentur, eiusmodi casuum multitudo adeo succrevit, ut frequentissimi hac de re ad supremam hanc Congregationem habeantur recursus, non sine porro partium incommodo, quibus inter informationes atque instructiones, quas pro re nata, ut aiunt, peti mittique necesse est, plurimum defluit temporis, quin possint ad optata vota convolare.

Quapropter S. eadem C. huiusmodi necessitatibus occurrere percupiens, simulque perpendens in dissitis praesertim missionum locis ecclesiasticos Praesides opportunis destitui subsidiis, quibus ex gravibus difficultatibus extricare se valeant, e re esse censuit uberiorem edere instructionem, in qua, iis quae iam tradita sunt nullo pacto abrogatis, regulae indigitentur, quas in eiusmodi casibus haec ipsa S. C. sequi solet, ut illarum ope, vel absque necessitate recursus ad S. Sedem, possint iudicia ferri, vel certe, si recurrendum sit, status quaestionis ita dilucide exponatur, ut impediri longiori mora sententia non debeat. Itaque:

1. Cum de coniugis morte quaestio instituitur, notandum primo loco, quod argumentum a sola ipsius absentia quantacumque (licet a legibus civilibus fere ubique admittatur), a sacris canonibus minime sufficiens ad iustam probationem habetur. Unde s. m. Pius VI ad Archiepiscopum Pragensem, die 11 iulii 1789, rescripsit, solam coniugis absentiam atque omnimodum eius silentium satis argumentum non esse ad mortem comprobandam, ne tum quidem cum edicto regio coniux absens evocatus (idemque porro dicendum est, si per publicas ephemerides id factum sit), nullum suimet indicium dederit. Quod enim non comparuerit, idem Pontifex, non magis mors in causa esse potuit, quam eius contumacia.

2. Hinc, ad praescriptum eorumdem sacrorum canonum, documentum authenticum obitus diligenti studio exquiri omnino debet; exaratum scilicet ex regestis paroeciae, vel xenodochii, vel militiae, vel etiam, si haberi nequeat ab auctoritate ecclesiastica, a gubernio civili loci in quo, ut supponitur, persona obierit.

3. Porro quandoque hoc documentum haberi nequit; quo casu testium depositionibus supplendum erit. Testes vero duo saltem esse debent, iurati, fide digni, et qui de facto proprio deponant, defunctum cognoverint, ac sint inter se concordes quoad locum et causam obitus, aliasque substantiales circumstantias. Qui insuper, si defuncti propinqui sint, aut socii itineris, industriae, vel etiam militiae, eo magis plurimi faciendum erit illorum testimonium.

4. Interdum unus tantum testis examinandus reperitur, et, licet ab omni iure testimonium unius ad plene probandum non admittatur, attamen, ne coniux, alias nuptias inire peroptans, vitam coelibem agere cogatur, etiam unius testimonium absolute non respuit S. C. in dirimendis huiusmodi casibus, dummodo ille testis recensitis conditionibus sit praeditus, nulli exceptioni obnoxius, ac praeterea eius depositio aliis gravibusque adminiculis fulciatur: sique alia extrinseca adminicula colligi omnino nequeant, hoc tamen certum sit, nihil in eius testimonio reperiri quod non sit congruum atque omnino verisimile.

5. Contingit etiam ut testes omnimoda fide digni testificentur se tempore non suspecto, mortem coniugis ex aliorum attestatione audivisse; isti autem, vel quia absentes, vel quia obierint, vel aliam ob quamcumque rationabilem causam examinari nequeunt; tunc, dicta ex alieno ore, quantenus omnibus aliis in casu concurrentibus circumstantis, aut saltem urgentibus respondeant, satis esse censentur pro secutae mortis prudenti iudicio.

6. Verum haud semel experientia compertum habetur, quo nec unus quidem reperiatur testis, qualis supra adstruitur. Hoc in casu probatio obitus ex coniecturis, praesumptionibus, indiciis, et adiunctis quibuscumque, sedula certe et admodum cauta investigatione curanda erit, ita nimirum ut, pluribus hinc inde collectis, eorumque natura perpensa, prout scilicet urgentiora vel leviora sunt, seu propiore vel remotiore nexu cum veritate mortis coniunguntur, inde prudentis viri iudicium ad eamdem morten affirmandam probabilitate maxima, seu morali certitudine, promoveri possit. Quapropter quandonam in singulis casibus habeatur ex huiusmodi coniecturis simul coniunctis iusta probatio, id prudenti relinquendum est iudicis arbitrio; hic tamen non abs re erit plures indicare fontes, ex quibus illae, sive urgentiores, sive etiam leviores, colligi et haberi possint.

7. Itaque in primis illae praesumptiones investigandae erunt, quae personam ipsius asserti defuncti respiciunt, quaeque profecto facile haberi poterunt a coniunctis, amicis, vicinis, et quoquo modo notis utriusque coniugis. In quorum examine requiratur, ex. gr.:

An ille, de cuius obitu est sermo, bonis moribus imbutus esset, pie religioseque viveret, uxoremque diligeret; nullam sese occultandi causam haberet; utrum bona stabilia possideret, vel alia a suis propinquis aut aliunde sperare posset.

An discesserit annuentibus uxore et coniunctis; quae tunc eius aetas et valetudo esset.

An aliquando et quo loco scripserit, et num suam voluntatem quamprimum redeundi aperuerit; aliaque eius generis indicia colligantur.

Alia ex rerum adiunctis pro varia absentiae causa colligi indicia sic poterunt:

Si ob militiam abierit, a Duce militum requiratur quid de eo sciat; utrum alicui pugnae interfuerit; utrum ab hostibus fuerit captus; num castra deseruerit, aut destinationes periculosas habuerit, etc.

Si negotiationis causa iter susceperit, inquiratur utrum tempore itineris gravia pericula fuerint ipsi superanda; num solus profectus fuerit, vel pluribus comitatus; utrum in regione ad quam se contulit, supervenerint seditiones, bella, fames et pestilentiae, etc.

Si maritimum iter fuerit aggressus, sedula investigatio fiat a quo portu discesserit; quinam fuerint itineris socii; quo se contulerit; quod nomen navis quam conscendit; quis eiusdem navis gubernator; an naufragium fecerit; an societas, quae navis cautionem forsan dedit, pretium eius solverit; aliaeque circumstantiae, si quae sint, diligenter perpendantur.

8. Fama quoque, aliis adiuta adminiculis, argumentum de obitu constituit, hisce tamen conditionibus, nimirum: quod a duobus saltem testibus fide dignis et iuratis comprobetur, qui deponant de rationabili causa ipsius famae; an eam acceperint a maiori et saniori parte populi, et an ipsi de eadem fama recte sentiant; nec sit dubium illam fuisse concitatam ab illis in quorum commodum inquiritur.

9. Tandem, si opus fuerit, praetereunda non erit investigatio per publicas ephemerides, datis directori omnibus necessariis personae indiciis, nisi ob speciales circumstantias saniori ac prudentiori consilio aliter censeatur.

10. Haec omnia pro opportunitate casuum S. haec C. diligenter expendere solet; cumque de re gravissima agatur, cunctis aequa lance libratis, atque insuper auditis plurium theologorum et iurisprudentum suffragiis, denique suum iudicium pronuntiat, an de tali obitu satis constet, et nihil obstet quominus petenti transitus ad alias nuptias concedi possit.

11. Ex his omnibus ecclesiastici Praesides certam desumere possunt normam, quam in huiusmodi iudiciis sequantur. Quod si, non obstantibus regulis hucusque notatis, res adhuc incerta et implexa illis videatur, ad S. Sedem recurrere debebunt, actis omnibus cum ipso recursu transmissis, aut saltem diligenter expositis.

APPENDIX II

DOCUMENTA PRO PROCESSU STATUS LIBERI AD MATRIMONIUM INEUNDUM

DECRETUM *emanatum in Congregatione generali S. Romanae et Universalis Inquisitionis habita feria V, die 21 Augusti 1670, in Palatio Apostolico Montis Quirinalis coram Sanctissimo Domino Nostro Clemente divina providentia Papa X, ac Eminentissimis et Reverendissimis DD. S. R. E. Cardinalibus in tota Republica Christiana contra haereticam pravitatem Generalibus Inquisitoribus a S. Sede Apostolica specialiter deputatis.*

Cum alias per Sacram Congregationem S. Officii, iteratis, instructionibus ab eadem emanatis de anno 1658, et 1665, locorumque Ordinariis transmissis, provisum fuerit, ut praescriptis interrogatoriis faciendis testibus, qui ad probandum statum liberum contrahentium matrimonium inducuntur, omnis prorsus secluderetur aditus iis, qui adhuc vivente altero conjuge, aut alias impediti ad secunda illicita vota transire satagebant: videns nihilominus Sanctissimus D. N. quamplures locorum Ordinarios, vel eorum Vicarios, et Deputatos ad excipiendas testium depositiones, nec non parochos, et notarios, in casibus expressis, aut omittere, aut non observare earumdem instructionum tenorem; et licet aliquando plene observent, non tamen interrogare testes super aliis impedimentis dirimentibus:

Ideo volens Sancititas Sua praedictis malis occurrere, re mature considerata cum Eminentissimis et Reverendissimis Dominis Cardinalibus Generalibus Inquisitoribus, praesenti decreto, perpetuis futuris temporibus duraturo, iterum injungit omnibus Vicariis, seu Deputatis pro examinandis testibus ad probandum statum liberum contrahentium matrimonium, nec non parochis, notariis, et quibuscumque aliis respective, sub poenis etiam gravibus corporalibus arbitrio S. Cong., ut instructionem infrascriptam ad unguem observent.

Ut autem praesens decretum, et instructio ad omnium notitiam facilius deveniant, decrevit, illa ad valvas Basilicae Principis Apostolorum, et Cancellariae Apostolicae, ac in acie Campi Florae de Urbe, ac Palatio S. Officii ejusdem Urbis per aliquem ex cursoribus Sanctitatis Suae publicari, ac eorum exempla ibidem affixa relinqui; illaque sic publicata omnes, et singulos, quos concernunt, post duos menses a die publicationis in Urbe faciendae numerandos, perinde afficere, ac arctare si illorum unicuique personaliter notificata, et intimata fuissent.

Instructio

Pro examine illorum testium, qui inducuntur pro contrahendis matrimoniis tam in Curia Eminentissimi et Reverendissimi D. Cardinalis Urbis Vicarii, quam in aliis Curiis caeterorum Ordinariorum.

In primis testis moneatur de gravitate juramenti in hoc praesertim negotio pertimescendi, in quo divina simul, et humana majestas laeditur ob rei, de qua tractatur, importantiam, et gravitatem; et quod imminet poena triremium et fustigationis deponenti falsum.

Secundo, interrogetur de nomine, cognomine, patria, aetate, exercitio et habitatione.

Tertio, an sit civis, vel exterus, et quatenus sit exterus, a quanto tempore est in loco, in quo testis ipse deponit.

Quarto, an ad examen acceserit sponte, vel requisitus; si dixerit accessisse sponte a nemine requisitum, dimittatur, quia praesumitur mendax. Si vero dixerit accessisse requisitum, interrogetur a quo, vel a quibus, ubi, quando, quomodo, coram quibus, at quoties fuerit requisitus, et an sciat adesse aliquod impedimentum inter contrahere volentes.

Quinto, interrogetur, an cognoscat ipsos contrahere volentes, et a quanto tempore, in quo loco, qua occasione, et cujus qualitatis, vel conditionis existant.

Septimo, interrogetur, an contrahere volentes sint cives vel exteri: si responderit esse exteros, supersederatur in licentia contrahendi, donec per litteras Ordinarii ipsorum contrahere volentium doceatur de eorum libero statu de eo tempore, quo permanserunt in sua civitate, vel dioecesi.

Ad probandum vero eorumdem contrahere volentium statum liberum pro reliquo temporis spatio, scilicet usque ad tempus, quo volunt contrahere, admittantur testes idonei, qui legitime, et concludenter deponant statum liberum contrahere volentium, et reddant sufficientem rationem causae eorum scientiae, absque eo quod teneantur deferre attestationes Ordinariorum locorum, in quibus contrahere volentes moram traxerunt.

Si vero responderit contrahere volentes esse cives:

Octavo, interrogetur, sub qua parochia hactenus contrahere volentes habitaverint, vel habitent de praesenti.

Item, an ipse testis sciat aliquem ex praedictis contrahere volentibus quandoque habuisse uxorem, vel maritum, aut professum fuisse in aliqua religione approbata, vel suscepisse aliquem ex ordinibus sacris, subdiaconatum scilicet, diaconatum, vel presbyteratum, vel habere aliud impedimentum, ex quo non possit contrahi matrimonium.

Si vero testis responderit non habuisse uxorem, vel maritum, neque aliud impedimentum, ut supra:

Nono, interrogetur de causa scientiae, et an sit possibile, quod aliquis ex illis habuerit uxorem, vel maritum, aut aliud impedimentum, et quod ipse testis nesciat.

Si responderint affirmative, supersedeatur, nisi ex aliis testibus probetur concludenter non habuisse uxorem, vel maritum, neque ullum aliud impedimentum, etc.

Decimo, interrogetur de causa scientiae, ex qua deinde judex colligere poterit, an testi sit danda fides.

Si responderit, contrahere volentes habuisse uxorem, vel maritum, sed esse mortuos:

Undecimo, interrogetur de loco, et tempore, quo sunt mortui, et quomodo ipse testis sciat fuisse conjuges, et nunc esse mortuos. Et si respondeat mortuos fuisse in aliquo hospitali, vel vidisse sepeliri in certa ecclesia, vel occasione militiae sepultos fuisse a militibus, non detur licentia contrahendi, nisi prius recepto testimonio authentico a rectore hospitalis in quo praedicti decesserunt, vel a rectore ecclesiae in qua humata fuerint eorum cadavera, vel si fieri potest a duce illius cohortis, in qua descriptus erat miles.

Si tamen hujusmodi testimonia haberi non possunt, S. Cong. non intendit excludere alias probationes, quae de jure communi possunt admitti, dummodo sint legitimae, et sufficientes.

Duodecimo, interrogetur, an post mortem dicti conjugis defuncti, aliquis ex praedictis contrahere volentibus transierit ad secunda vota.

Si responderit negative:

Decimo tertio, interrogetur, an esse possit, quod aliquis ex illis transierit ad secunda vota, absque eo quod ipse testis sciat.

Si responderit affirmative, supersedeatur in licentia, donec producantur testes, per quos negativa coarctetur concludenter.

Si vero negative:

Decimo quarto, interrogetur de causa scientiae, qua perpensa judex poterit judicare an sit concedenda licentia, vel non.

Si contrahentes sunt vagi, non procedatur ad licentiam contrahendi, nisi doceant per fides Ordinariorum suorum esse liberos, et in aliis servata forma Concilii Tridentini *in cap. Multi, Sess. 24.*

Fides, aliaque documenta, quae producuntur de partibus, non admittantur, nisi sint munita sigillo, et legalitate Episcopi Ordinarii, et recognita saltem per testes, qui habeant notam manum, et sigillum, et attente consideretur, quod fides seu testimonia bene et concludenter identificent personnas, de quibus agitur.

Pro testibus in hac materia recipiantur magis consanguinei, quam extranei, quia praesumuntur melius informati, et cives magis, quam exteri; nec admittantur homines vagi et milites, nisi data causa, et maturo consilio; et notarius exacte describat personam testis, quem si cognoscit, utatur clausula: *Mihi bene cognitus.* Sin minus examen non recipiat, nisi una cum persona testis aliqua alia compareat cognita notario, et quae attestetur de nomine, et cognomine ipsius testis, nec non de idoneitate ejusdem ad testimonium ferendum.

Et hujusmodi examinibus debet interesse in Urbe, ultra notarium, officialis specialiter deputandus ab Eminentissimo Vicario, et extra Urbem vel Vicarius Episcopi, vel aliqua alia persona insignis, et idonea ab Episcopo specialiter deputanda; alias puniatur notarius arbitrio S. Cong., et Ordinarius non permittat fieri publicationes.

Ordinarii praecipiant omnibus, et singulis parochis in eorum dioecesibus existentibus, ut pro matrimoniis cum exteris contrahendis non faciant publicationes in eorum ecclesiis, nisi certiorato Ordinario, a quo, vel ejus Generali Vicario, prius teneantur authenticam reportare, quod pro tali matrimonio fuerunt examinati testes in eorum tribunali, qui probant statum liberum contrahere volentium, etc.

Contravenientes autem severe punientur.

Anno a Nativatate D. N. J.-C. millesimo sexcentesimo septuagesimo, indictione octava, die vero 30 mensis Augusti, Pontificatus autem Sanctiss. in Christo Patris, et D. N. D. Clementis Divina Providentia Papae X anno primo, supradictum decretum affixum, et publicatum fuit ad valvas basilicae Principis Apostolorum, Cancellariae Apostolicae, et in acie Campi Florae de Urbe, ac Palatio S. Officii ejusdem Urbis per me Petrum Paulum Desiderium ejusdem Sanctiss. D. N. Papae, et Sacrae Inquisitionis cursorem.

APPENDIX III

S. CONGREGATIO DE DISCIPLINA SACRAMENTORUM

Instructio ac Revmos Ordinarios Locorum

Super Probatione Status Liberi
ac Denuntiatione Initi Matrimonii

ITERUM conquesti sunt haud pauci Ordinarii locorum quod parochi, praesertim in exteris dissitisque regionibus ad quas frequentes demigrant ex Europa opifices, horum aliquando matrimoniis assistant, quin praescripta iuris tum de statu libertatis tum de initi matrimonii denuntiatione rite serventur; ex quo fit ut non raro novum contra fas attentetur matrimonium ab iis qui adhuc priore vinculo adstringuntur.

Ad huiusmodi malum praecavendum, quo sacra familiae christianae iura pessumdantur, parentes vinculis damnationis illaqueantur, et filii perversionis periculo facile obiiciuntur, haec Sacra Congregatio de disciplina Sacramentorum die 6 mensis martii anni 1911 Instructionem Ordinariis dedit, quae in Commentario Officiali *Acta Apostolicae Sedis,* Vol. III, pag. 102, sub die 15 eiusdem mensis evulgata est.

Verum ne quis, in negotio tam gravi, huic Instructioni aliquid a Codice iuris canonici derogatum esse putet, Emi Patres huius Sacrae Congregationis in generali conventu die 26 mensis iunii currentis anni habito, eam, ipsius Codicis praescriptionibus suffultam. Ordinariis iterum sequentis tenoris dandam censuerunt.

1. Ordinarii in parochorum memoriam revocare satagant haud licere ipsis adstare matrimonio, ne praetextu quidem et intentione avertendi fideles a turpi concubinatu, aut praecavendi scandalum coniugii, quod vocant, civilis, nisi constito sibi legitime de libero statu contrahentium, servatis de iure servandis (can. 1020 et 1097 § 1 n. 1°, Cod. iur. can.), iidemque moneantur ne omittant, ad normam can. 1021, baptismi testimonium a contrahentibus exigere, si hic in alia paroecia fuerit illis collatus.

2. Vi can. 1103 § 2 parochus, qui matrimonio interfuit, ad parochum baptismi transmittere festinet initi contractus denuntiationem, quae, ut praescripta eiusdem canonis rite serventur, contineat oportet coniugum eorumque parentum nomina et agnomina, aetatem contrahentium, locum diemque nuptiarum, testium pariter nomina et agnomina, denique ipsum parochi nomen et agnomen una cum paroeciali sigillo.

Accurate autem edoceatur de paroecia, de dioecesi, ac de baptismi coniugum loco; ceteraque alia serventur, quae ad scripta per publicos portitores tuto transmittenda pertinent.

3. Quo securius sive testimonium de statu libero a parocho nupturientium habeatur, sive denuntiatio de secuto matrimonio ad parochum baptismi perveniat, parochi haec documentat petant vel transmittant per cancellariam Ordinarii loci.

4. Id autem perpendant parochi oportet, aliqua huiusmodi opificum emigrantium matrimonia, quasi vagorum matrimonia habenda esse, quibus, iuxta can. 1032, *parochus assistere non debet nisi debitam licentiam assistendi ab Ordinario loci obtinuerit.* Quod si de vagis non agatur, tamen difficulter quoad alios emigrantes *abest dubium de exsistentia impedimenti,* ideoque, iuxta can. 1031 § 1 n. 3, parochus *eorum matrimonio assistere nequit inconsulto Ordinario;* habito etiam prae oculis praescripto can. 1023 § 2. Hisce de causis haec Sacra Congregatio iubet et mandat ut parochi matrimoniis fidelium de quibus agitur in hac Instructione non assistant, excepto casu necessitatis seu potissimum periculo mortis, inconsulto Ordinario loci.

5. Si forte accidat ut, adhibitis etiam cautelis de quibus in n. 1, baptismi parochus in recipienda denuntiatione matrimonii comperiat alterutrum contrahentium aliis nuptiis iam esse alligatum, rem quantocius significabit, per cancellariam Ordinarii, parocho contra fas attentati matrimonii.

6. Ordinarii sedulo advigilent ut haec praescripta religiose serventur, horumque violatores, siquos repererint, curent ad officium revocare, adhibitis etiam, si opus sit, canonicis sanctionibus.

Ssm̃us Dominus Noster Benedictus Pp. XV, in audientia habita ab infrascripto Secretario huius Sacrae Congregationis die 26 iunii 1921, hanc Instructionem approbavit et confirmavit, eamque ab omnibus quibus spectat servari mandavit.

Datum Romae ex aedibus S. C. de Sacramentis, die 4 iulii 1921.

M. Card. Lega, *Praefectus.*

BIBLIOGRAPHY

Sources

Acta Apostolicae Sedis, Commentarium Officiale, Romae, 1909-

Acta et Decreta Concilii Plenarii Baltimorensis Tertii, A. D. MCXXXLXXXIV, Baltimorae: John Murphy, 1866.

Acta et Decreta Sacrorum Conciliorum Recentiorum, Collectio Lacensis, 7 vols., Friburgi Brisgoviae, 1870-1892.

Acta Sanctae Sedis, 41 vols., Romae, 1865-1908.

Bullarii Romani Continuatio Summorum Pontificum, 19 vols., Prato, 1756-1883.

Bullarium Clementis XI, Romae: Typographia Rev. Camerae Apostolicae, 1723.

Bullarium SSmi Domini Nostri Benedicti Papae XIV, 4 vols., 4. ed., Venetiis, 1778.

Codex Iuris Canonici Pii X Pontificis Maximi iussu digestus, Benedicti Papae XV auctoritate promulgatus, Romae: Typis Polyglottis Vaticanis, 1917.

Codicis Iuris Canonici Fontes cura Emi, Petri Card. Gasparri editi, 7 vols., Romae: Typis Polyglottis Vaticanis, 1923-1935. (Vol. VII, ed. cura et studio Emi. Iustiniani Card. Serédi.)

Collectanea S. Congregationis de Propaganda Fide, 2 vols., Romae: Typographia Polyglotta, S. C. de Propaganda Fide, 1907.

Concilii Plenarii Baltimorensis II, in Ecclesia Metropolitana Baltimorensi, a die VII. ad diem XXI. Octobris, A. D. MDCCCLXVI, *Habiti, et a Sede Apostolica Recogniti, Acta et Decreta,* Baltimorae: John Murphy, 1894.

Corpus Iuris Canonici, Editio Lipsiensis II (Richter-Friedberg), 2 vols., Lipsiae, 1922.

Corpus Iuris Civilis, 3 vols., Berolini, 1928-1929.
Institutiones, quas recognovit P. Kreuger;
Digesta, quae recognovit et retractavit P. Kreuger;
Codex Iustinianus, quem recognovit et rectractavit P. Kreuger;
Novellae, quas recognovit R. Schoell, et absolvit G. Kroll.

Corpus Scriptorum Ecclesiasticorum Latinorum, editum consilio et impensis Academiae Litterarum Vindobonensis, 68 vols., Vindobonae: Hoelder-Pichler-Tempsky, A. G., 1866-

Harduin, Jean, *Acta Conciliorum et Epistolae Decretales ac Constitutiones Summorum Pontificum,* 12 vols., Parisiis, 1715.

Hinschius, Paulus, *Decretales Pseudo-Isidorianae et Capitula Angilramni,* Lipsiae, 1863.

Mansi, J. D., *Sacrorum Conciliorum Nova et Amplissima Collectio,* 58 vols., Paris-Leipzig-Arnheim, 1901-1927.

Migne, P. J., *Patrologiae Cursus Completus,* Series Graeca, 161 vols., Parisiis, 1856-1866.

———, *Patrologiae Cursus Completus,* Series Latina, 221 vols., Parisiis, 1858-1864.

Monumenta Germaniae Historica, Leges, 5 vols., Lipsiae, Hiersemann, 1925.

Quinque Compilationes Antiquae, Friedberg, Aemilius, Lipsiae, 1882.

Sacrae Romanae Rotae Decisiones seu Sententiae, 21 vols., 1909-

Thesaurus Resolutionum Sacrae Congregationis Concilii, 167 vols., Romae, 1718-1908.

AUTHORS

A Coronata, Matthew, *Institutiones Iuris Canonici Ad Usum Utriusque Cleri et Scholarum,* 5 vols., Taurini: Marietti, 1928-1936.

Aertnys-Damen, *Theologia Moralis,* 2. ed., Taurinorum Augustae: Marietti, 1928.

Aichner, Simon, *Compendium Iuris Ecclesiastici,* 6. ed., Brixinae, 1887.

Alford, Culver Bernardus, *Ius Matrimoniale Comparatum,* Romae: Anonima Libraria Cattolica Italiana, 1938.

Antonelli, I., *De Conceptu Impotentiae et Sterilitatis relate ad Matrimonium,* Romae, 1900.

———, *Medicina Pastoralis in Usum Confessariorum et Curiarum Ecclesiasticarum,* Romae, 1932.

Ayrinhac-Lydon, *Marriage Legislation in the New Code of Canon Law,* New York: Benziger, 1932.

[Bachofen], Charles Augustine, *A Commentary on the New Code of Canon Law,* 4. ed., 8 vols., St. Louis: B. Herder, 1921-1929.

Ballerini, A., *Opus Theologicum Morale,* 7 vols., Prati, 1898-1901.

Bangen, Joannes, *Instructio Practica in Sponsalibus et Matrimonio,* Monasterii: Typis et sumptibus Librariae Aschendorffinae, 1858.

Bastnagel, Clement Vincent, *The Appointment of Parochial Adjutants and Assistants,* The Catholic University of America, Canon Law Studies, n. 58, Washington: The Catholic University of America, 1930.

Batzill, P. Hartmann, *Decisiones Sanctae Sedis de Usu et Abusu Matrimonii,* Taurini: Marietti, 1937.

Bellarminus, Card. Robertus, *Opera Omnia ex Editione Veneta,* iterum edidit Justinus Fèvre, 12 vols., Parisiis, 1870-1874.

Benedict XIV, *De Synodo Dioecesana,* 2 vols., Romae: Typographia S. C. de Propaganda Fide, 1806.

Berardi, C., *Gratiani Canones Genuini ab Apocryphis Discreti, Corrupti ad emendatiorum Codicum Fidem Exacti, Difficiliores Commoda interpretatione illustrati,* 3 vols. in 4, Venetiis, 1777.

Boudinhon, A., *Le Mariage ed Les Fiançailles,* 4. ed., Lethielleux, Paris, 1907.

Bouix, D., *Tractatus de Iudiciis Ecclesiasticis,* 2. ed., 2 vols., Parisiis, 1855.

Bouscaren, T. Lincoln, *The Canon Law Digest,* 2 vols., Milwaukee: Bruce, 1934-1937.

Brennan, James H., *The Simple Convalidation of Marriage,* The Catholic University of America, Canon Law Studies, n. 102, Washington: The Catholic University of America, 1937.

Bucceroni, I., *Institutiones Theologiae Moralis,* Vol. IV, *De Matrimonio,* Romae, 1915.

Cappello, Felix M., *Tractatus Canonico-Moralis de Sacramentis,* Vol. III, *De Matrimonio,* 2. ed., Romae: Marietti, 1927.

———, *Tractatus Canonico-Moralis de Sacramentis,* Vol. III, *De Matrimonio,* 3. ed. emendata et aucta, Romae: Apud Aedes Univ. Gregorianae, 1933.

Carberry, John J., *The Juridical Form of Marriage,* The Catholic University of America, Canon Law Studies, n. 84, Washington: The Catholic University of America, 1930.

Cerato, Prosdocimus, *Matrimonium a Codice Iuris Canonici Desumptum,* 4. ed., Patavii: Typis Seminarii, 1929.

Chelodi, Joannes, *Ius Matrimoniale iuxta Codicem Iuris Canonici,* 3. ed., Tridenti: Libr. Edit. Tridentum, 1921.

Cicognani, Amleto Giovanni, *Canon Law,* 2. ed., Philadelphia: The Dolphin Press, 1935.

Coady, John Joseph, *The Appointment of Pastors,* The Catholic University of America, Canon Law Studies, n. 52, Washington: The Catholic University of America, 1929.

Coffey, P., *The Science of Logic,* 2. ed., 2 vols., London: Longmans, Green Company, 1918.

Corbett, Percy Ellwood, *The Roman Law of Marriage,* Oxford: Clarendon Press, 1930.

Costello, John Michael, *Domicile and Quasi-Domicile,* The Catholic University of America, Canon Law Studies, n. 60, Washington: The Catholic University of America, 1930.

Coucke-Walsh, *The Sterile Period in Family Life,* New York: Wagner, 1933.

Creagh, John T., *A Commentary on the Decree "Ne Temere,"* Baltimore: Furst Co., 1908.

Cronin, Charles J., *The New Matrimonial Legislation,* New York: Benziger, 1908.

D'Annibale, J., *Summula Theologiae Moralis,* 3. ed., 3 vols., Romae, 1892.

De Becker, Julius, *De Sponsalibus et Matrimonio Praelectiones Canonicae,* Lovanii, 1903.

Declareuil, J., *Rome the Lawgiver,* New York: Alfred Knopf, 1926.

De Justis, Vincentius, *De Dispensationibus Matrimonialibus Tractatus in tres libros digestus,* Lucae, 1726.

De Meester, A., *Iuris Canonici et Iuris Canonico-Civilis Compendium,* 3 vols. in 4, Bruges, 1921-1928.

Denziger, H—Banwart, C., *Enchiridion Symbolorum Definitionum et Declarationum de Rebus Fidei et Morum,* 17 ed., Friburgi Brisgoviae: Herder, 1928.

De Smet, Aloysius, *Betrothment and Marriage,* Bruges, 1909.

——— *De Sponsabilis et Matrimonio,* Bruges, 1912.

Donohue, John F., *The Impediment of Crime,* The Catholic University of America, Canon Law Studies, n. 69, Washington: The Catholic University of America, 1931.

Durieux, P., *The Busy Pastor's Book on Matrimony,* translation by Oliver Dolphin, Faribault, 1926.

Eichman, Eduard, *Das katholische Mischehenrecht nach dem Codex Iuris Canonici,* Paderborn: Schöningh, 1921.

——— *Das Prozessrecht des Codex Iuris Canonici,* Paderborn: Schöningh, 1921.

Eschbach, A. R. D., *Casus de Feminae Impotentia,* Romae, 1899.

——— *Disputationes Physiologico-Theologicae,* 2. ed., Romae, 1901.

Esmein, A., *Le Mariage en Droit Canonique,* 2. ed., 2 vols., Paris: Libraire de Reçueil, Sirey, 1929.

Fanfani, Ludovicus, *De Iure Parochorum ad norman Codicis Iuris Canonici,* Turin: Marietti, 1924.

Farren, Neil, *Domicile and Quasi-Domicile,* Dublin: Gill, 1920.

Farrugia, P. Nicolaus, *De Matrimonio et Causis Matrimonialibus, Tractatus Canonico-Moralis iuxta Codicem Iuris Canonici,* Taurini-Romae: Marietti, 1924.

Feije, Henricus Joannes, *De Impedimentis et Dispensationibus Matrimonialibus,* 3. ed., 2 vols. Lovanii, 1885.

Ferreres, P. Joannes, *De Vasectomia Duplici necnon de Matrimonio Mulieris Excisae,* ed. altera, Madrid, 1913.

Fourneret, Pierre, *Le Domicile Matrimonial,* Paris, 1906.

——— *Le Mariage Chrètien,* Paris, 1909.

Funk, Francis Xavier, *Didascalia et Constitutiones Apostolorum,* Paderbornae, 1905.

Gasparri, Petrus, *Tractatus Canonicus de Matrimonio,* 2 vols., Paris, 1891.

——— *Tractatus Canonicus de Matrimonio,* 2. ed., 2 vols., Paris, 1892.

——— *Tractatus Canonicus de Matrimonio,* 3. ed., 2 vols., 1904.

——— *Tractatus Canonicus de Matrimonio,* ed. nova, ad mentem Codicis I. C., 2 vols., Romae: Typis Polyglottis Vaticanis, 1932.

Genicot, Eduardus, *Institutiones Theologiae Moralis,* 10. ed., 2 vols., Bruxellis: A. Dewit, 1922.

Gougnard, Armandus, *Tractatus de Matrimonio,* 7. ed., Mechliniae: H. Dessain, 1931.

Giovine, Petrus, *De Dispensationibus Matrimonialibus Consultationes Canonicae,* 2 vols., Neapoli, 1863.

Hartman, Sylvester J., *A Textbook of Logic,* New York: American Book Co., 1936.

Hefele, Carl Joseph von, *Conciliengeschichte,* 2. ed., 9 vols., Freiburg im Breisgau, 1875-1890.

Hefele-Leclerque, *Histoire des Conciles,* 5 vols., Paris, 1910.

Heiss, M., *De Matrimonio Tractatus Quinque,* Monachi, 1861.

Hughes, James Austin, *Witnesses in Criminal Trials of Clerics,* The Catholic University of America, Canon Law Studies, n. 106, Washington: The Catholic University of America, 1937.

Journel, M. J. Rouet de, *Enchiridion Patristicum,* 3. ed., Friburgi Brisgoviae: Herder, 1920.

Joyce, George Hayward, *Christian Marriage,* London and New York: Sheed & Ward, 1933.

Kaas, L., *Kriegsverschollenheit und Wiederverheiratung nach staatlichem und kirchlichem Recht,* Paderborn: Schöningh, 1919.

Kay, Thomas Henry, *Competence in Matrimonial Procedure,* The Catholic University of America, Canon Law Studies, n. 53, Washington: The Catholic University of America, 1929.

Kearney, Raymond A., *The Principles of Delegation,* The Catholic University of America, Canon Law Studies, n. 55, Washington: The Catholic University of America, 1929.

Kelly, James Patrick, *The Jurisdiction of the Simple Confessor,* The Catholic University of America, Canon Law Studies, n. 43, Washington: The Catholic University of America, 1927.

Kennedy, Edwin Joseph, *The Special Matrimonial Process in Cases of Evident Nullity,* The Catholic University of America, Canon Law Studies, n. 93, Washington: The Catholic University of America, 1935.

King, James Ignatius, *The Administration of the Sacraments to Dying Non-Catholics,* The Catholic University of America, Canon Law Studies, n. 23, Washington: The Catholic University of America, 1924.

Konings-Putzer, *Commentarium in Facultates Apostolicas,* 3. ed., New York, 1893.

Koudelka, Charles, *Pastors, Their Rights and Duties According to the New Code of Canon Law,* The Catholic University of America, Canon Law Studies, n. 11, Washington: The Catholic University of America, 1921.

Kubelbeck, William J., *The Sacred Penitentiaria and its Relations to the Faculties of Ordinaries and Priests,* The Catholic University of America, Canon Law Studies, n. 5, Washington: The Catholic University of America, 1918.
1918.

Laymann, Paulus, *Theologia Moralis,* 5 vols. in 1, Paris, 1627.

Leage, R. W., *Roman Private Law,* 2. ed., London: MacMillan, 1932.

Lehmkuhl, Augustinus, *Theologia Moralis,* 3. ed., 2 vols., Friburgi Brisgoviae, 1886.

Leinz, A., *Die Ehevorschrift des Concils von Trient,* Freiburg im Breisgau, 1888.

Leitner, M., *Lehrbuch des katholischen Eherechts,* 3. ed., Paderborn: Schöningh, 1920.

Lightfoot, J. B., *The Apostolic Fathers,* 2. ed., 3 vols., London: MacMillan, 1889.

Linneborn, J., *Grundriss des Eherechts nach dem Codex Iuris Canonici*, 2. and 3. ed., Paderborn: Schöningh, 1922.

——— *Grundriss des Eherechts nach dem Codex Iuris Canonici*, 4. ed., Paderborn, Schöningh, 1933.

Lombardus, Petrus, *Libri IV Sententiarum studia et cura PP. Collegii S. Bonaventurae in lucem editi*, Ad Claras Aquas: Typographia Collegii S. Bonaventurae, 1916.

Mazzeus, Franciscus, *De Matrimonio Conscientiae*, Romae, 1766.

Meaker, Samuel Raynor, *Human Sterility*, Baltimore: Williams & Wilkins Co., 1934.

Michiels, Gommarus, *Normae Generales Iuris Canonici*, 2 vols., Lublin-Polonia, Universitas Catholica, 1929.

Moran, William, *The Government of the Church in the First Century*, New York, 1913.

Moriarty, Eugene James, *Oaths in Ecclesiastical Courts*, The Catholic University of America, Canon Law Studies, n. 110, Washington: The Catholic University of America, 1937.

Motry, Hubert Louis, *Diocesan Faculties According to the Code of Canon Law*, The Catholic University of America, Canon Law Studies, n. 16, Washington: The Catholic University of America, 1922.

Muratori, Ludovicus Antonius, *Liturgia Romana Vetus*, 2 vols., Venetiis, 1748.

Nau, Louis J., *Manual of the Marriage Laws of Canon Law*, New York: Pustet, 1933.

Noldin, H., *Summa Theologiae Moralis*, 3 vols., 14. ed., Oeniponte: Typis et sumptibus Rauch, 1921.

Noval, P. Josephus, *Commentarium Codicis Iuris Canonici*, lib. IV, *De Processibus*, 2 vols., Augustae Taurinorum: Marietti, 1920.

Ottaviani, Alaphridus, *Institutiones Iuris Publici Ecclesiastici*, Vol. I, *Ius Publicum Interum*, ed. altera emendata et aucta, Romae: Typis Polyglottis Vaticanis, 1935.

Ojetti, Benedictus, *Synopsis Rerum Moralium et Iuris Pontificii*, Romae, 1899.

O'Keeffe, Gerald Michael, *Matrimonial Dispensations, Powers of Bishops, Priests and Confessors*, The Catholic University of America, Canon Law Studies, n. 45, Washington: The Catholic University of America, 1927.

O'Malley-Walsh, *Essays in Pastoral Medicine*, New York: Longmans, Green & Co., 1925.

O'Mara, William A., *Canonical Causes for Matrimonial Dispensations*, The Catholic University of America, Canon Law Studies, n. 96, Washington: The Catholic University of America, 1935.

O'Neill, W. H., *Papal Rescripts of Favor*, The Catholic University of America, Canon Law Studies, n. 57, Washington: The Catholic University of America, 1930.

Payen, G., *De Matrimonio in Missionibus ac Potissimum in Sinis Tractatus Practicus et Casus*, 3 vols., Zi-ka-wei: Typographia T'OU-SE-WE, 1928-1929.

Perrone, J., *De Matrimonio Christiano*, 3 vols., Leodii, 1861.

Petrovits, Joseph, *The New Church Law on Matrimony*, Philadelphia: McVey, 1921.

Pighi, Jo. Bapta, *De Sacramento Matrimonii Tractatio Canonico-Moralis*, 2. ed., Veronae, 1921.

Pirhing, Henricus, *Ius Canonicum Novo Methodo Explicatum*, 5 vols., Dilingae, 1728.

Quigley, Joseph A. M., *Condemned Societies*, The Catholic University of America, Canon Law Studies, n. 46, Washington: The Catholic University of America, 1927.

Reiffenstuel, Anacletus, *Ius Canonicum Universum*, 4 vols., Venetiis, 1735.

Ramstein, Matthew, *The Pastor and Marriage Cases*, New York: Benziger, 1936.

Rimlinger, Herbert Theodore, *Error Invalidating Matrimonial Consent*, The Catholic University of America, Canon Law Studies, n. 82, Washington: The Catholic University of America, 1932.

Roberts, James Brendan, *The Banns of Marriage*, The Catholic University of America, Canon Law Studies, n. 64, Washington: The Catholic University of America, 1931.

Rossi, Joseph, *De Impedimento Impotentiae*, Romae, 1910.

——— *De Matrimonii Celebratione iuxta Codicem Iuris Canonici*, Romae: Pustet, 1923.

Sanchez, Thomas, *De Sancto Matrimonii Sacramento Disputationum*, Tomi tres, Lugduni, 1669.

Sangmeister, Joseph V., *Force and Fear as Precluding Matrimonial Consent*, The Catholic University of America, Canon Law Studies, n. 80, Washington: The Catholic University of America, 1932.

Santi-Leitner, *Praelectiones Iuris Canonici*, 5 vols., Ratisbonae: Pustet, 1905.

Schäfer, Timotheus, *Compendium de Religiosis ad Normam Codicis Iuris Canonici*, Münster i. Westf., Ex Typographia Aschendorff, 1931.

——— *Das Eherecht*, 6. and 7. ed., Münster: Aschendorff, 1921.

Schenk, Francis J., *The Matrimonial Impediments of Mixed Religion and Disparity of Cult*, The Catholic University of America, Canon Law Studies, n. 51, Washington: The Catholic University of America, 1929.

Schmiedeler, Edgar, *An Introductory Study of the Family*, New York: The Century, 1930.

Schmalzgrueber, Franciscus, *Ius Ecclesiasticum Universum*, 12 vols., Romae, 1843-1845.

Schulte, J., *Handbuch des katholischen Eherechts nach dem gemeinen katholischen Kirchenrechte und dem österreichischem, preussischem, französischem Particularrechte, mit Rüksichtsnahme auf noch andere Civilgesetzgebungen*, Giessen, 1875.

Suarez, Franciscus, *Opera Omnia*, Venetiis, 1740-1757.

Tanquerey, *Synopsis Theologiae Moralis*, 9. ed., 3 vols., Romae, 1922.

Ter Haar, Francis, *Mixed Marriages and Their Remedies,* translation by Aloysius Walter, New York: Pustet, 1933.

Thaner, Friedrich, *Die Summa Magistri Rolandi nochmals Papstes Alexander III,* Innsbruck, 1874.

Thomassinus, Ludovicus, *Vetus et Nova Ecclesiae Disciplina,* 3 vols., Venetiis, 1730.

Ursprung, W., *Verschollenheit und Todeserklärung,* Aarau: H. R. Saurlander & Co., 1918.

Van Hove, A., *Commentarium Lovaniense in Codicem Iuris Canonici,* Vol. I, *Prologomena,* Mechliniae: H. Dessain, 1928.

Vecchiotti, Septimus, *Institutiones Canonici,* 3. ed., 3 vols., Paris, 1880.

Vermeersch, A., *De Castitate,* Romae: Università Gregoriana, 1919.

Vermeersch-Creusen, *Epitome Iuris Canonici,* 4. ed., 3 vols., Mechliniae: Dessain, 1929.

Vlaming, Thomas, *Praelectiones Iuris Matrimonii ad normam Codicis Iuris Canonici,* 3. ed., 2 vols., Bussum: Paul Brand, 1919.

Vromant, G., *Ius Missionarium,* Vol. V, *De Matrimonio,* Louvain: Museum Lessianum, 1931.

Wanenmacher, Francis, *Canonical Evidence in Marriage Cases,* Philadelphia: Dolphin Press, 1935.

Wahl, Francis X., *The Matrimonial Impediments of Consanguinity and Affinity,* The Catholic University of America, Canon Law Studies, n. 90, Washington: The Catholic University of America, 1934.

Weigl, Edward, *Das Kirchliche Brautexamen,* München: J. G. Manz, 1932.

Wernz, Franciscus, *Ius Decretalium,* 6 vols., Romae: 1908-1913.

Wernz-Vidal, *Ius Canonicum,* Romae: Apud Aedes Universitatis Gregorianae, 1923-1928.

Whalen, Donald, *The Value of Testimonial Evidence in Matrimonial Procedure,* The Catholic University of America, Canon Law Studies, n. 99, Washington: The Catholic University of America, 1935.

White, Robert J., *Canonical Ante-nuptial Promises and the Civil Law,* The Catholic University of America, Canon Law Studies, n. 91, Washington: The Catholic University of America, 1934.

Winslow, Francis Joseph, *Vicars and Prefects Apostolic,* The Catholic University of America, Canon Law Studies, n. 24, Washington: The Catholic University of America, 1924.

Wouters, L., *De Forma Promissionis et Celebrationis Matrimonii,* 4. ed., Bussum: P. Brand, 1919.

Woywod, Stanislaus, *A Practical Commentary on the Code of Canon Law,* 3. ed., 2 vols. New York: Wagner, 1929.

Young, Hugh Hampton, *Genital Abnormalities, Hermaphroditism and Related Adrenal Diseases,* Baltimore: The Williams & Wilkins Co., 1937.

Zitelli, Zepherinus, *De Dispensationibus Matrimonialibus,* Romae, 1887.

Articles

Capobianco, Pacificus, "De Notione Fori Interni in Iure Canonico," *Apollinaris* IX (1936), 343-365.

Cappello, F. M., "De Vicario Substituto," *Periodica,* XIX (1930), 1-10*.

Carberry, John J., "Legal Relationship as an Impediment of Marriage in the United States," *AER,* XC (1934), 394-403.

Harrington, J. C., "The Importance of the Cautiones in Disparity of Worship," *AER,* LXV (1921), 257-262.

O'Donnell, M. J., "'Vagi' and a Months' Residence," *IER,* XVII (1921), 622-627.

——— "The Ne Temere and the Code," *ITQ,* XIV (1919), 133-155.

Oesterle, G., "De Cautionibus Matrimonialibus," *JP,* XIV (1934), 270-276; XV (1935), 64-81, 191-195.

O'Neill, P., "Disparity of Worship and Fictitious Guarantees," *IER,* LXIX (1933), 630-635.

Park, Charles E., "Insincere Ante-nuptial Guarantees," *AER,* XCI (1934), 446-459.

Schaaf, Valentine, "Are Protestant Baptisms Ordinarily Valid?" *AER,* LXXV (1926), 136-151.

——— "Proof of Death of Husband or Wife," *AER,* LXXXIX (1935), 282-286.

——— "The Invalidity of Sectarian Baptisms," *AER,* LXXV (1926), 358-370.

Toso, A., "Consultationes de Cautionibus Matrimonialibus," *JP,* XIII (1933), 207-214.

Turner, John F., "Preliminary Arrangements for Marriage," *AER,* LXXIV (1926), 489-495.

Woywod, Stanislaus, "Delegation of Priest to Assist at Marriage," *HPR,* (1924), 957-965.

Periodicals

American Ecclesiastical Review, Philadelphia, 1889—

Apollinaris Commentarium Iuridico-Canonicum, Romae, 1928—

Archiv für katholisches Kirchenrecht, Mainz, 1857—

Ephemerides Theologicae Lovaniensis, Lovanii, 1924—

Homiletic and Pastoral Review, The, New York, 1900—

Irish Ecclesiastical Record, Dublin, 1864—

Irish Theological Quarterly, Dublin, 1906—

Ius Pontificium, Romae, 1921—

Nouvelle Revue Théologique, Parisiis, 1869—

Periodica de re canonica et morali, Brugis, 1905—

LIST OF ABBREVIATIONS

AAS—*Acta Apostolicae Sedis.*

AER—*American Ecclesiastical Review.*

AKKR—*Archiv für katholisches Kirchenrecht.*

ASS—*Acta Sanctae Sedis.*

C.—*Codex* (Justinianus).

c.—canon.

cc.—canones.

Coll.—*Collectanea S. C. de Propaganda Fide,* ed. 1907.

Coll. Lac.—*Collectio Lacensis.*

ETL—*Ephemerides Theologicae Lovaniensis.*

Fontes—*Codicis Iuris Canonici Fontes cura . . . Gasparri editi.*

HPR—*Homiletic and Pastoral Review.*

IER—*Irish Ecclesiastical Record.*

ITQ—*Irish Theological Quarterly.*

JP—*Jus Pontificium.*

Mansi—*Sacrorum Conciliorum Nova et Amplissima Collectio.*

MGH—*Monumenta Germaniae Historica.*

MPG—Migne, *Patrologia Graeca.*

MPL—Migne, *Patrologia Latina.*

Nov.—*Novellae* (Justinianae).

NRT—*Nouvelle Revue Théologique.*

Periodica—*Periodica de Re Canonica et Morali Utili praesertim Religiosis et Missionariis.*

Pont. Comm. Interp. Cod.—*Pontifical Commission for the Authentic Interpretation of the Code.*

Thesaurus—*Thesaurus. Resolutionum Sacrae Congregationis Concilii.*

ALPHABETICAL INDEX

BIOGRAPHICAL NOTE

JAMES JOSEPH DONOVAN was born at Castlefarm, Knocklong, County Limerick, Ireland, on January 9, 1909. He received his primary education at Presentation School and at De La Salle Brothers' Elementary School, Hospital, County Limerick. He obtained his secondary education at De La Salle Brothers' Intermediate School and at Mount St. Joseph College, Roscrea, County Tipperary. His philosophical studies and his first three years of theological studies were made at St. Patrick's College, Thurles, County Tipperary. At the desire of his bishop, Most Reverend Edwin V. O'Hara, D.D., LL.D., he entered St. Thomas Seminary, Denver, Colorado, in September, 1931, for his final year of Theology, and was ordained to the priesthood on May 21, 1932, at St. Ann's Cathedral, Great Falls, Montana. For three years he was assistant priest at St. Patrick's Church, Billings, Montana. In September, 1935, he enrolled in the School of Canon Law at the Catholic University of America, Washington, D. C., receiving the degree of J.C.B. in June, 1936, and the degree of J.C.L. in June, 1937.

CANON LAW STUDIES

1. Freriks, Rev. Celestine A., C.PP.S., J.C.D., Religious Congregations in Their External Relations, 121 pp., 1916.
2. Gallliher, Rev. Daniel M., O.P., J.C.D., Canonical Elections, 117 pp., 1917.
3. Borkowski, Rev. Aurelius L., O.F.M., J.C.D., De Confraternitatibus Ecclesiasticis, 136 pp., 1918.
4. Castillo, Rev. Cayo, J.C.D., Disertacion Historico-Canonica sobre la Potestad del Cabildo en Sede Vacante o Impedida del Vicario Capitular, 99 pp., 1919 (1918).
5. Kubelbeck, Rev. William J., S.T.B., J.C.D., The Sacred Penitentiaria and Its Relation to Faculties of Ordinaries and Priests, 129 pp., 1918.
6. Petrovits, Rev. Joseph, J.C., S.T.D., J.C.D., The New Church Law on Matrimony, X-461 pp., 1919.
7. Hickey, Rev. John J., S.T.B., J.C.D., Irregularities and Simple Impediments in the New Code of Canon Law, 100 pp., 1920.
8. Klekotka, Rev. Peter J., S.T.B., J.C.D., Diocesan Consultors, 179 pp., 1920.
9. Wanenmacher, Rev. Francis, J.C.D., The Evidence in Ecclesiastical Procedure Affecting the Marriage Bond, 1920 (Printed 1935).
10. Golden, Rev. Henry Francis, J.C.D., Parochial Benefices in the New Code, IV-119 pp., 1921 (Printed 1925).
11. Koudelka, Rev. Charles J., J.C.D., Pastors, Their Rights and Duties According to the New Code of Canon Law, 211 pp., 1921.
12. Melo, Rev. Antonius, O.F.M., J.C.D., De Exemptione Regularium, X-188 pp., 1921.
13. Schaaf, Rev. Valentine Theodore, O.F.M., S.T.B., J.C.D., The Cloister, X-180 pp., 1921.
14. Burke, Rev. Thomas Joseph, S.T.D., J.C.D., Competence in Ecclesiastical Tribunals, IV-117 pp., 1922.
15. Leech, Rev. George Leo, J.C.D., A Comparative Study of the Constitution "Apostolicae Sedis" and the "Codex Juris Canonici," 179 pp., 1922.
16. Motry, Rev. Hubert Louis, S.T.D., J.C.D., Diocesan Faculties According to the Code of Canon Law, II-167 pp., 1922.
17. Murphy, Rev. George Lawrence, J.C.D., Delinquencies and Penalties in the Administration and the Reception of the Sacraments, IV-121 pp., 1923.
18. O'Reilly, Rev. John Anthony, S.T.B., J.C.D., Ecclesiastical Sepulture in the New Code of Canon Law, II-129 pp., 1923.
19. Michalicka, Rev. Wenceslas Cyrill, O.S.B., J.C.D., Judicial Procedure in Dismissal of Clerical Exempt Religious, 107 pp., 1923.

20. DARGIN, REV. EDWARD VINCENT, S.T.B., J.C.D., Reserved Cases According to the Code of Canon Law, IV-103 pp., 1924.
21. GODFREY, REV. JOHN A., S.T.B., J.C.D., The Right of Patronage According to the Code of Canon Law, 153 pp., 1924.
22. HAGEDORN, REV. FRANCIS EDWARD, J.C.D., General Legislation on Indulgences, II-154 pp., 1924.
23. KING, REV. JAMES IGNATIUS, J.C.D., The Administration of the Sacraments to Dying Non-Catholics, V-141 pp., 1924.
24. WINSLOW, REV. FRANCIS JOSEPH, O.F.M., J.C.D., Vicars and Prefects Apostolic, IV-149 pp., 1924.
25. CORREA, REV. JOSE SERVELION, S.T.L., J.C.D., La Potestad Legislativa de la Iglesia Catolica, IV-127 pp., 1925.
26. DUGAN, REV. HENRY FRANCIS, A.M., J.C.D., The Judiciary Department of the Diocesan Curia, 87 pp., 1925.
27. KELLER, REV. CHARLES FREDERICK, S.T.B., J.C.D., Mass Stipends, 167 pp., 1925.
28. PASCHANG, REV. JOHN LINUS, J.C.D., The Sacramentals According to the Code of Canon Law, 129 pp., 1925.
29. POINTEK, REV. CYRILLUS, O.F.M., S.T.B., J.C.D., De Indulto Exclaustrationis necnon Saecularizationis, XIII-289 pp., 1925.
30. KEARNEY, REV. RICHARD JOSEPH, S.T.B., J.C.D., Sponsors at Baptism According to the Code of Canon Law, IV-127 pp., 1925.
31. BARTLETT, REV. CHESTER JOSEPH, A.M., LL.B., J.C.D., The Tenure of Parochial Property in the United States of America, V-108 pp., 1926.
32. KILKER, REV. ADRIAN JEROME, J.C.D., Extreme Unction, V-425 pp., 1926.
33. MCCORMICK, REV. ROBERT EMMETT, J.C.D., Confessors of Religious, VIII-266 pp., 1926.
34. MILLER, REV. NEWTON THOMAS, J.C.D., Founded Masses According to the Code of Canon Law, VII-93 pp., 1926.
35. ROELKER, REV. EDWARD G., S.T.D., J.C.D., Principles of Privilege According to the Code of Canon Law, XI-166 pp., 1926.
36. BAKALARCZYK, REV. RICHARDUS, M.I.C., J.U.D., De Novitiatu, VIII-208 pp., 1927.
37. PIZZUTI, REV. LAWRENCE, O.F.M., J.U.L., De Parochis Religiosis, 1927. (Not Printed.)
38. BLILEY, REV. NICHOLAS MARTIN, O.S.B., J.C.D., Altars According to the Code of Canon Law, XIX-132 pp., 1927.
39. BROWN, MR. BRENDAN FRANCIS, A.B., LL.M., J.U.D., The Canonical Juristic Personality with Special Reference to its Status in the United States of America, V-212 pp., 1927.
40. CAVANAUGH, REV. WILLIAM THOMAS, C.P., J.U.D., The Reservation of the Blessed Sacrament, VIII-101 pp., 1927.
41. DOHENY, REV. WILLIAM J., C.S.C., A.B., J.U.D., Church Property: Modes of Acquisition, X-118 pp., 1927.

42. Feldhaus, Rev. Aloysius H., C.PP.S., J.C.D., Oratories, IX-141 pp., 1927.
43. Kelly, Rev. James Patrick, A.B., J.C.D., The Jurisdiction of the Simple Confessor, X-208 pp., 1927.
44. Neuberger, Rev. Nicholas J., J.C.D., Canon 6 or the Relation of the Codex Juris Canonici to the Preceding Legislation, V-95 pp., 1927.
45. O'Keefe, Rev. Gerald Michael, J.C.D., Matrimonial Dispensations, Powers of Bishops, Priests, and Confessors, VIII-232 pp., 1927.
46. Quigley, Rev. Joseph A. M., A.B., J.C.D., Condemned Societies, 139 pp., 1927.
47. Zaplotnik, Rev. Johannes Leo, J.C.D., De Vicariis Foraneis, X-142 pp. 1927.
48. Duskie, Rev. John Aloysius, A.B., J.C.D., The Canonical Status of the Orientals in the United States, VIII-196 pp., 1928.
49. Hyland, Rev. Francis Edward, J.C.D., Excommunication, Its Nature, Historical Development and Effects, VIII-181 pp., 1928.
50. Reinmann, Rev. Gerald Joseph, O.M.C., J.C.D., The Third Order Secular of Saint Francis, 201 pp., 1928.
51. Schenk, Rev. Francis J., J.C.D., The Matrimonial Impediments of Mixed Religion and Disparity of Cult, XVI-318 pp., 1929.
52. Coady, Rev. John Joseph, S.T.D., J.U.D., A.M., The Appointment of Pastors, VIII-150 pp., 1929.
53. Kay, Rev. Thomas Henry, J.C.D., Competence in Matrimonial Procedure, VIII-164 pp., 1929.
54. Turner, Rev. Sidney Joseph, C.P., J.U.D., The Vow of Poverty, XLIX-217 pp., 1929.
55. Kearney, Rev. Raymond A., A.B., S.T.D., J.C.D., The Principles of Delegation, VII-149 pp., 1929.
56. Conran, Rev. Edward James, A.B., J.C.D., The Interdict, V-163 pp., 1930.
57. O'Neil, Rev. William H., J.C.D., Papal Rescripts of Favor, VII-218 pp., 1930.
58. Bastnagel, Rev. Clement Vincent, J.U.D., The Appointment of Parochial Adjutants and Assistants, XV-257 pp., 1930.
59. Ferry, Rev. William A., A.B., J.C.D., Stole Fees, V-136 pp., 1930.
60. Costello, Rev. John Michael, A.B., J.C.D., Domicile and Quasi-Domicile, VII-201 pp., 1930.
61. Kremer, Rev. Michael Nicholas, A.B., S.T.B., J.C.D., Church Support In the United States, VI-136 pp., 1930.
62. Angulo, Rev. Luis, C.M., J.C.D., Legislation de la Iglesia sobre la intencion en la application de la Santa Misa, VII-104 pp., 1931.
63. Frey, Rev. Wolfgang Norbert, O.S.B., A.B., J.C.D., The Act of Religious Profession, VIII-174 pp., 1931.
64. Roberts, Rev. James Brendan, A.B., J.C.D., The Banns of Marriage, XIV-140 pp., 1931.
65. Ryder, Rev. Raymond Aloysius, A.B., J.C.D., Simony, IX-151 pp., 1931.

66. CAMPAGNA, REV. ANGELO, PH.D., J.U.D., Il Vicario Generale del Vescovo, VII-205 pp., 1931.
67. COX, REV. JOSEPH GODFREY, A.B., J.C.D., The Administration of Seminaries, VI-124 pp., 1931.
68. GREGORY, REV. DONALD J., J.U.D., The Pauline Privilege, XV-165 pp., 1931.
69. DONOHUE, REV. JOHN F., J.C.D., The Impediment of Crime, VII-110 pp., 1931.
70. DOOLEY, REV. EUGENE A., O.M.I., J.C.D., Church Law on Sacred Relics IX-143 pp., 1931.
71. ORTH, REV. CLEMENT RAYMOND, O.M.C., J.C.D., The Approbation of Religious Institutes, 171 pp., 1931.
72. PERNICONE, REV. JOSEPH M., A.B., J.C.D., The Ecclesiastical Prohibition of Books, XII-267 pp., 1932.
73. CLINTON, REV. CONNELL, A.B., J.C.D., The Paschal Precept, IX-108 pp., 1932.
74. DONNELLY, REV. FRANCIS B., A.M., S.T.L., J.C.D., The Diocesan Synod, VIII-125 pp., 1932.
75. TORRENTE, REV. CAMILO, C.M.F., J.C.D., Las Processiones Sagradas, V-145 pp., 1932.
76. MURPHY, REV. EDWIN, J., C.PP.S., J.C.D., Suspension Ex Informata Conscientia, XI-122 pp., 1932.
77. MACKENZIE, REV. ERIC F., A.M., S.T.L., J.C.D., The Delict of Heresy in Its Commission, Penalization, Absolution, VII-124 pp., 1932.
78. LYONS, REV. AVITUS E., S.T.B., J.C.D., The Collegiate Tribunal of First Instance, XI-147 pp., 1932.
79. CONNOLLY, REV. THOMAS A., J.C.D., Appeals, XI-195 pp., 1932.
80. SANGMEISTER, REV. JOSEPH V., A.B., J.C.D., Force and Fear as Precluding Matrimonial Consent, V-211 pp., 1932.
81. JAEGER, REV. LEO A., A.B., J.C.D., The Administration of Vacant and Quasi-Vacant Episcopal Sees in the United States, IX-229 pp., 1932.
82. RIMLINGER, REV. HERBERT T., J.C.D., Error Invalidating Matrimonial Consent, VII-79 pp., 1932.
83. BARRETT, REV. JOHN D. M., S.S., J.C.D., A Comparative Study of the Third Plenary Council of Baltimore and the Code, IX-221 pp., 1932.
84. CARBERRY, REV. JOHN J., PH.D., S.T.D., J.C.D., The Juridical Form of Marriage, X-177 pp., 1934.
85. DOLAN, REV. JOHN L., A.B., J.C.D., The Defensor Vinculi, XII-157 pp., 1934.
86. HANNAN, REV. JEROME D., A.M., S.T.D., LL.B., J.C.D., The Canon Law of Wills, IX-517 pp., 1934.
87. LEMIEUX, REV. DELISLE A., A.M., J.C.D., The Sentence in Ecclesiastical Procedure, IX-131 pp., 1934.
88. O'ROURKE, REV. JAMES J., A.B., J.C.D., Parish Registers, VII-109 pp., 1934.

89. Timlin, Rev. Bartholomew, O.F.M., A.M., J.C.D., Conditional Matrimonial Consent, X-381 pp., 1934.
90. Wahl, Rev. Francis X., A.B., J.C.D., The Matrimonial Impediments of Consanguinity and Affinity, VI-125 pp., 1934.
91. White, Rev. Robert J., A.B., LL.B., S.T.B., J.C.D., Canonical Ante-Nuptial Promises and the Civil Law, VI-152 pp., 1934.
92. Herrera, Rev. Antonio Parra, O.C.D., J.C.D., Legislacion Ecclesiastica sobrael Ayuno y la Abstinencia, XI-191 pp., 1935.
93. Kennedy, Rev. Edwin J., J.C.D., The Special Matrimonial Process in Cases of Evident Nullity, X-165 pp., 1935.
94. Manning, Rev. John J., A.B., J.C.D., Presumption of Law in Matrimonial Procedure, XI-111 pp., 1935.
95. Moeder, Rev. John M., J.C.D., The Proper Bishop for Ordination and Dimissorial Letters, VII-135 pp., 1935.
96. O'Mara, Rev. William A., A.B., J.C.D., Canonical Causes for Matrimonial Dispensations, IX-155 pp., 1935.
97. Reilly, Rev. Peter, J.C.D., Residence of Pastors, IX-81 pp., 1935.
98. Smith, Rev. Mariner T., O.P., S.T.Lr., J.C.D., The Penal Law for Religious, VII-169 pp., 1935.
99. Whalen, Rev. Donald W., A.M., J.C.D., The Value of Testimonial Evidence in Matrimonial Procedure, XIII-297 pp., 1935.
100. Cleary, Rev. Joseph F., J.C.D., Canonical Limitations on the Alienation of Church Property, VIII-141 pp., 1936.
101. Glynn, Rev. John C., J.C.D., The Promoter of Justice, XX-337 pp., 1936.
102. Brennan, Rev. James H., S.S., M.A., S.T.B., J.C.D., The Simple Convalidation of Marriage, VI-135 pp., 1937.
103. Brunini, Rev. Joseph Bernard, J.C.D., The Clerical Obligations of Canons 139 and 142, X-121 pp., 1937.
104. Connor, Rev. Maurice, A.B., J.C.D., The Administrative Removal of Pastors, VIII-159 pp., 1937.
105. Guilfoyle, Rev. Merlin Joseph, J.C.D., Custom, XI-144 pp., 1937.
106. Hughes, Rev. James Austin, A.B., A.M., J.C.D., Witnesses in Criminal Trials of Clerics, IX-140 pp., 1937.
107. Jansen, Rev. Raymond J., A.B., S.T.L., J.C.D., Canonical Provisions for Catechetical Instruction, VII-153 pp., 1937.
108. Kealy, Rev. John James, A.B., J.C.D., The Introductory Libellus in Church Court Procedure, XI-121 pp., 1937.
109. McManus, Rev. James Edward, C.SS.R., J.C.D., The Administration of Temporal Goods in Religious Institutes, XVI-196 pp., 1937.
110. Moriarty, Rev. Eugene James, J.C.D., Oaths in Ecclesiastical Courts, X-115 pp., 1937.
111. Rainer, Rev. Eligius George, C.SS.R., J.C. D., Suspension of Clerics, XVII-249 pp., 1937.

112. Reilly, Rev. Thomas F., C.SS.R., J.C.L., Visitation of Religious.
113. Moriarty, Rev. Francis E., C.SS.R., J.C.L., The Extraordinary Absolution from Censures.
114. Connolly, Rev. Nicholas P., J.C.L., The Canonical Erection of Parishes.
115. Donovan, Rev. James Joseph, J.C.L., The Pastor's Obligation in Prenuptial Investigation.
116. Harrigan, Rev. Robert J., M.A., S.T.B., J.C.L., The Radical Sanation of Invalid Marriages.

www.ingramcontent.com/pod-product-compliance
Lightning Source LLC
LaVergne TN
LVHW050258080826
844660LV00012B/654

* 9 7 8 0 8 1 3 2 2 3 0 4 9 *